CONSTRUCTION DRAWINGS AND DETAILS FOR INTERIORS: BASIC SKILLS

W. OTIE KILMER
ROSEMARY KILMER

WILEY

John Wiley & Sons, Inc.

Library of Congress Cataloging-in-Publication Data:

Kilmer, W. Otie.
  Construction drawings and details for interiors : basic skills / by W.
Otie Kilmer and Rosemary Kilmer.
     p. cm.
Includes bibliographical references and index.
  ISBN 0-471-10953-3 (Paper)
  1. Building--Details--Drawings. 2. Interior architecture. 3.
Structural drawing. I. Kilmer, Rosemary. II. Title.
  TH2031.K54 2003
  729--dc21

                                   2003000582

Printed in the United States of America.

10 9 8 7 6 5 4 3

Contents

Preface

The design process for architectural interiors involves a series of phases, each of which may call for drawings. At the outset, these may include programming, schematic, preliminary, and design development drawings. Such presentation drawings are created to convey program elements, spatial relationships, materials, color schemes, furnishings, and equipment, as necessary to set the design concept for an interior. Construction drawings are then produced that follow the design intent developed through these earlier drawings. Construction drawings, also known as working drawings, are graphic representations that communicate how to construct, remodel, or install a project. These drawings also include related information, such as room designations, door, window, and fixture locations; dimensions; materials; and other details.

Construction drawings involve considerable time and attention to detail. In many professional design firms, over 50 percent of a project fee (payment from the client to the designer) might be allocated to preparing construction drawings and the related specifications. This attests to the importance of construction drawings in the overall process of designing and constructing environments.

Interior designers are taking an increasing role in coordinating interior projects and for producing construction drawings. Interior design and construction requires some unique types of drawing not commonly addressed in textbooks or curricula. It is to speak to this need that this book was created—as a handbook on preparing construction drawings solely for the field of interior design.

The book has been designed for two groups of users: students in interior design schools and interns in the offices that design interiors; and professional interior designers and architecturs who need a basic, yet comprehensive set of standards and techniques. For students or interns, these pages are best used with an instructor or mentor who can present the published materials, but augment them with supplemental information and other exercises.

Computer-aided drawing (CAD) and computer-aided drawing and drafting (CADD) are tools that have become integral to interior design. This book thus provides a general introduction to using the computer. It briefly discusses electronically storing and retrieving documents for current and future projects. Many elements of a current project can be copied and easily modified for future application in other projects. In this manner, designers can build a design database. Today, images, drawings and other information are sent electronically to clients, consultants, suppliers, builders, and other professionals. This is a far leap ahead of such past methods as copying and mailing or sending telephonic facsimile. Working electronically has changed many of the ways designers communicate their work, and is continually evolving.

However, this is not a textbook on how to draft with the computer, or on the use of specific drafting software. Computer hardware and software are constantly being upgraded and improved. For this reason, this book focuses on how to incorporate a generic CAD approach into the construction drawing process. Examples are presented throughout the book of both electronic and hand-drawn creations. Although many designers use CAD heavily in their work, a significant number do not fully use it for all aspects of the drawing process, or at all. Well-executed hand drawings can still be effective design exploration and communication tools, and sometimes they are even works of art.

This book is organized in two parts. Part 1 (Chapters 1 through 4) first discusses graphic language as a communication tool in design and architecture. Chapters 2 and 3 present equipment needs and basic drafting principles for the beginning student. Chapter 4 presents the drawing classification systems and how they are used for idea generation and communication.

Part 2 (Chapters 5 throuth 16) detail the construction document process. Overall concepts and organization are discussed, as are specific examples. Chapter 16 discusses the use of computers and the various systems for reproducing construction drawings.

Examples used in the book include both residential and commercial interiors. However, more emphasis is placed on commercial projects, as these installations usually require more in-depth detailing, coordination, and often multiple drawings/sheets due to the larger spaces and number of building trades required. The illustrations represent high standards and can serve as guides for design: linework, lettering, notation, and dimensioning that students can aspire to in their own work. In addition to the authors' drawings, examples are included from practicing professionals.

Drawings and details of interiors are included from a variety of geographical areas—as design ideas, material, environmental factors, and accepted standards vary throughout the world. Projects are also shown in relation to their compliance with the American Disabilities Act and other code requirements. Dimensions are often indicated in feet and inches, with metric equivalents for Canadian and international applications.

A glossary and appendices are included listing commonly used terms, graphic standards, and other information related to the preparation of construction drawings for interiors.

Acknowledgments

The authors wish to express their sincere thanks to the following people, who helped in the development and preparation of this book.

We are deeply grateful to the dedicated staff at John Wiley & Sons. Without their guidance, assistance, and dedicated work, this project would have never become a reality. Among these individuals the authors are particularly indebted to Amanda Miller, Associate Publisher. Her support, understanding, and perseverance to complete this project are very much appreciated. Also, we wish to thank Paul Drougas, Acquisitions Editor, for his help in the development and final preparation of this project. To David Sassian, Associate Managing Editor, for his diligence in editing and attending to the many details that turned the manuscript into a finished book.

Special appreciation is expressed to the professionals and organizations that provided us with illustrations and permissions to use their materials to make this book a truly visual experience. We are especially thankful to The Construction Specifications Institute, American Society of Interior Designers, Hillenbrand Mitsch Design, KJG Architecture, Inc., KraftMaid Cabinetry, Océ-USA, Inc., and Hewlett-Packard Company. Every effort has been made to correctly supply the proper credit information.

We are grateful to a number of interior design educators throughout the country for their in-depth reviews, criticism, and helpful suggestions as to the needs of students and instructors in interior design.

Finally, we would like to express our deep appreciation to Courtney and Jeff Johnston for their tireless help with the illustrations and for their suggestions, based on their professional experience, as to contemporary standards and practices. Special thanks also to Lisa Kilmer, for assistance and encouragement in the early stages of this project.

Part I
Drawings, Equipment, and Fundamentals

DRAWING AS COMMUNICATION 1

Ideas and plans are formed in the interior designer's mind, but to be transformed into reality, they have to be communicated to others. Although a designer may have a great idea, it must be effectively communicated or it will remain just an idea and never move beyond conception. Interior designers and other professionals in the building industry use drawings as the primary means of developing and sharing their ideas. Interior designers and architects do a lot of sketching and drawing. They develop their skills in freehand drawing by sketching existing objects and spaces in the environment (Figure 1-1). These same skills of observation and sketching are then used in visualizing designs for new spaces and objects (Figure 1-2).

This process of brain, eye, and hand coordination is an intrinsic part of design. Architectural drawings can be grouped into three basic types: drawing as idea generation, drawing as a design and presentation medium, and drawing as a guide for the construction process. There are distinct differences between each of these types, yet they all contain some common drawing tools, techniques, standards, and graphic language.

Drawing for Idea Generation

Idea generation assists the designer in working through and visualizing the solution to a problem. Designers use many different types of drawings to generate and bring to reality their creative ideas. These drawings can be in the form of quick freehand sketches illustrating different kinds of views (Figure 1-3). Many times these types of drawings are not shown to clients but are used solely to help designers shape their ideas. The drawings are not

Figure 1-1 Sketching existing objects and spaces helps designers develop their freehand drawing skills.

intended to be the final solution to a problem but rather to allow the designer to explore alternatives or refine an idea. They also help to record a designer's two- and three-dimensional thinking. These concept sketches and drawings are part of a sequence of design steps referred to as the design process (Figure 1-4).

Figure 1-2 Designers can use their freehand drawing skills to visualize and sketch new spaces and objects.

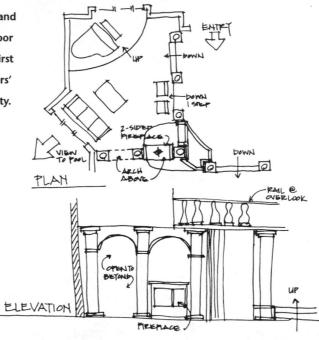

Figure 1-3 Quick freehand sketches such as this floor plan can be used as a first step in turning designers' creative ideas into reality.

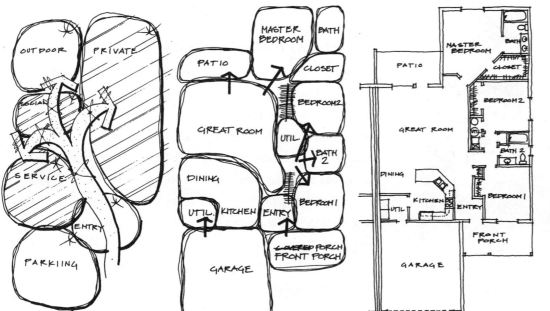

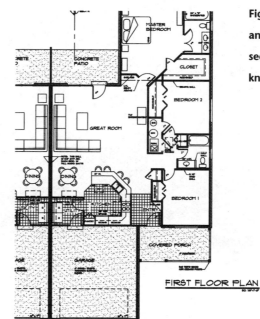

Figure 1-4 Concept sketches and drawings are part of a sequence of design steps known as the design process.

Drawing as Design and Presentation Media

Once a designer has developed an idea to a point that visual communication is needed to show it to the client or others, new drawings must be created for use as presentation media. These drawings depict the parameters of an idea in more detail, yet are not totally worked out to a point that they serve as an accurate construction guide. Design drawings can range from pictorial renderings of an idea (Figure 1-5) to rendered plan views of a building's interiors (Figure 1-6). In the first example, a rendering is often done as a perspective view (Chapter 4), which resembles a photograph. The receding lines of an object are purposely drawn to a distant vanishing point — similar to the effect of railroad tracks that appear to touch at the horizon. Design drawings are also done using techniques other than perspectives, such as in the isometric shown in Figure 1-7. Different types of drawings are discussed further in Chapter 4.

Drawing as a Guide for Construction

Drawings serve as the prime means of communication for constructing buildings, interior spaces, cabinets, furniture, and other objects. Construction drawings are scaled, detailed, and accurate representations of how an object looks and how it is constructed, as well as the materials used (Figure 1-8). The drawings follow established architectural graphic conventions to indicate sizes, material, and related information that is needed to bring the objects or spaces into reality (Figure 1-9). The builder needs clear, concise drawings that are directly related to the different views of an object, such as plans, elevations, sections (Figure 1-10), and other drawing types that are discussed in later chapters.

Figure 1-5 Design drawings such as this pictorial rendering show ideas in more detail.

Figure 1-6 Design drawings can also take the form of plan views.

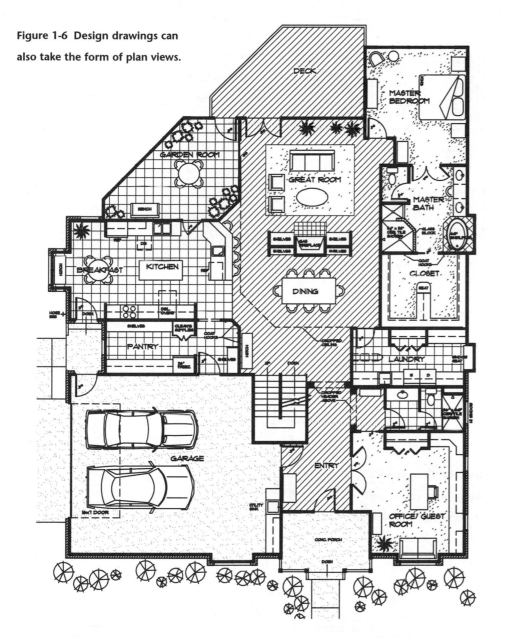

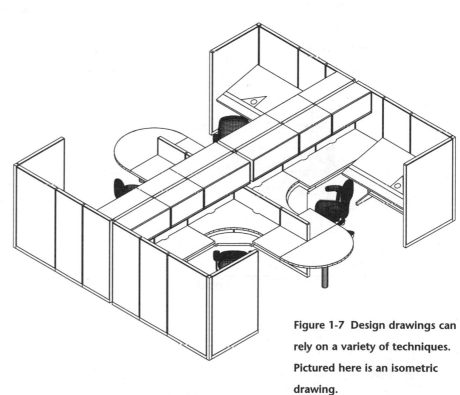

Figure 1-7 Design drawings can rely on a variety of techniques. Pictured here is an isometric drawing.

Figure 1-8 Drawings used to communicate how something should be constructed are scaled, detailed, and accurate; they also show materials to be used.

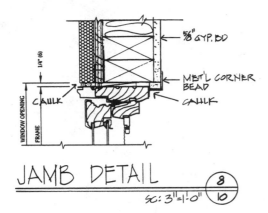

JAMB DETAIL
SC: 3"=1'-0" 8/10

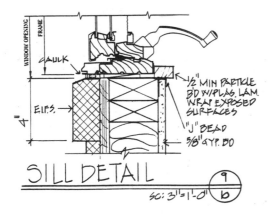

SILL DETAIL
SC: 3"=1'-0" 9/6

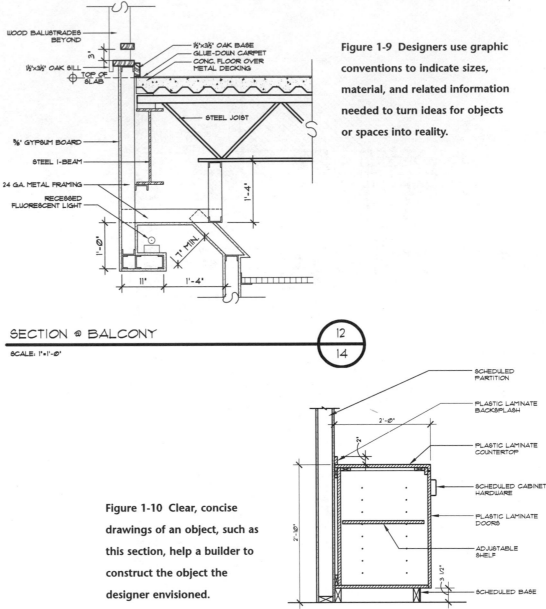

Figure 1-9 Designers use graphic conventions to indicate sizes, material, and related information needed to turn ideas for objects or spaces into reality.

SECTION @ BALCONY
SCALE: 1"=1'-0" 12/14

Figure 1-10 Clear, concise drawings of an object, such as this section, help a builder to construct the object the designer envisioned.

SECTION OF BASE CABINET
SCALE: 1" = 1'-0"

To do any job accurately and expediently, a designer must have the proper tools. Tools are important in all work — whether it be surgery or carpentry, designing or drafting. Quality tools and equipment will also make drawing and drafting more enjoyable. Investing in good equipment for designing and drafting can benefit both students and professionals.

The advent of computer-aided design and drafting, commonly referred to as CAD, has reduced the need for much of the basic equipment described in the following pages. However, many students and professionals still prefer to draw manually in some situations, such as sketching initial design concepts or construction details. To this end, basic manual equipment and techniques are described in the next few chapters.

A designer or draftsperson need not buy every piece of new equipment or software available. However, one should buy a new product if it will improve one's work, both in quality and efficiency. Manufacturers often produce a range of models of varying quality. One can decide which model will produce the best effects in relation to the purchase price — sometimes not the top-of-the-line model. One should purchase tools and equipment of good quality, as they are an investment that will pay off throughout one's career.

Drawing Tables and Surfaces

To produce quality drawings for interior design projects, it is necessary to establish a dedicated workplace. Designs can be drawn manually on a drawing board set on a tabletop surface, on a handmade drafting table, or on a ready-made drafting table. Or they can be drawn using computer drafting hardware and software that augments a drawing board or replaces it totally. In this chapter, commonly used manual drafting tables, equipment and tools are discussed. Computer drawing and drafting are discussed in more detail in Chapter 16.

For interior designers, a fairly large layout and drawing surface is needed most of the time. It is vital to have a drawing surface that will hold large presentation boards and standard sheets up to 24 x 36 inches (731 x 914 mm). Even larger sheets may be necessary for perspective drawings and full-size furniture drawings. A drawing board or table approximately 30 x 50 inches (.762 x 1.27 m) should be obtained if possible. This will allow adequate space around the actual drawing sheet to place and maneuver the drawing tools and materials.

Ready-made drafting tables are manufactured in a wide variety of shapes, sizes, materials, and prices (Figure 2-1). Some styles have an adjustable top and rest on four legs. Other models have a single or double pedestal base with a top that can be raised or lowered according to the chair or stool height. This enables drafters to sit in a chair with a comfortable back and thus to work with less fatigue. The newer models also allow the top to tilt at various angles for comfort. This allows the drafter to work whether sitting or standing. Space-saving folding tables are also produced, although they are not generally as sturdy as the fixed models.

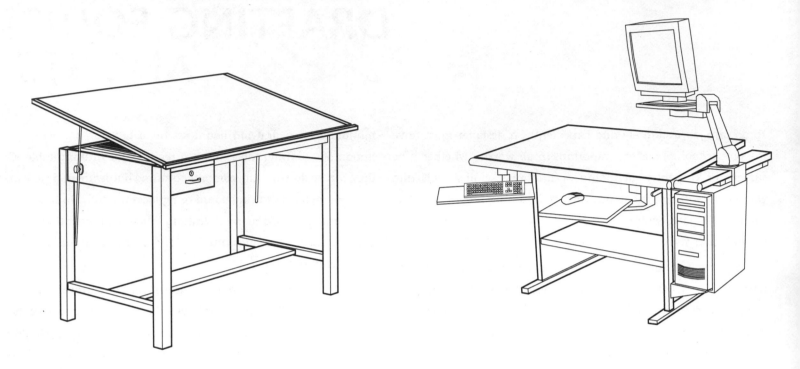

Figure 2-1 A variety of pre-manufactured drafting tables are available to designers. They range from very basic, with few options for adjustment, to quite sophisticated, with electronic controls.

Manufactured tables have drawing surfaces that range in size from 30 x 48 inches (762 x 1.21 mm) to 30 x 60 inches (.762 x 1.52 m) and are usually made of wood or hardboard over a cellular core. However, a wood drawing surface can become scored and grooved over time, which affects the drawing quality of the surface. It is best to cover the bare wood top with a protective finish such as plastic melamine or a vinyl drawing-board cover that gives a bit of resiliency and is easy to keep clean. The latter covering is often produced with an off-white and a colored side. Which side to leave faceup is left to the individual.

Drawing-board and table surfaces do not have to be manufactured, as a self-made surface can also be satisfactory and less expensive. For example, a hollow-core, flush door can be supported on blocks or handmade legs made of 2x4 lumber with metal brackets. However, the height and angle that suits individual work

habits must first be determined, as this type of drawing area will be fixed and not adjustable.

Drawing Papers and Plastic Film

Interior design drawings can be produced on paper or plastic film. The quality of paper or film will help determine the quality of linework. A variety of papers and plastic films are manufactured today in many standard sheet sizes and rolls. The choice of which to use is dependent upon the designer's overall intent, office standards, and the intended method selected for making a copy from the original.

Papers

Drafting papers are made in a large variety of types, based on stability, translucency, permanence, strength, and cost. There are two basic categories: opaque and translucent. Opaque papers are thicker than translucent ones and cannot be reproduced through methods such as the diazo printing process (see Chapter 16 for reproduction methods). Therefore, they are not suitable for construction drawings that are to be copied in this manner. They are more suitable for plotting directly from a computer (in single sheets or rolls) and for concept and presentation drawings, as they are available in a variety of colors ranging from white to gray, cream, green, and blue. Some opaque papers are made smooth on one side and rough on the other. The smooth side is more appropriate for inking and the rough side for pencil drawings. Most papers will accept ink or pencil. However, the quality of their application and possible bleed-through varies according to the composition of the paper and its thickness.

Translucent papers, such as tracing paper and vellum, are used for drawings that are to be reproduced through the diazo process. However, they can also be reproduced photostatically. Tracing paper is generally a natural, untreated translucent paper. It is used primarily for exploratory ideas and sketches. It is commonly sold in inexpensive rolls (in white or yellow shades) and called "tracing," "trash," "flimsy," or "bum wad." It is fairly strong and durable, but not as transparent as vellums, and will not produce line work as crisp and clear as vellums.

Vellum is a translucent tracing paper that is treated to improve strength, surface texture, and transparency. Vellums also have a high rag content that gives them strength so they can withstand erasing. Vellum is sold in rolls or standard sheet sizes and can be used for hand or computer drafting. Standard sheet sizes for architectural drawings are shown in Table 2-1.

Plastic Films

Plastic drafting films are tough, translucent, polyester sheets. Their common thickness ranges from 0.002, 0.003, 0.004, 0.005, and

Table 2-1 Standard Paper Sizes			
Architectural Drawing			**Metric**
Type	Size (in.)	Type	Size (mm)
A	8½ x 11	A4	210 x 297
B	11 x 17	A3	297 x 420
C	17 x 22	A2	420 x 594
D	24 x 36	A1	594 x 841
E	36 x 48	A0	841 x 1189

0.0075 inch to 0.05, 0.08, 0.10, 0.14, and 0.19 mm. The sheets may be frosted on one side and smooth on the other or frosted on both sides. Drawing is done on the frosted side, which accepts pencil or pen more readily than the smooth side.

Special plasticized lead pencils were at one time commonly used with plastic films, but they are not as prevalent as they once were. These are discussed in the paragraph under leads in the next section. Special ink is also available for drawing on plastic film. Both pencil and ink lines are very clear and crisp on plastic films and produce very clear, clean prints. Plastic films are sold in rolls and standard sheet sizes. The films are generally more expensive than tracing paper or vellum and used primarily for permanent records or tough originals for multiple reproductions.

Pencils, Leads, and Pens

Pencils are one of the most basic and primary drawing tools of the professional designer. There are three basic types of pencils available to a designer for producing quality drawings (Figure 2-2). The selection is a matter of preference and the particular level of performance needed by the user.

Wood-Cased Pencil

The oldest manufactured pencil is of wood with a lead encased inside. It is seldom used for repetitive work in today's office, yet is still a reliable tool for occasional use for convenience and when

Figure 2-2 The three types of pencils available for designers are the wood-cased pencil, the traditional leadholder, and the fine-line mechanical pencil.

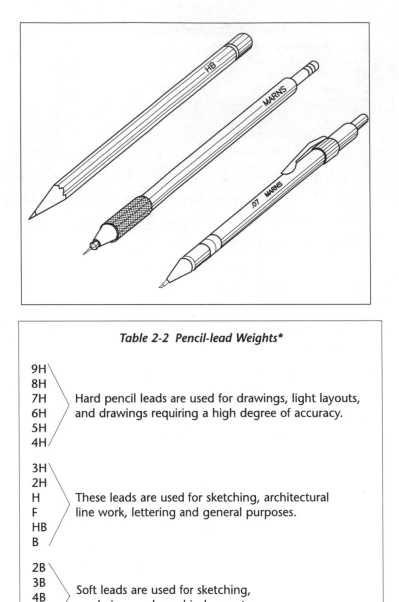

Table 2-2 Pencil-lead Weights*

9H 8H 7H 6H 5H 4H	Hard pencil leads are used for drawings, light layouts, and drawings requiring a high degree of accuracy.
3H 2H H F HB B	These leads are used for sketching, architectural line work, lettering and general purposes.
2B 3B 4B 5B 6B	Soft leads are used for sketching, rendering, and graphical accents.

The gradations can vary with different brands and types of drawing media. When in doubt, try a sample or test first.

pencil line control is needed. To expose the lead, the wood shell is cut away by a draftsman's pencil sharpener. However, the sharpener only cuts the wood and does not touch the lead. To "point" the lead, the designer can use a lead pointer, which forms the lead into a conical point. If a wedge point is desired, rubbing the lead on sandpaper can form it. Wood-cased pencils come in a variety of different lead weights, ranging from 9H (extremely hard) to 6B (extremely soft). These leads are explained later in this chapter.

Traditional Leadholder

This type of mechanical pencil is made of metal or plastic, with special individual leads inserted in a permanent holder. Different lead weights may be inserted to produce a variety of sharp line weights. Pencil leads are graded from 9H (hard) to F (firm) to 6B (black). Beginners should sharpen the point frequently for a clear, sharp line until they develop the ability to rotate the pencil while drawing to wear the point more evenly. The lead is sharpened by rubbing and rotating on sandpaper, on regular paper, or in a special mechanical lead pointer. When using sandpaper to sharpen the lead, it should be slanted at a low angle to achieve a good taper and point.

Fine-Line Mechanical Pencil

This type of mechanical pencil does not require sharpening and is loaded with multiple leads of the same diameter and hardness. The pencil generally is made to hold 0.3, 0.5, 0.7, or 0.9 mm diameter lead. The size of the lead determines the line width. This type of pencil is also generally rotated while drawing, and capable of producing consistently sharp, clean lines. Like the traditional leadholder, the mechanical pencil offers the convenience of a steady supply of lead, as the leads are inserted in the bottom of the holder and pushed out the tip by pressing a button on the end of the pencil. It is the most widely used pencil in today's schools and offices for sketching, note-taking, and even drafting.

Leads

A variety of leads are available for both wood and mechanical pencils. Leads used on tracing paper and drafting paper are composed of graphite. Leads range in grades from 9H (extremely hard) to 6B (extremely soft). (See Table 2-2.) The softer the lead, the darker the image or line it will produce. For most drafting work, where clean, crisp lines are necessary, H and 2H leads are used. For sketching, softer leads are better, such as F and HB. Very soft leads, such as the B grades, are best for pencil renderings and shadowing work. For light, preliminary layout work, 3H and 4H leads are best.

Generally, the more "tooth" or roughness a paper has, the harder the lead should be. Also, the harder the drawing surface, the softer the lead will feel. If you are in high humidity conditions, the apparent hardness of the lead tends to increase.

As noted before, there are also special plastic-leaded pencils available for drawing on plastic drafting film. These plastic leads are available in five grades of hardness, ranging from E1 (soft) to E5 (super hard). They are water-resistant and bond well to the plastic film. A vinyl eraser is also available for use with these special leads.

Pens

Some designers prefer ink and use a technical fountain pen (Figure 2-3), as it is capable of precise line width. It can be used for both freehand and drafted ink drawings. As with drafting pencils, pens are available in a variety of forms and price ranges. However, most technical drawing pens consist of a tubular point, which has an ink-flow-regulating wire inside it. The size of the tubular point is what determines the finished width. Standard widths of ink lines are measured according to a line-width code, such as .30/00, which

means the line width is .30 mm or the American standard size of 00. Metric widths range from .13 to 2.0 mm, while the American standard widths range from 000000 to 6. These sizes correspond to line-width designations developed by the American National Standards Institute (ANSI) and are coordinated with metric sizes. For a starter pen set, a good range of point sizes would be 3x0 (.25 mm), 2x0 (.3 mm), 1 (.45 mm), and 3 (.80 mm). Technical pens that produce the same line widths are also available with felt tips. These are less costly, however their felt tips tend to wear out faster than the metal tips.

An advantage to using ink, especially on plastic drafting film, is that it will last several years longer than pencil, will not smudge, and will produce excellent reproductions. When using technical pens, remember to keep points screwed in securely to prevent the ink from clogging. Always replace the cap firmly after each use to

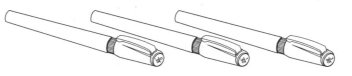

Figure 2-3 Technical fountain pens and ink refill.

keep the ink from drying, and store the pens with their points up when not in use.

Use a good waterproof black drawing ink. Good nonclogging ink that is specially made for use in fountain and technical pens is the best choice.

Parallel Bar, T-Square, and Drafting Machines

It is extremely important to make sure lines on design drawings and construction drawings are exactly straight and, when required, parallel. To make sure lines are straight in a horizontal, vertical, and angular direction, there are several tools available. The most common of these instruments are the T-square and parallel bar (Figure 2-4). A device called a drafting machine (Figure 2-5) is also sometimes used.

T-Square

A T-square consists of a straightedge with a head set at right angles that can be set flush against the edge of a drawing board or table. The head is generally very sturdy and immovable. T-squares come in different lengths to coordinate with various drawing board sizes. The most common lengths are 36 and 42 inches (.91 and 1.06 m). They are available with opaque or transparent edges, the latter making it easier to see through to existing lines when spacing by eye. To use a T-square, one holds it with one hand (usually the left) at the head so it can be moved into position and held in place while a line is drawn along the straightedge with the other hand. The T-square is inexpensive and portable, which makes it convenient for students. However, in modern practice the T-square has been replaced by the parallel bar and the drafting machine, as they do not require a constant hand to steady the head.

Parallel Bar

A parallel bar is attached by cleats and pulleys to a particular drawing surface. The bar moves up and down on thin wire that moves runs over pulleys inside the bar. When properly installed, the bar can be moved up and down the drawing board and always be parallel with the top of it. Parallel bars are available in a variety of lengths to fit different drawing board sizes. The parallel bar is easy to use. It permits the drafter to draw long horizontal lines and serves as a base for the placement of triangles and other instruments for precision drawing.

Drafting Machines

A drafting machine is a combination of several conventional drafting tools. It is fixed to the drawing board and consists of vertical and horizontal blades that serve as scales for linear measurement, eliminating the need for a triangle and T-square for drawing vertical and horizontal lines. There is also a scale in angular degrees on the head that replaces the protractor.

There are two basic types of drafting machines — the arm type and the track type. The arm type has two arms that pivot in the center with a head at the end of the lower arm — which is clamped to the top edge of the drafting table. The drafter moves the head up and down and right and left. The head and the scales on it remain parallel to their original setting. The track type has a horizontal track mounted to the top edge of the drafting table with a vertical track attached to it that slides left and right. The head with the scales on it is fastened to the vertical track and slides up and down.

Drafting machines are available for right- or left-handed people. Right-handed people hold the head in place with the left hand. Left-handed people hold the head in their right hand with the scales facing the opposite direction.

The scales on drafting machines can be set at angles by releasing a lock, pressing a release button and turning the head. Frequently used angles such as 30, 45, and 60 degrees have positive set points. Scales are available in several lengths, in either architectural or metric measurements. They are also available in either plastic or aluminum finishes.

Triangles, Templates, and Compasses

A variety of other drawing tools are available for constructing vertical or inclined lines as well as circles, curvilinear shapes not based on fixed-radius circular forms, and other special shapes such as representations of furniture, plumbing fixtures, and other interior equipment and furnishings.

Triangles

A triangle is a three-sided instrument used with the T-square or parallel straightedge for drawing vertical and angular lines (Figure 2-6). The most common are 45-degree and 30/60-degree triangles, each named for the angles they form. A range of sizes is available, with a size of 8 or 10 inches (203 x 254 mm) being in the middle of the range. Their size is based on the length of the longest side of the right angle. It is best to begin with these; then larger and smaller sizes can be added as needed. For example, small triangles, such as 4 inches (101 mm), are useful for hand-lettering and crosshatching small areas.

Adjustable triangles can be set for any angle from 0 to 45 degrees. The adjustable triangle is convenient for situations requiring a variety of sloping lines, such as for stairs or slanted ceilings.

Some triangles are available with recessed edges for use when inking. This keeps the edge up off of the paper so the ink doesn't run under the triangle and become smeared. Triangles are available in a clear (nonyellowing) or colored plastic. They are scratch-resistant and generally have good edge retention. They should not be used as a cutting edge as they are easy to nick, and they must be used and stored carefully.

Templates

Templates are prepunched patterns representing various shapes commonly used in interior design and architectural plans (Figure 2-7). Templates help to speed up the drafting process and aid in the production of accurate drawings. There are a variety of templates available, some of which are used regularly, while others are needed for special purposes only. There are templates that are used to draw circles, squares, windows, doors, electrical symbols, plumbing fixtures, furnishings, and hundreds of other features.

The circle template is a very basic and highly useful timesaving device for drawing accurate circles of various sizes as well as curves that are parts of circles. Circles range in size from $\frac{1}{16}$ inch (1.58 mm) up to 2 inches (50.8 mm) in diameter. Ellipse templates come in similar sizes, but since ellipses vary from near flat to near circular, a series of templates may be needed for each size. However, a single guide with the most commonly used proportions is available.

French curved templates are excellent tools for drawing irregular curved lines that are not part of a circle or ellipse. These guides consist of at least a dozen traditional forms that can help a designer draw almost any flowing curve needed. There are also flexible drawing curves available that can be bent as needed to fit an irregular curved line. They can hold the shape as the line is drawn, then straightened out after use.

Other useful templates include forms for both residential and commercial furniture, as well as plumbing fixtures, retail fixtures, and lighting and electrical symbols. Lettering templates are also

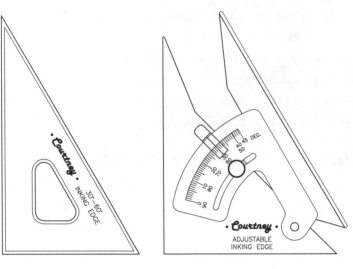

Figure 2-6 Triangles are also used to create straight lines when drawing. When used with a parallel bar or T-square, angular and vertical lines can be drawn. Shown on the left is a fixed 30-60 triangle; on the right is an adjustable triangle.

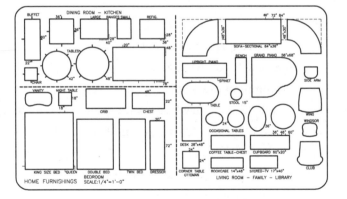

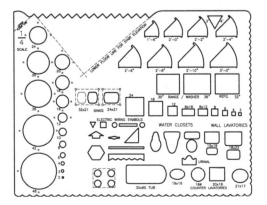

Figure 2-7 Templates are used to speed up the drafting process by tracing the punched shapes directly onto a drawing. Templates come in a variety of patterns and scales.

available, but even though they may be convenient they often appear stiff and are not frequently used in design offices. Lettering templates are best used for very large letters and numbers that may be difficult to form freehand.

Compass

A compass is an inverted V-shaped instrument used for drawing circles and arcs (Figure 2-8). It has a pin at the end of one leg and a leadholder at the end of the other. A special device will allow technical pen points to be used with the compass. The best way to use a compass is to mark a centerpoint and the radius desired on a piece of paper and adjust the compass to that measurement by setting the pin on the center point and setting the pencil or pen point on the radius mark. Hold the compass firmly at the top, leaning it a little in the direction the circle will be drawn, then rotate it. Generally, rotating it in a clockwise direction is easier. Press hard enough to get the desired line weight. Be careful to match line weights of circles and arcs to the rest of the drawing.

Scales

Measuring tools are extremely important to the interior designer, because a designer's plans, elevations, sections, and details must always be drawn with all their dimensions at the same fractional part of their real (full-size) dimensions. Architectural and interior design line work generally represents objects that are much larger than the drawing paper; therefore, a proportional measuring system must be used. This *scale* of the drawing is always stated on the drawing. When a drawing is drawn *to scale,* this means that all dimensions on the drawing are related to the real object, or space, by an appropriate selected scale ratio. For example, when drawing at a scale of ⅛" = 1'0", each ⅛" increment in the drawing represents a foot in the full-size object.

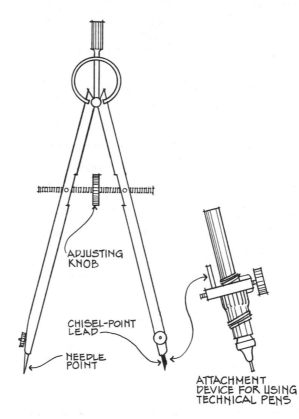

ADJUSTING KNOB

CHISEL-POINT LEAD

NEEDLE POINT

ATTACHMENT DEVICE FOR USING TECHNICAL PENS

Figure 2-8 Compasses are used to draw circles and arcs; this illustration shows a compass with a lead point, and the attachment used when drawing with ink.

The term *scale* also refers to the physical measuring device used by designers to accurately reduce linear distances to their correct scaled lengths. Scales are special rulers that can be used for measuring in a variety of units and that enable the designer to draw an object larger than, smaller than, or the same size as the real (full-size) object. Scales are calibrated in inches or millimeters much like a regular ruler. They are available in either a flat or a triangular shape (Figure 2-9). Triangular scales are very popular because as many as four scales can be printed on each face. Generally, a triangular scale has as many as 11 different scales on it. The shape also makes them convenient to pick up and use. Flat scales generally have either a two-bevel or four-bevel edge,

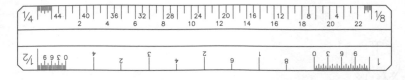

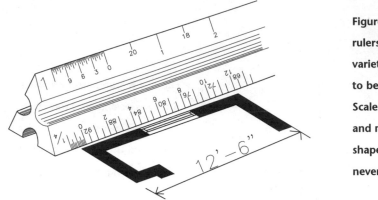

Figure 2-9 Scales are special rulers designed to measure in a variety of units, enabling objects to be drawn at various sizes. Scales are available in English and metric units, and in various shapes and sizes. A scale should never be used as a straightedge.

When using the architect's scale, begin at the 0 point, then count off the number of feet, using the major subdivisions that are marked along the length of the scale. The scaled inches are located on the other side of the 0 point.

The **engineer's scale** is a full divided scale, as it has the inches marked along its edge, which are then divided into decimal parts of an inch. The engineer's scale generally contains 6 different divisions/scales. These divisions are indicated as 10, 20, 30, 40, 50, and 60. These numbers mean "parts to an inch." For example, the 40 scale means 1 inch = 40 feet. As there are 40 subdivisions within an inch, each mark represents 1 foot. This scale can also be used to represent larger units such as 400 or 4,000 feet per inch. Engineer's scales are generally used for drawing large-scale site plans and maps.

Metric scales are used when drawing architectural and interior plans in metric units. The millimeter is the basic unit of the metric scale. Metric scales are based on ratios, such as 1:50, which means 1 mm on the scale represents 50 mm. Typical ratios are 1:10, 1:25, 1:50, 1:100, 1:200, and 1:500. To enlarge a drawing, scales are available in 2:1 and 5:1 ratios. Since metric scales are based on the metric system, using the base 10, it is possible to use single-ratio scales for other ratios. For example, a 1:1 scale with 1-mm markings could also be used to represent 1 mm, 10 mm, 100 mm, or 1000 mm. A 1:2 metric scale could be used for 1 mm to represent 20 mm, 200 mm, and so forth.

Erasers, Erasing Shields, and Brushes

To be able to erase errors and correct drawings is very important to the interior designer. Erasability is one of the key advantages of using a pencil or pen for drawings. Erasers, erasing shields, and brushes are convenient tools of almost equal importance.

depending on the number of scales they carry. Good-quality scales must have sharply defined graduations that are close to the edge for accurate measurements. Scales are not meant to be a straightedge, and should never be used as a pencil or inking guide when drawing a straight line.

There are several different types of scales, but the interior designer will mainly use the architect's scale, engineer's scale, and metric scale.

The **architect's scale** is the one most frequently used by an interior designer. It is used for laying out accurate design and construction drawings in feet and inches. Architectural scales generally contain 11 different divisions, where each major division represents 1 foot. The major divisions are indicated as $3/32$, $1/16$, $1/8$, $3/16$, $1/4$, $3/8$, $1/2$, $3/4$, 1, $1\frac{1}{2}$, and 3. Each one of these divisions represents one foot on the scale. For example, the $1/4$ scale means $1/4$ of an inch on the scale represents 1 foot.

Erasers

A wide variety of both rubber and synthetic erasers are available. A good eraser must be capable of completely removing pencil or ink lines without leaving smudge marks or roughing the surface of the paper. For vellum drafting paper, soft rubber erasers should generally be used. There are also special erasers designed to remove ink. However, be careful, as these erasers are too abrasive for some drawing surfaces. Some ink erasers claim to have a solvent incorporated into them for better erasing of ink. Erasers are available in either block form or stick form inserted into a holder much like a leadholder (Figure 2-10). Vinyl and other plastic erasers are designed for use on plastic drafting film.

Electric erasers are extremely useful when a great amount of erasing is necessary. Electric erasers are small handheld tools that hold long round lengths of eraser that are rotated when turned on. The cordless variety is the most convenient (Figure 2-11).

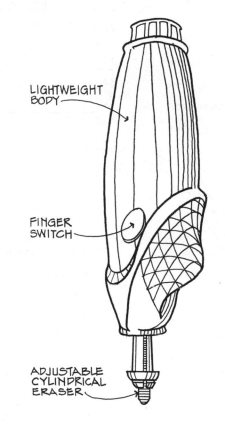

LIGHTWEIGHT BODY

FINGER SWITCH

ADJUSTABLE CYLINDRICAL ERASER

Figure 2-11 An electric eraser can be very handy when erasing large areas of a drawing and is especially convenient when cordless.

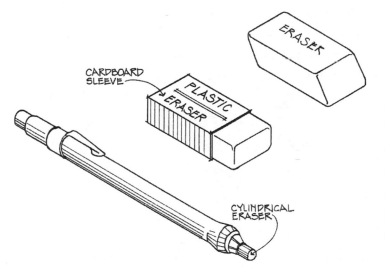

CARDBOARD SLEEVE

ERASER

PLASTIC ERASER

CYLINDRICAL ERASER

Figure 2-10 Erasers come in various shapes and sizes, and different kinds can erase pencil or ink. Shown are a mechanical eraser-holder, a plastic block eraser in a sleeve, and a basic block eraser.

Figure 2-12 An eraser shield allows for precise erasing, as it shields the parts of the drawing that are to remain. The prepunched holes allow the designer to erase only those lines needing to be erased.

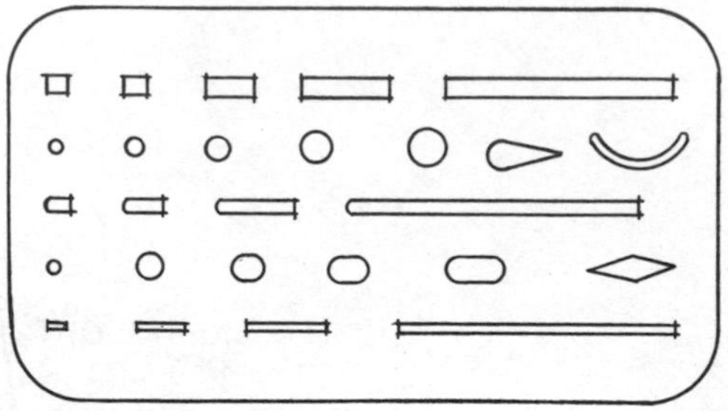

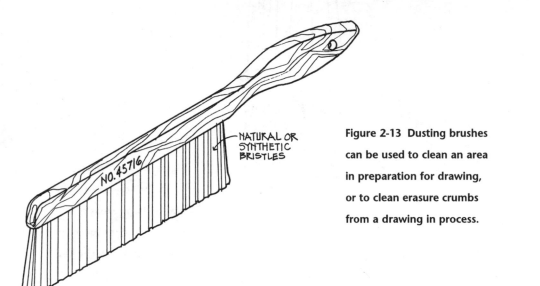

NATURAL OR
SYNTHETIC
BRISTLES

NO. 45716

Figure 2-13 Dusting brushes can be used to clean an area in preparation for drawing, or to clean erasure crumbs from a drawing in process.

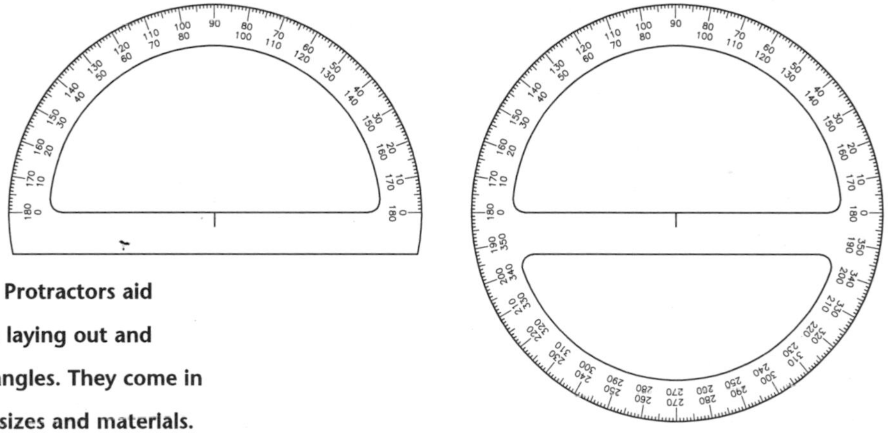

Erasing Shield

A small metal or plastic card with prepunched holes and slots is used to erase precise areas of a drawing, as shown in Figure 2-12. The prepunched holes come in a variety of sizes and shapes, allowing the designer to erase small details and control the erasure up to a particular point. It is also helpful for protecting the drawing surface while using an electric eraser. Although the transparency of a plastic shield can be convenient, a metal shield generally lasts longer.

Brushes

A dusting brush is useful for keeping drafting surfaces clean and free of debris (Figure 2-13). Erasure crumbs are sometimes left on a drawing surface to help prevent smudges, but if they become too abundant they can cause lines to skip, so it is helpful to brush the drawing surface often.

Additional Equipment

A number of additional tools may assist the designer. For example, full-circular (360 degrees) and half-circular (180 degrees) protractors aid in the layout and measuring of angles on a drawing. They are manufactured in a variety of sizes in both metal and plastic (Figure 2-14).

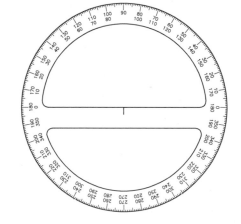

Figure 2-14 Protractors aid designers in laying out and measuring angles. They come in a variety of sizes and materials.

DRAWING AND DRAFTING FUNDAMENTALS 3

Drawing and drafting are forms of visual language that use lines, pictorial images, and symbols to convey specific meanings. Like spoken language, written language, and body language, this visual language has its own unique applications. In the design field, drawing, also called sketching or idea generation, is used as a technique for developing and communicating ideas. Preliminary sketches are used to initiate and explore basic concepts, as illustrated in Figure 3-1. These can be presented to others as is, or refined into presentation drawings that are developed to scale and rendered in more detail. Drawing is thus a means of communication used by designers to effectively convey ideas and converse with one another about how to turn them into reality.

Drafting is a particular type of drawing that conveys specific information about something's size, composition, assembly, and other exacting characteristics. Drafting is usually a means to an end; that is, it serves as a guide on how to make something. For these reasons, drafting is founded on a number of basic premises and rules. A draftsperson's specialized drawings, generally referred to as working drawings or construction drawings, help the designer to develop ideas and communicate to the builder the exact parameters of their design concepts — assisting in the construction of a physical interior environment or building (Figure 3-2). Construction drawings require a great deal of effort to draw, as they must be clear, concise, and accurate, with high-quality lines and legible dimensions and notes.

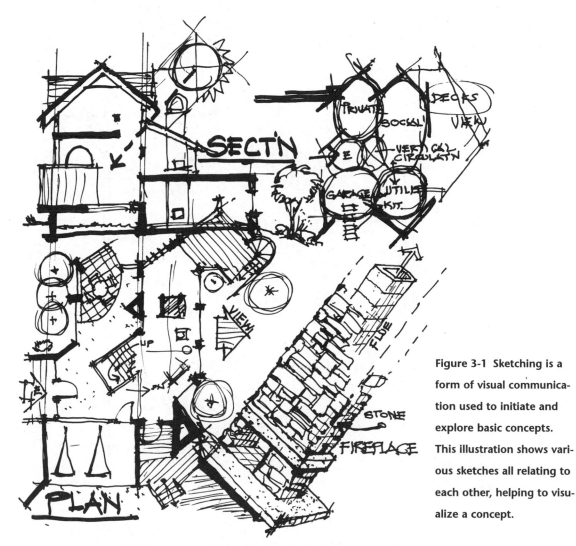

Figure 3-1 Sketching is a form of visual communication used to initiate and explore basic concepts. This illustration shows various sketches all relating to each other, helping to visualize a concept.

21

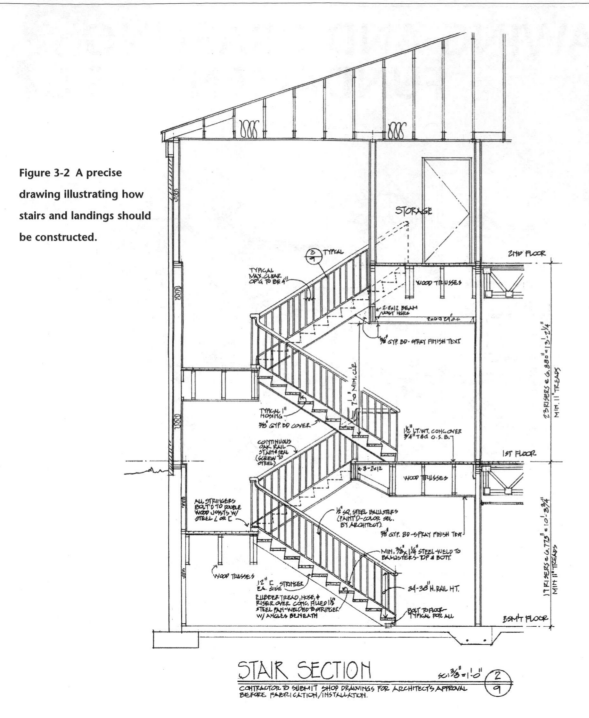

Figure 3-2 A precise drawing illustrating how stairs and landings should be constructed.

STORAGE

③ TYPICAL

TYPICAL MAX. CLEAR OP'G TO BE 4"

WOOD TRUSSES

2-3x12 BEAM JOIST HERE

3x8 EA/22

⅝ GYP. BD.-SPRAY FINISH TEXT

TYPICAL 1" NOSING

⅜ GYP. BD. COVER

CONTINUOUS OAK RAIL STAIN & SEAL (SCREW TO STEEL)

7'-0 MIN. CLR.

½" LT. WT. CONC COVER ¾" T&G O.S.B.

1ST FLOOR

ALL STRINGERS BOLT TO DOUBLE WOOD JOISTS W/ STEEL L OR C

3-2x12

WOOD TRUSSES

½" SQ. STEEL BALUSTERS (PAINT'D-COLOR SEL. BY ARCHITECT)

⅝ GYP. BD-SPRAY FINISH TEXT

MIN. ⅜" x ¼" STEEL WELD TO BALUSTERS-TOP & BOTT.

WOOD TRUSSES

12" C STRINGER EA. SIDE

RUBBER TREAD, NOSE, & RISER OVER CONC. FILLED 1⅛ STEEL PAN-WELDED TO STRINGER W/ ANGLES BENEATH

34-38 H. RAIL HT.

BOLT TO FLOOR TYPICAL FOR ALL

BSM'T FLOOR

2ND FLOOR

23 RISERS @ G. 880"=13-2¼ MIN. 11" TREADS

17 RISERS @ G. 775"=10-8¾ MIN. 11" TREADS

STAIR SECTION

SC: ⅜"=1'-0"

②/⑨

CONTRACTOR TO SUBMIT SHOP DRAWINGS FOR ARCHITECT'S APPROVAL BEFORE FABRICATION/INSTALLATION.

To draw and draft at a professional level, one must learn some basic skills and techniques. This chapter will introduce the basics needed to produce quality and easily readable drawings and so effectively communicate with others.

Starting the Drawing

Drawings are executed on a paper or plastic sheet that is placed on the drawing board or surface. It is usually held in place on the drawing surface with drafting tape placed at the four corners, as illustrated in Figure 3-3. The opposite corners are pulled and taped alternately to stretch and flatten the sheet. When one is finished with the drawing or needs to remove it for a short period of time, the tape is carefully removed and discarded. The sheet can then be stored flat or rolled for convenience. There is a tendency for beginners to roll original drawings and prints with the original line work or printed side on the inside, probably in an effort to protect the line work. However, the preferred way to roll a drawing is to do it with the printed information on the outside. In this way, as the drawing is unrolled, it will tend to curl away from the viewer and toward the surface it is placed on (Figure 3-4). This keeps the drawing from constantly curling up toward the viewer. This technique is also effective for multiple copies stapled together in sets.

Drawings are produced on a variety of surfaces with varying types of media, as discussed in Chapter 2. One of the first steps in composing a properly scaled drawing is to select the best size and format for the surface. To do this effectively, a number of variables must be taken into account. These include the complexity and scale of the drawing, the reproduction technique selected, and the viewing conditions the reader will be under.

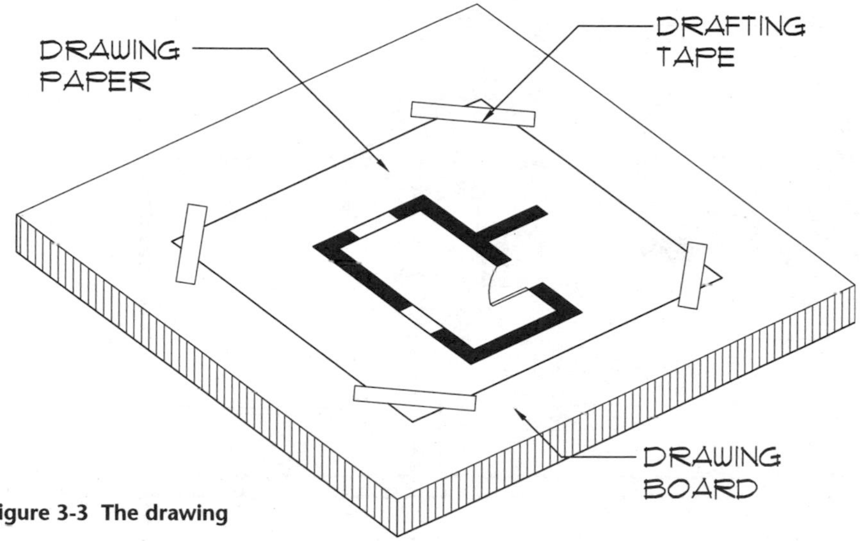

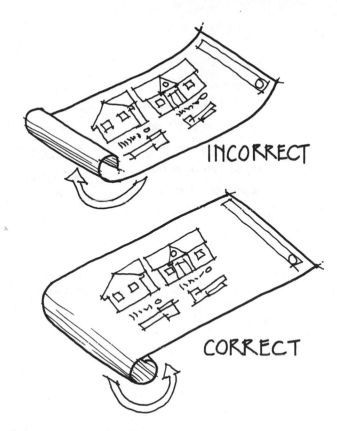

DRAWING PAPER

DRAFTING TAPE

DRAWING BOARD

Figure 3-3 The drawing paper is held in place on the drawing surface with small pieces of drafting tape.

INCORRECT

CORRECT

Figure 3-4 Rolling drawings with the printed information on the inside causes them to curl and hide the drawing from the viewer when unrolled and laid flat. Rolling them with the information on the outside allows the viewer to look at the drawings without having the paper curl up and hide the drawing.

Drawing Page Layout

Original drawings, particularly those done in pencil, need to be kept clean to provide for the clearest reproduction. Smudged drawings will often produce smudged prints that are difficult and time-consuming to read. Graphite from pencils is the greatest threat to drawing cleanliness. Sliding hands, elbows, and equipment over pencil lines will blur them and produce an undesirable patina over the entire drawing surface. The same is true with ink drawings, whether they are done by hand or computer. Time must be allowed for the ink to dry. Equipment should be lifted and placed over drawings, not slid from one area to another. Regular washing of hands and equipment will also help prevent smudging of line work.

In manual drawing, one should start with very light lines and darken those as needed for the final drawing (Figure 3-5). On the computer, "pen" settings determine the value or thickness of a line (Figure 3-6). There is no preliminary stage of drawing with light lines. In manual drawings, it is good practice to start drawing at the upper portion of the sheet and progress toward the bottom of the paper. In this way, most drawings will not be disturbed as you move the equipment and hands down the sheet. Of course, computer drawing allows one to begin almost anywhere on the sheet, compose the drawings, and print out the results in one clean plot. The machine doesn't worry about top to bottom or left to right — it follows the composition set by the designer.

Figure 3-5 When drawing manually, light lines should be used to lay out an image or text. Final lines can then be darkened according to the desired line hierarchy.

Figure 3-6 When using the computer to create a drawing, various "pen" weights/widths can be assigned to lines for the desired line hierarchy.

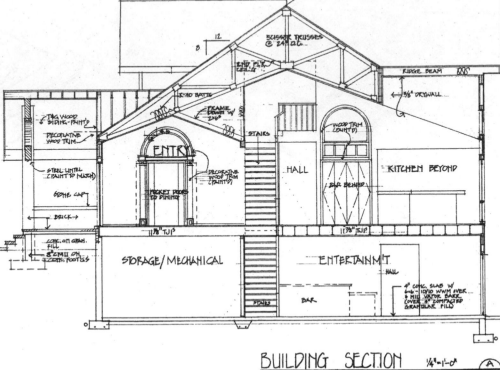

BUILDING SECTION ¼"=1'-0" A/4

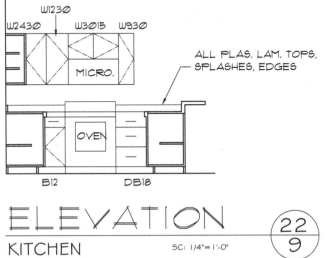

ELEVATION

KITCHEN   SC: 1/4"= 1'-0"   22/9

Line Types

Lines are drawn to describe objects, hidden conditions, and important relationships between components and space. A line drawn on a surface has both direction and weight. The weight of a line refers to its thickness and intensity; a line can also be continuous or dashed. The direction can be straight, curved, diagonal, or a combination of these. In drafting, continuous lines of various weights are used to represent objects and major elements such as structural walls and columns. Dotted lines are usually used to denote objects hidden from view. However, they can also be used to denote other things, such as a wheelchair turning radius or ceiling height changes on a floor plan. The following are the most commonly used line types. Examples are shown in Figure 3-7.

- Cutting lines: show major slices in a building or object.

- Object lines: show major outlines of building elements or objects.

- Hidden lines: indicate areas or objects not visible on the surface, or objects hidden behind others. They are also used to show objects above the cutting plane of a floor plan, such as wall cabinets, beams, arches, etc.

- Centerlines: locate the symmetrical center of objects such as windows, doors, beams, and walls.

- Dimension lines and extension lines: indicate the physical dimensions of objects. Dimensions are placed directly above the dimension line or inserted within it.

- Leaders: line extending from text and ending with an arrow, pointing to an object or place.

- Break lines: indicate where an object or area is not drawn in its entirety.

- Layout lines: are used in the preliminary blocking out of components and for lettering guidelines.

Line Weights and Their Uses

Line weight refers to the blackness (intensity) and width of a line on the drawing surface. In general, heavy (dark) lines are used to represent cutting planes and contours (or outer boundaries) of an object. In a floor-plan view, it is often the walls that are drawn with the darkest lines in order to define the spaces (Figure 3-8). These lines appear to be the closest to the viewer and are perceived as major elements. Medium and lighter lines appear to be farther away from the viewer and are used for secondary emphasis.

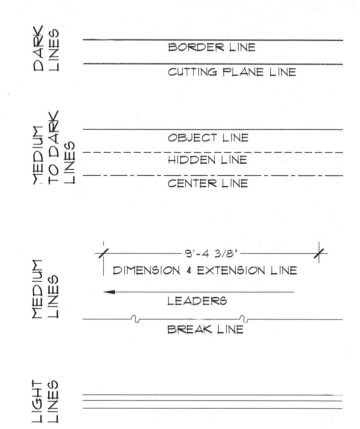

Figure 3-7 **These are common line types used in drawings to describe objects, hidden conditions, and important relationships between components and space.**

Drawings for interior design projects generally use three line widths: thick (dark), medium, and thin (light). Thick lines are generally twice as wide as thin lines, usually $\frac{1}{32}$ inch or about 0.8 mm wide. Thin lines are approximately $\frac{1}{64}$ inch or 0.4 mm wide. Medium lines fall between these two extremes. In pencil drawings, each type can be further broken down, depending on the variety of lead and level of pressure. With the variety of mechanical pencils on the market today, it is easy to control line widths. As discussed in Chapter 2, fine-line mechanical pencils are available in a 0.3, 0.5, 0.7, or 0.9 mm lead. By switching to different pencils, the drafter can vary line weight easily.

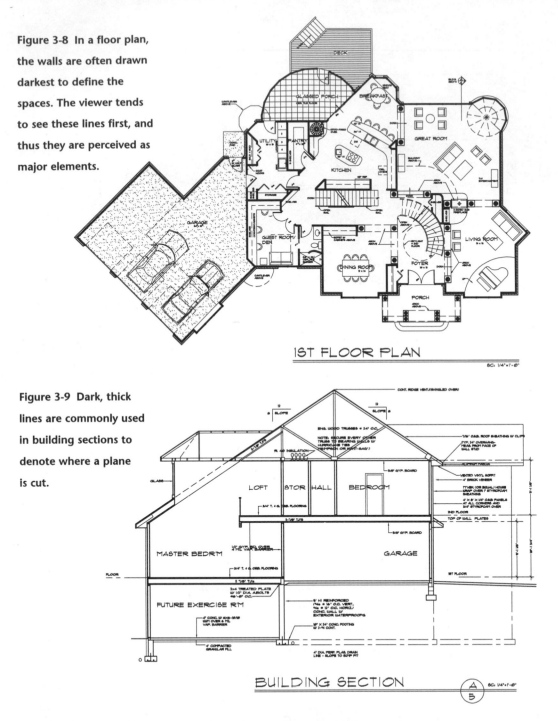

Figure 3-8 In a floor plan, the walls are often drawn darkest to define the spaces. The viewer tends to see these lines first, and thus they are perceived as major elements.

1ST FLOOR PLAN

Figure 3-9 Dark, thick lines are commonly used in building sections to denote where a plane is cut.

BUILDING SECTION

Thick, Dark Lines

Thick, dark lines are used for major sections (Figure 3-9), details, borderlines, and cutting plane lines. A thick, intense line can represent the walls on a floor plan or structural members, such as fireplaces or stairways, the outline of a ceiling on a reflected ceiling plan, or the outline of a building on a site plan. Thick, intense lines are also used to emphasize an object or element.

Medium Lines

Medium-weight lines are used for hidden objects and are usually drawn dashed or dotted. They are also used for outlining the planes of objects and for centerlines, as well as for furniture and equipment.

Thin, Light Lines

Thin, light lines are generally used as guidelines, drawn to help line up certain details or to help with lettering height. These lines should be barely visible and should disappear when a print or copy is made. Lines that are a little darker are used for dimension and extension lines, leaders, door swings, and break lines.

Drafting Standards, Abbreviations, and Symbols

A designer's drawings are used to communicate specific information to many other individuals, such as owners, architects, engineers, and builders. To do this effectively, a number of drafting standards, abbreviations, and symbols have been developed over time that have become uniformly acceptable in the building industry. Although an office may use variations of the standard conventions presented here, most follow some version of these conventions. Many construction terms are abbreviated to save drawing space and eliminate the need for detailed drawings or notes. For example, a W8x31 is a standard steel beam whose exact physical and structural properties are detailed out in industrywide steel manuals. Another example is the commonly used term "above finished floor," which is abbreviated as A.F.F. and used in floor plans and electrical plans. The most commonly used abbreviations are discussed in Chapter 5 and shown in the Appendix.

Symbols are used to represent objects that cannot be depicted accurately or would take too much time to draw. For example, the details of a window in plan or a wall electrical outlet are impractical to draw with clarity at such a small scale. These are represented in the plan by an acceptable symbol that is cross-referenced to a legend or note to more clearly define the object (Figure 3-10). Various components such as sinks, doors, windows, and electrical devices are drawn as symbols. These will be discussed in more depth in later chapters.

Sections cut through the building and materials are depicted using common symbols to represent their elements rather than drawing them as they might appear. For example, a section through a piece of plywood is shown schematically instead of drawn realistically to show the intricate layers of cross-grained wood veneers and glue. Symbols for materials are often drawn differently in a plan view and section view. In most cases, an attempt is made to portray as closely as possible what the actual cross-section would look like (Figure 3-11). Again, typical symbols for architectural materials are discussed more in Chapter 5 and shown in the Appendix.

Lettering

Lettering is used to communicate ideas and to describe elements that cannot be effectively explained with just drawings. In some cases, words are actually a clearer and more economical way to

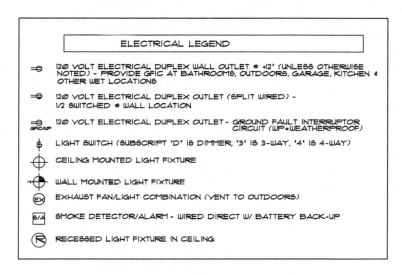

ELECTRICAL LEGEND

120 VOLT ELECTRICAL DUPLEX WALL OUTLET @ +12' (UNLESS OTHERWISE NOTED) - PROVIDE GFIC AT BATHROOMS, OUTDOORS, GARAGE, KITCHEN & OTHER WET LOCATIONS

120 VOLT ELECTRICAL DUPLEX OUTLET (SPLIT WIRED) - 1/2 SWITCHED @ WALL LOCATION

120 VOLT ELECTRICAL DUPLEX OUTLET - GROUND FAULT INTERRUPTOR CIRCUIT (WP=WEATHERPROOF)

LIGHT SWITCH (SUBSCRIPT 'D' IS DIMMER, '3' IS 3-WAY, '4' IS 4-WAY)

CEILING MOUNTED LIGHT FIXTURE

WALL MOUNTED LIGHT FIXTURE

EXHAUST FAN/LIGHT COMBINATION (VENT TO OUTDOORS)

SMOKE DETECTOR/ALARM - WIRED DIRECT W/ BATTERY BACK-UP

RECESSED LIGHT FIXTURE IN CEILING

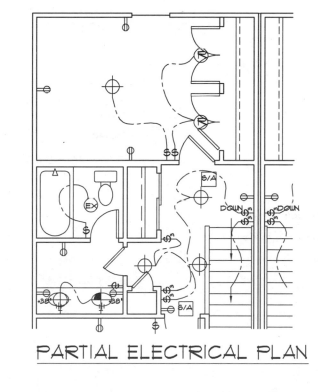

PARTIAL ELECTRICAL PLAN

Figure 3-10 In this illustration, an electrical plan is shown with various electrical symbols, and the legend above describes what each symbol represents.

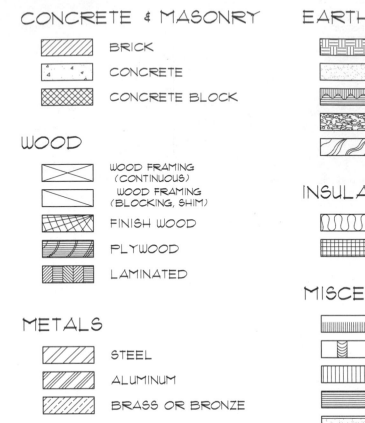

CONCRETE & MASONRY

- BRICK
- CONCRETE
- CONCRETE BLOCK

WOOD

- WOOD FRAMING (CONTINUOUS)
- WOOD FRAMING (BLOCKING, SHIM)
- FINISH WOOD
- PLYWOOD
- LAMINATED

METALS

- STEEL
- ALUMINUM
- BRASS OR BRONZE

EARTH & STONE

- EARTH
- SAND OR LIMESTONE
- ROCK
- GRAVEL
- MARBLE

INSULATION

- BATT (OR LOOSE FILL IN ATTICS)
- RIGID SHEATING

MISCELLANEOUS

- CARPET
- CAULKING
- CERAMIC OR QUARRY TILE
- GLASS
- GYPSUM BOARD

Figure 3-11 Materials that are cut through in section are depicted graphically. An attempt is made to represent the material, but in general it is drawn simplistically, since drawing all the intricate details would be too time-consuming.

communicate. To ensure written words are quickly understood, a universal lettering style is commonly employed by designers and architects (Figure 3-12). This style, based on the Roman alphabet, generally consists of all capital letters for ease of reading. Although most designers employ a universal-looking style, individual styles do develop and are often recognized and associated with the person who uses them. However, stylistic differences must not be so extreme that letters and words become difficult or time-consuming to read. The intent of architectural lettering is to communicate quickly and clearly. Many firms attempt to unify lettering among their personnel by adopting an office standard.

Today, computer software quickly produces lettering in many styles that appear to be hand-lettered or typed (Figure 3-13). Some of these are so realistic it is difficult to tell whether they really are done by hand or by computer. However, this does not mean that there is not a need for a student or designer to learn and produce good hand-lettering. The ability to hand-letter is still much alive and needed. We still need to have effective handwriting when communicating with clients, builders, and many others in the field. A designer's lettering style can also be a kind of professional trademark that distinguishes him or her as a creative individual.

Basic Guidelines for Lettering

Good lettering is made by consistency. This includes height of letters, style, and spacing between letters. To maintain consistency in height, hand-lettering is always done using two or more horizontal guidelines. To maintain consistency between lines of lettering, the distance between these lines should be measured with a scale or other device. Then, when the draftsperson gains more proficiency, this distance can be fairly accurately "eyeballed" in. The two lines serve as the upper and lower limits of the letters. A third line can serve as a consistent guide for parts of letters or even lower-case let-

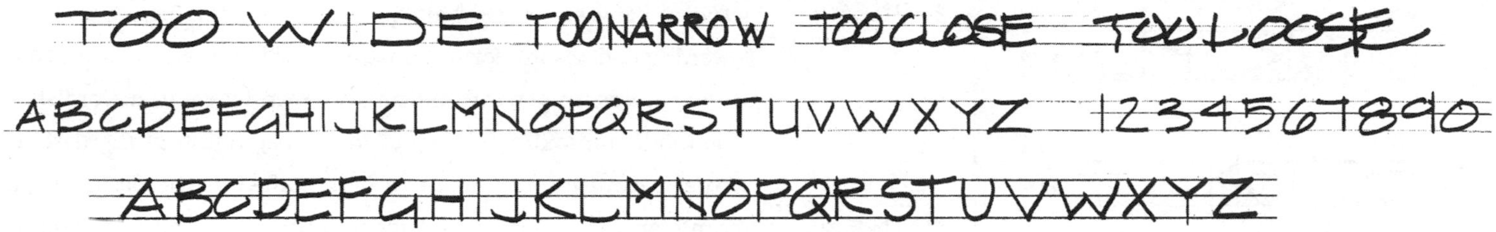

Figure 3-12 In order to make words and letters in drawings quickly and easily understood, a universal style of lettering is used that is usually done in all capital letters.

Figure 3-13 Lettering on the computer can be done in many styles, even one that simulates hand-lettering.

STYLE	SAMPLE
ARCHSTYL.SHX	A B C D E F G H I J K L M N O P Q R S T U V W X Y Z 1 2 3 4 5 6 7 8 9 0
ARIAL	ABCDEFGHIJKLMNOPQRSTUVWXYZ 1234567890
BELL MT	ABCDEFGHIJKLMNOPQRSTUVWXYZ 1234567890
BERLIN SANS FB	ABCDEFGHIJKLMNOPQRSTUVWXYZ 1234567890
BOOK ANTIQUA	ABCDEFGHIJKLMNOPQRSTUVWXYZ 1234567890
CENTURY	ABCDEFGHIJKLMNOPQRSTUVWXYZ 1234567890
CITY BLUEPRINT	ABCDEFGHIJKLMNOPQRSTUVWXYZ 1234567890
COPPERPLATE GOTHIC	ABCDEFGHIJKLMNOPQRSTUVWXYZ 1234567890
COUNTRY BLUEPRINT	ABCDEFGHIJKLMNOPQRSTUVWXYZ 1234567890
ERAS MEDIUM ITC	ABCDEFGHIJKLMNOPQRSTUVWXYZ 1234567890
GILL SANS MT	ABCDEFGHIJKLMNOPQRSTUVWXYZ 1234567890
LUCIDA CONSOLE	A B C D E F G H I J K L M N O P Q R S T U V W X Y Z 1 2 3 4 5 6 7 8 9 0
ROMANS	A B C D E F G H I J K L M N O P Q R S T U V W X Y Z 1 2 3 4 5 6 7 8 9 0
STYLUS BT	ABCDEFGHIJKLMNOPQRSTUVWXYZ 1234567890
TAHOMA	ABCDEFGHIJKLMNOPQRSTUVWXYZ 1234567890
TIMES NEW ROMAN	ABCDEFGHIJKLMNOPQRSTUVWXYZ 1234567890
VERDANA	ABCDEFGHIJKLMNOPQRSTUVWXYZ 1234567890

ters (Figure 3-14). The draftsperson must endeavor to keep the letters within the top and bottom lines, and not let parts of the letters extend beyond these. In most cases, the guidelines are produced with such a light line that they are left in and not erased. In pen-and-ink drawing, these lines might be laid out in nonreproducible blue pencil lines.

Most designers prefer vertical strokes in lettering, although slanted characters are often faster to produce. Letters should be produced with bold strokes, not drawn with a series of sketched and ragged lines. There should be a distinct start and stop to each line stroke within a letter. Shapes and proportions of lettering should be consistent throughout a drawing (Figure 3-15). Close attention

Figure 3-14 Horizontal guidelines can be used for height consistency when lettering. Two or three guidelines can be used, and these lines can remain on the drawing if produced lightly.

Figure 3-15 Lettering should be consistent throughout a drawing; the shapes and proportions should be similar.

should be given to the width of a letter, as well as the proportional spaces between letters. This spacing is very important, as it gives words good visual formation and clarifies their relationship to other words. In general, spacing between letters in a word should be made approximately equal in the beginning of the designer's career. However, this rule can be modified as the designer gains confidence, as proportional spacing can vary a bit, depending on the shapes of the letters.

One shortcut used for lettering by some designers is the aid of a small triangle carried along the parallel bar (or other horizontal device) and quickly brought into play for vertical strokes within a letter. This technique produces a very consistent vertical lettering style, but some designers see it as a crutch. If this technique is used, it should be discontinued once the draftsperson gains the ability and confidence to produce accurate vertical lines.

To effectively learn proper lettering, one should produce words and numbers, not just individual letters. Practice by copying phrases from articles and books, or writing a story. This will give you better skills in forming properly proportioned letters and spaces between them.

DRAWING CLASSIFICATION SYSTEMS 4

Design drawings enable the professional designer to visualize and communicate the features of a three-dimensional object or interior space. Then, detailed construction drawings are made to accurately describe what materials are to be used and how the object or space is to be constructed. The design drawing can be a three-dimensional pictorial sketch that shows what the object looks like in reality (Figure 4-1), or a series of related yet different views of the object, such as a plan or top view and an elevation, as illustrated in Figure 4-2. The first approach, the single view, attempts to portray the object as the eye would see it. The second approach, the multiview, relies on the eye to view a series of images and the mind to then put these views together into a whole. For example, a floor plan shows width and length of objects within a space. An elevation view is then drawn to illustrate height, but no third dimension or true depth is visually indicated. Figure 4-3 classifies the various drawing systems according to these two broad categories. Many computer software programs now can produce some very convincing single-view drawings from multiviews, then allow designers to quickly flip back and forth between these two types of drawings.

Multiview Drawings

Multiview drawings can be visualized by what is commonly called the glass box theory. In this process, a three-dimensional object is imagined to be surrounded by a clear glass box (Figure 4-4). If the viewer looks along the perpendicular through any plane on the glass box, the object can be imagined to be a flat, two-dimensional image on that particular glass pane. The object can be viewed

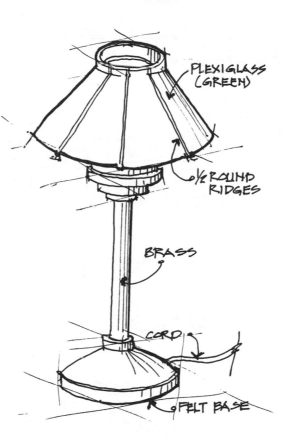

Figure 4-1 Design drawings may consist of pictorial sketches that show an object as the eye might see it.

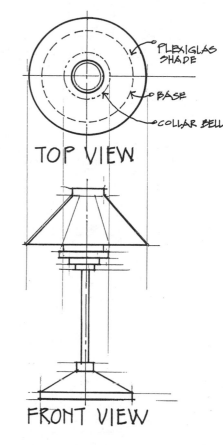

Figure 4-2 Different views of an object help the eye understand the object as a whole.

31

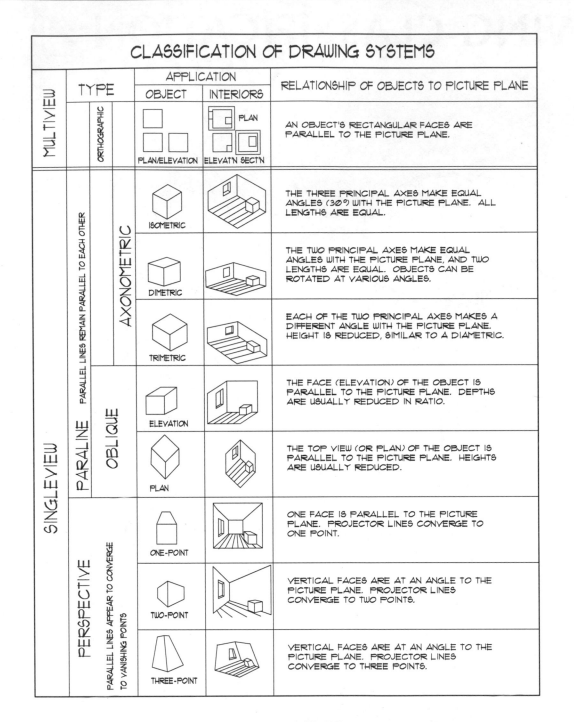

CLASSIFICATION OF DRAWING SYSTEMS

	TYPE	APPLICATION		RELATIONSHIP OF OBJECTS TO PICTURE PLANE
		OBJECT	INTERIORS	
MULTIVIEW	ORTHOGRAPHIC	PLAN/ELEVATION	PLAN / ELEVAT'N SECT'N	AN OBJECT'S RECTANGULAR FACES ARE PARALLEL TO THE PICTURE PLANE.
SINGLE VIEW — PARALINE (PARALLEL LINES REMAIN PARALLEL TO EACH OTHER) — AXONOMETRIC		ISOMETRIC		THE THREE PRINCIPAL AXES MAKE EQUAL ANGLES (30°) WITH THE PICTURE PLANE. ALL LENGTHS ARE EQUAL.
		DIMETRIC		THE TWO PRINCIPAL AXES MAKE EQUAL ANGLES WITH THE PICTURE PLANE, AND TWO LENGTHS ARE EQUAL. OBJECTS CAN BE ROTATED AT VARIOUS ANGLES.
		TRIMETRIC		EACH OF THE TWO PRINCIPAL AXES MAKES A DIFFERENT ANGLE WITH THE PICTURE PLANE. HEIGHT IS REDUCED, SIMILAR TO A DIAMETRIC.
OBLIQUE		ELEVATION		THE FACE (ELEVATION) OF THE OBJECT IS PARALLEL TO THE PICTURE PLANE. DEPTHS ARE USUALLY REDUCED IN RATIO.
		PLAN		THE TOP VIEW (OR PLAN) OF THE OBJECT IS PARALLEL TO THE PICTURE PLANE. HEIGHTS ARE USUALLY REDUCED.
PERSPECTIVE (PARALLEL LINES APPEAR TO CONVERGE TO VANISHING POINTS)		ONE-POINT		ONE FACE IS PARALLEL TO THE PICTURE PLANE. PROJECTOR LINES CONVERGE TO ONE POINT.
		TWO-POINT		VERTICAL FACES ARE AT AN ANGLE TO THE PICTURE PLANE. PROJECTOR LINES CONVERGE TO TWO POINTS.
		THREE-POINT		VERTICAL FACES ARE AT AN ANGLE TO THE PICTURE PLANE. PROJECTOR LINES CONVERGE TO THREE POINTS.

from above (called a plan view) or the side (called an elevation view). In turn, if these images are drawn separately, the viewer reverses the process and projects (by imagining) the multiviews onto a whole three-dimensional object.

Orthographic Projections

The word *orthographic* refers to the projection system that is used to derive multiview drawings based on the glass box model. Drawings that appear on a surface are the view a person sees on the transparent viewing plane that is positioned perpendicular to the viewer's line of sight and the object. In the orthographic system, the object is placed in a series of positions (plan or elevation) relative to the viewing plane.

The most common types of orthographic drawings are the plan, elevation, and section (Figure 4-5). However, no single one of these drawings can communicate the actual configuration of a three-dimensional object or space. They must be used together to accurately depict spatial and solid elements. In fact, more complex objects and spaces will require several more of each of these drawings. Multiview drawings lack the pictorial effect of perspectives (which are a type of single-view drawing), yet are more accurate for conveying correctly scaled objects, interiors, and buildings.

Single-view Drawings

Single-view drawings attempt to picture an object or space as we normally see it in reality with all three dimensions appearing simultaneously. They present relationships of objects, space, and materials in a realistic or photographic-looking manner. Single-view drawings can be either paraline or perspective views. In paraline drawings, lines are drawn parallel to one another, and object features retain this relationship as they appear to recede in the dis-

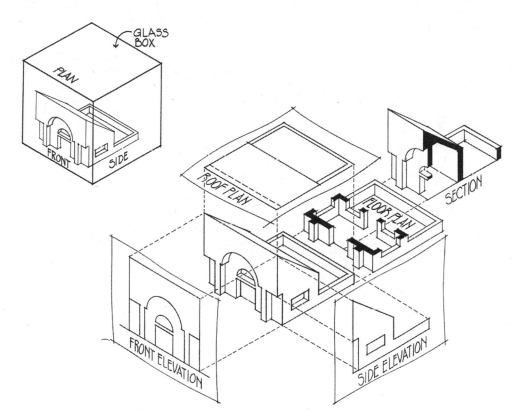

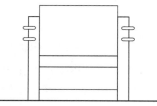

Figure 4-4 The glass box theory portrays a three-dimensional object as though surrounded by a clear glass box, with the corresponding view projected to the glass plane.

Figure 4-3 *(opposite page)* This chart classifies various drawing systems into two broad categories: single-view and multiview.

FRONT ELEVATION

SIDE ELEVATION

PLAN

tance (Figure 4-6). This parallel phenomenon is what gives this drawing system the name *paraline*.

The perspective view produces a more realistic picture, as it attempts to duplicate the way our eyes actually see objects and space. In perspective drawing, parallel lines in space or on an object appear to converge to a common distant vanishing point, as illustrated in Figure 4-7. Perspective drawings resemble a photograph and are the most convincing of the drawing systems. They generally take more time to produce by hand, but computer generation has made the process less time-consuming.

Figure 4-5 The plan, elevation, and section are the most common multiview drawings.

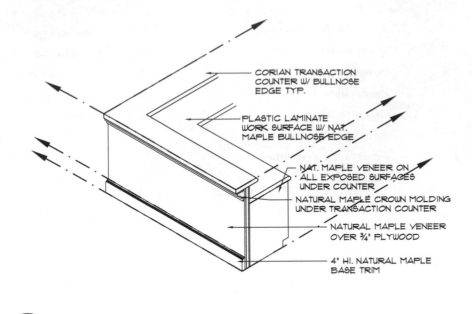

CORIAN TRANSACTION
COUNTER W/ BULLNOSE
EDGE TYP.

PLASTIC LAMINATE
WORK SURFACE W/ NAT.
MAPLE BULLNOSE EDGE

NAT. MAPLE VENEER ON
ALL EXPOSED SURFACES
UNDER COUNTER

NATURAL MAPLE CROWN MOLDING
UNDER TRANSACTION COUNTER

NATURAL MAPLE VENEER
OVER ¾" PLYWOOD

4" HI. NATURAL MAPLE
BASE TRIM

RECEPTION DESK SECTION

Ⓐ SCALE: 1"=1'-0"

Figure 4-6 Lines are drawn parallel to one another in a paraline drawing, a form of single-view drawing.

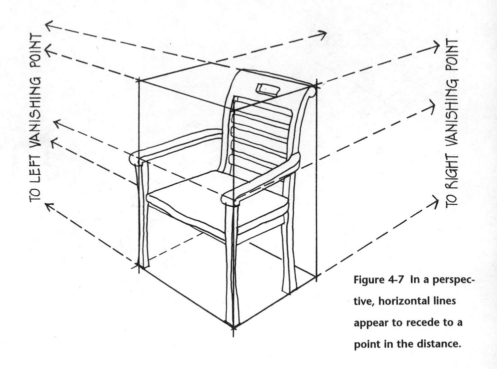

Figure 4-7 In a perspective, horizontal lines appear to recede to a point in the distance.

Paraline Drawings

Paralines are usually faster and easier to develop than perspectives, as receding horizontal lines can be drawn with instruments, without calculating depths or drawing lines to a common vanishing point as is necessary in perspective drawings. However, when using computer-aided design (CAD), the speed of the rendering programs will govern which of these is produced the quickest. Paraline drawings are categorized according to the projection method used to develop them, and can be subdivided into two distinct types, axonometric and oblique (Figure 4-8).

Axonometric Projections

Some interior designers refer to all paralines as axonometrics; however, axonometric drawings are technically just one form of paraline drawing. *Axonometric* means "measurable along the axes."

Axonometric drawings include three axes that relate to width, depth, and height. Each line drawn parallel to these axes is drawn at an exact scale with the true length of the object depicted. The axonometric projection system consists of three primary views: isometric, dimetric, and trimetric. These views are distinguished by the degree of variation visible of the principal faces of the object. In the isometric view, all faces represent true scales. The latter two systems show one or more faces in a reduced scale.

Isometric (derived from the Greek words meaning "equal measure") drawings present the three primary faces of an object equally and at the same angle with the viewing plane. The planes of width and depth are drawn at 30 degrees and the height is held vertical (Figure 4-9). Dimensions are scaled equally along all three axes. Isometric drawings are the easiest of the axonometric systems

PARALINE (AXONOMETRIC)

Figure 4-8 There are two types
of paraline drawings:
axonometric and oblique.

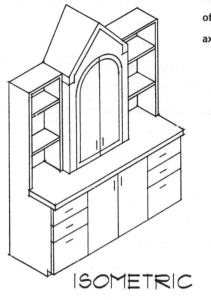

ISOMETRIC

Figure 4-9 Isometric drawings
present the three primary
faces of an object equally and
at the same angle with the
viewing plane.

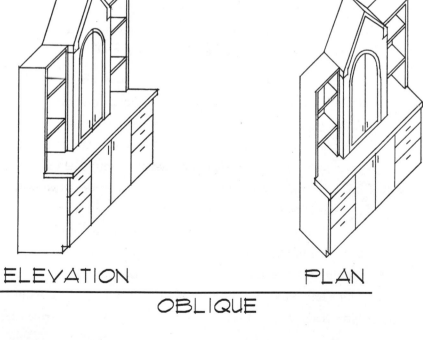

ELEVATION

PLAN

OBLIQUE

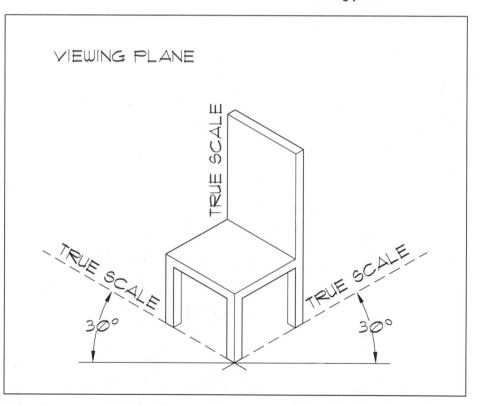

VIEWING PLANE

TRUE SCALE

TRUE SCALE

TRUE SCALE

30°   30°

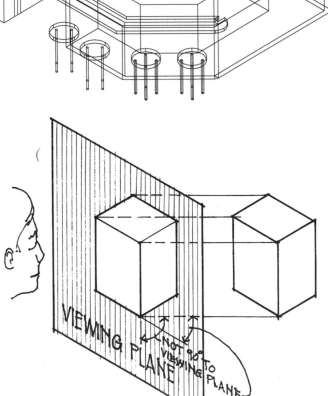

Figure 4-10 Isometric drawings are generally constructed as "wire frames" showing the construction lines.

to construct, but the visual distortion caused by parallel lines not appearing to converge to a distant vanishing point gives them a distinctly pictorial effect. Computer software now allows the designer to program in dimensions for width, height, and depth. Then, isometric "wire frames" that show the construction lines can be quickly generated on the screen, as illustrated in Figure 4-10. Hidden or unwanted lines can also be easily turned off or removed from the image.

In dimetric and trimetric drawings, all principal faces are not held at equal angles to the picture plane (Figure 4-11). The dimetric drawing makes two faces equally visible and shortens the third face. The trimetric rotates an object so that all three faces are at different angles to the picture plane.

In both dimetric and trimetric drawings, the scale along one or more of the principal faces is reduced proportionately to emphasize or deemphasize a feature of the object. Both dimetric and trimetric drawings are more time-consuming to construct than isometric drawings, but have the advantage of presenting an object's best features and more closely resembling perspective drawings.

Oblique Projections

Oblique projections are popular among interior designers. Although there are several types of oblique drawings, the plan oblique and elevation oblique are the most commonly used. In these drawings, the floor plan or elevation serves as the true face on the picture plane, and parallel lines are projected vertically or horizontally at an angle other than 90 degrees from this face. The viewer's lines of sight are parallel, but are not at right angles with the viewing plane (Figure 4-12). Oblique drawings also have the feature that one face of an object is always parallel to the viewing plane and represented in true proportion, such as an elevation or plan view. The parallel lines are sometimes reduced in scale (short-

Figure 4-12 In a plan oblique drawing, the true plane can be rotated at any angle, although the 30-60 degree and 45-45 degree are most popular.

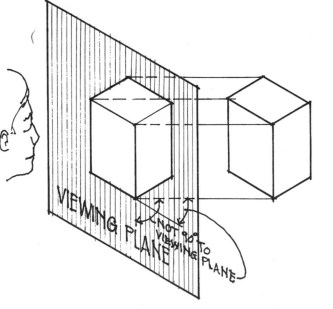

VIEWING PLANE

NOT 90° TO VIEWING PLANE

ened) from true size to reduce the visual distortion. With the use of specialized computer software, these views can be generated or extruded from a plan or elevation view with the click of a mouse.

To produce a plan oblique, the true shaped plan can be rotated to any angle, although the 30/60-degree and 45/45-degree are the most popular. The advantage of the plan oblique is that the building's floor plan can be used directly to generate this kind of drawing. By contrast, isometrics are more time-consuming because of the extra projections and dimensioning required. A floor plan or elevation cannot be used directly to produce an isometric drawing.

Perspective Drawings

A perspective drawings is a type of single-view drawing that is more realistic-looking than an oblique or axonometric drawing. In a perspective drawing, objects appear to diminish in size as they recede into the distance, and lines that are parallel in the actual object appear to converge at some distant point on the horizon (termed the *vanishing point*). Perspectives are used primarily as presentation drawings to portray a finished object, building, or interior space (Figure 4-13). Perspectives most closely duplicate what our eye or a camera sees.

Perspectives have characteristics that distinguish them from paraline and orthographic drawings. These characteristics are:

- Convergence of parallel lines
- Diminution of size
- Foreshortening
- Overlapping of forms

These properties, as illustrated in Figure 4-14, help make perspectives very realistic compared to the other types of drawings. Perspective drawings are broken into three basic categories accord-

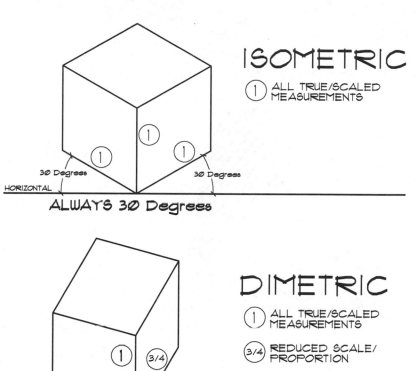

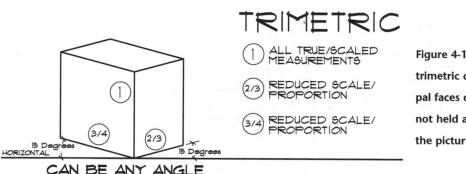

Figure 4-11 In diametric and trimetric drawings, all principal faces of an object are not held at equal angles to the picture plane.

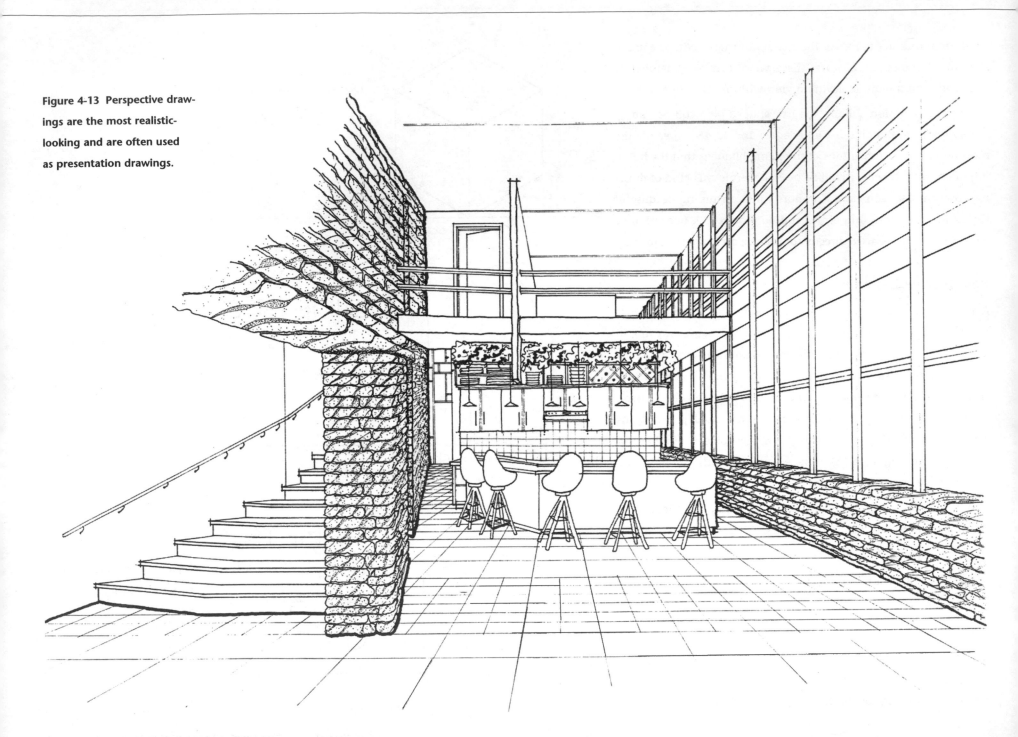

Figure 4-13 Perspective drawings are the most realistic-looking and are often used as presentation drawings.

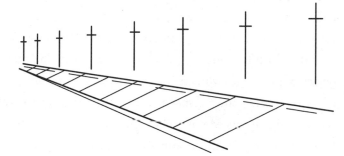

CONVERGENCE OF PARALLEL LINES

PARALLEL LINES APPEAR TO GET CLOSER TO ONE ANOTHER INTO THE DISTANCE AND MERGE INTO A DISTANT POINT

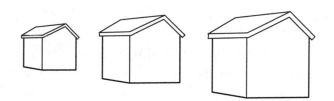

DIMINUTION OF SIZE

OBJECTS APPEAR TO BECOME SMALLER AS THEY RECEDE INTO THE DISTANCE

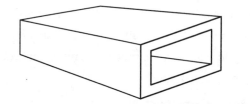

FORESHORTENING

OBJECTS APPEAR TO LOSE HEIGHT, WIDTH, AND LENGTH TOWARD A VANISHING POINT

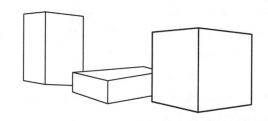

OVERLAPPING OF FORMS

OBJECTS APPEAR TO LAY OVER ONE ANOTHER, GIVING A CLUE TO WHICH ARE IN FRONT OR BEHIND

Figure 4-14 Perspective drawings use four properties that make them more realistic than paraline and orthographic drawings.

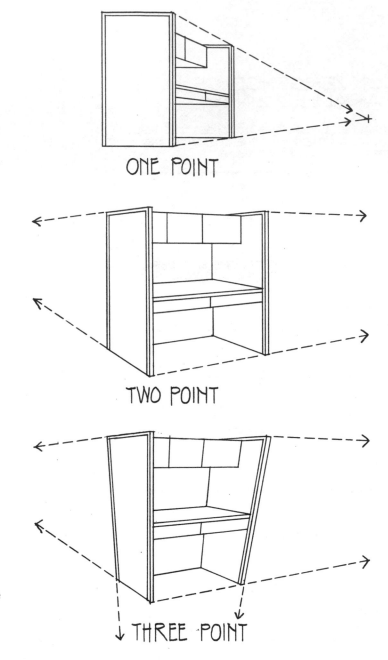

ONE POINT

TWO POINT

↓ THREE POINT

Figure 4-15 There are three basic categories of perspective drawings, depending on the number of vanishing points.

ing to the number of vanishing points used to construct them (Figure 4-15). To construct perspectives, an imaginary picture plane is placed between the observer and the object (or interior) to be drawn. If this plane can be placed parallel to one plane of an object, parallel lines will appear to converge to only one point, producing the one-point perspective, as shown in Figure 4-16. If the picture plane is placed parallel to only one set of lines (the vertical lines, for example), the results are termed a *two-point perspective* (Figure 4-17). The parallel lines then appear to converge to two vanishing points. A three-point perspective is produced when all the lines or faces of an object are oblique (not parallel) to the picture plane. This method is not often used for interior spaces, but rather for tall buildings. Each of these perspective types can be hand-drawn in a number of different ways. A projection system can be used to produce an individualistic drawing for a specific object or space (Figure 4-18). Or a preconstructed perspective grid can be made and overlay sheets placed over it to draw a perspective. One method for constructing a grid is shown in Figure 4-19. Perspective grids can be drawn for each project, or preprinted grids can be made with the lines already drawn in true perspective. These grids can be generated by hand or computer, or one can purchase preprinted grids.

One-Point Perspectives

Of the three types of perspective, the one-point is perhaps the easiest to understand and construct. In one-point perspectives, receding lines or sides of an object appear to vanish to a single point on the horizon. These types of perspectives are often used to produce room interiors, either from an elevation (front view) or plan (top view), depending on where the observer is standing (called the *station point*), as illustrated in Figure 4-20. The setup for both of these

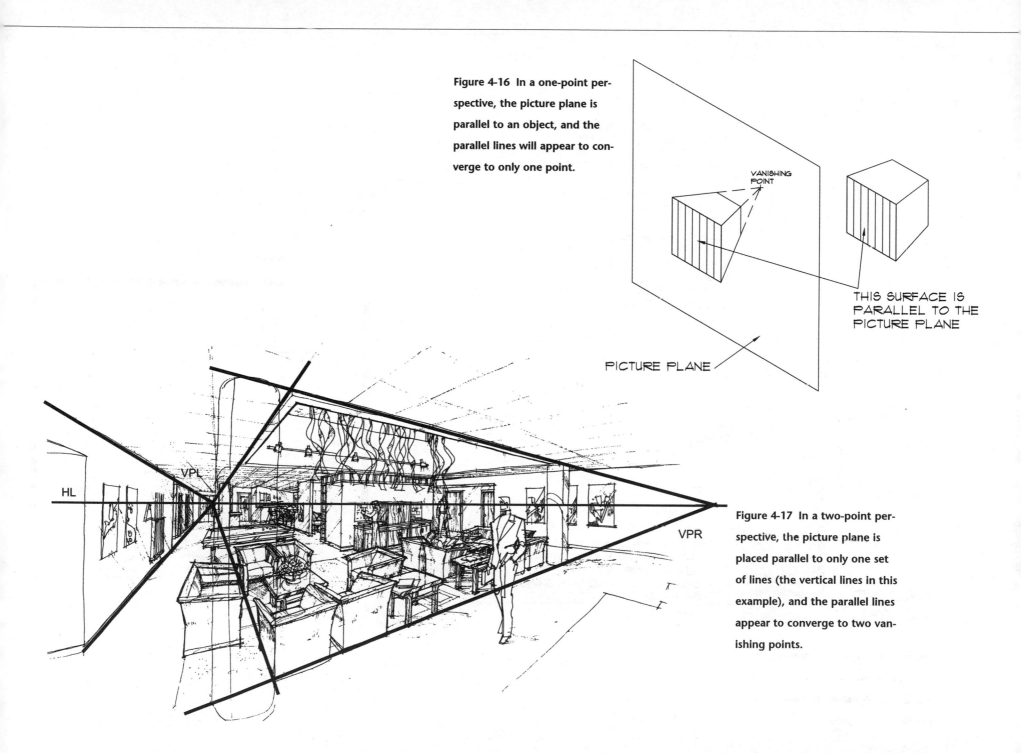

Figure 4-16 In a one-point perspective, the picture plane is parallel to an object, and the parallel lines will appear to converge to only one point.

VANISHING POINT

THIS SURFACE IS PARALLEL TO THE PICTURE PLANE

PICTURE PLANE

HL

VPL

VPR

Figure 4-17 In a two-point perspective, the picture plane is placed parallel to only one set of lines (the vertical lines in this example), and the parallel lines appear to converge to two vanishing points.

PLAN PROJECTION METHOD

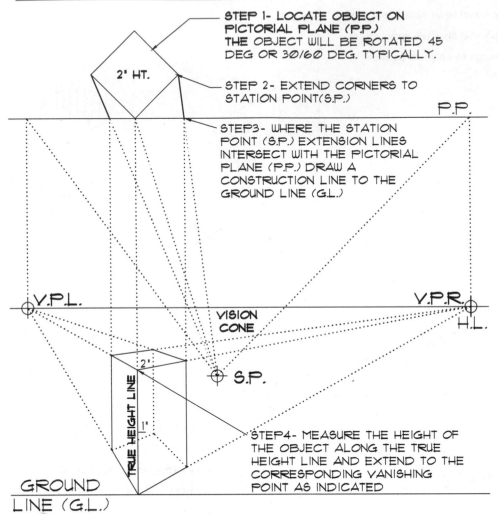

STEP 1- LOCATE OBJECT ON PICTORIAL PLANE (P.P.) THE OBJECT WILL BE ROTATED 45 DEG OR 30/60 DEG. TYPICALLY.

2' HT.

STEP 2- EXTEND CORNERS TO STATION POINT(S.P.)

P.P.

STEP 3- WHERE THE STATION POINT (S.P.) EXTENSION LINES INTERSECT WITH THE PICTORIAL PLANE (P.P.) DRAW A CONSTRUCTION LINE TO THE GROUND LINE (G.L.)

V.P.L.

V.P.R.

VISION CONE

H.L.

S.P.

2'

TRUE HEIGHT LINE

1"

STEP 4- MEASURE THE HEIGHT OF THE OBJECT ALONG THE TRUE HEIGHT LINE AND EXTEND TO THE CORRESPONDING VANISHING POINT AS INDICATED

GROUND LINE (G.L.)

Figure 4-18 In the hand-drawn method, a plan projection system is used to produce an individualistic drawing for a specific object or space.

Figure 4-20 The station point, shown in this plan view, represents the point from which the interior of the room will be seen in perspective.

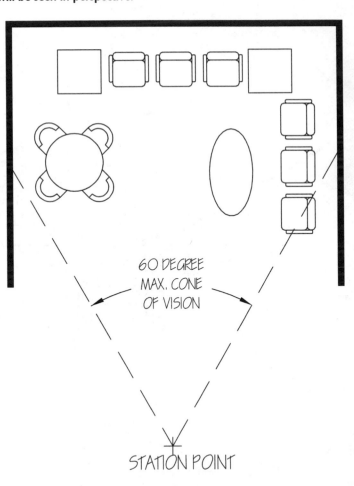

60 DEGREE MAX. CONE OF VISION

STATION POINT

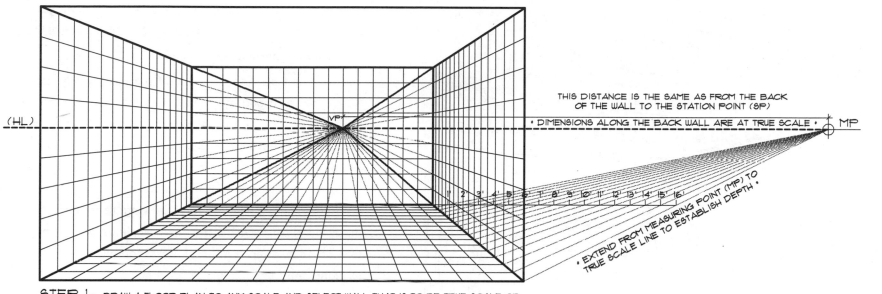

THIS DISTANCE IS THE SAME AS FROM THE BACK OF THE WALL TO THE STATION POINT (SP)

• DIMENSIONS ALONG THE BACK WALL ARE AT TRUE SCALE •   MP

(HL)

• EXTEND FROM MEASURING POINT (MP) TO TRUE SCALE LINE TO ESTABLISH DEPTH •

STEP 1- DRAW A FLOOR PLAN TO ANY SCALE AND SELECT WALL THAT IS TO BE TRUE SCALE OR BACK PARALLEL WALL IN THE PERSPECTIVE. PICK STATION POINT SP OF OBSERVER IN PLAN, NOTING THIS POINT SHOULD BE APPROXIMATELY A 30-60 DEG. CONE OF VISION TO INCORPORATE SOME OF THE SIDE WALLS. MEASURE & RECORD THIS DISTANCE (IN SCALED FEET) FROM SP TO WALL B, WHEN CONSTRUCTING A PERSPECTIVE GRID WITHOUT PLAN MEASUREMENT, THIS DISTANCE CAN OFTEN BE ASSUMED TO BE 1 TO 1 1/2 TIMES THE WIDTH OF WALL B.

STEP 2 - MAKING THE GRID: TO WHATEVER SCALE DESIRED (OFTEN 1/2' = 1'-0'), DRAW WALL B IN TRUE VERTICAL PROJECTION AND MARK OFF IN ONE FOOT INCREMENTS. DRAW A HORIZON LINE FIVE FEET ABOVE THE FLOOR OR BASELINE. PLACE A DOT ON HORIZON LINE CORRESPONDING TO YOUR POSITION FROM SIDEWALLS ON FLOOR PLAN (SAME DISTANCE FROM WALLS B & C), AND CALL THIS THE VANISHING POINT VP. DRAW LINES FROM ROOM CORNERS (WALL B) THROUGH VP.

STEP 3 - EXTEND BASELINE AT WALL B AND MARK IN ONE FOOT INCREMENTS (SAME SCALE AS WALL B). MEASURE DISTANCE FROM VP TO MEASURING POINT MP EQUAL TO DISTANCE FROM SP TO WALL B (STEP 1).

STEP 4 - DRAW LINES FROM MP THROUGH THE ONE FOOT INCREMENTS ALONG BASELINE AND EXTEND TO FLOOR AND WALL C JUNCTION. FROM THESE MARKS, DRAW HORIZONTAL LINES ALONG THE FLOOR, WHICH MARK OFF ONE FOOT INCREMENTS RECEDING TOWARD WALL B. DRAW VERTICAL LINES ON WALLS A & C FROM ENDS OF EACH OF THESE FLOOR LINES. EXTEND THESE LINES HORIZONTALLY TO GRID OFF THE CEILING.

STEP 5 - EXTEND LINES FROM THE VP THROUGH THE FOOT INCREMENTS ON THE PERIMETER OF WALL B, FINISHING THE GRID PERSPECTIVE TO BE ONE FOOT SQUARES AS THEY LOOK IN PERSPECTIVE.

STEP 6 - IF YOU DREW THE GRID NICE AND NEAT, TRACE IT IN INK AND KEEP IT FOR FUTURE USAGE WITH OVERLAY PAPER. MAKE A SERIES OF GRIDS WITH VARYING STATION POINTS, DIMENSIONS, ETC. FOR VARIETY. NOTE THAT YOU CAN TURN THE GRID ON END, UPSIDE DOWN, OR REVERSE TO PRODUCE DIFFERENT ROOM AND VANISHING POINT CONFIGURATIONS.

Figure 4-19 An example of how to draw a one-point perspective grid.

Figure 4-21 The two-point perspective is used more often than the one-point and three-point perspectives, because it portrays a more realistic view of an object or space.

is exactly the same, the difference being whether the observer is positioned above or at the horizon. The station point can also be moved to the left or right to emphasize the particulars of the space.

Two-Point Perspective

The two-point perspective is one of the most widely used of the three types, as it portrays the most realistic view for the observer (Figure 4-21). By placing the object at unequal angles from the right and left vanishing points (which corresponds to the viewer's position in the space), dynamic views can be produced. However, if the viewer's position is moved too far over to one side or the other, distortions can occur in the final drawing. In most interior views, the eye-level perspective is the preferred choice. Two-point perspectives are more difficult to hand-draw than one-point perspectives, as planes must be projected to two vanishing points, as illustrated in Figure 4-22.

Three-Point Perspective

Three-point perspectives are generally drawn with the viewer at a distance above the horizon (bird's-eye view) or below the horizon (worm's-eye view). The three-point perspective is used mostly for very tall buildings and is rarely used in interior spaces, unless they are multistoried. Three-point perspectives are more complicated than the former two types, as a third vanishing point is introduced, which precludes all parallel lines.

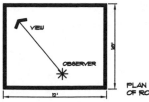

MEASURE THE DIMENSIONS OF THE ROOM AND ASSUME YOUR DIRECTION OF VIEW (AND YOUR GENERAL LOCATION IN THE ROOM.)

Figure 4-22 How to draw a two-point perspective grid.

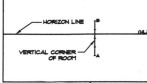

USE A LARGE SHEET OF PAPER FOR YOUR DRAWING AND SCALE THE PERSPECTIVE TO THE PAPER. SCALE THE HEIGHT OF THE FAR CORNER OF THE ROOM (LINE AB) ON THE PAPER AT A CONVENIENT SCALE, SAY ½"=1'-Ø". DRAW THE HORIZON LINE (HL) AT APPROXIMATE EYE LEVEL (5'-Ø') AND EXTEND ACROSS THE PAPER.

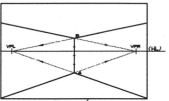

SKETCH IN THE APPROXIMATE CORNER VIEW YOU WOULD SEE IN THE ROOM BY EXTENDING THE LINES TO THE HL TO GAIN YOUR LEFT AND RIGHT VANISHING POINTS (VPL & VPR)

A GOOD RULE OF THUMB ON PLACING THE VANISHING POINTS IS TO PLACE THE CLOSEST VP APPROXIMATELY 1½ TIMES THE WIDTH OF THE BACK WALL OF THE ROOM (NOT THE WALL ADJACENT TO YOU) FROM THE VERTICAL LINE AB ON THE HL. PLACE THE OTHER VP AT A FATHER DISTANCE THAN THIS. THIS WILL ASSURE THAT THE ENTIRE BACK WALL WILL BE IN THE PICTURE.

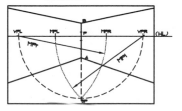

MEASURE A POINT (P) MIDWAY BETWEEN VPL & VPR ON THE HORIZON LINE. CONSTRUCT AN ARC CONNECTING VPL & VPR USING POINT P AS THE CENTER OF THE ARC. LOCATE YOUR STATION POINT (SP) ON THAT ARC, DIRECTLY VERTICAL FROM THE FAR CORNER OF THE ROOM. SWING AN ARC FROM THIS STATION POINT (SP) TO THE HORIZON LINE USING EACH VANISHING POINT (VP) AS THE CENTER TO LOCATE THE MEASURING POINT LEFT (MPL) AND THE MEASURING POINT RIGHT (MPR).

ALONG THE GROUND LINE (GL), SCALE THE WIDTH AND DEPTH OF THE ROOM FROM POINT A USING THE SAME SCALE AS LINE AB. DRAW LINES FROM THE MPL & MPR THROUGH THE INCREMENTS ALONG THE GL UNTIL THEY TOUCH THE LINES AC & AD (JUNCTION OF EACH WALL WITH THE FLOOR)

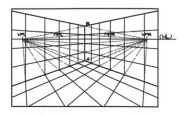

FROM THESE POINTS ALONG AC & AD EXTEND LINES ON THE FLOOR TOWARD YOU FROM THE RESPECTIVE VANISHING POINTS, CREATING A PERSPECTIVE OF SQUARE GRIDS ON THE FLOOR. EXTEND VERTICAL LINES FROM THE POINTS ALONG AC & AD TO PRODUCE LINES RECEDING IN PERSPECTIVE ALONG THE WALL. DRAW LINES FROM THE SCALED POINTS ALONG LINE AB THAT EXTEND TO THE PROPER VANISHING POINTS, PRODUCING PERSPECTIVE GRIDS ON THE WALLS

Part II
Contract Documents

CONSTRUCTION DRAWINGS, SPECIFICATIONS, AND CONTRACTS 5

Specifications, contracts, and construction drawings are an integral part of what is referred to as the contract documents. These documents form a guide for the various workers and suppliers to follow in constructing the project. The construction drawings show the location, size, and particulars of a structure to be built. The specifications set the standards of the workmanship and materials in writing. The drawings and specifications complement one another and are used together. For example, the drawings show the color and location of paint to be applied to a wall surface, but do not tell how it is to be applied (sprayed, rolled, or brushed) and the resulting quality of workmanship required. In this case, the subsurface must first be prepared to receive the paint, adjacent areas need to be protected from the painting, the minimum skills of the painter must be specified, and the cleanup needed must be called out. These particulars are all detailed in written specifications for the painting, and similar instructions are prepared for all the other work to be carried out on the project.

Specifications

Specifications are written documents that clearly describe the required materials, requirements for the execution of the work, and workmanship expected. Generally, for small, simple projects the written specifications may be placed directly in the drawings, either typed on transparent adhesive film or in text form in CAD on a separate drawing sheet. However, for most projects, the specifications are included in a "job book" or "project manual" and

issued with the contract agreements and construction drawings as the complete set of contract documents.

The job book can be a bound or loose-leaf manual and contains the technical specifications. A project manual may include the specifications as well as other documentation for the total project, such as the contract(s), bidding requirements (if needed), and general and supplementary conditions of the contract.

Specification Types

Specifications should complement the construction drawings, not duplicate them. Their main purpose is to describe the type and quality of materials and finishes; quality and method of construction and installation; acceptable testing methods; alternate provisions; and warranties and their requirements. Specifications are referred to as "closed" or "open" for bidding purposes. "Closed" means no product can be used on the project other than what is specified. Open specifications allow for the substitution of products specified, or for the contractor to suggest a number of products for the item that is specified or being bid on. There are four main types of specifications: proprietary, descriptive, reference, and performance.

Proprietary

Proprietary specifications, which are closed, call out a specific manufacturer's products by name, model or part number, and color or finish, if applicable. Proprietary specifications are the most restrictive, as they give the interior designer complete control over what is

Table 5-1 Sample Proprietary Specifications

LOUNGE AREA

Item	Quantity	Description
1	3	Manufacturer #10-123, Black Leather Lounge Chair
2	4	Manufacturer # 9-321, Dark Oak, Side Table

to be installed in a project. Sometimes the specifications include an "or equal" clause (sometimes referred to a base-bid specification), which means the substitution of other products will be allowed if the contractor thinks they are equal to the one specified. Proprietary specifications tend to be easier to write, as the designer needs to provide only the basic descriptive information, such as the manufacturer, product number, and finish/fabrics, as shown in Table 5-1.

If more detail is needed, the manufacturer will supply the information to the designer so that it can be incorporated into the specifications.

Descriptive

Descriptive specifications are open, and do not specify a manufacturer or trade name for the materials and/or finishes required for a project. Descriptive specifications call out in detail the materials, finishes, fabrication methods, acceptable workmanship, and installation methods. Descriptive specifications may be more difficult to write, because all the pertinent information and requirements for the construction and installation of a product must be specified. However, when a tremendous number of similar products are on the market, descriptive specifications allow the designer to prescribe the exact standards he or she wants for a project without selecting a particular manufacturer.

Reference

Reference specifications are similar to descriptive ones, insofar as they describe a material, finish, or other product based on the designer's requirements rather than a trade name. However, reference specifications are generally based on standards that are set by an established authority or testing facility, such as the American Society for Testing and Materials (ASTM) or the American National Standards Institute (ANSI).

These authorities provide minimum performance criteria for various materials and products. Reference specifications are generally short, because only the standard must be stated, and they are fairly easy to write. Chances for error are minimal, as industry standards and generally recognized methods of building are being used. However, the designer must be completely familiar with and updated on the standard and how to write the appropriate specification. Sometimes the standard includes more provisions than are needed for a particular project.

Performance

Performance specifications describe the expected performance of the item(s) being specified. This type of specification is also considered open, as no trade names are included. Any item that meets the performance criteria can be used in the project. The means by which the required results are met is not specified, but left up to the contractor, subcontractor, or vendor. Performance specifications are often used for custom components when the designer wants to achieve a particular result that is not already manufactured. This type of specification can be more difficult to write, because the designer must know all the criteria expected as well as methods for testing (if required). Also, there is a risk that the designer could lose his or her original design concept along with control over the products used if it is not carefully written.

Organization of Specifications

The organization of written specifications has been standardized in accordance with the building trades. Many architects and interior designers use the specification system developed by the Contract Specifications Institute (CSI), known as the Masterformat system. This system standardizes the format and numbering of project information used in specifications and cost estimating, and organizes the job book or project manual. The Masterformat model, as shown in Table 5-2, contains 16 divisions that are based on major categories of work. Each of these major divisions is coded with a five-digit number, such as 09300 for tile. Each division, known as a broadscope, is then subdivided into narrowscope categories. The first two digits represent the broadscope, the last three digits detail the narrowscope subdivision. For example, under Painting, 09900 is a broadscope category that includes several different types of painting. Specifications within a job book or project manual could also incorporate narrowscope categories, such as 09920 Interior Painting. The level of information the designer uses depends on the complexity of the job and specifications. (See Appendix for complete listing of broadscope and narrowscope categories.)

The Masterformat system further establishes a way of organizing any broadscope or narrowscope category. Each division is broken down into three parts as listed in the Section Format outline. General information about each division, such as its scope, required submittals, warranties, etc., is included in Part 1. Part 2 includes the specific materials, finishes, and products. This part also includes what standards and/or test methods the material and products must conform to, and how items are to be constructed. Part 3 describes how the materials, finishes, and products are to be installed or applied in the project. This part also covers any preparation or examination of materials or products required prior to installation as well as how quality control will be maintained on the job. Any requirements for adjusting, cleaning, and protecting the finished work are also covered in Part 3. (See Appendix for the Masterformat Section Format Outline.) The designer or specifier (if

Table 5-2 Breakdown of Masterformat, by Construction Specifications Institute (CSI)			
Masterformat's 16 Divisions		**Example of Division 12—Furnishings**	
Division 1–	General Requirements	12050	Fabrics
Division 2–	Sitework	12100	Artwork
Division 3–	Concrete	12300	Manufactured Casework
Division 4–	Masonry	12301	Metal Casework
Division 5–	Metals	12302	Wood Casework
Division 6–	Wood and Plastics	12500	Window Treatment
Division 7–	Thermal and Moisture Protection	12510	Blinds
Division 8–	Doors and Windows	12515	Interior Shutters
Division 9–	Finishes	12520	Shades
Division 10–	Specialties	12540	Curtains
Division 11–	Equipment	12600	Furniture and Accessories
Division 12–	Furnishings	12620	Furniture
Division 13–	Special Construction	12670	Rugs and Mats
Division 14–	Conveying Systems	12700	Multiple Seating
Division 15–	Mechanical	12800	Interior Plants and Planters
Division 16–	Electrical		

they are different) can select the areas of the Masterformat that are appropriate for the materials, finishes, and other products to be specified for their project and utilize this information to complete a job book or project manual where the information can be easily and reliably found.

Contracts

Various contractual agreements are needed between the parties involved in a building project. These agreements detail each party's responsibilities and can be in oral or written form. However, it is preferable to put down in writing the responsibilities of each party and what is expected. This can prevent future disagreements and serves as a legal contract binding the various parties. Contracts can be simple written agreements, or preprinted docu-

Abbreviated Form of Agreement for Interior Design Services

THIS DOCUMENT HAS IMPORTANT LEGAL CONSEQUENCES: CONSULTATION WITH AN ATTORNEY IS ENCOURAGED WITH RESPECT TO ITS COMPLETION OR MODIFICATION.

1994 EDITION

AGREEMENT

made as of the   day of   in the year of
(In words, indicate day, month and year)

BETWEEN the Owner:
(Name and address)

and the Designer:
(Name and address)

For the following Project:
(Include detailed description of Project, location, address and scope.)

The Owner and the Designer agree as set forth below.

ments (Figure 5-1), such as those provided by the AIA (American Institute of Architects), ASID (American Society of Interior Designers), and IIDA (International Interior Design Association). One important contract is that between the owner and contractor to do the work based on the drawings and specifications. There may also exist a whole series of other contracts between the contractor and subcontractor, or contractor and material supplier.

Construction Drawings

Construction drawings (often called working drawings) visually communicate the design and the information required to bring it into reality to everyone who is involved in the building process. These drawings generally follow a set of architectural drawing conventions that are widely accepted in the industry. However, there is not just one right way to do construction drawings. The office staff and project size, office standards, and the detail needed for custom fabrications can require construction drawings that vary from the conventions.

Organization of Construction Drawings

A variety of types of drawings are needed to accurately describe a project to the various tradespeople who will do the work. Two main types are what are generally called architectural and engineering drawings. For example, a concrete wall may be described as to its size and finish on the architectural drawings, but an engineering drawing is also needed to spell out the exact structural components, such as size and spacing of steel reinforcing in the wall. In addition to these two categories of drawings, there might be other specialty drawings that do not fit neatly within either one. For example, an architectural floor plan might show exact information about rooms, doors, windows, and other particulars, but items such as the exact placement of office desks and files would be found on a separate furniture installation plan, as seen in Figure 5-2. In interiors projects, the interior partition plans, details, and furniture drawings could be included with the architectural set, or they could be a completely separate set of drawings. Another type of specialized drawing might be a drapery installation plan for detailing specific window coverings.

Construction drawings are sequentially arranged by major components, as illustrated in Table 5-3. This sequence generally follows how the building is constructed, from the ground to the shell of the building to the interiors. However, the exact sequence of drawings and their content will vary from project to project and office to office. For example, the number of sheets of construction drawings

Figure 5-1 *(opposite page)* **A preprinted ASID contract document.**

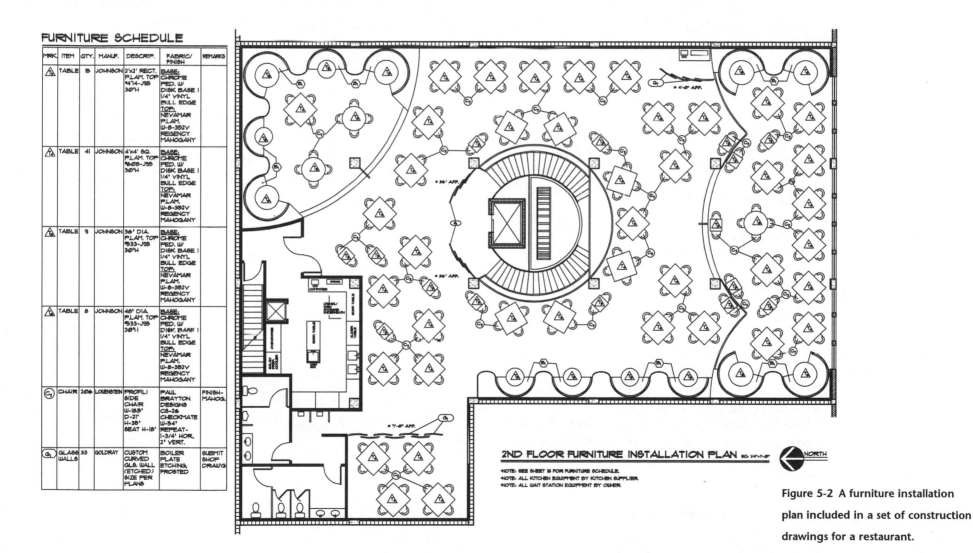

FURNITURE SCHEDULE

2ND FLOOR FURNITURE INSTALLATION PLAN SC. 1/4"=1'-0"

NOTE: SEE SHEET 18 FOR FURNITURE SCHEDULE.
NOTE: ALL KITCHEN EQUIPMENT BY KITCHEN SUPPLIER.
NOTE: ALL WAIT STATION EQUIPMENT BY OWNER.

NORTH

Figure 5-2 A furniture installation plan included in a set of construction drawings for a restaurant.

Table 5-3 Typical Sheet Sequence for a Set of Construction Drawings

SHEET NO.	DESCRIPTION
1.	TITLE/COVER SHEET Client, project, designer Index of sheets Architectural symbols & abbreviations Perspective or other visuals
2.	LOCATION OR SITE PLAN This information might be on cover sheet
3.	FOOTING AND FOUNDATION PLAN (If required)
4.	FLOOR PLAN (S) Begin with lowest floor first
5.	BUILDING SECTIONS Key to floor plans
6.	EXTERIOR ELEVATIONS (If required)
7.	WALL SECTIONS Drawn at large scale
8.	INTERIOR ELEVATIONS Show most prominent elevations
9.	DETAILS Drawn at large scale
10.	FINISH PLAN (S) Include legend and specific finishes
11.	FURNITURE INSTALLATION PLAN (S) Include legend and furniture placement
12.	FURNISHINGS AND EQUIPMENT PLAN (S) (If required)
13.	REFLECTED CEILING PLAN (S) Include legend and coordinate with Electrical & Mechanical
14.	ELECTRICAL PLAN (S) AND/OR POWER/COMMUNICATION PLAN (S) Include legend and reference to reflected ceiling plan
15.	MECHANICAL PLAN (S)
16.	SPECIFICATIONS (If required, or put in separate booklet)

for a small residence may be smaller than for a commercial project. Figures 5-3, 5-4, and 5-5 show the example of a small model home where only three sheets comprise the whole set of construction drawings. A more complex commercial project might include as many as 21 sheets of drawings, as illustrated in Figure 5-6, which shows the cover sheet for a restaurant project with a table of contents listing the 21 sheets. In both cases, however, the sheet order remains similar. The sheets are numbered and bound sequentially as a set, for clarity and ease of use by contractors, subcontractors, and others involved in the project.

The sheet numbering system can vary according to the complexity of the project and office preference. For small projects, a simple numeric system can be used. Most offices prefer to use a system that identifies each area of specialty by a prefix, such as "A" for the architecture or "S" for structural. A list of the most common prefixes follows; however, other prefixes may be added as needed.

A Architecture

S Structural

M Mechanical

E Electrical

P Plumbing

I Interiors

F Finishes or Furniture

Q Equipment

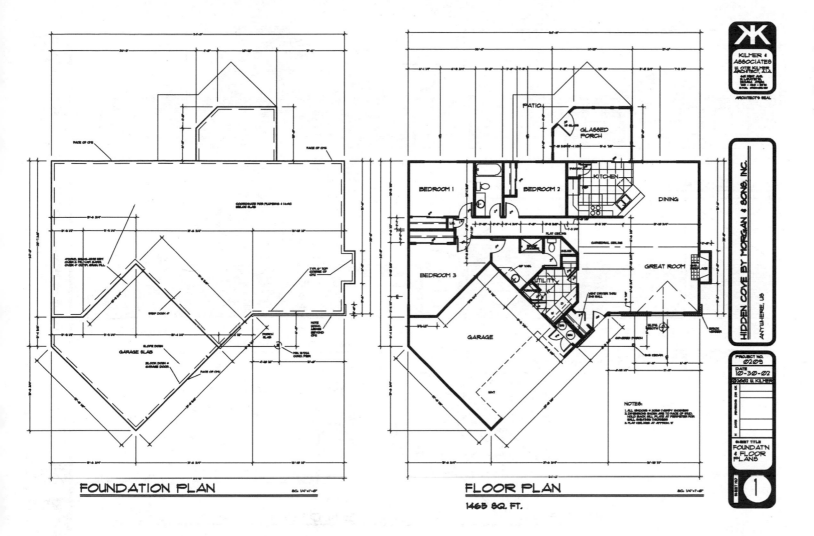

FOUNDATION PLAN   SC: 1/4"=1'-0"

FLOOR PLAN   SC: 1/4"=1'-0"

1463 SQ. FT.

Figure 5-3 This small set of construction drawings consists of only 3 sheets. Sheet 1 of 3 includes the foundation plan, floor plan, and a footing detail.

Figure 5-4 Sheet 2 of 3 for this small house includes four exterior elevations, a roof plan, and a building section.

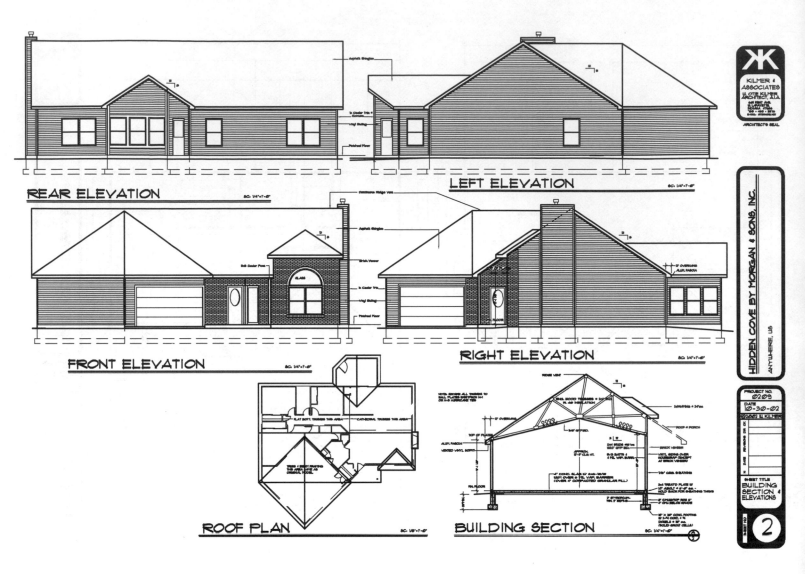

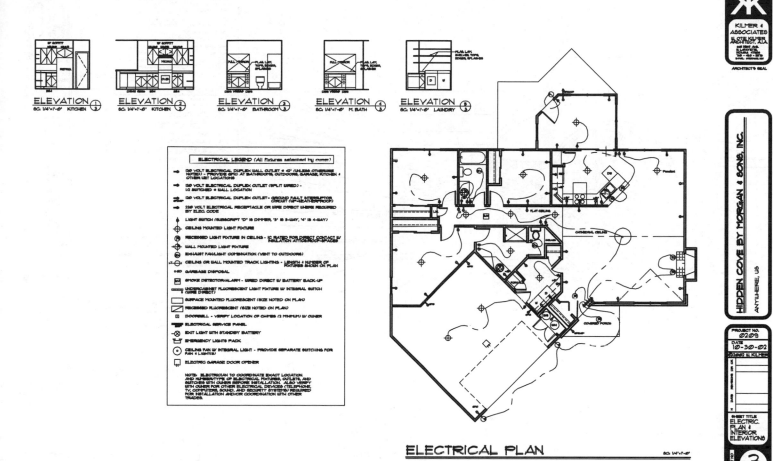

ELECTRICAL PLAN

Figure 5-6 This cover sheet for a set of construction drawings for a commercial restaurant and lounge indicates the set consists of 21 sheets. The table of contents lists what can be found on each sheet.

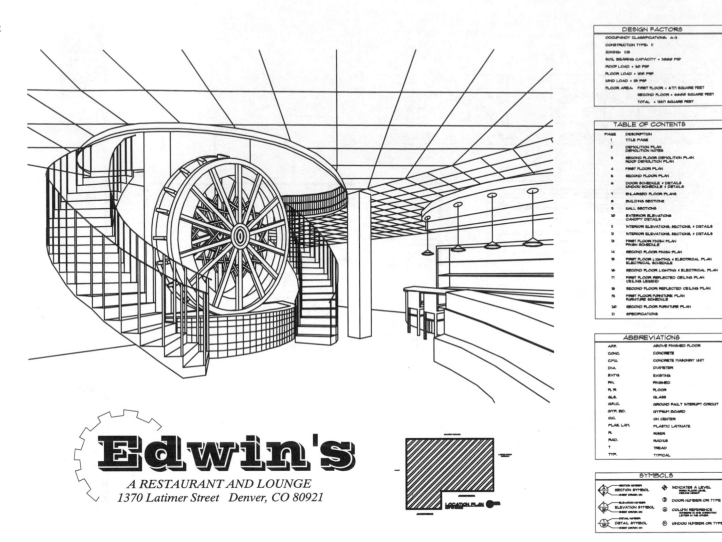

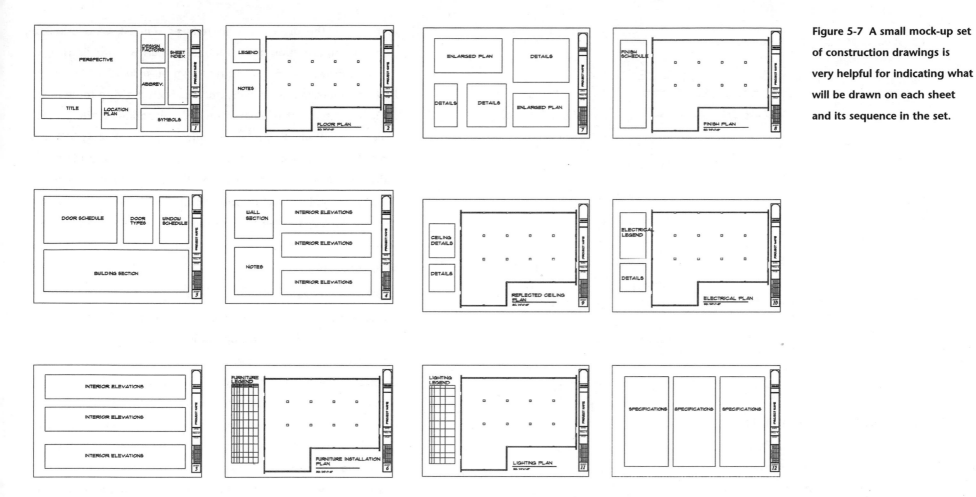

Guidelines for Preparing Construction Drawings

Before construction drawings are executed, a considerable amount of work must precede their preparation, such as programming, preparing schematic drawings, and developing the design. The overall design of the project, general materials, finishes, and other particulars must already be established. Preliminary information from other consultants, such as electrical and acoustical engineers,

must be collected and available for input into the drawings. A building-code analysis must be done to confirm the project meets requirements for the protection of the public's health, safety, and welfare.

Before the construction drawings are drafted up, a mock-up set is first created to give an overview of the sequence of sheets and their individual contents, as shown in Figure 5-7. This process helps

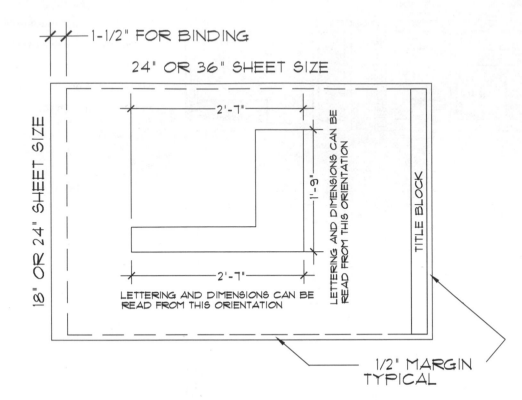

1-1/2" FOR BINDING

24" OR 36" SHEET SIZE

18" OR 24" SHEET SIZE

2'-7"

1'-9"

LETTERING AND DIMENSIONS CAN BE READ FROM THIS ORIENTATION

TITLE BLOCK

2'-7"

LETTERING AND DIMENSIONS CAN BE READ FROM THIS ORIENTATION

1/2" MARGIN TYPICAL

Figure 5-8 Most information should be readable with the sheets right side up, similar to a bound book. However, some information can also be placed to be read from the right side of the sheet.

to organize the drawings and reduces the risk of overlooking important information and relationships between drawings. These mock-up drawings are generally drawn on a small scale, such as half-size, quarter-size, or even smaller. Each drawing to be placed on a separate sheet is blocked out as a rectangle at the properly scaled size with its title, reference number, and the scale it is to be drawn to. This mock-up set of drawings serves as a guide for the individual or team when preparing the construction drawing set. On a small project, a small number of mock-up drawings may be required, whereas larger projects demand a carefully planned out mock-up set, which usually requires a greater number of drawings and more details.

Sheet Size

The size of sheets that drawings are done on can vary among professional firms, depending upon office standards, the type of project, and the form of reproduction selected for the drawings. Generally, sheets are composed in a horizontal format, and multiple sheets (which comprise a set) are bound on the left side, as for a book. In this case, the left border of the sheet becomes the binding side, and drawings are placed no closer than 1 – 1½ inch (25–38 mm) from this edge. Drawings, lettering, and dimensions are composed so they can be read from the bottom of the sheet when viewed in the horizontal position, as illustrated in Figure 5-8. It occasionally becomes necessary to arrange for dimensions and some notes to be read from the right side of the sheet, but never from the top or left side.

The most common sheet sizes used by offices are 18 x 24 inches (457 x 609 mm), 24 x 36 inches (609 x 914 mm), and 36 x 48 inches (914 x 1218 mm). Small drawings, such as revisions or additions to a large drawing, are typically drawn on 8½ x 11 inches (213 x

275 mm), 8½ x 14 inches (213 x 350 mm), or 11 x 17 inches (275 x 425 mm). These smaller sizes are based on standard photocopier, inkjet, and laser printer machines.

Standard paper sizes include A, B, C, D, and E in inches in architectural sizes. Metric sizes are measured in millimeters and include A4, A3, A2, A1, and A0 (see Table 2-1, page 11).

Sheet Composition

When sheets are bound into a set and a person leafs through the sheets, the information on the right-hand side of the sheet is generally seen first. For this reason, title blocks and important information are often placed to the right side of the sheet, as seen in Figure 5-9. This is particularly important if the sheet is not completely filled with drawings, schedules, etc. The blank, unused areas should appear to the left. As mentioned, the left-hand side has the largest margin, while the other sheet margins should be held to a minimum of ½ inch (12 mm). Some firms prefer to draw a borderline around the entire sheet, which graphically "surrounds" or encompasses all the drawings. In that case, the borderline is held to the same margins as discussed above.

Title Blocks

Title blocks on a construction-drawing sheet serve a number of key functions. These blocks are standardized for each office and are generally placed along the right side of the sheet, running the full height of that edge, minus the ½ inch (12 mm) top and bottom borders or margins. Title blocks can also be placed along the bottom of the sheet, or in the case of engineering drawings might be simply a block in the lower right-hand corner. Figure 5-10 illustrates the most common placement of title blocks.

Title blocks are drawn on sheets in a variety of ways. Many firms

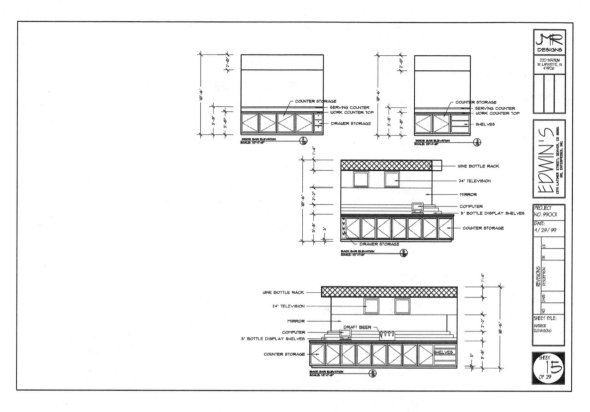

have them preprinted on the sheets or programmed into the computer to print out when the drawings are produced. Other methods include making reproducible title blocks with photocopiers on transparent sticky-back sheets and individually adding them to the drawing sheets. In these latter cases, additional information can be filled in with pencil, pen, or other transfer mediums.

Title blocks typically contain information that identifies the project, its location, the name of the client, the designer's (or firm's) name and address, names or initials of the drafters and checkers, revision blocks, and space for professional seals. It might also include information on others involved in the project, such as consulting engineers. The title block tells contractors, suppliers, and

Figure 5-9 Important information is placed on the lower right of the sheet for ease of finding. Sets of drawings can then be "thumbed" through as with pages in a book.

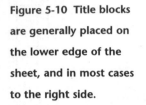

Figure 5-10 **Title blocks are generally placed on the lower edge of the sheet, and in most cases to the right side.**

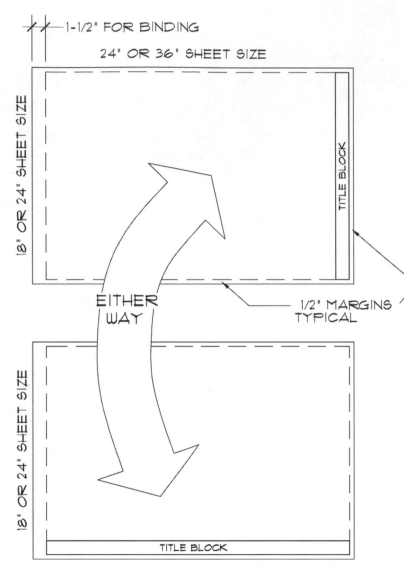

1-1/2" FOR BINDING

24" OR 36" SHEET SIZE

18" OR 24" SHEET SIZE

TITLE BLOCK

EITHER WAY

1/2" MARGINS TYPICAL

18" OR 24" SHEET SIZE

TITLE BLOCK

other interested parties the location of the project and who to contact for specific information. Title blocks, as shown in Figure 5-11, generally include:

- Design firm's name/logo, address, telephone/fax number, and e-mail address (if applicable)
- Date, professional seals, sheet title, sheet number
- Job number and how many sheets comprise a set

Title blocks might also include an area for the initials of the person who drew the sheet, and the person who checked it. The block generally includes a "revisions" section (Figure 5-12) to indicate changes made to the original drawing after the initial date it was issued to the various parties. When several revisions are made to a sheet, they are listed as Revision A, B, etc., to indicate which changes are most recent.

Lettering on Drawings

The most important aspect of lettering in construction drawings is its readability. It should be consistent in style and easy to follow. Most offices use upper-case lettering for quick readability, but a clear lower-case alphabet can also be employed. When several drafters are working on a set of drawings, it is important that all the lettering from the design firm appear in the same style. In both manual and computer-aided lettering, a consistent style or font should be selected and used by all participants.

The height of lettering on construction drawings varies according to the hierarchy of the information being presented and the type of reproduction being used. If the drawings are to be reproduced at the same size, the following standards are generally used:

1. Sheet numbers in the title block — ½ in. (12 mm)

2. Main titles under individual drawings — ³⁄₁₆–¼ in. (5–6 mm)

3. Subtitles, such as room names — ³⁄₁₆ in. (5 mm)

4. Majority of lettering, such as notes and dimensions — ³⁄₃₂–⅛ in. (2.4–3 mm)

If the drawings are to be reduced by photocopying, plotting, or other means, the lettering sizes should be increased, depending upon the reduction ratio, in order for the final notes, dimensions, etc., to be clear and readable.

Notes

Notes are used on construction drawings for the identification of features or information that cannot be conveyed by drawings or by a symbol. Notes should be concise, easy to read, and clear in their meaning. Notes should be grouped and aligned vertically to the right or left side, as illustrated in Figure 5-13. They should also be placed close to the elements described in order to keep leaders as short and direct as possible. Leaders are drawn away from the beginning or end of the note and generally end in an arrow pointing to the object the note refers to. Leaders can be either straight or curved lines, depending upon the office standards. If curved lines are used, they should be gradual sweeping curves, and not crooked or wavy. Leaders should never cross one another, as this can create visual confusion. Notes that pertain to several items, such as the height of electrical outlets, can be pulled out separately and organized below the drawing. If there is more than one note, they should be numbered and organized chronologically on the drawing sheet, as shown in Figure 5-14.

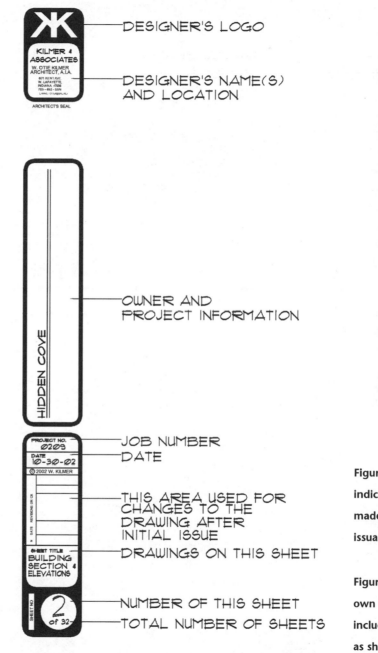

DESIGNER'S LOGO

DESIGNER'S NAME(S) AND LOCATION

OWNER AND PROJECT INFORMATION

JOB NUMBER
DATE

THIS AREA USED FOR CHANGES TO THE DRAWING AFTER INITIAL ISSUE

DRAWINGS ON THIS SHEET

NUMBER OF THIS SHEET

TOTAL NUMBER OF SHEETS

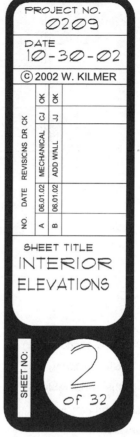

Figure 5-12 A revision block clearly indicates the date and type of changes made to the drawings after the initial issuance date of the sheet.

Figure 5-11 Professionals design their own unique title blocks, but most include certain common information, as shown in this example.

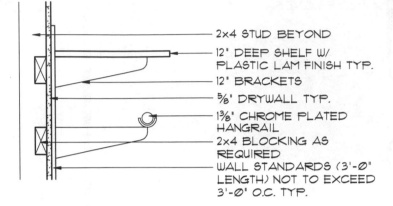

SHELF & GARMENT ROD DETAIL

6

SCALE: 3⁄8" = 1'-0"

- 2×4 STUD BEYOND
- 12" DEEP SHELF W/ PLASTIC LAM FINISH TYP.
- 12" BRACKETS
- 5⁄8" DRYWALL TYP.
- 13⁄8" CHROME PLATED HANGRAIL
- 2×4 BLOCKING AS REQUIRED
- WALL STANDARDS (3'-0" LENGTH) NOT TO EXCEED 3'-0" O.C. TYP.

Figure 5-13 It is good drafting practice to align lettering where possible (preferably to the left), and minimize the length of leaders.

Notes should be placed in open areas of the drawings so line work, textures, and dimensions will not be drawn over them (Figure 5-15).

Drawing Conventions and Representations

Construction drawings communicate how something is built by showing specific assemblies and by employing architectural drawing conventions. These conventions are fairly standard throughout the industry and are used to reduce the drawing time and space needed to convey information. For example, in Figure 5-16, a graphic symbol with an arrow drawn on a cabinetry section denotes the exact place the section was cut and the direction of the view taken in the resulting section drawing.

Abbreviations, graphic symbols, keys, and legends are used as shorthand to reduce drawing time while conveying important information. Another convention governs how dimensions are recorded in a drawing. Dimensioning standards ensure that exact sizes and placement of assemblies are communicated by using a system that is recognized by both the designer and the builder.

Abbreviations

Abbreviations for words and short phrases are often used in construction drawings. Commonly used abbreviations can be found in the Appendix, but it should be noted they are not universal. Abbreviations can vary among the different trades, as, for example, QT can mean "quarry tile" or "quart." The architect, engineer, interior designer, drafter, and contractor must all be able to recognize what each abbreviation stands for. The drafter should include a legend of abbreviations (often shown on the title sheet of a set of drawings) to ensure their meaning is understood. See Figure 5-17

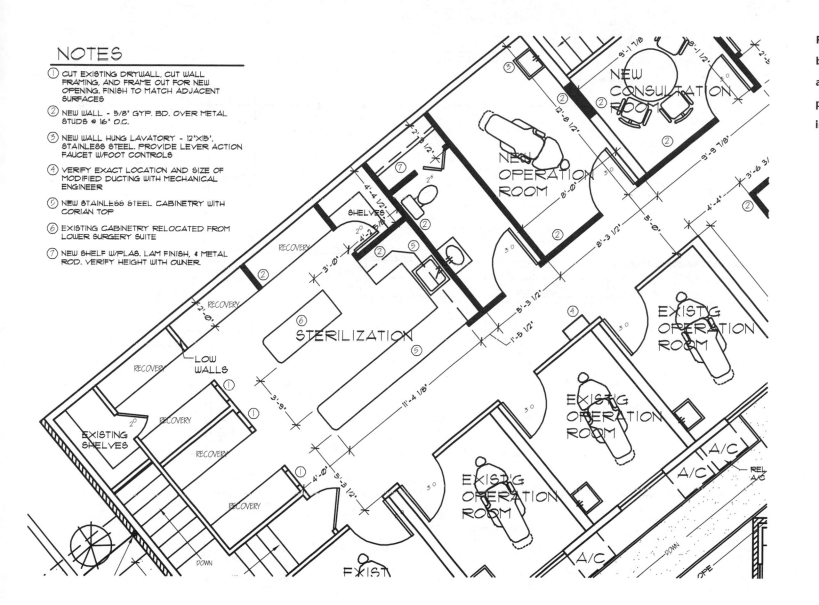

NOTES

1. CUT EXISTING DRYWALL, CUT WALL FRAMING, AND FRAME OUT FOR NEW OPENING. FINISH TO MATCH ADJACENT SURFACES

2. NEW WALL - 5/8" GYP. BD. OVER METAL STUDS @ 16" O.C.

3. NEW WALL HUNG LAVATORY - 12"X15", STAINLESS STEEL. PROVIDE LEVER ACTION FAUCET W/FOOT CONTROLS

4. VERIFY EXACT LOCATION AND SIZE OF MODIFIED DUCTING WITH MECHANICAL ENGINEER

5. NEW STAINLESS STEEL CABINETRY WITH CORIAN TOP

6. EXISTING CABINETRY RELOCATED FROM LOWER SURGERY SUITE

7. NEW SHELF W/PLAS. LAM FINISH, & METAL ROD. VERIFY HEIGHT WITH OWNER

Figure 5-14 Notes can be numbered, organized into a block, and cross-referenced to the plan just by placing the number in the drawings.

Figure 5-15 Notes should be placed in positions that do not block dimensions or other parts of the drawings.

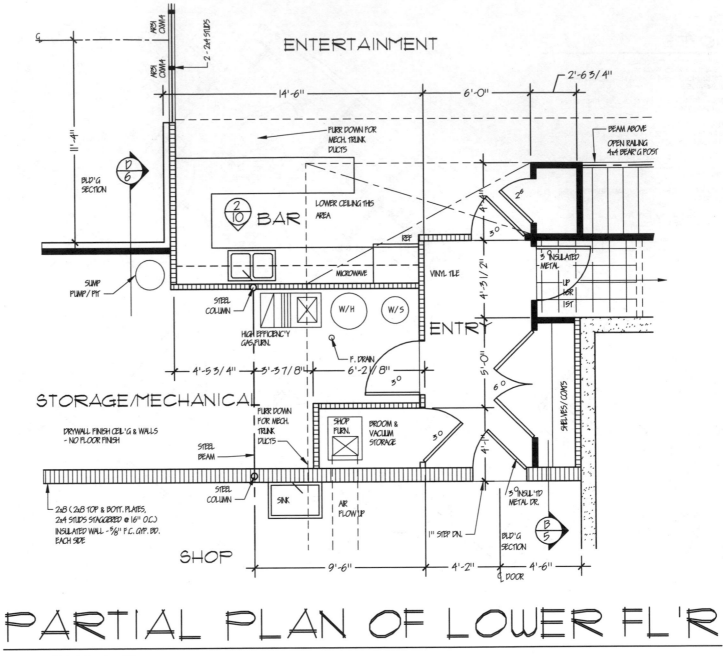

ENTERTAINMENT

ARCH CXW4

2 - 2x4 STUDS

14'-6"

6'-0"

2'-6 3/4"

11'-4"

FURR DOWN FOR MECH. TRUNK DUCTS

BEAM ABOVE
OPEN RAILING
4x4 BEAR'G POST

D/6 BLD'G SECTION

2⁶

2⁶

2/10 BAR

LOWER CEILING THIS AREA

4'-3"

3⁰

REF

3⁰ INSULATED METAL

SUMP PUMP/ PIT

MICROWAVE

VINYL TILE

UP FOR 1ST

STEEL COLUMN

W/H

W/S

ENTRY

4'-3 1/2"

HIGH EFFICIENCY GAS FURN.

F. DRAIN

SHELVES/ COATS

STORAGE/MECHANICAL

4'-5 3/4"

3'-3 7/8"

6'-2 1/8"

3⁰

5'-0"

6⁰

DRYWALL FINISH CEIL'G & WALLS - NO FLOOR FINISH

FURR DOWN FOR MECH. TRUNK DUCTS

SHOP FURN.

BROOM & VACUUM STORAGE

STEEL BEAM

3⁰

STEEL COLUMN

SINK

AIR FLOW UP

4'-1"

3⁰ INSUL'TD METAL DR.

2x8 (2x8 TOP & BOTT. PLATES, 2x4 STUDS STAGGERED @ 16" O.C.) INSULATED WALL - ⁵⁄₈" F.C. GYP. BD. EACH SIDE

SHOP

9'-6"

4'-2"

1" STEP DN.

C DOOR

BLD'G SECTION

B/5

4'-6"

PARTIAL PLAN OF LOWER FL'R

SCALE: 1/4"=1'-0"

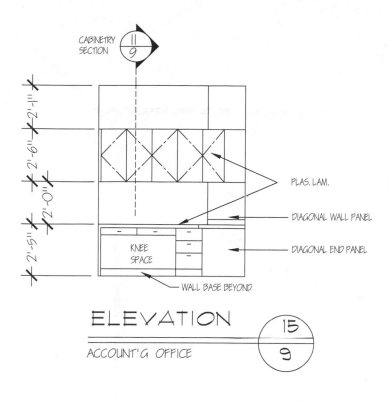

CABINETRY SECTION $\frac{11}{9}$

2'-1"
2'-6"
2'-0"
2'-5"

PLAS. LAM.

DIAGONAL WALL PANEL

DIAGONAL END PANEL

KNEE SPACE

WALL BASE BEYOND

ELEVATION $\frac{15}{9}$

ACCOUNT'G OFFICE

ABBREVIATIONS	
A.F.F.	ABOVE FINISHED FLOOR
CONC.	CONCRETE
C.M.U.	CONCRETE MASONRY UNIT
DIA.	DIAMETER
EXT'G	EXISTING
FIN.	FINISHED
FL 'R	FLOOR
GLS.	GLASS
G.F.I.C.	GROUND FAULT INTERRUPT CIRCUIT
GYP. BD.	GYPSUM BOARD
O.C.	ON CENTER
PLAS. LAM.	PLASTIC LAMINATE
R.	RISER
RAD.	RADIUS
T	TREAD
TYP.	TYPICAL

Figure 5-16 Example of a graphic symbol showing where a cabinet is cut through for a section drawing.

Figure 5-17 To reduce the amount of space needed for notes, many abbreviations are commonly accepted in the design fields.

for an example of abbreviated terms used in a set of construction drawings. See page 231 for an expanded list.

Graphic Symbols

Graphic symbols are used in construction drawings as a pictorial shorthand to reduce drawing time and coordinate separate drawings. For example, symbols can be used on a floor-plan drawing to indicate placement and type of specific equipment such as electrical outlets and wall light switches (Figure 5-18). Although symbols may vary from office to office, there are generally accepted types used by all architectural and interior design firms. Each symbol must communicate clearly specific directives to be followed.

Symbols are divided into several types: material symbols, line symbols, graphic symbols, and component symbols.

Material symbols are used in drawings to represent the construction materials used in a component. Designers should use the symbols most widely accepted in the industry, such as those shown in Figure 5-19, indicating materials cut in section. Symbols are also used to indicate materials in elevation drawings, as illustrated in Figure 5-20. A detailed list of materials and their section symbols is shown in the Appendix.

Line symbols use the graphic look, line weight, and thickness of elements represented in the drawings to communicate information

Figure 5-18 Graphic symbols used on electrical plans to indicate the location of the electrical outlets and wall switches.

Figure 5-19 Materials shown in section view are rendered with commonly recognized marks, as seen in this partial example.

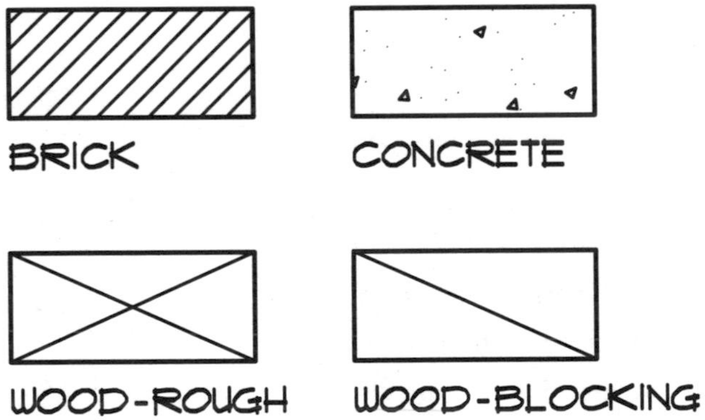

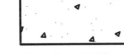

BRICK

CONCRETE

WOOD-ROUGH

WOOD-BLOCKING

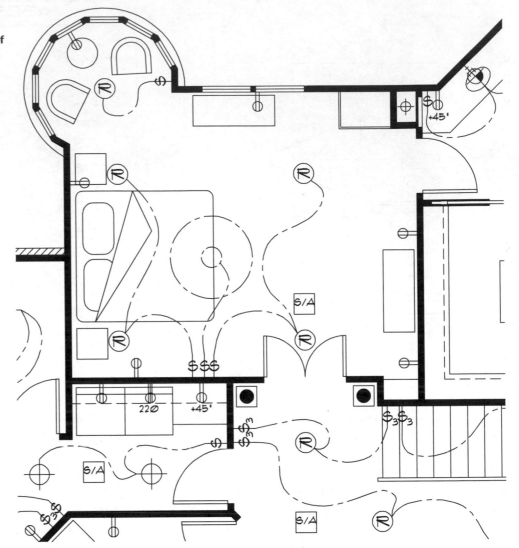

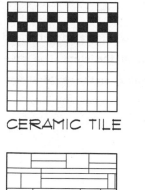

CERAMIC TILE BRICK

CUT STONE STUCCO

GLASS BLOCK WOOD PANELING

Figure 5-20 Standard techniques can also be used to represent materials seen in elevation views.

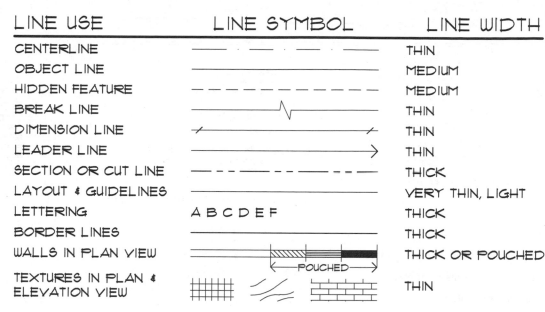

LINE USE	LINE SYMBOL	LINE WIDTH
CENTERLINE		THIN
OBJECT LINE		MEDIUM
HIDDEN FEATURE		MEDIUM
BREAK LINE		THIN
DIMENSION LINE		THIN
LEADER LINE		THIN
SECTION OR CUT LINE		THICK
LAYOUT & GUIDELINES		VERY THIN, LIGHT
LETTERING	A B C D E F	THICK
BORDER LINES		THICK
WALLS IN PLAN VIEW	POUCHED	THICK OR POUCHED
TEXTURES IN PLAN & ELEVATION VIEW		THIN

Figure 5-21 Line widths and types are used as graphic symbols with specific meanings.

to the viewer. For example, a dashed line can indicate a hidden feature or object. See Figure 5-21 for typical line symbols and their meanings.

Graphic symbols can be used to index related parts of drawings, either on the same sheet or multiple sheets. Letters, numbers, and notes can be placed within the symbol to organize it with other symbols and refer to other sheet numbers. Symbols can also be used to denote a specific height on a floor elevation or structural column designation. These basic symbols are shown in Figure 5-22. See a more complete list of symbols in the Appendix.

Legends

Construction drawing legends combine graphic symbols with notes. They are used on a variety of drawings, such as floor plans, furniture plans, electrical plans, and lighting plans. For example, a wall legend (Figure 5-23) can be used on a floor plan to designate a specific wall construction assembly. An electrical legend is used

SYMBOLS

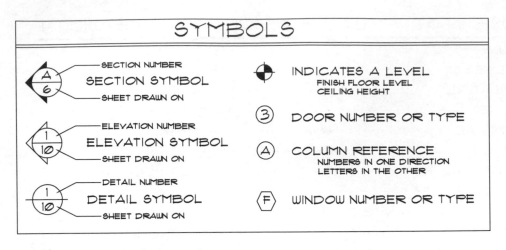

SECTION NUMBER
SECTION SYMBOL
SHEET DRAWN ON

ELEVATION NUMBER
ELEVATION SYMBOL
SHEET DRAWN ON

DETAIL NUMBER
DETAIL SYMBOL
SHEET DRAWN ON

INDICATES A LEVEL
FINISH FLOOR LEVEL
CEILING HEIGHT

③ DOOR NUMBER OR TYPE

Ⓐ COLUMN REFERENCE
NUMBERS IN ONE DIRECTION
LETTERS IN THE OTHER

⬡ WINDOW NUMBER OR TYPE

Figure 5-22 This example shows a few of the most commonly recognized architectural symbols.

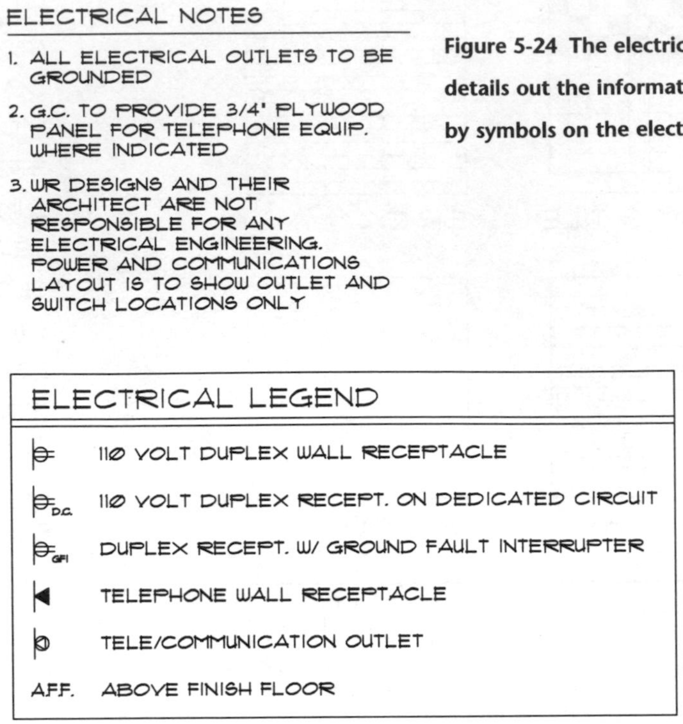

ELECTRICAL NOTES

1. ALL ELECTRICAL OUTLETS TO BE GROUNDED

2. G.C. TO PROVIDE 3/4' PLYWOOD PANEL FOR TELEPHONE EQUIP. WHERE INDICATED

3. WR DESIGNS AND THEIR ARCHITECT ARE NOT RESPONSIBLE FOR ANY ELECTRICAL ENGINEERING. POWER AND COMMUNICATIONS LAYOUT IS TO SHOW OUTLET AND SWITCH LOCATIONS ONLY

Figure 5-24 The electrical legend details out the information represented by symbols on the electrical plan.

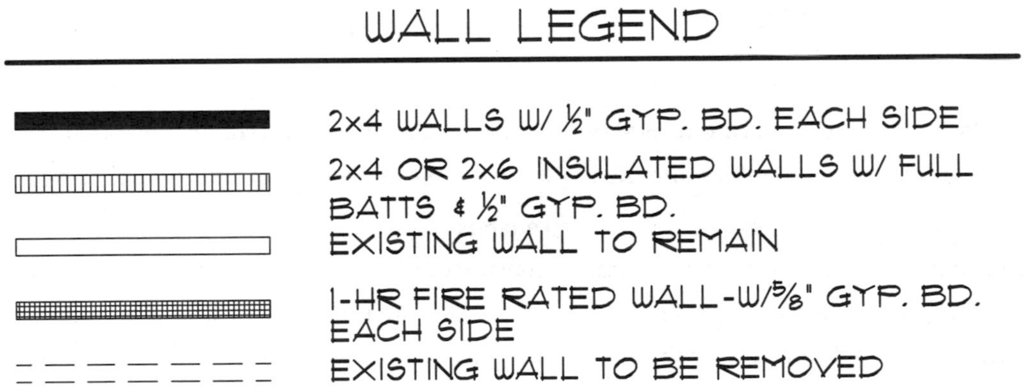

ELECTRICAL LEGEND

110 VOLT DUPLEX WALL RECEPTACLE

110 VOLT DUPLEX RECEPT. ON DEDICATED CIRCUIT

DUPLEX RECEPT. W/ GROUND FAULT INTERRUPTER

TELEPHONE WALL RECEPTACLE

TELE/COMMUNICATION OUTLET

A.FF. ABOVE FINISH FLOOR

WALL LEGEND

Figure 5-23 A wall legend is helpful for designating specific wall types in a floor plan drawing.

2x4 WALLS W/ ½" GYP. BD. EACH SIDE

2x4 OR 2x6 INSULATED WALLS W/ FULL BATTS & ½" GYP. BD.

EXISTING WALL TO REMAIN

1-HR FIRE RATED WALL-W/⅝" GYP. BD. EACH SIDE

EXISTING WALL TO BE REMOVED

in conjunction with an electrical plan to denote specific equipment. Figure 5-24 illustrates an electrical legend in conjunction with additional electrical notes.

Although there are many commonly recognized legends and graphic symbols, the drafter should always include the specifics of what is being shown. Legends should be concise and graphically presented: as small as possible on the sheet, yet easily readable in the field by the builder.

Dimensioning

Dimensioning involves incorporating numerical values in a drawing to accurately locate and size various objects and assemblies in buildings and interiors. Dimension lines and arrows (or tick marks) are used to identify exactly where the dimension begins and ends, as shown in Figure 5-25. Dimensions are grouped, where possible, and ordered in a hierarchical manner. First the overall, or outside, dimension of a space or object is indicated, then the dimension of smaller details within the space are noted, as illustrated in Figure 5-26.

Dimensions are required on all construction drawings and must be accurate, complete, and readable. At the present time, most construction drawings are dimensioned in the English or metric systems, using feet and inches, or meters.

When feet and inches (English system) are used for dimensioning, the symbol (') is used for feet and (") for inches. Dimensions less than 12" are specified in inches, with no zero before them. Dimensions 12" or above are specified in feet and inches, with a dash placed between the feet and inches, such as 2'-6". If a dimension is an even number of feet, the inches are generally shown as a zero, such as 5'-0". However, some firms prefer to leave the inch-

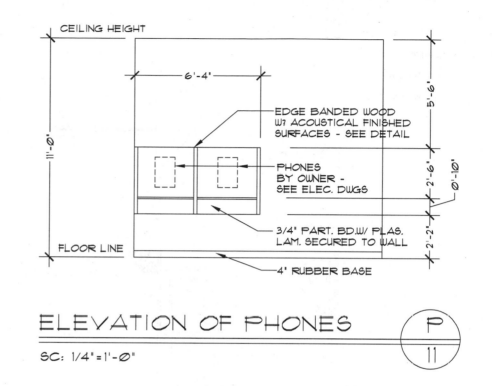

ELEVATION OF PHONES

SC: 1/4"=1'-∅"

Figure 5-25 The 45-degree slash marks in this example show where a dimension begins and ends.

es off when they are zero, such as 5'. If a distance is a fraction of an inch without a whole number before it, some prefer to put a zero before it for clarity, such as 0'-⅜". In most drawings using the metric system, all dimensions are in millimeters, such as 5 mm.

Dimensioning should remain consistent with respect to how materials and assemblies are measured, whether to subsurface or finish surfaces. For example, if a wall is dimensioned to the finished face, subsequent walls should also be dimensioned to their finished faces. A note should be placed on the drawing to denote

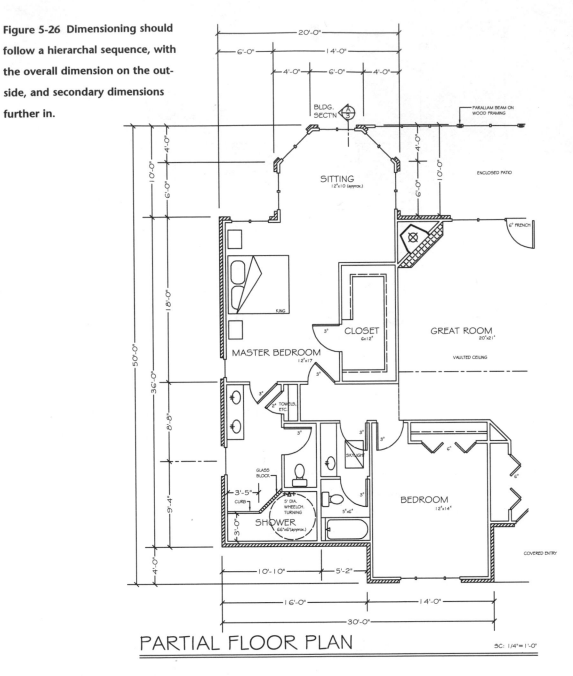

Figure 5-26 Dimensioning should follow a hierarchal sequence, with the overall dimension on the outside, and secondary dimensions further in.

PARTIAL FLOOR PLAN

SC: 1/4"=1'-0"

how items are to be measured. If there are any exceptions to this overall rule, these should be called out on the sheet.

The most common method of dimensioning is the framing technique. The advantage of this system is that it most closely follows the construction sequence in the field and informs the particular trades of the dimensions most important to their area of construction. The framing technique is to the face of a stud, concrete, or masonry wall, as illustrated in Figure 5-27. With this technique, the builder first locates the framing or foundation wall, to which other assemblies or finish materials are applied at a later date. The dimension can be placed to either the face of the sub wall (depending on the location and how easy it is for the builder to make a mark), or to each side, with an indication of the total sub wall thickness.

For example, a wood stud partition wall on a plan with a layer of ½ inch (12 mm) gypsum board on each side is dimensioned as 3½ inch (88 mm). This is the actual stud width, and not the total wall thickness, which would be 4½ inch (100 mm). This way, the builder who is erecting the wall does not have to be concerned with the finish materials at this time and mentally subtract these thicknesses to arrive at the exact location for the wall stud. However, if there is indeed a critical dimension that needs to be maintained relative to the finish material, typically for fit with another object (such as a wall or cabinet to be installed later), a note can be added to the dimension stating it is a "clear" or "face of finish" dimension, as shown in Figure 5-28.

The other method of dimensioning involves locating the centerline of a wall. In this case the builder must subtract from the centerline to find where to run the face of the wall studs, or make a center mark on the stud. This takes extra time and introduces the

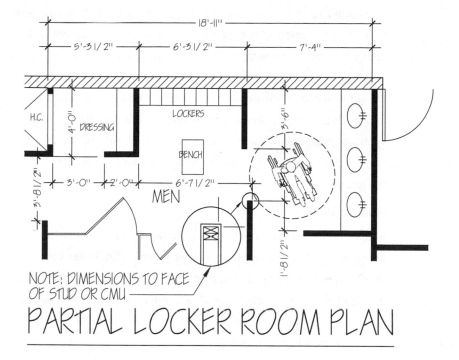

NOTE: DIMENSIONS TO FACE OF STUD OR CMU

PARTIAL LOCKER ROOM PLAN

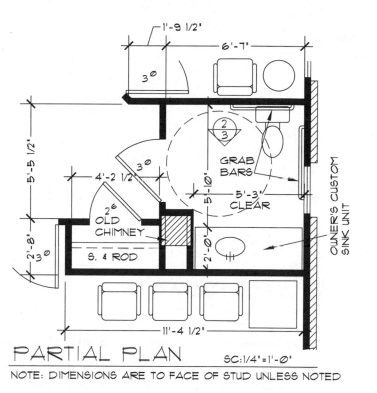

PARTIAL PLAN SC: 1/4" = 1'-0"

NOTE: DIMENSIONS ARE TO FACE OF STUD UNLESS NOTED

possibility of errors. However, this method is appropriate in a plan where one wants to locate a wall in the exact center of a space, or in the center of a structural frame gridwork.

Dimension standards discussed here primarily apply to the floor plan. Different drawings, such as elevations, ceiling plans, details, etc., have their own unique dimension standards, but are similar to the floor-plan font size, style, and units. These other drawing types might be dimensioned to the frame member or the finished face of a material. In the field of kitchen design, specialized cabinetry is almost exclusively dimensioned only in inches (or millimeters) instead of feet and inches, to the finish faces (Figure 5-29).

English and Metric Dimensioning Systems

Although many plans are dimensioned using the English system (feet and inches), the metric system is slowly replacing it as the preferred method. In the metric system, units are based on the standard meter, which is then subdivided by tenths to arrive at decimeters, centimeters, and millimeters. This system is simple to use, as the decimal can simply be moved to the right or left to change from one unit to another. There are no fractions to memorize or convert when adding. In architectural drawings, the meter or millimeter is used more than the decimeter or centimeter.

Figure 5-27 An example of dimensioning to face of stud, concrete, or masonry wall.

Figure 5-28 This example shows how dimensions are applied to the face of the finish where the "clear" opening is critical.

Figure 5-29 An elevation of cabinetry that is dimensioned in inches.

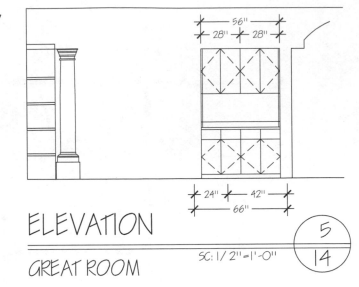

Converting from the English to the metric system can be done in several ways. The choice will depend upon whether one is dealing with elements still manufactured under the English system and on what accuracy is required in the final assembly, which will be a judgment call on the part of the designer or builder.

In the first and most accurate method, if a piece of metal is made at ½ inch thickness (as the manufacturer has not converted to the metric system), the ½ inch must be converted to metric by multiplying ½ x 2.54, which would equal 1.27 cm or 0.0127 meters.

Another method of converting is to estimate the number in the metric system according to a scale one is familiar with. Note that one inch equals 2.54 centimeters, and that ½ inch is a bit more than one centimeter. Also, ¼ inch is more than half a centimeter, and ¹⁄₁₆ inch is more than one millimeter. Using these rough guides, the final number in metrics can be estimated to a tolerance that is acceptable in the field during construction.

Another factor to consider when converting is whether the item or detail dimension can be rounded up or down to arrive at the metric number. For example, if the current spacing of some fastening anchors is 6'-0" on center, one cannot round up when converting into metrics, because then one will exceed the specified spacing. In this case, the dimension would have to be rounded down. Typically, when conversions are needed, one should round off fractions to the nearest 5 mm, inches to the nearest 25 mm, and feet to the nearest meter.

Modular Units

Buildings can be constructed using modular components that are manufactured in standard sizes. This process eliminates considerable waste of materials, labor, and time. Modules manufactured in the English system of dimensioning come in 16-, 24-, and 48-inch (40.6, 60.9 and 121.9 cm) sizes, as shown in Figure 5-30. Even brick and concrete block are installed on approximately 4-inch (101.1 cm) and 8-inch (20.32 cm) modular coursing.

A modular grid (based on common building material sizes) can be used in the design process to conform the floor plan (or section when working vertically) to a standard module. For example, if a small building is 28 feet (8.53 m) by 40 feet (12.19 m), its dimensions correspond to the 2-foot (.6 m) module. However, if the building is 27 feet (8.22 m) by 39 feet (11.88 m), it falls short of the module. In this situation, approximately one foot (.3 m) must be cut off the modular material, resulting in wasted material and increased labor costs for cutting.

During the construction drawing process, the modular layout should also be followed wherever possible. When dimensioning new spaces, walls, and other elements, it is preferable to set the dimensions on the module to avoid creating more work for the car-

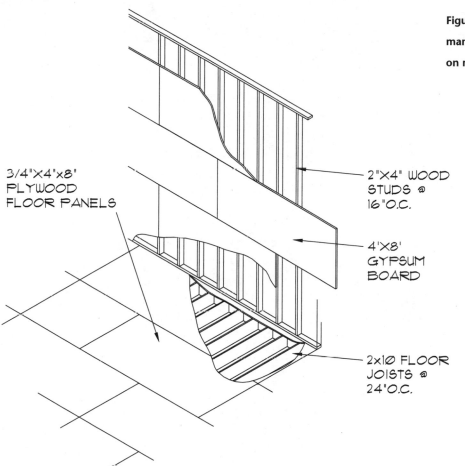

3/4"X4"X8"
PLYWOOD
FLOOR PANELS

2"X4" WOOD
STUDS @
16"O.C.

4'X8'
GYPSUM
BOARD

2x10 FLOOR
JOISTS @
24'O.C.

Figure 5-30 Building materials are manufactured and installed based on modular units.

penter and wasting material. For example, if a wall is to be located in a new space, it should be placed at 12 feet (3.65 m) from an existing wall rather than 11 feet, 10⅛ inches (3.6 m).

It is good design practice to try to always design with a modular unit in mind. In the design of corporate spaces, the spacing of the windows generally sets the modular unit, which is generally 5'0" (1.52 m) or 6'0" (1.83 m).

FLOOR PLANS 6

The floor plan is perhaps the most significant architectural drawing, as it contains a tremendous amount of information about the design and construction of a building or space (see Figure 6-1). It also serves as the primary drawing to which many of the other specialty drawings can be keyed.

A floor plan is an orthographic view of a total building or an area within a building, seen as if a horizontal cutting plane were passed through it at a height of approximately 4 feet (1219 mm) above the floor line (Figure 6-2). In some cases, it may be necessary to assume a higher cutting plane to show an item such as a high window or the space above a tall cabinet. The viewer is looking straight down into the building, as illustrated in Figure 6-3. In multiple-level buildings, a separate floor plan is drawn for each level. In turn, each level is aligned with the one above for bearing walls, stairways, ductwork, and other vertical elements related to both floors. Stairways are labeled "up" on one level and "down" on the level above. When viewing a floor plan of a building that includes a mezzanine or loft, the upper level is shown in plan, with the lower level also shown or simply labeled "open" (Figure 6-4).

In construction drawings, floor plans are drawn to scale and detailed to show walls, doors, windows, plumbing fixtures, appliances, stairs, cabinetry, and any other built-in or free-standing interior features. Most of these items are drawn as viewed from above. Figure 6-5 illustrates how a lavatory, appliances, and plumbing fixtures are drawn. Doors are drawn in the plan view in an open position showing the direction of their operation. Their size might be called out simplistically in plan, such as 3°, denoting that the door is 3 feet (91.4 cm) wide, as shown in Figure 6-6. More

detailed information regarding doors is shown in a door schedule (see Chapter 10) and keyed on the plan. Windows and their operation are difficult to describe in a floor-plan view. They are drawn simplistically in plan and referenced with specific symbols that relate to the type of their action and listed in a window schedule.

In addition to symbols, line weights and different types of lines can be used to relay information with the floor-plan drawing. For example, broken lines can denote items such as upper cabinets and high windows that are above the cutting plane, as shown in

Figure 6-1 A construction drawing of a floor plan conveys a significant amount of information to the builder, such as dimensions, door/window locations, cabinetry, and symbols that correspond to interior elevations.

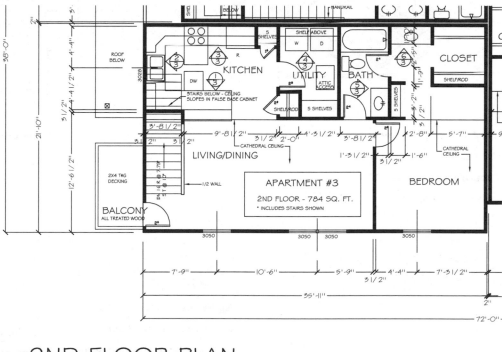

2ND FLOOR PLAN

SC: 1/4"=1'-0"

1. ALL WALLS TO BE 2X4 STUDS @ 16" O.C. GYP. BOARD - UNLESS NOTED OTHERWISE
2. FIELD VERIFY ALL CABINETRY BEFORE ORDERING/INSTALLING

77

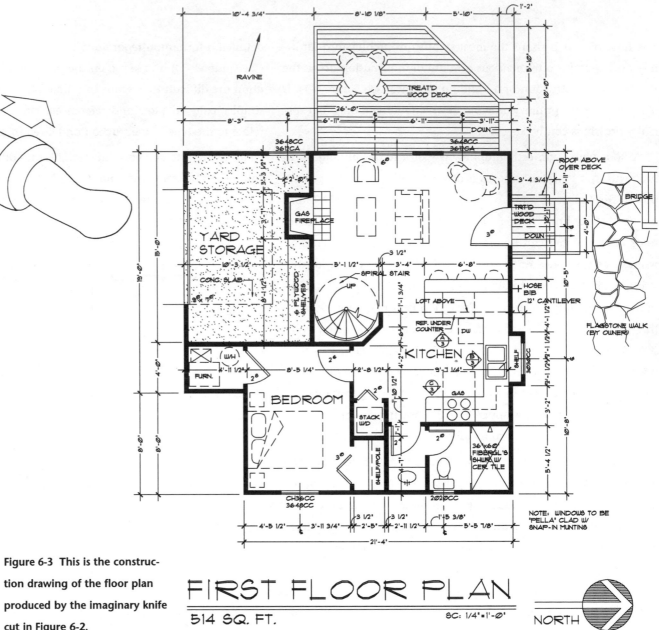

Figure 6-2 A floor-plan drawing is visualized as if an imaginary knife sliced approximately 4 feet (1219 mm) above the floor.

Figure 6-3 This is the construction drawing of the floor plan produced by the imaginary knife cut in Figure 6-2.

FIRST FLOOR PLAN

514 SQ. FT.   SC: 1/4"=1'-0'

NORTH

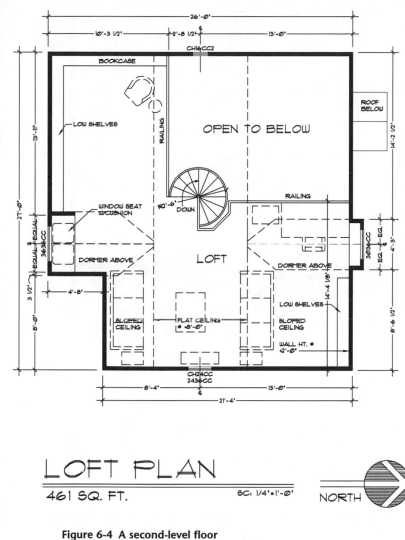

LOFT PLAN

461 SQ. FT.

SC: 1/4"=1'-0"

NORTH

OPEN TO BELOW

BOOKCASE

LOW SHELVES

ROOF BELOW

WINDOW SEAT w/CUSHION

DOWN

RAILING

LOFT

DORMER ABOVE

DORMER ABOVE

SLOPED CEILING

FLAT CEILING @ 8'-0'

SLOPED CEILING

LOW SHELVES

WALL HT. @ 2'-0'

Figure 6-4 A second-level floor plan can also show part of the space below. This helps to visualize what one can see when looking from this upper floor to the lower one.

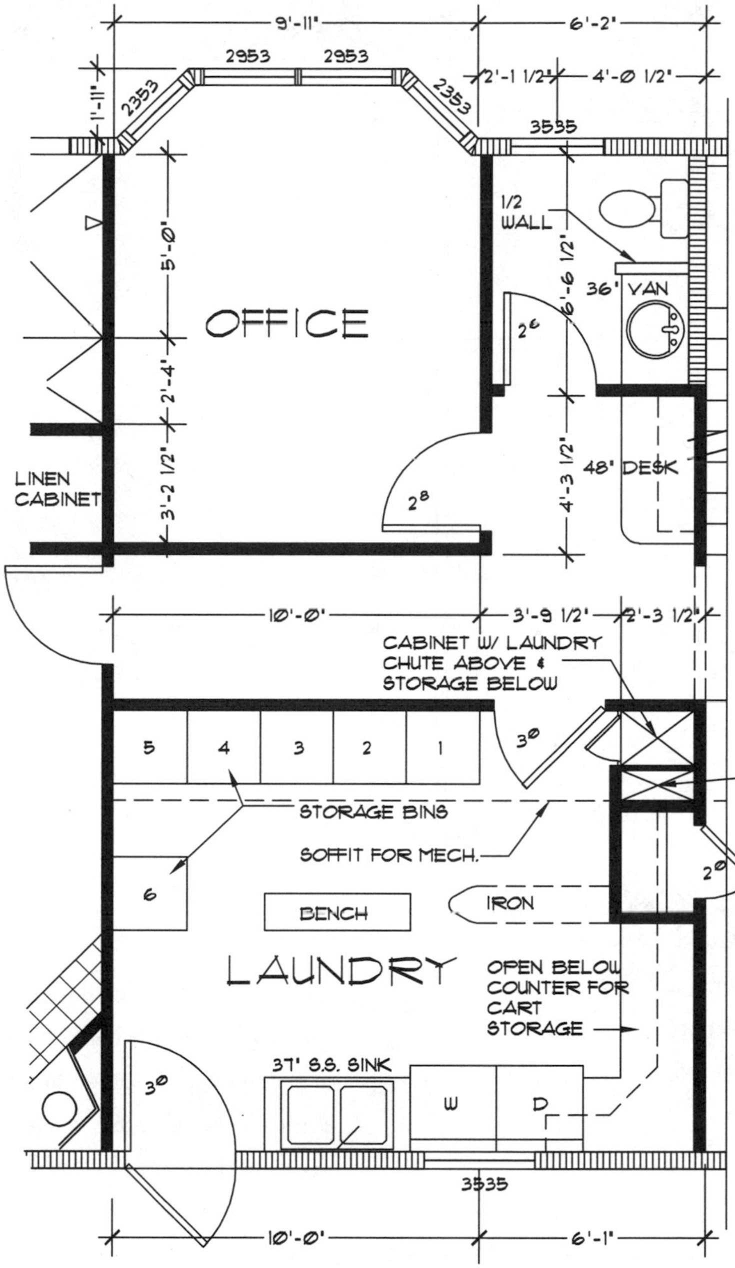

OFFICE

1/2 WALL

36' VAN

48' DESK

LINEN CABINET

CABINET W/ LAUNDRY CHUTE ABOVE & STORAGE BELOW

STORAGE BINS

SOFFIT FOR MECH.

BENCH

IRON

LAUNDRY

OPEN BELOW COUNTER FOR CART STORAGE

37' S.S. SINK

Figure 6-5 Built-in features such as sinks, cabinetry, and water closets are drawn as viewed from above.

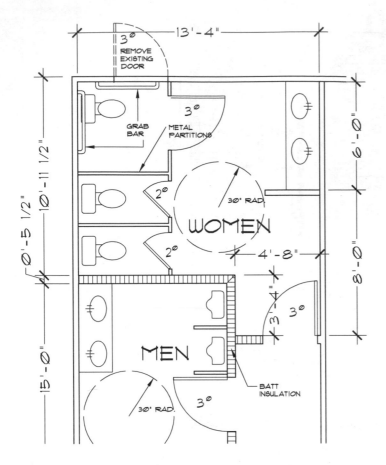

Figure 6-6 In this partial floor plan, doors are drawn simply, just showing their size and direction of swing. For example, 3° means a door that is 3 feet in width.

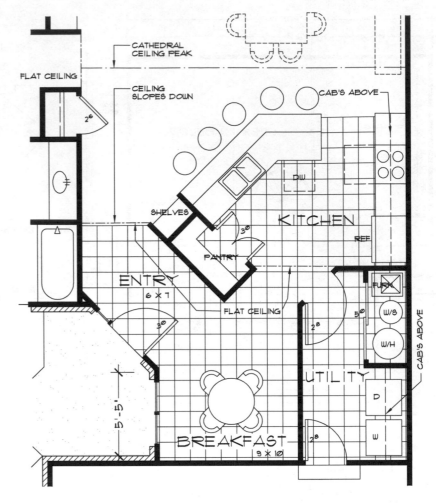

Figure 6-7 Dashed and dotted lines are used in this floor plan to indicate upper cabinets in the kitchen and utility areas, as well as ceiling changes.

Figure 6-7. Also, a different pattern can be used on the floor plan to denote a change in the floor treatment, such as the grid pattern in the kitchen and utility room in Figure 6-7. Much of the other information given on a floor plan is more general, with the items spelled out in more detail in other drawings or specifications. For example, a water heater or handrail is designated as such on the plan, and its detailed specifications are found elsewhere in the construction drawings or written specifications.

Scale of Floor Plans

The floor plan tends to be one of the largest single drawings in a construction set and often is placed on a sheet by itself. However, if space permits, other minor elements might be drawn around it to fill up the sheet. The sheet size a floor plan is drawn on is often the governing factor of the scale of that drawing. Floor plans are drawn at a scale that best presents the information to be conveyed without being too small to read. Residential floor plans are relatively small in overall square footage and are generally drawn at a scale of ¼" = 1'-0" (1:50 in metric scale). As commercial spaces can be quite large, a scale of ⅛" =1'-0" (1:100 metric) or even 1/16" = 1'-0" (1:200 metric) might be more appropriate. In these latter examples, auxiliary enlarged plans can be drawn and keyed to the base floor plan, as shown in Figure 6-8. One should always indicate the scale of the floor plan on the sheet, generally under the title.

Drafting Standards

Many decisions must be made before a floor plan is complete. The designer will probably spend more time drafting the floor plan than any other element. Drafting floor plans is more efficient if a logical sequence is followed; that is, first lay out the walls, openings, door swings, fixtures, and cabinets; then add dimensions, symbols, and any necessary notes.

Walls in Plan View

Floor plans should be drawn with a hierarchy of line weights for easy reading and for graphic excitement. Generally, a minimum of three line weights should be used, as illustrated in Figure 6-9. Walls should be drawn with the darkest and thickest lines. These lines can be double or filled in to indicate the thickness of the wall. The actual wall thickness will vary with the construction, but there

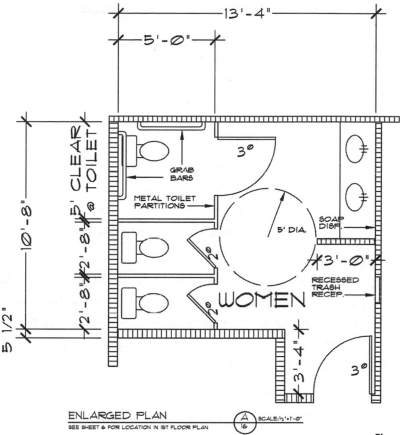

ENLARGED PLAN
SEE SHEET 6 FOR LOCATION IN 1ST FLOOR PLAN

SCALE: ½"=1'-0"

Figure 6-8 Some spaces can be drawn at a large scale, such as ½" = 1'0" (1:20 metric), to convey detailed information. These are then cross-referenced to a smaller-scale floor plan.

are some typical widths. Most walls in residential and small commercial construction are built with 2x4 wood studs, which are actually 3½ inches (89 mm) in width. When ½ inch (13 mm) gypsum board is added on each face, the wall thickness becomes 4½ inches (114 mm) finished. The same wall thickness is also often used in large commercial interiors where the studs are made of steel, although steel stud widths are produced in many other sizes as well. For both residential and commercial projects, interior 2x4 walls are generally drafted at approximately 5 inches (127 mm)

Figure 6-9 A minimum of three distinct line weights should be used in floor-plan drawings.

LIGHT LINE WEIGHT _____

MEDIUM LINE WEIGHT _____

HEAVY LINE WEIGHT _____

Figure 6-10 A variety of line weights and types are used to depict specific kinds of wall construction in floor-plan drawings.

thick in plan view. Exterior walls are drawn at about 6–8 inches (152–203 mm) thick, depending upon what materials they are constructed of. See Figure 6-10 for an example of different wall materials and how they are constructed as well as designated in a plan view drawing.

Built-in and free-standing objects such as countertops, plumbing fixtures, stairs, furniture, and other items that have contours should be drawn with slightly lighter line weights than the walls. Finally, textures, door swings, and dimension lines are the thinnest and lightest lines, as shown in Figure 6-11.

Doors and Windows in Plan View

Doors and windows are drawn in the floor plan using various symbols and images, and are further dimensioned and referenced to schedules in the construction drawings. The symbols used will depend upon the operating action of the door or window, the specifics needed to describe it, and the scale of the floor-plan drawing. In hand-drafting, these symbols are generated for each new project. However, when using a computer, door and window symbols can be stored in a symbol library and merely called up and inserted in the proper location.

Doors

Doors are generally classified by their action, as illustrated in Figure 6-12, and whether they are interior or exterior units.

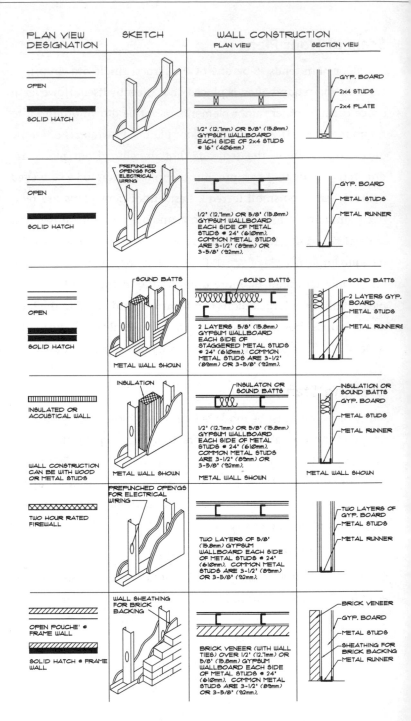

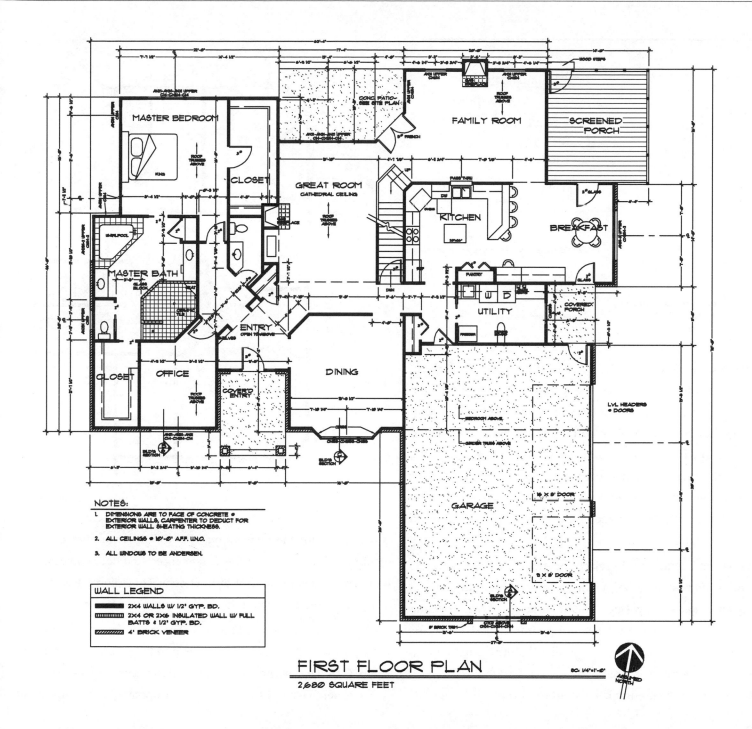

Figure 6-11 In this drawing, walls are drawn with heavy lines. Built-in furniture, cabinetry, and other objects are drawn with medium lines. Textures are represented with light lines.

FIRST FLOOR PLAN
2,680 SQUARE FEET

NOTES:
1. DIMENSIONS ARE TO FACE OF CONCRETE @ EXTERIOR WALLS, CARPENTER TO DEDUCT FOR EXTERIOR WALL SHEATING THICKNESS.
2. ALL CEILINGS @ 10'-0" AFF. U.N.O.
3. ALL WINDOWS TO BE ANDERSEN.

WALL LEGEND
2X4 WALLS W/ 1/2" GYP. BD.
2X4 OR 2X6 INSULATED WALL W/ FULL BATTS & 1/2" GYP. BD.
4" BRICK VENEER

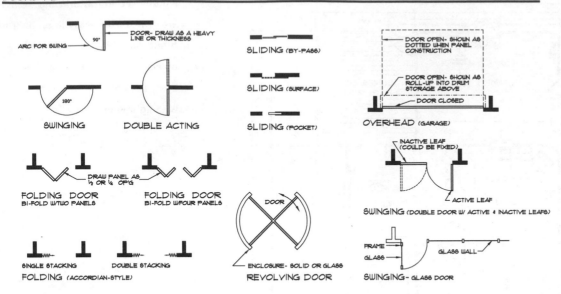

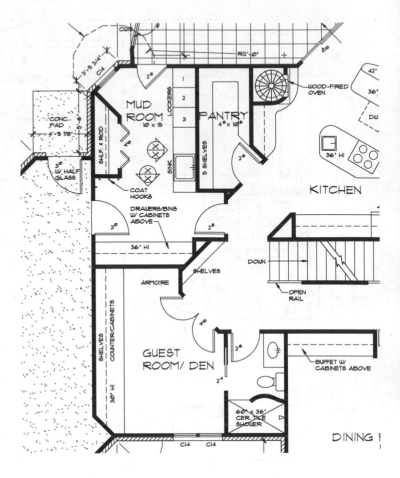

Figure 6-12 Doors drawn in plan view to show their method of operation.

Figure 6-13 The doors in this second-floor plan are generically called out according to their widths, such as 3°. They are all of the same materials, style, and other matching features.

Although a wide variety of styles exists within these general classifications, it is difficult to denote the specific style in a plan view. Refer to Chapter 10 for the most common door types, their operation, styles, hardware, and other features. Doors are drawn in plan view as a heavy line in small-scale drawings, or as a double line, to indicate their thickness, in larger-scaled plans. A swing door has a thinner curved line drawn to denote the direction of its swing. In small projects (particularly residential work) the door size is noted on the plan (Figure 6-13).

In larger and commercial projects, openings that are to receive doors can be addressed by two methods. The first and simplest is to treat openings generically. Doors might be labeled "A," for example, and all be of the same type, finish, frame, and hardware. "B" doors would represent another group. The other method is to address each opening as a unique design feature and assign each door its own independent number, as shown in Figure 6-14. A circle

is drawn within the door swing, and the door number is placed within it. In turn, this number is referenced to a door schedule that provides the details for that distinct door. This information is then cross-referenced to a door schedule, as explained in Chapter 10.

Doors and windows in plan view are generally dimensioned to the centerline of the door or window and frame unit, as shown in Figure 6-15. This method allows the designer to locate the door fairly accurately, leaving the actual rough opening, trim, and other

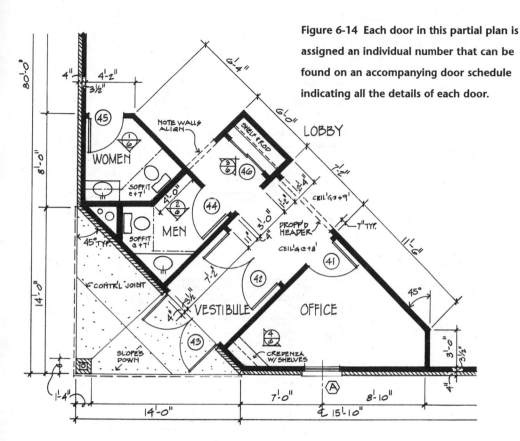

Figure 6-14 Each door in this partial plan is assigned an individual number that can be found on an accompanying door schedule indicating all the details of each door.

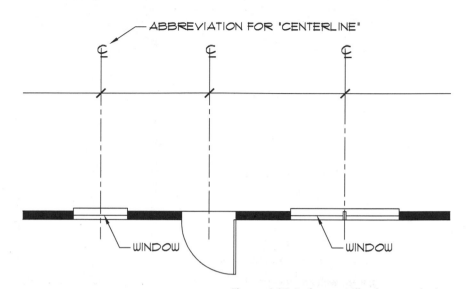

Figure 6-15 In frame walls, doors and windows are dimensioned to their centerlines, noted as a C/L. From these, the builder establishes the "rough" openings.

clearance details to the builder. In masonry, the door or window assembly (which has an exact unit size) is listed. The builder provides (in both cases) a slightly larger size, to set and shim the unit to fit the opening. The rough opening size is listed on the plan or in the schedule and abbreviated "R.O." This R.O. includes the door, frame, and proper clearances to install the unit within the frame wall, as illustrated in Figure 6-16. In many cases where a door hinge is close to an adjacent wall, it is not necessary to dimension the center of the door (or frame). The builder knows the door is to be located tight to the wall and will allow the proper exact clearances for operation and trim work, as shown in Figure 6-17.

Figure 6-16 In masonry walls, door and window openings are dimensioned to the edges rather than the centerline. The door or window unit is centered in the space.

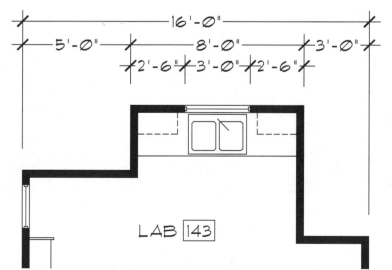

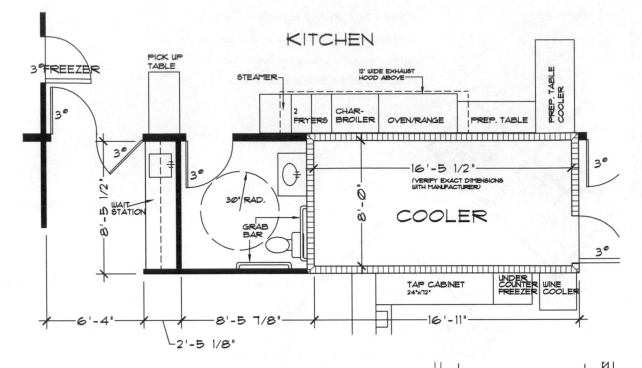

KITCHEN

3° FREEZER

PICK UP TABLE

STEAMER

12" WIDE EXHAUST HOOD ABOVE

PREP. TABLE COOLER

2 FRYERS

CHAR-BROILER

OVEN/RANGE

PREP. TABLE

3°

3°

3°

16'-5 1/2"

(VERIFY EXACT DIMENSIONS WITH MANUFACTURER)

8'-5 1/2"

30" RAD.

WAIT STATION

GRAB BAR

8'-0"

COOLER

3°

6'-4"

8'-5 7/8"

16'-11"

2'-5 1/8"

TAP CABINET 24"x12"

UNDER COUNTER FREEZER

WINE COOLER

Figure 6-17 When a door is adjacent to a wall, as in this partial restaurant plan, it is often not necessary to dimension the door location. The builder knows the door is to be located tight to the adjacent wall and will provide the proper details and clearances.

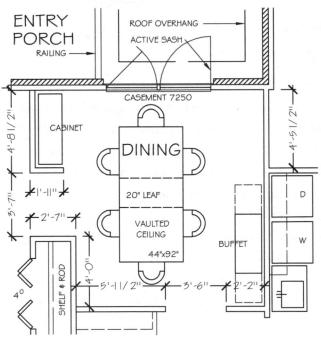

ENTRY PORCH

RAILING

ROOF OVERHANG

ACTIVE SASH

CASEMENT 7250

4'-8 1/2"

CABINET

4'-5 1/2"

DINING

5'-7"

1'-11"

2'-7"

20" LEAF

VAULTED CEILING

44"x92"

BUFFET

D

W

4'-0"

4°

SHELF & ROD

5'-1 1/2"

3'-6"

2'-2"

Figure 6-18 The windows in the dining room of this partial plan are drawn in some detail, as the scale of the drawing is fairly large.

Windows

Windows are drawn in floor plans in a variety of ways according to the scale of the plan and office standards. Generally, if the scale is large enough, windows are drawn based on their style and type of operation. A double casement window is shown in Figure 6-18. See Figure 6-19 for a complete list of the different styles of windows and how they would be drawn in plan view. If the scale of the drawing is small, such as ⅛" = 1'-0" (1:100 metric) or 1/16" = 1'-0" (1:200 metric) on large commercial projects, then a simple single line should be used with a symbol referring to the window schedule for more detailed information (Figure 6-20).

Graphic and Text Notation on Floor Plans

As a floor plan is the central or core drawing of any set of construction documents, it must be cross-referenced to other drawings and background materials. Graphic symbols and text notation are incorporated into the floor plan to make it as clear as possible.

Room Names and Notes

There are a number of items in a floor plan that cannot be portrayed graphically and need to be noted. These will vary according to the scale of the floor plan, its complexity, and whether it is a design or construction drawing (Figure 6-21). Room use is generally spelled out in both design and construction drawings. In small projects, only the room name is listed, whereas in large commercial spaces, a number might be assigned (or both a name and number). If the room is too small to write in the name or number on the floor plan, it is written just outside the space with a leader pointing to the room, as seen in Figure 6-22. Approximate room size is sometimes indicated beneath the room name; however, this is done mostly in presentation drawings, as the dimension is generally not accurate enough for a construction drawing. In a construction drawing,

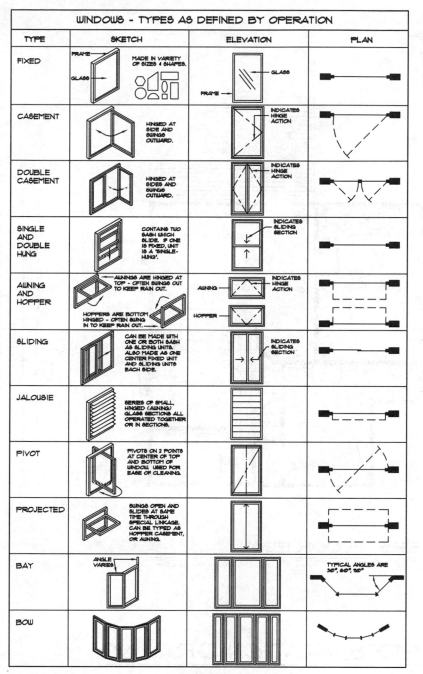

Figure 6-19 Different types of windows defined by their operation are illustrated in plan view and elevation.

Figure 6-21 A presentation
drawing, as shown on the left,
shows spaces, furniture, and
other items, including some
textures. A construction
drawing, shown on the right,
indicates the exact dimensions
and other particulars in
more detail.

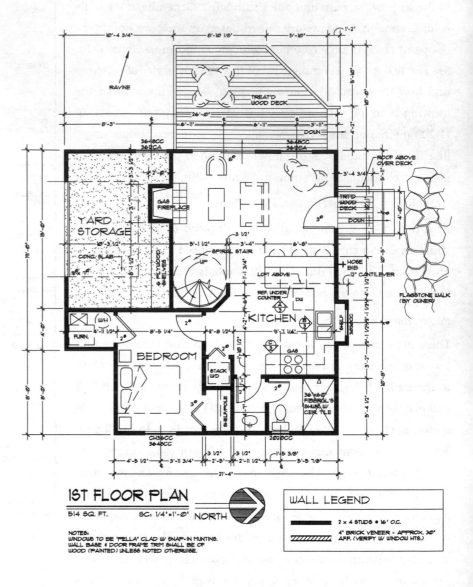

PRESENTATION DRAWING

CONSTRUCTION DRAWING

other dimensions noted on the plan will govern the size of the rooms, as it controls the exact placement of the studs. The finishes placed over the studs reduce the dimensions of the room by the material thickness. Some materials such as ceramic tile have an uneven base, which varies the room dimensions slightly.

Various notes are also added to the floor plan to convey specific information to the client or builder. These items might include handrails on stairs, soffits above, floor-level changes, and so forth, as shown in Figure 6-23. However, these notes are kept to a minimum in order not to clutter the drawing and are lettered at a smaller height than the room names. Figure 6-24 shows an example of how notes might be added to floor-plan drawings.

Architectural Symbols

A number of specialized symbols are used on the floor plan. For example, columns are usually assigned a grid number and referenced to the column centerline for dimensioning purposes (Figure 6-25). The grid consists of numbers along one axis and letters of the alphabet along the other, so that one can easily pinpoint a specific column, such as D-2 or C-4. A centerline is drafted as a series of single dashes and long lines passing through the column. A column designation bubble (sized for the appropriate lettering within it) is placed at the end of this line. In some cases, such as at an end column, the reference line might be to the face of a column, instead of the center. In this case, a notation is added to point out this exception, as shown in Figure 6-26.

Wall and building section cuts are shown on the floor plan with a symbol that indicates the approximate location of the cut and the direction of view, as illustrated in Figure 6-27. A circle is generally used that is divided in two sections. In the top portion, a letter, such as A, B, or C, generally indicates how many sections are cut.

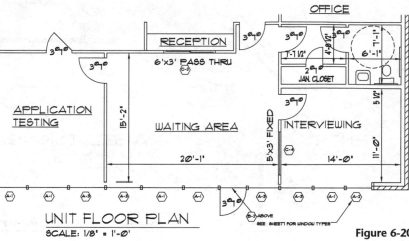

Figure 6-20 In commercial plans, such as this tenant space drawn at ⅛" scale, windows are shown as a single line. A symbol is added that is referenced to a detailed window schedule.

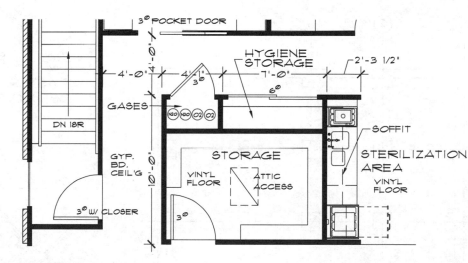

Figure 6-22 The small gas and hygiene storage rooms in this partial floor plan are labeled just outside of the space, as the lettering is too large to fit within it.

Figure 6-23 In addition to room names, this partial plan has notes added at a small scale to call out various items in the space.

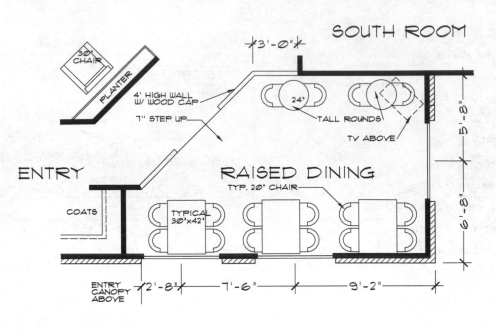

Figure 6-25 Columns can be identified in a floor plan by assigning numbers and letters to a grid locating their centerlines or faces.

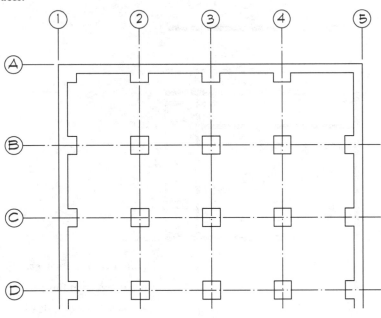

Figure 6-24 Several notes are added to this partial floor plan for clarity.

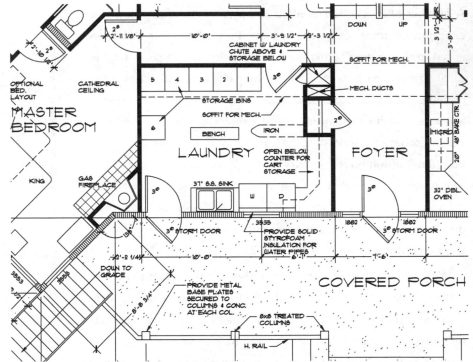

(Numbers can also be used.) The bottom section of the circle contains a number that refers to the sheet number this section is drawn on. In small projects where there is a limited number of sheets, bottom numbers are not used. The circle is just big enough to contain the letter and number. If more than one building section cut is needed, the symbols are drawn at a similar size to adhere to a uniform standard. Figure 6-28 shows how building section cuts are indicated on floor plans.

Interior and exterior elevations are noted on the floor plan in much the same way as building section cuts (Figure 6-29). Once again, a circle containing numbers is used, with an arrow indicating the direction of view. Some designers prefer to make a distinct visual difference between sections and elevations to help the viewer easily distinguish them. In Figure 6-30, for example, the arrow is blackened in on sections and not on elevations. Another way to denote the difference is to use an arrow on the section cut and eliminate the arrow "tails" on an elevation mark.

Sometimes the scale of the floor plan is too small to place all the required detail or notes within a small space such as toilet rooms and stairs. In such situations, an enlarged plan is drawn elsewhere of these spaces and cross-referenced on the plan. The area to be enlarged can simply have a note within (or adjacent) that says "see sheet x for enlarged plan." In most cases, however, a heavy broken line is placed around the area to be enlarged, as illustrated in Figure 6-31. A circle and number(s) are assigned to it, similar to the section or elevation symbol. This enlarged plan can appear on the floor-plan sheet or another sheet. This same method can also be used to show detail on other features, such as a column or another specialized assembly.

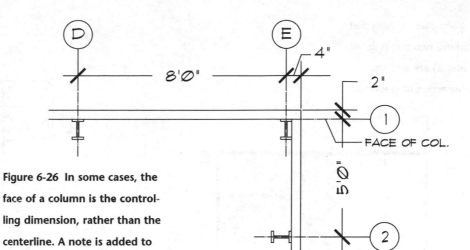

Figure 6-26 In some cases, the face of a column is the controlling dimension, rather than the centerline. A note is added to point this feature out.

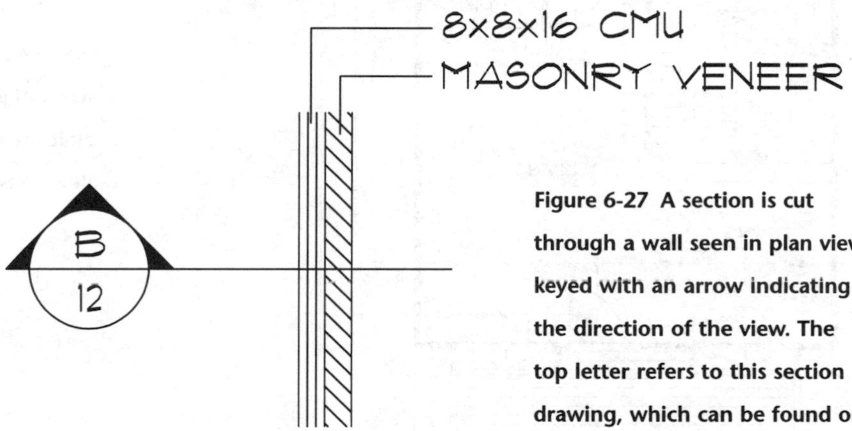

Figure 6-27 A section is cut through a wall seen in plan view, keyed with an arrow indicating the direction of the view. The top letter refers to this section drawing, which can be found on the sheet identified in the lower half of the circle.

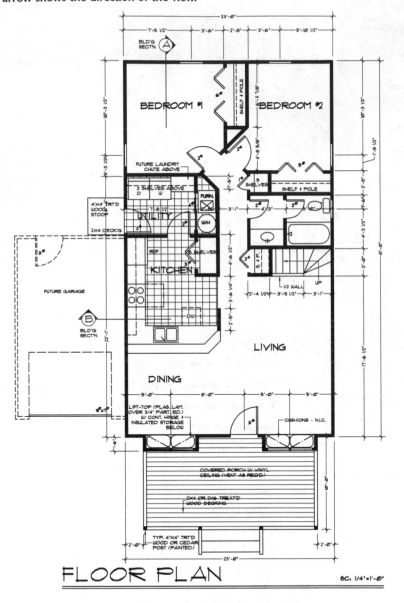

FLOOR PLAN

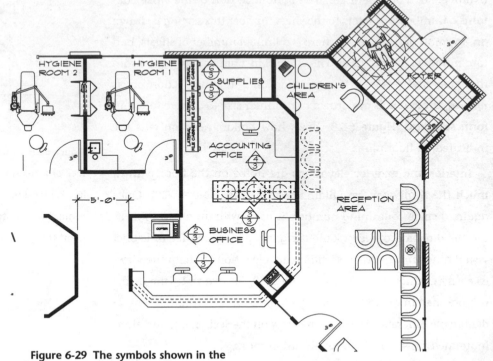

Figure 6-29 The symbols shown in the accounting and business offices of this dental clinic are referenced to sheet 3, where interior elevations of these offices are drawn.

Figure 6-30 Coloring in the arrow or leaving it uncolored can make the difference between a section and elevation symbol. Or the tails of the arrow can be eliminated to make one different from the other.

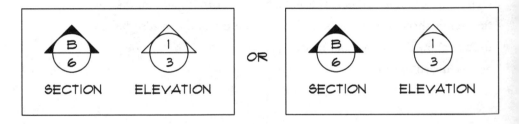

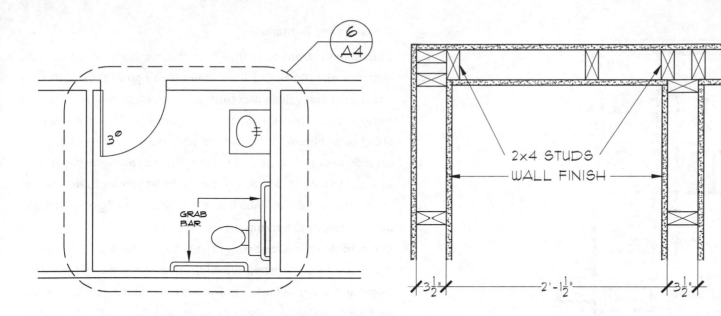

Figure 6-31 A portion of a floor plan can be keyed with a symbol to a larger, more detailed plan that is drawn elsewhere. For example, this part of the plan is referenced as area 6 and enlarged on sheet A4.

Figure 6-32 Dimensions on a floor plan generally locate the framework of the building, such as the face of these 2x4 studs.

Dimensioning Floor Plans

A floor plan is carefully dimensioned to ensure that items such as walls, columns, doors, windows, openings, stairs, and other particulars are correctly located for construction. Sometimes after a plan is drawn accurately to a scale, its reproduction causes a slight enlargement or reduction of the drawing. In such cases, the floor plan is slightly out of true scale, but this is acceptable because the written dimensions are the controlling factors. In fact, most designers add a note on the drawing that says, "do not scale drawing, follow written dimensions."

Generally, elements such as walls are dimensioned to the frame (Figure 6-32), as the builder first erects this and then adds the finishes to it. This dimensioning technique gives the exact location of the studs, columns, and beams and is generally placed to the face of these. In some cases, however, the centerline of the wall might be located and dimensioned, as illustrated in Figure 6-33.

As noted in Chapter 5, dimensioning is done in a hierarchical manner. Buildings, structural framework, rooms, and fixtures are dimensioned in decreasing size order. The actual number of dimensions on a plan is dependent upon how much latitude the designer affords the contractor. A very detailed and dimensioned plan gives the builder little room for deviation from the original design. However, if only a few key dimensions are shown, the builder is trusted to determine exact locations of interior components. A good guideline for dimensioning falls somewhere between these two approaches. An overdimensioned plan allows the builder little freedom to make field adjustments or substitute cost-saving techniques. However, too few dimensions can produce a lot of guesswork and increase the chances for error in the field and in coordination between subcontractors.

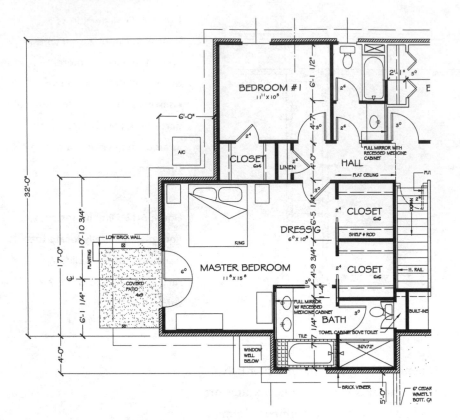

Dimensioning Techniques

Dimensions are placed on the floor plan as shown in Figure 6-34. Note that the dimension lines are drafted lighter than wall lines and are generally done as a continuous group or string of numbers along a line. The extension line begins slightly away from the object (a minimum of $\frac{1}{16}$ inch or 1.58 mm), never touching it. It extends about $\frac{1}{8}$ inch (3.17 mm) beyond the dimension line. Arrows, dots, or 45-degree tick marks (most common) are used at the extension line and dimension line junction (Figure 6-35). The arrows, dots, or tick marks are drawn with a thicker and/or darker line to make them stand out graphically. The 45-degree tick marks are drawn in a consistent direction. However, some draftspersons slope the tick marks for vertically read dimensions from left to right and horizontally read dimensions from right to left. When using the computer, any of these three graphic symbols (arrows, dots, or ticks) can be called up and consistently inserted for all dimensions.

Figure 6-33 All dimensions in this floor plan are to the face of a stud, except for the wall between the closets. It is dimensioned to the centerline of the wall. The centerline technique can also be used to locate exterior windows and doors, as seen in this example.

Figure 6-34 Note that the dimensions on this partial floor plan are placed outside of the spaces. The extension lines do not touch the walls, and dark 45-degree tick marks indicate the extent of the dimensions.

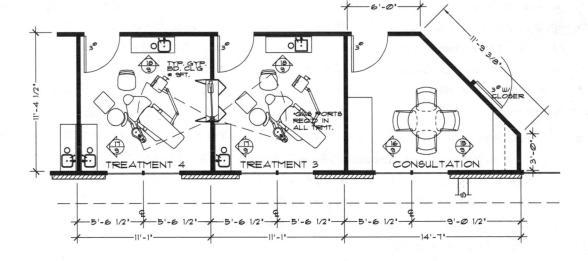

Dimensioning on a floor plan usually requires two or three continuous dimension lines to locate exterior walls, wall jogs, interior walls, windows, doors, and other elements, as shown in Figure 6-36. Exterior walls of a building are dimensioned outside the floor plan. The outermost dimension line is the overall building dimension. The next dimension line, moving toward the plan, indicates wall locations and centerlines to doors and windows. Other miscellaneous details in the plan (such as minor offsets, jogs, or cabinetry and fixtures) are located on a third dimension line. This hierarchy of line work allows the carpenters and other trades to quickly locate major framing elements and minor details by referring to the appropriate dimension line.

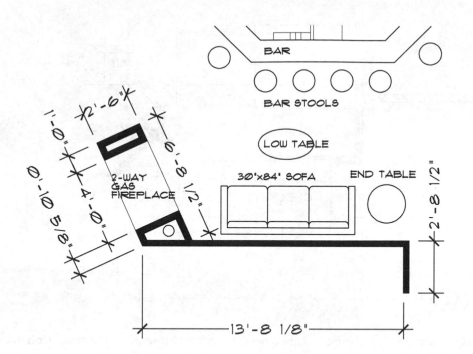

Figure 6-35 Dark tick marks at 45 degrees to a dimension's extension line are the most common technique for indicating junction points.

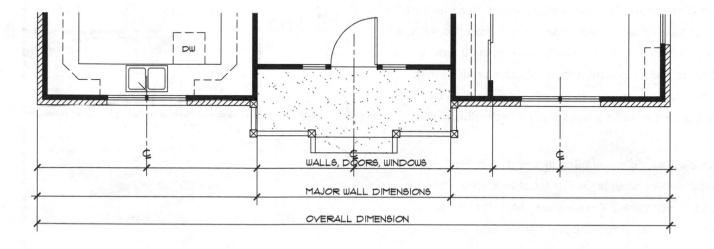

Figure 6-36 Dimensioning on a floor plan is grouped hierarchically, working from the overall dimension of the exterior walls to the smaller components of a building or space, such as wall jogs, interior walls, windows, doors, and other important elements.

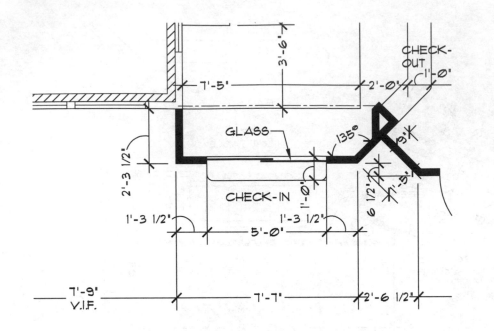

Figure 6-37 A leader is used to indicate the distance of 1'-3½" from a wall corner to the check-in shelf on this partial plan, as the space within the dimension line is too small to letter in.

Designation of Materials

Floor plans are generally not used to designate specific materials, as finishes might be too small to show in plan and their selections might be changed later. The amount of material information provided on a floor plan depends on the size and complexity of the proposed construction. The plans for a small residential project may contain more detailed information, such as the finished floor materials, because the design may be simpler and very few materials used, as illustrated in Figure 6-38.

The few materials that might be designated on the floor plan are the walls, which can be pouched to indicate wood or other wall material designations such as block, brick, or concrete. Floor and wall finish materials are better indicated on the finish plans. See Chapter 11 for further information on drafting finish plans.

Numerals are placed above and centered on the dimension line, being drafted at a height of ⅛–³⁄₁₆ inch (3.17–4.76 mm). The numbers do not rest on the dimension line, as they might blend in with the line and become unreadable. In computerized drafting, the machine often is programmed to automatically place the numbers centered in the broken dimension line, rather than above it. Dimensions are oriented to read from the base or right side of a drawing. When an area is too small for the dimension to go in the usual place, the numbers are placed outside (or sometimes below) the extension line and a leader is used to point to the dimensioned area (Figure 6-37).

The preferred area for dimensioning all items on a floor plan is outside the walls where possible, as this tends to keep the interior of the floor plan uncluttered. However, it is difficult to accurately dimension most projects without having some dimension lines within the floor plan. This is especially true of interior projects.

Figure 6-38 Floor plans in small residential projects often depict material finishes, such as this tiled floor in the entry, kitchen, breakfast area, and utility room.

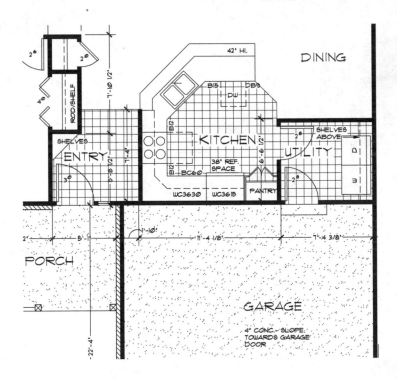

Checklist for Floor Plans

General

- Title the drawing, note its scale, and indicate north (or reference direction).

- Draw all doors and direction of operation (swings, folding, etc.).

- Draw all windows to scale and show mullions.

- Number and symbol-code all doors and windows.

- Check door swings and window operations for possible conflicts with other elements and views.

- Number or name all rooms/spaces.

- Show stairways and include an arrow to indicate "up" or "down" from that floor level. Call out the number of risers and treads and cross-reference if a detailed drawing is made of the stairs elsewhere.

- Draw dash lines for major soffits or openings above and call them out in a note, including attic and other access panels.

- Draw dash lines for wheelchair access circles to show compliance with ADA standards (where applicable).

- Draw handrails, guardrails, and half-height walls and call out with a note, where necessary.

- Pouche walls and reference to a wall type legend.

- Draw in fixed cabinets, shelves, plumbing fixtures, and other built-in items.

Notations

- Note any floor level changes, slopes, and ramps.

- Call out floor drains where applicable.

- Cross-reference the floor plan with section and elevation symbols for information about the building structure, walls, ceilings, floors, and built-in items such as cabinetry.

- Label major components such as fireplaces, bookcases, built-in furniture, refrigerators, dishwashers, compactors, furnaces, and water heaters.

- Call out miscellaneous items such as medicine cabinets, drinking fountains, and other built-in items. Include here or reference to another drawing information and locations of towel dispensers, soap dispensers, waste containers, electric hand dryers, mirrors, and towel bars.

- Label shelves and rod in closets.

- Note ceiling heights here (small projects) or on the reflected ceiling plan (larger projects).

Dimensions

- Dimension all wall locations, and place a general note indicating whether the dimensions are to face of a wall, centerline, or other surface (such as face of a stud, concrete, etc.).

- Dimension walls and other items to structural components such as columns or existing walls.

- Give the angle in degrees of walls that are not placed ninety degrees to one another and supply exact reference points where these walls start and end.

- Give radius or diameter of all circular elements, such as curved walls, openings, curved handrails, etc.

- Dimension all horizontal openings, partitions, and general cabinetry.

- Locate all stairs and dimension properly. See Chapter 9 for stair details and dimension standards.

An elevation is a scaled drawing that shows a vertical surface or plane seen from a point of view perpendicular to the viewers' picture plane. An elevation is also a type of orthographic multiview drawing (discussed in Chapter 4). The various elevation views include the front, sides, and rear. Planes perpendicular to the picture plane are seen on edge, and other angles are seen foreshortened. Elevations are drawn as straight-on views, so there is no distortion as in a perspective or isometric drawing. Architectural elevations illustrate the finished appearance of an exterior or interior wall of a building, as shown in Figure 7-1.

Elevations serve as a primary source to show heights, materials, and related information that cannot be seen in floor plans, sections, or other drawings. For example, a lavatory and vanity shown on a floor plan gives no information about the number, heights, and sizes of doors and drawers located beneath the basin unit. An elevation is drawn to convey this information. Elevations are drawn as exterior or interior views of a building, or they might be specialized views of objects such as furniture or free-standing cabinetry. Elevations generally show:

1. Object profiles and finish materials (Figure 7-2).

2. Relationships of different parts of objects such as doors, drawers, and top surfaces of a cabinet (Figure 7-3).

3. Vertical dimensions of an object that cannot be found in a plan view. In some cases, horizontal dimensions are also shown for clarity (Figure 7-4).

Figure 7-1 Elevations can provide detailed information about wall finishes, cabinetry, doors, windows, and other design features.

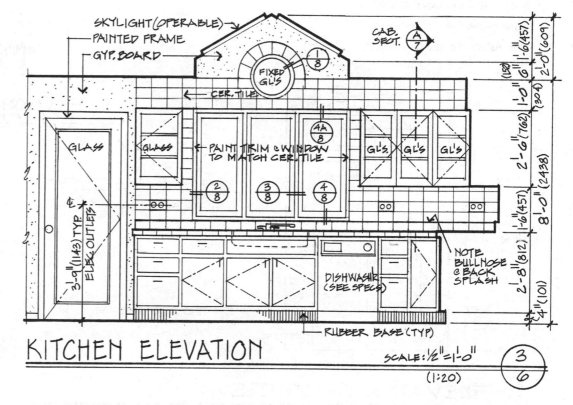

99

Figure 7-4 Elevations are used to convey vertical dimensions of objects that can't be indicated in a plan view. Detailed horizontal dimensions can also be shown.

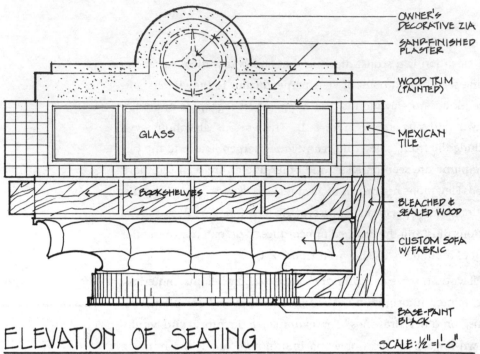

ELEVATION OF SEATING

OWNER'S DECORATIVE ZIA

SAND-FINISHED PLASTER

WOOD TRIM (PAINTED)

MEXICAN TILE

GLASS

BOOKSHELVES

BLEACHED & SEALED WOOD

CUSTOM SOFA W/FABRIC

BASE-PAINT BLACK

SCALE: ½"=1'-0"

Figure 7-2 In this elevation, the sofa is drawn in profile on the left, and the various materials are called out and delineated with a texture.

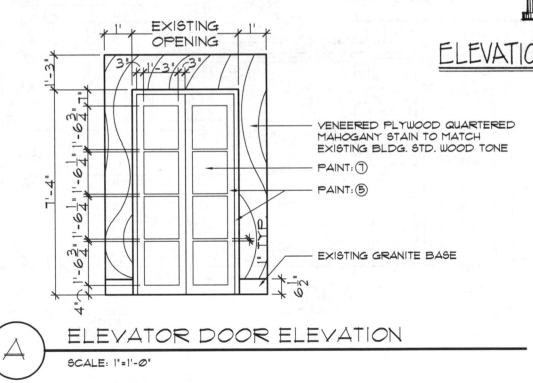

EXISTING OPENING

VENEERED PLYWOOD QUARTERED MAHOGANY STAIN TO MATCH EXISTING BLDG. STD. WOOD TONE

PAINT: ①

PAINT: ⑤

EXISTING GRANITE BASE

ELEVATOR DOOR ELEVATION

Ⓐ

SCALE: 1"=1'-0"

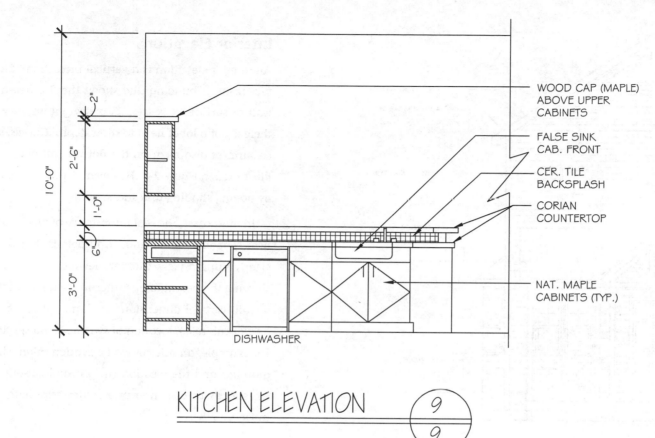

WOOD CAP (MAPLE) ABOVE UPPER CABINETS

FALSE SINK CAB. FRONT

CER. TILE BACKSPLASH

CORIAN COUNTERTOP

NAT. MAPLE CABINETS (TYP.)

DISHWASHER

KITCHEN ELEVATION

Figure 7-3 A cabinet elevation can show heights, widths, and layout of doors, drawers, and items such as sinks and backsplashes.

Exterior Elevations

Exterior elevations illustrate the finished appearance of an exterior wall of a building. They convey the types of materials proposed, types of doors and windows, the finished grade, roof slope, foundation, footings, and selected vertical dimensions. Elevations assist the designer in visualizing how proposed door and window types and locations on the floor plan will influence the appearance and style of the structure (Figure 7-5).

Exterior elevations are identified with a title and scale. Generally, exterior elevations are titled according to the compass direction they are facing, either North Elevation, East Elevation, South Elevation, or West Elevation. If a building is not facing true north, the side that is oriented the most nearly north is identified as such. Then the other elevations are titled according to the compass direction most closely related to them. In some cases, exterior elevations are titled Front, Rear, Left, and Right.

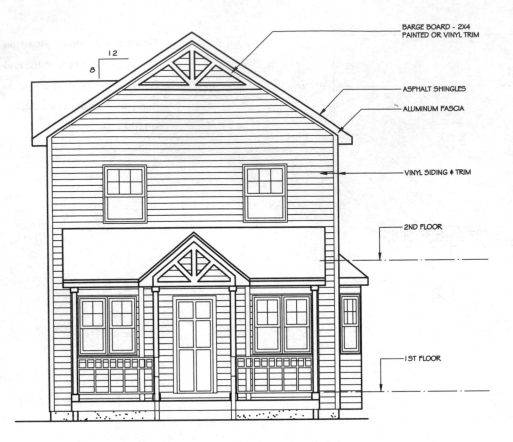

BARGE BOARD - 2X4
PAINTED OR VINYL TRIM

12
8

ASPHALT SHINGLES

ALUMINUM FASCIA

VINYL SIDING & TRIM

2ND FLOOR

1ST FLOOR

FRONT ELEVATION

SC: 1/4"= 1'-0"

Figure 7-5 Exterior elevations convey the materials used and particulars of doors, windows, roofs, and footings, as well as important vertical dimensions.

In most cases, architects and engineers draw exterior elevations. However, interior designers may be required to draw exterior elevations for residential or small commercial projects, such as retail store facades, as shown in Figure 7-6. When remodeling a building or adding space to an existing structure, it may be necessary for the interior designer to draw partial exterior elevations for clarity and understanding.

Interior Elevations

An interior elevation is a vertical projection of a wall or other surface inside a building and shows the finished appearance of that wall or surface. It is seen as a straight-on view of the surface, as there is not a lot of need to show depth. Curves, spheres, and slanted surfaces disappear on the flat vertical plane of an elevation, as illustrated in Figure 7-7. However, depth can be indicated if desired by adding shading and shadowing.

In most cases, the real importance of an elevation is to show vertical elements, dimensions, and details that cannot be explained clearly in plan view. Interior elevations are particularly useful for showing the height of openings in a wall, materials and finishes of a wall, vertical dimensions, wall-mounted items (such as shelves and/or cabinets), location of switches, and special wall treatments. For example, an interior wall elevation might show the height of a grab bar and the location (height and cut-out size required) of a recessed tissue dispenser in a commercial bathroom, as illustrated in Figure 7-8.

Scale of Interior Elevations

The scale at which an interior elevation should be drawn will depend upon the complexity and detail of items, information, and finishes to be shown. Generally, interior elevations are drawn to the same scale as the floor plan(s). If the wall plane and other items are fairly simple, then a scale of ¼" = 1'-0" (1:50 metric) is acceptable. This is especially applicable in large public spaces. However, in very large commercial interior spaces a smaller scale of ⅛" = 1'-0" (1:100 metric) might be required. In small projects or spaces, elevations might be drawn at a larger scale, such as ½" = 1'-0" (1:20 metric) or ⅜" = 1'-0" (1:30 metric) to show small details.

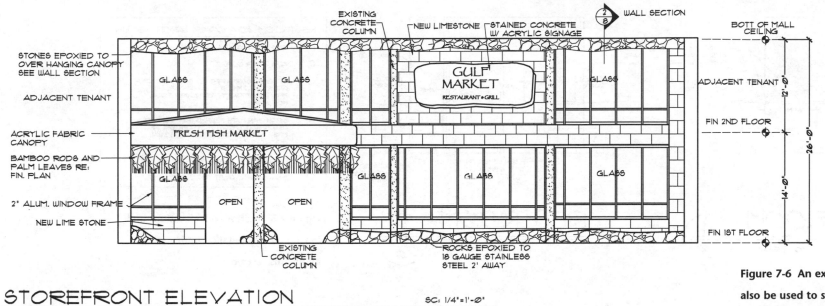

STONES EPOXIED TO
OVER HANGING CANOPY
SEE WALL SECTION

ADJACENT TENANT

ACRYLIC FABRIC
CANOPY

BAMBOO RODS AND
PALM LEAVES RE:
FIN. PLAN

2" ALUM. WINDOW FRAME

NEW LIME STONE

EXISTING
CONCRETE
COLUMN

NEW LIMESTONE

STAINED CONCRETE
W/ ACRYLIC SIGNAGE

WALL SECTION

BOTT OF MALL
CEILING

ADJACENT TENANT

FIN 2ND FLOOR

FIN 1ST FLOOR

GLASS

GLASS

GLASS

GULF
MARKET
RESTAURANT • GRILL

GLASS

FRESH FISH MARKET

GLASS

GLASS

GLASS

OPEN

OPEN

EXISTING
CONCRETE
COLUMN

ROCKS EPOXIED TO
18 GAUGE STAINLESS
STEEL 2' AWAY

12'-0"

14'-0"

26'-0"

STOREFRONT ELEVATION

SC: 1/4"=1'-0"

Figure 7-6 An exterior elevation may also be used to show a storefront in a shopping mall, such as this facade for the Gulf Market Restaurant and Grill.

Figure 7-7 A curved reception desk looks flat in an elevation. Its curved surface is only apparent in the floor plan.

TEMPERED
GLASS TOP
1/4" REVEAL TYP.

WOOD PANELS

3'-6"

3'-1"

1 RECEPTION DESK - ELEVATION

SCALE: 1/4"=1'-0"

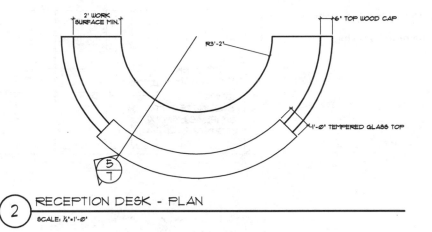

2' WORK
SURFACE MIN.

6" TOP WOOD CAP

R3'-2"

1'-0" TEMPERED GLASS TOP

5
7

2 RECEPTION DESK - PLAN

SCALE: 1/4"=1'-0"

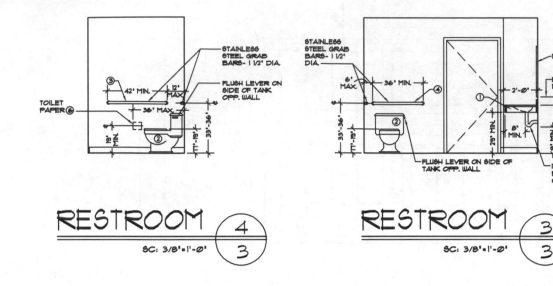

RESTROOM

SC: 3/8"=1'-0" 4/3

RESTROOM

SC: 3/8"=1'-0" 3/3

RESTROOM ADA COMPLIANCE LEGEND

① ADA CERAMIC WALL HUNG SINK

② ADA WATER CLOSET

③ GRAB BAR (WITH PEENED GRIP SURFACE)-
   (SIDE WALL) MOUNT @ 33" CENTERLINE
   MFG: BOBRICK OR APPROVED EQUAL
   NO: 6206-42"

④ GRAB BAR (WITH PEENED GRIP SURFACE)-
   (BACK WALL) MOUNT @ 33" CENTERLINE
   MFG: BOBRICK OR APPROVED EQUAL
   NO: 6206-36"

⑤ WALL MIRROR- MOUNT BOTTOM @ 40" AFF.

⑥ SINGLE ROLL TOILET TISSUE DISPENSER

Figure 7-8 Interior wall elevations and legend convey detailed information about this restroom.

Figure 7-9 The scale an elevation is drawn to is recorded directly beneath the drawing, along with the title of the drawing.

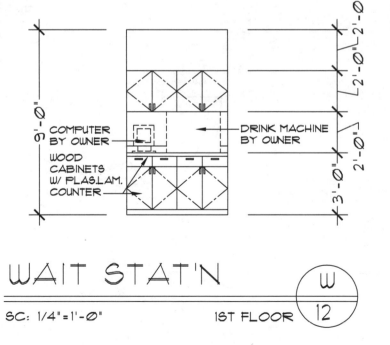

WAIT STAT'N

SC: 1/4"=1'-0"   1ST FLOOR W/12

The scale of the drawing is noted directly beneath the drawing, as shown in Figure 7-9, or elsewhere on the sheet if the same scale is used throughout the entire sheet.

Drafting Standards for Interior Elevations

Interior elevations are drafted to clearly indicate surfaces, edges, and the intersections of materials and forms. The elevation is drawn to scale, with the limits of the ceiling, floor, and adjacent walls (or other forms) shown with a dark outline. There are two basic methods that professional firms use to draw interior elevations. These methods are illustrated in Figure 7-10. The first method is to outline all the elements (such as cabinets, beams, soffits, etc.) that project toward the viewer and establish the limits of the wall elevation, as shown in Figure 7-11. The other method depicts these items in cross-section, often showing construction details, materials, and other hidden items. This method is useful

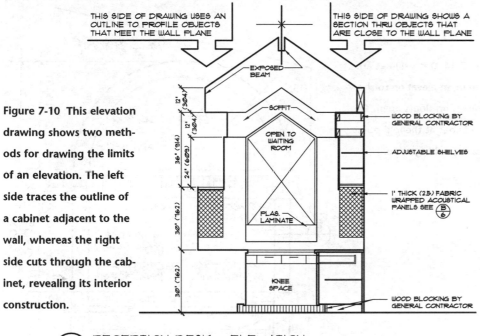

THIS SIDE OF DRAWING USES AN OUTLINE TO PROFILE OBJECTS THAT MEET THE WALL PLANE

THIS SIDE OF DRAWING SHOWS A SECTION THRU OBJECTS THAT ARE CLOSE TO THE WALL PLANE

EXPOSED BEAM

SOFFIT

OPEN TO WAITING ROOM

WOOD BLOCKING BY GENERAL CONTRACTOR

ADJUSTABLE SHELVES

1" THICK (25) FABRIC WRAPPED ACOUSTICAL PANELS SEE B/6

PLAS. LAMINATE

KNEE SPACE

WOOD BLOCKING BY GENERAL CONTRACTOR

① RECEPTION DESK - ELEVATION

SCALE: ¼"=1'-0"

Figure 7-10 This elevation drawing shows two methods for drawing the limits of an elevation. The left side traces the outline of a cabinet adjacent to the wall, whereas the right side cuts through the cabinet, revealing its interior construction.

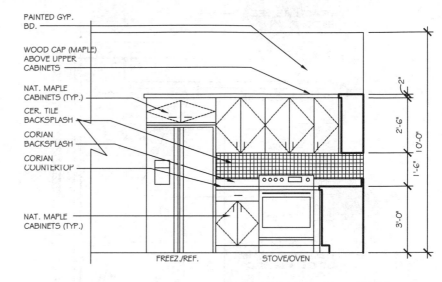

PAINTED GYP. BD.

WOOD CAP (MAPLE) ABOVE UPPER CABINETS

NAT. MAPLE CABINETS (TYP.)

CER. TILE BACKSPLASH

CORIAN BACKSPLASH

CORIAN COUNTERTOP

NAT. MAPLE CABINETS (TYP.)

FREEZ./REF.   STOVE/OVEN

Figure 7-11 The cabinetry in this wall elevation is shown in outline form, rather than with its interior construction.

for explaining the details of an adjacent object (a cabinet interior, for example) without having to generate a separate drawing elsewhere. See Figure 7-12 for an example of this type of drawing. The choice between these techniques is dependent upon the complexity of the interior, the information that needs to be conveyed, and the established office standards.

Drawing interior elevations does not always follow a rigid set of architectural rules. Decorative elements or embellishment may need to be added to convey the character of the space. Many interior designers and architects take some liberty with elevations to convey important features, even if that means departing from "architecturally correct" drafting standards. For example, wall coverings,

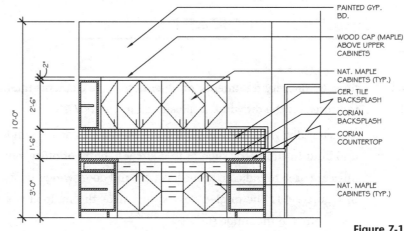

PAINTED GYP. BD.

WOOD CAP (MAPLE) ABOVE UPPER CABINETS

NAT. MAPLE CABINETS (TYP.)

CER. TILE BACKSPLASH

CORIAN BACKSPLASH

CORIAN COUNTERTOP

NAT. MAPLE CABINETS (TYP.)

Figure 7-12 In this elevation, the adjacent cabinets are drawn showing their interior construction.

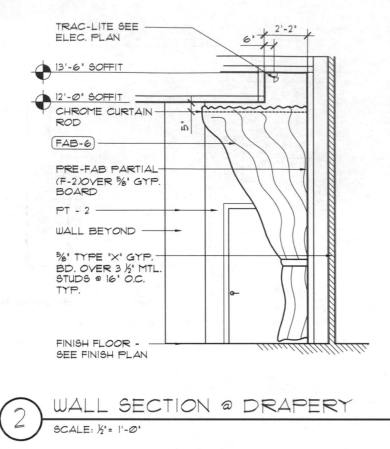

TRAC-LITE SEE ELEC. PLAN

13'-6" SOFFIT

12'-0" SOFFIT

CHROME CURTAIN ROD

FAB-6

PRE-FAB PARTIAL (F-2)OVER ⅝" GYP. BOARD

PT - 2

WALL BEYOND

⅝" TYPE "X" GYP. BD. OVER 3 ½" MTL. STUDS @ 16' O.C. TYP.

FINISH FLOOR - SEE FINISH PLAN

2'-2"

6'

5"

② WALL SECTION @ DRAPERY

SCALE: ½"= 1'-0"

Figure 7-14 Dashed lines are drawn in an elevation to show the direction doors open. The dashed lines at the mid-point indicate the hinge side.

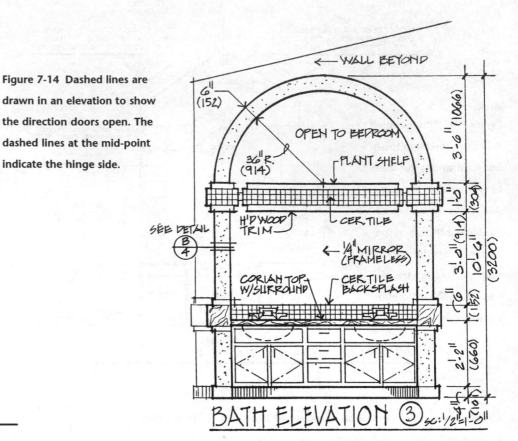

WALL BEYOND

6" (152)

3'-6" (1066)

OPEN TO BEDROOM

PLANT SHELF

36" R. (914)

SEE DETAIL B/4

H'D WOOD TRIM

CER. TILE

¼" MIRROR (FRAMELESS)

CORIAN TOP W/SURROUND

CER. TILE BACKSPLASH

2'-2" (660)

6" (152)

3'-0" (914)

1'-0" (304)

10'-6" (3200)

BATH ELEVATION ③ SC: ½"=1'-0"

Figure 7-13 This wall section shows the drapery and wall beyond in elevation view.

finishes, drapery treatments, or other decorative elements might be indicated on the drawing, as illustrated in Figure 7-13.

Generally, when drawing interior elevations of doors, windows, and built-in cabinetry, such as in a kitchen, bath, or office, dashed lines are used to indicate hinge location and door swings, as shown in Figure 7-14. The angled dashed line near the midpoint of the door points to the hinge side.

In theory, construction drawings include a sheet (or more) dedicated specifically to interior elevations. In practice, however, this is not always the case. A small project with seven or eight interior ele-

vations may not warrant a separate sheet, and so the elevations are drawn with other details in the construction set. Sometimes on small projects that involve built-in cabinetry, it is advantageous to place the interior elevations on the same sheet as the floor plan if space permits. This way, the elevations can be studied without flipping sheets back and forth. The actual number of interior elevations is proportional to the complexity of the project. On large, complex projects, interior elevations may be placed together on one or more sheets and referenced back to the floor plans, as illustrated in Figure 7-15.

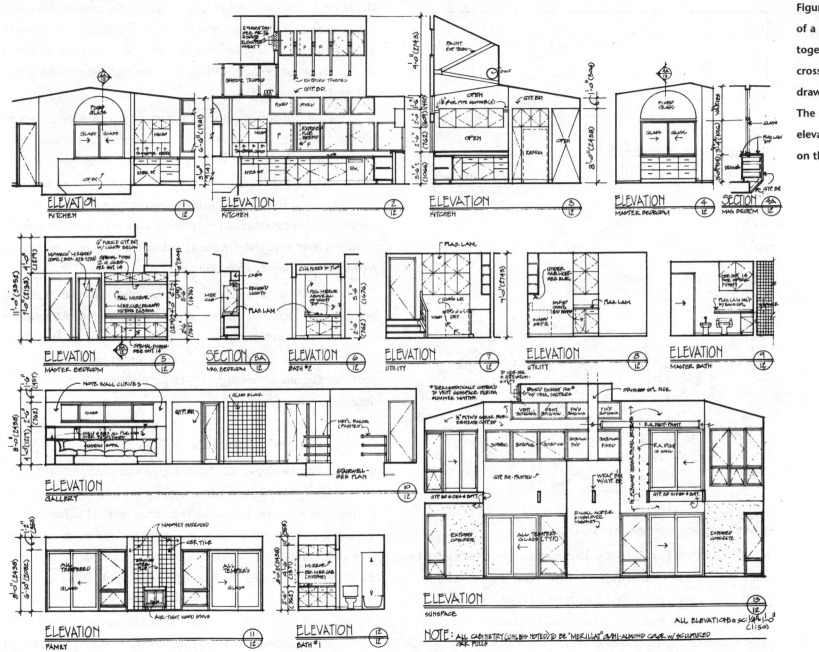

Figure 7-15 Interior elevations of a project are grouped together on one sheet and cross-referenced, below each drawing, to the floor plan. The scale is the same for all elevations and noted as such on the lower right side.

Figure 7-16 Interior elevations can be named according to the compass direction the viewer is facing.

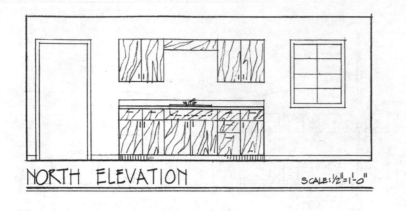

NORTH ELEVATION   SCALE: ½"=1'-0"

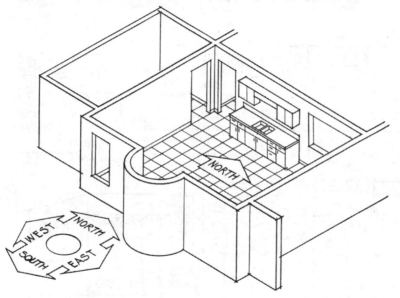

Referencing and Naming Interior Elevations

Interior elevations can be named in several different ways. An interior elevation can be assigned a compass orientation according to the direction the viewer would be facing if looking at the surface depicted — north, south, east, or west. For example, an elevation drawn from the point of view of a person standing inside an office and facing to the north is called a north elevation, as shown in

Figure 7-16. However, using compass names for interior elevations can be confusing at times, particularly if the building is oriented in a direction such as southwest or northeast. A wall might even run at a diagonal to others within a room, further confusing the assigned compass names.

Reference symbols are the preferred way to assign names to interior elevations. A reference symbol is shown on the floor plan and a number is assigned to each interior elevation view, as illustrated in Figure 7-17. An arrow is drawn around the elevation symbol on the plan to indicate the direction the viewer is looking, and another number is assigned to indicate on what sheet the interior elevation may be found. On the elevation sheet, these numbers are repeated just below the elevation view.

The full title of an elevation often includes the room name or number by which it is referenced on the floor plan. Although it may seem obvious that the viewer is looking at an interior elevation, most firms prefer to identify the drawing, as in "Master Bedroom Elevation." See Figure 7-18 for an example of this procedure.

Designation of Materials

Materials can be shown on interior elevations simplistically with notes only, or various line textures can be drawn to help visually convey differences in materials. This latter method is particularly helpful when an interior elevation is complex and needs to convey a lot of information — which can be difficult with just simple line drawings, as illustrated in Figure 7-19. In small-scaled elevation drawings, some liberty can be taken in simplifying an object or material that is complicated and cannot be accurately drawn at that scale. For example, a highly decorative raised wood panel on a kitchen cabinet may have to be blocked out in panel proportions

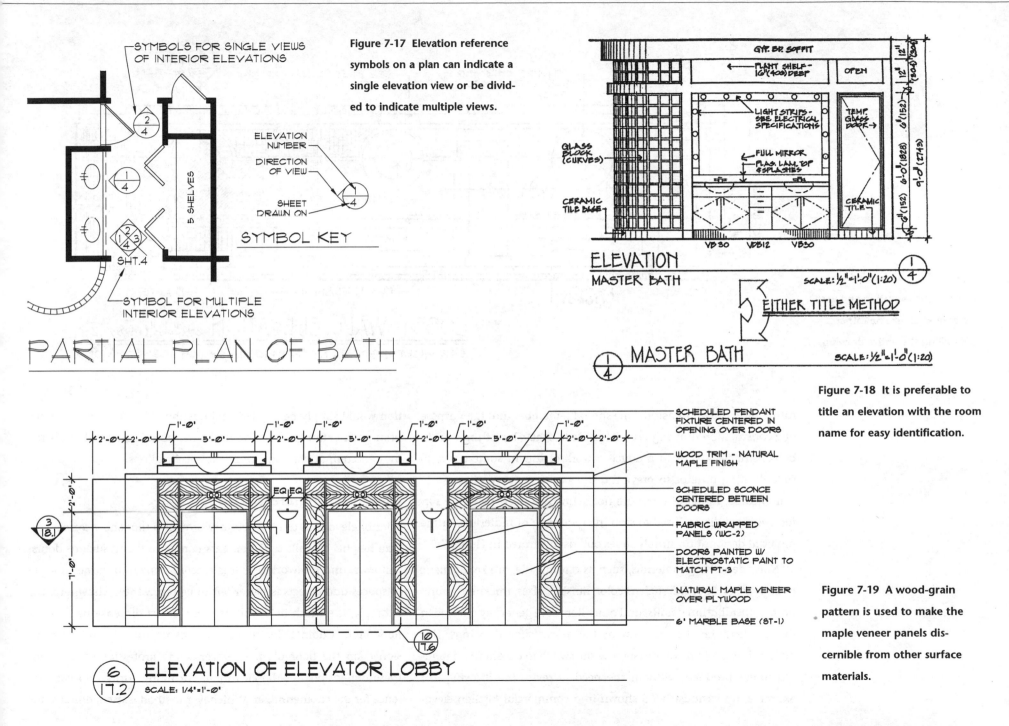

SYMBOLS FOR SINGLE VIEWS OF INTERIOR ELEVATIONS

Figure 7-17 Elevation reference symbols on a plan can indicate a single elevation view or be divided to indicate multiple views.

ELEVATION NUMBER

DIRECTION OF VIEW

SHEET DRAWN ON

SYMBOL KEY

5 SHELVES

SHT.4

SYMBOL FOR MULTIPLE INTERIOR ELEVATIONS

PARTIAL PLAN OF BATH

GYP. BD. SOFFIT

PLANT SHELF - 16"(400) DEEP

OPEN

LIGHT STRIPS - SEE ELECTRICAL SPECIFICATIONS

GLASS BLOCK (CURVES)

FULL MIRROR

PLAS. LAM. TOP & SPLASHES

TEMP. GLASS DOOR

CERAMIC TILE BASE

CERAMIC TILE

VB 30   VDB12   VB30

ELEVATION
MASTER BATH

SCALE: ½"=1'-0"(1:20)

EITHER TITLE METHOD

MASTER BATH

SCALE: ½"=1'-0"(1:20)

Figure 7-18 It is preferable to title an elevation with the room name for easy identification.

SCHEDULED PENDANT FIXTURE CENTERED IN OPENING OVER DOORS

WOOD TRIM - NATURAL MAPLE FINISH

SCHEDULED SCONCE CENTERED BETWEEN DOORS

FABRIC WRAPPED PANELS (WC-2)

DOORS PAINTED W/ ELECTROSTATIC PAINT TO MATCH PT-3

NATURAL MAPLE VENEER OVER PLYWOOD

6' MARBLE BASE (ST-1)

EQ EQ

ELEVATION OF ELEVATOR LOBBY

SCALE: 1/4"=1'-0"

Figure 7-19 A wood-grain pattern is used to make the maple veneer panels discernible from other surface materials.

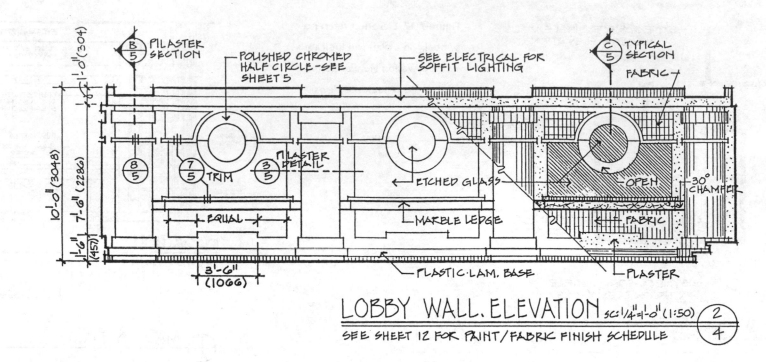

Figure 7-20 The detailed textures on this elevation end with a diagonal break line rather than filling the entire drawing.

rather than drawn in detail. One should remember that the purpose of a construction drawing is to delineate to others how things are to be constructed — not to produce a work of art. In some cases, to save drafting time or to prevent a drawing from becoming overly complicated, material types are not delineated over the entire surface. A break line is used to stop the rendering of materials, or the material designation simply fades out, as illustrated in Figure 7-20.

Notes describing materials, such as ceramic tile, are kept generic in most cases. Specifics such as color, finishes, sizes, thickness, brand names, installation details, and other items are generally covered in the specifications that accompany the construction drawings. This allows changes to be made (such as the switch to an alternate manufacturer's products) without the need to revise the drawing. For example, an exhaust hood shown in a commercial kitchen eleva-

tion would simply be labeled "exhaust hood." The manufacturer's brand name, fan speed, color, and other particulars would be listed in an accompanying note or in the specifications.

Dimensioning Elevations

Interior elevations are the primary drawings that show correct vertical heights of walls and elements related to them, such as doors, windows, and millwork. For this reason, horizontal dimensioning of spaces and objects is better left to be represented elsewhere. For example, the width of a wall or room is best dimensioned on the floor plan. Cabinet depths and widths are also usually dimensioned on the floor plan. However, some professionals do place these dimensions on the elevations for more clarity and convenience for the cabinetmaker. Whichever method is used, dimensions should not be repeated in both places, as errors can be made when one drawing or the other is revised.

In construction drawings, dimensions are generally indicated in feet and inches (or metric). However, in specialized drawings (such as interior elevations in the kitchen and bath industry), cabinetry, doors, windows, and other items are dimensioned only in inches (or metric), as shown in Figure 7-21. In laying out the dimensions, one should indicate overall heights and similar cumulative dimensions of important elements (Figure 7-22).

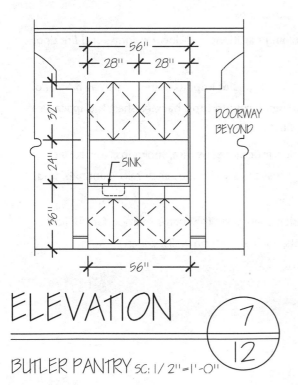

ELEVATION

BUTLER PANTRY SC: 1/2"=1'-0"

Figure 7-21 In specialized drawings, such as for this butler pantry in a kitchen, dimensions are indicated in inches or metric units only.

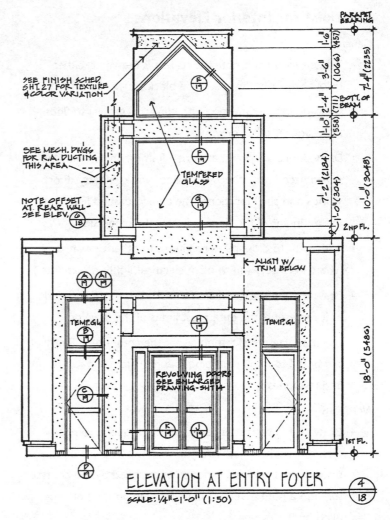

ELEVATION AT ENTRY FOYER

SCALE: 1/4"=1'-0" (1:50)

Figure 7-22 Vertical dimensions can be shown on elevations to indicate overall heights and dimensions of other important elements.

Checklist for Interior Elevations

General

- Title elevation and note the scale it is drawn at, either below title or in the sheet title block.

- Cross-reference drawing (with correct symbols) to floor plans and/or other drawings.

- Draw doors, windows, and their frames. Show (with hidden/dotted lines) direction of door and cabinetry door swings and shelf locations. The angled dashed line near the midpoint of the door indicates the hinge side.

- Add notes to cross-reference items to other drawings where necessary (finish plan, electrical/lighting plan, etc.).

- Draw the outline (profile) of the elevation nice and dark, as it represents the outermost limits of the drawing.

- Use manufacturers' templates, or the computer "library of symbols," to draw plumbing fixtures, such as water closets and lavatories.

Notations

- Draw and note appliances/equipment such as refrigerators, dishwasher, washer/dryer, microwave, trash compactor, etc. If an item is not to be supplied by the contractor, add a note that it is N.I.C. (not in contract) or supplied by the owner.

- Call out (with generic names) wall and base cabinet materials, wainscot, moldings, chair rails, and shelves (adjustable or fixed).

- Call out generic wall finishes (vinyl, ceramic tile, brick, wood paneling, gypsum board, fabric, etc.) and refer to the finish plan for detailed information.

- Call out glass, mirrors, metal frames, and other related information.

- Key window or glazing wall details to the appropriate enlarged drawings.

- Note folding partitions, roll-down security, and fire doors.

Dimensions

- Dimension heights of important items such as base and wall cabinetry, countertops, backsplashes, toe spaces, soffits, and fixtures.

- Dimension miscellaneous trim, moldings, wall surface treatments such as wainscots, chair rails, handrails, and grab bars.

- Dimension walls and other items to important building elements, such as existing walls, concrete walls, or columns.

We have seen how elevations and floor plans show finish materials, heights, room layouts, and locations of doors and windows. However, many of the details and subsurface parts of a building or interior space cannot be completely understood through only these types of drawings. To gain more information as to how a building, interior space, or object is to be constructed, one or more slices may have to be cut through the assembly in a vertical direction.

Section drawings take such an imaginary slice through an object or building, as illustrated in Figure 8-1. They give information on heights and relationships between floors, ceilings, spaces, walls, and in some instances details of the specific construction techniques used. Sections can be cut on a vertical (most common) or horizontal plane. In fact, a floor plan is really a horizontal section drawing. Two or more sections are often cut at 90 degrees to one another to give additional information, unless the space or object is very simple. Sections should ideally be cut in a continuous, straight plane, without many jogs. This slice should be taken where it will best illustrate the relationships between significant components of an object or interior space, as shown in Figure 8-2. The location of this cut is indicated on the floor plan or elevation (whichever is the base drawing) with a graphical symbol, as seen in Figure 8-3. This symbol gives the section an identification number with an arrow that shows the direction the person is looking when viewing the final sectional drawing. If there are a number of sheets in a designer's set of construction drawings, the indicator mark also shows which sheet the particular section is drawn on.

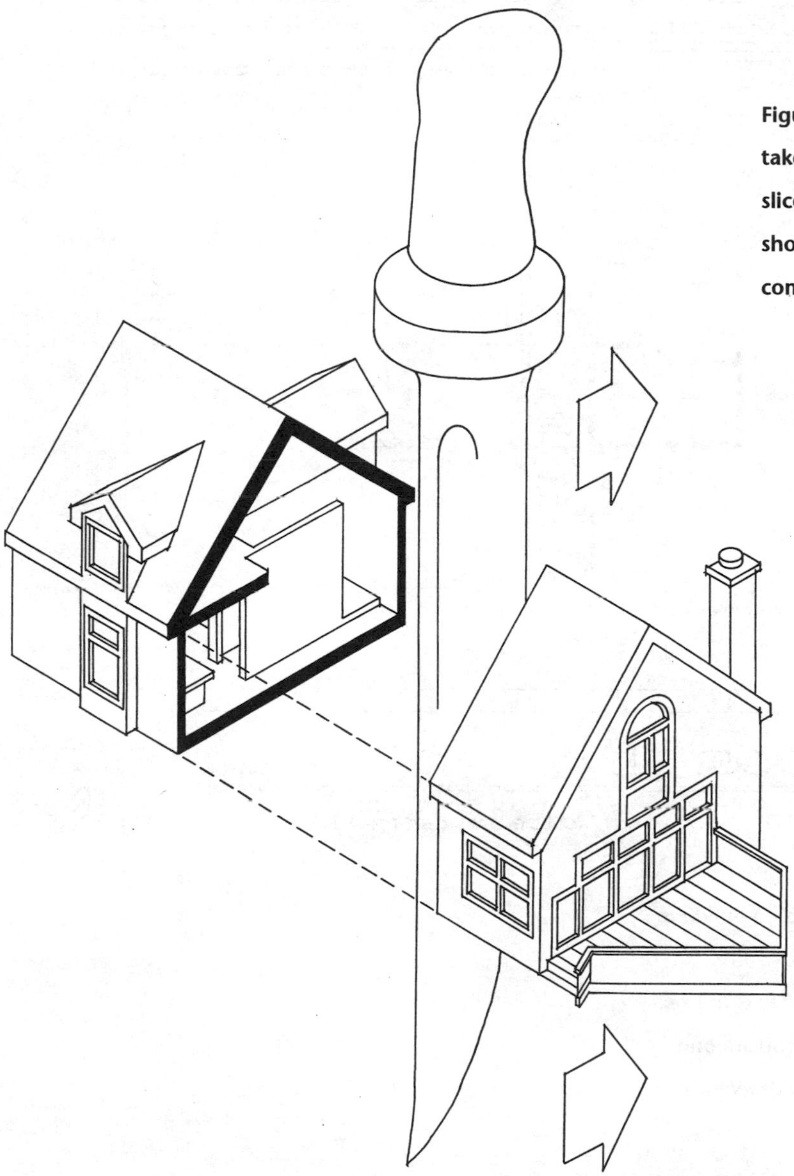

Figure 8-1 A section drawing takes an imaginary vertical slice through a structure, showing its materials and components.

113

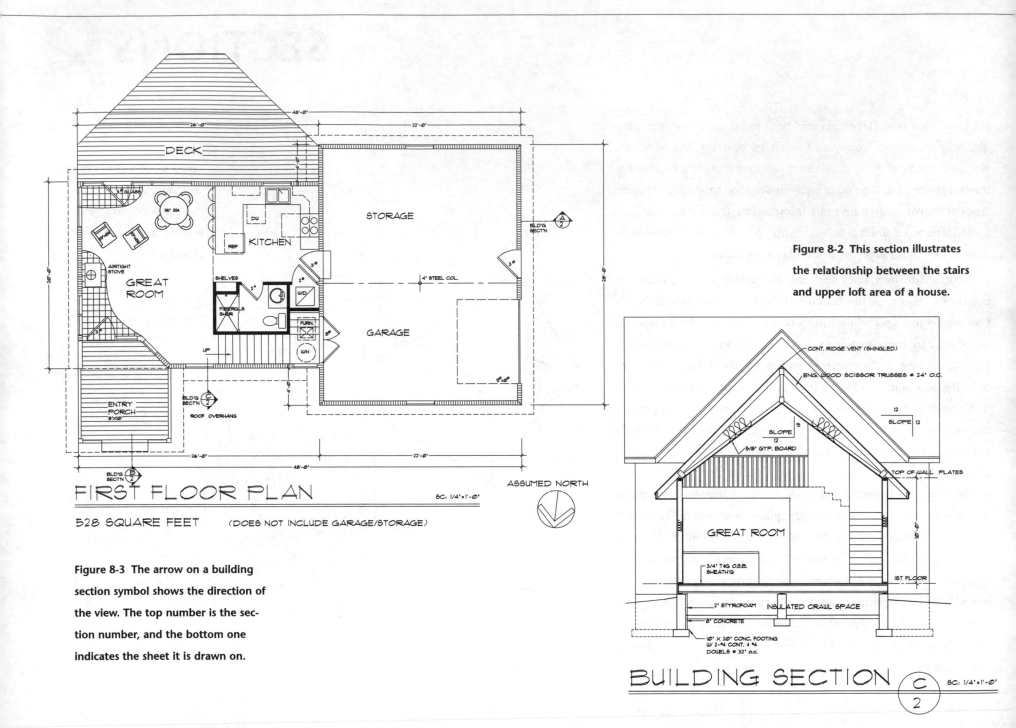

DECK

36" DIA

KITCHEN

DW

REF

SHELVES

AIRTIGHT
STOVE

GREAT
ROOM

FIBERGLS
SHWR

W/D

FURN

W/H

UP

STORAGE

4" STEEL COL.

GARAGE

BLD'G
SECT'N

A
2

BLD'G
SECT'N

C
2

ROOF OVERHANG

ENTRY
PORCH
8'X10'

BLD'G
SECT'N

B
2

FIRST FLOOR PLAN

SC: 1/4"=1'-0"

528 SQUARE FEET   (DOES NOT INCLUDE GARAGE/STORAGE)

ASSUMED NORTH

Figure 8-2 This section illustrates the relationship between the stairs and upper loft area of a house.

Figure 8-3 The arrow on a building section symbol shows the direction of the view. The top number is the section number, and the bottom one indicates the sheet it is drawn on.

CONT. RIDGE VENT (SHINGLED)

ENG. WOOD SCISSOR TRUSSES @ 24" O.C.

SLOPE 12

SLOPE 12

3/8" GYP. BOARD

TOP OF WALL PLATES

GREAT ROOM

3/4" T&G O.S.B.
SHEATH'G

1ST FLOOR

2" STYROFOAM   INSULATED CRAWL SPACE

8" CONCRETE

10" X 20" CONC. FOOTING
W/ 2-#4 CONT. & #4
DOWELS @ 32" O.C.

BUILDING SECTION

C
2

SC: 1/4"=1'-0"

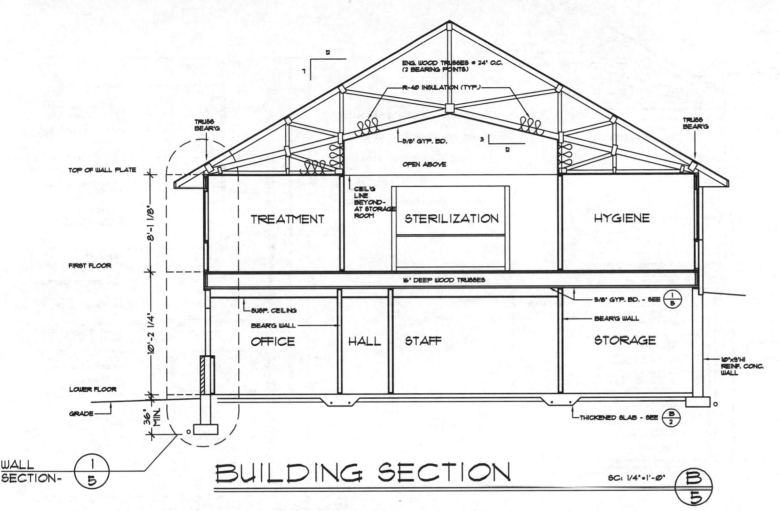

TRUSS
BEAR'G

TOP OF WALL PLATE

8'-1 1/8'

FIRST FLOOR

10'-2 1/4'

LOWER FLOOR

GRADE

36'
MIN.

WALL
SECTION- ① / ⑤

TREATMENT

CEIL'G
LINE
BEYOND-
AT STORAGE
ROOM

STERILIZATION

HYGIENE

SUSP. CEILING

BEAR'G WALL

OFFICE

HALL

STAFF

STORAGE

ENG. WOOD TRUSSES @ 24' O.C.
(2 BEARING POINTS)

R-40 INSULATION (TYP.)

5/8' GYP. BD.

OPEN ABOVE

16' DEEP WOOD TRUSSES

5/8' GYP. BD. - SEE ① / ⑤

BEAR'G WALL

10'x9'HI
REINF. CONC.
WALL

THICKENED SLAB - SEE ⑧ / ②

TRUSS
BEAR'G

BUILDING SECTION

SC: 1/4'=1'-0' ⑧ / ⑤

**Figure 8-4 The wall section
ballooned on the left side of
this building section can be
found enlarged on sheet 5.**

Types of Section Drawings

Sections can be drawn of a total building, interior space, or object. These are referred to as full sections. However, if only an isolated area needs to be illustrated, a partial section can also be drawn. Sections can be cut in a variety of ways to show more detailed information. A section might be cut all the way through a building (called a building section), or only through a wall (wall section).

Both may be needed, because the small scale and complexity of a building section generally means the materials and details related to the walls cannot be drawn there. A symbol on the building section shown in Figure 8-4 marks the wall area to be enlarged. The wall section (Figure 8-5) is drawn to accurately show the many details and materials that are needed in the assembly.

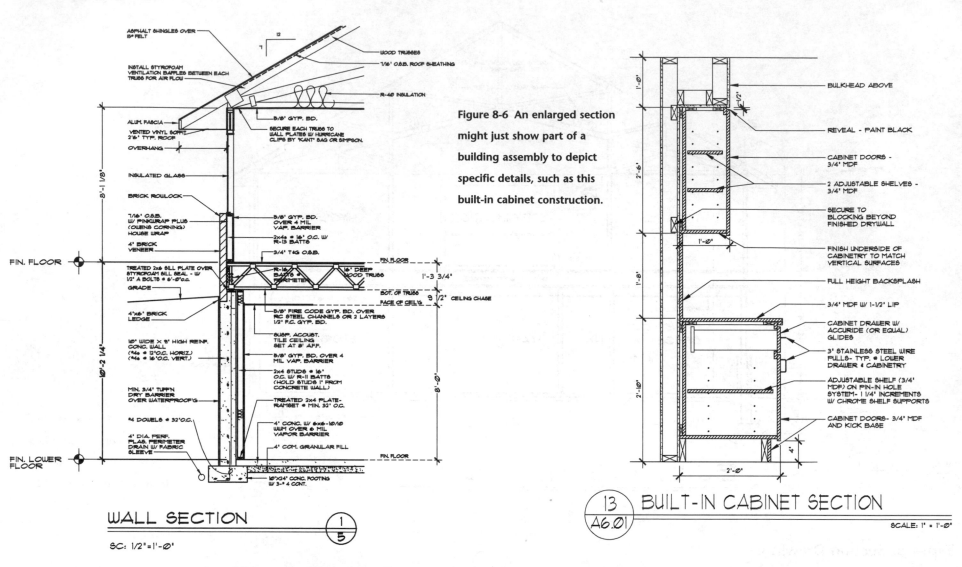

ASPHALT SHINGLES OVER
15# FELT

INSTALL STYROFOAM
VENTILATION BAFFLES BETWEEN EACH
TRUSS FOR AIR FLOW

ALUM. FASCIA
VENTED VINYL SOFFIT
2'-6" TYP. ROOF
OVERHANG

INSULATED GLASS

BRICK ROWLOCK

7/16" O.S.B.
W/ PINKWRAP PLUS
(OWENS CORNING)
HOUSE WRAP
4" BRICK
VENEER

TREATED 2x6 SILL PLATE OVER
STYROFOAM SILL SEAL - W/
1/2" A BOLTS @ 6'-0"o.c.
GRADE

4"x6" BRICK
LEDGE

10" WIDE X 8" HIGH REINF.
CONC. WALL
(#4 @ 12"O.C. HORIZ.)
(#4 @ 16"O.C. VERT.)

MIN. 3/4" TUFF'N
DRY BARRIER
OVER WATERPROOF'G

#4 DOWELS @ 32"O.C.

4" DIA. PERF.
PLAS. PERIMETER
DRAIN W/ FABRIC
SLEEVE

WOOD TRUSSES
7/16" O.S.B. ROOF SHEATHING

R-40 INSULATION

5/8" GYP. BD.

SECURE EACH TRUSS TO
WALL PLATES W/ HURRICANE
CLIPS BY 'KANT' SAG OR SIMPSON.

5/8" GYP. BD.
OVER 4 MIL
VAP. BARRIER
2x4s @ 16" O.C. W/
R-13 BATTS
3/4" T&G O.S.B.

R-16
BATTS @
PERIMETER

16" DEEP
WOOD TRUSS

5/8" FIRE CODE GYP. BD. OVER
RC STEEL CHANNELS OR 2 LAYERS
1/2" F.C. GYP. BD.

SUSP. ACOUST.
TILE CEILING
SET AT 8' A.F.F.
5/8" GYP. BD. OVER 4
MIL VAP. BARRIER

2x4 STUDS @ 16"
O.C. W/ R-11 BATTS
(HOLD STUDS 1" FROM
CONCRETE WALL)

TREATED 2x4 PLATE-
RAMSET @ MIN. 32" O.C.

4" CONC. W/ 6x6-10/10
W.W.M. OVER 6 MIL
VAPOR BARRIER

4" COM. GRANULAR FILL

FIN. FLOOR

BOT. OF TRUSS
FACE OF CEIL'G

FIN. FLOOR

10"x24" CONC. FOOTING
W/ 3-#4 CONT.

FIN. FLOOR

FIN. LOWER
FLOOR

8'-1 1/8"

10'-2 1/4"

1'-3 3/4"

9 1/2" CEILING CHASE

8'-0"

WALL SECTION

⊕ 1 / 5

SC: 1/2"=1'-0"

Figure 8-5 This is the enlarged wall section keyed on the building section in Figure 8-4.

Figure 8-6 An enlarged section might just show part of a building assembly to depict specific details, such as this built-in cabinet construction.

BULKHEAD ABOVE

REVEAL - PAINT BLACK

CABINET DOORS -
3/4" MDF

2 ADJUSTABLE SHELVES -
3/4" MDF

SECURE TO
BLOCKING BEYOND
FINISHED DRYWALL

FINISH UNDERSIDE OF
CABINETRY TO MATCH
VERTICAL SURFACES

FULL HEIGHT BACKSPLASH

3/4" MDF W/ 1-1/2" LIP

CABINET DRAWER W/
ACCURIDE (OR EQUAL)
GLIDES

3" STAINLESS STEEL WIRE
PULLS- TYP. @ LOWER
DRAWER & CABINETRY

ADJUSTABLE SHELF (3/4"
MDF) ON PIN-IN HOLE
SYSTEM- 1 1/4" INCREMENTS
W/ CHROME SHELF SUPPORTS

CABINET DOORS- 3/4" MDF
AND KICK BASE

1'-0"
2'-6"
1'-8"
2'-10"

1/2"
1'-0"

2'-0"

4"

⊕ 13 / A6.01 **BUILT-IN CABINET SECTION**

SCALE: 1" = 1'-0"

In addition to building and wall sections, there may also be a need to draw a section through built-in or custom components within a space, such as shelving, reception desks, credenzas, bars, display cases, cabinets, and counters. Figure 8-6 shows a built-in cabinet section. These types of sections are discussed in more detail in Chapter 9.

In interior construction drawings, sometimes the terms *section* and *detail* are interchanged, thus causing some confusion. Section cuts through small portions of construction or objects, for example, are often referred to as details. But details are not always drawn in section. They may also include enlarged portions of the floor plan or elevation.

The scale of section drawings may range from ⅛" to 3" (3.17 mm to 76 mm), depending upon the size of the drawing paper, the size of the building (or component), and the desired features to be shown. The specific information a section shows may vary, depending on whether it is a design or construction drawing. Construction drawings show only the items or components of a space that are built in or attached to the structure. Movable furniture is not shown in this type of drawing.

Drafting Standards

Section drawings are shown as cut through solid elements and spaces (voids) within an object or building. To graphically represent these, certain accepted techniques are often employed. For example, solid materials cut through in the section slice are pouched with standard material designations, such as wood, brick, concrete, and so forth. Some fairly common material designations are listed in the Appendix. Many offices use these, but variations on these graphic standards also occur. Legends or keys are used in the drawings to explain what the material designations stand for. The lines or outlines around these sliced materials are drawn with heavy thick lines to accent the cut. To differentiate these materials from adjacent construction or objects seen beyond the cut plane, lighter and thinner lines are used (Figure 8-7).

Building Sections

Building sections can effectively show the construction details of single or multilevel structures, including the floors, walls, and ceiling/roof. The location and number of building sections to be cut will depend upon the amount of information to be shown about the structure and its features (Figure 8-8). Building sections are typically drawn at a scale of ⅛" = 1'-0" or ¼" = 1'-0" (1:100 or 1:50 met-

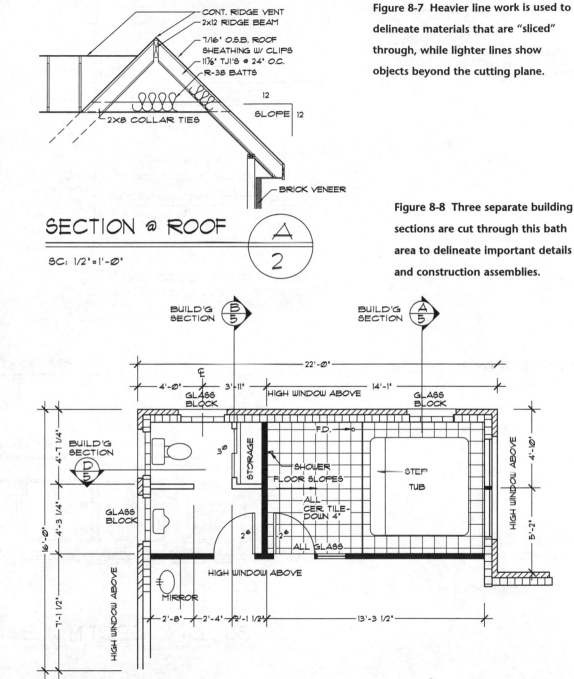

Figure 8-7 Heavier line work is used to delineate materials that are "sliced" through, while lighter lines show objects beyond the cutting plane.

Figure 8-8 Three separate building sections are cut through this bath area to delineate important details and construction assemblies.

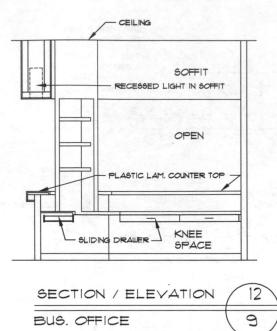

Figure 8-9 The countertop, overhead soffit, and sliding drawer are shown cut in cross-section in this interior elevation.

CEILING

SOFFIT

RECESSED LIGHT IN SOFFIT

OPEN

PLASTIC LAM. COUNTER TOP

SLIDING DRAWER

KNEE SPACE

SECTION / ELEVATION — 12 / 9

BUS. OFFICE

ric). A section cut through the length of a building is called a longitudinal section, and one cut at 90 degrees to this, through the narrow width of a building, is a transverse section. If a detail or other assembly (such as a wall) needs to be presented in a way that conveys more information, indicator marks are drawn on the building section for cross-reference to another location where this detail is drawn at a larger scale.

Sections of Interior Spaces

When working with interior spaces, it may not be necessary to include a building section in its entirety. For example, if the extent of construction work is primarily limited to an interior remodel of an existing space, the section may not need to include all the structural details. Full assemblies such as the concrete floor thickness, granular fill, and below-ground footings do not really need to be

Figure 8-10 This partial section view of the basement level of a residence also shows the fireplace wall and bathroom in elevation.

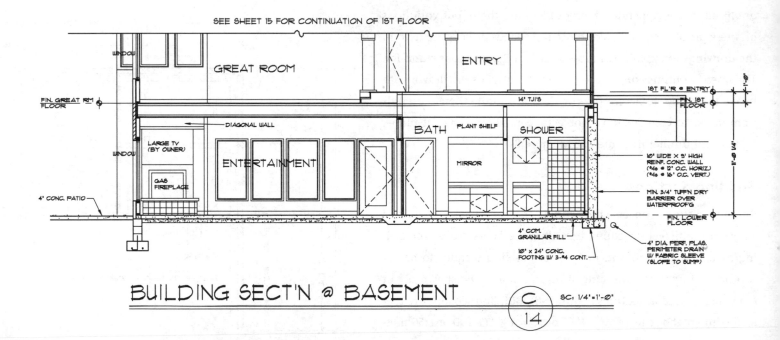

SEE SHEET 15 FOR CONTINUATION OF 1ST FLOOR

WINDOW

GREAT ROOM

ENTRY

FIN. GREAT RM FLOOR

14' TJI'S

1ST FL'R @ ENTRY

FIN. 1ST FLOOR

DIAGONAL WALL

BATH

PLANT SHELF

SHOWER

WINDOW

LARGE TV (BY OWNER)

ENTERTAINMENT

MIRROR

10' WIDE X 9' HIGH REINF. CONC. WALL (#4s @ 12" O.C. HORIZ.) (#4s @ 16" O.C. VERT.)

GAS FIREPLACE

MIN. 3/4" TUFF'N DRY BARRIER OVER WATERPROOF'G

4' CONC. PATIO

FIN. LOWER FLOOR

4" COM. GRANULAR FILL

4' DIA. PERF. PLAS. PERIMETER DRAIN W/ FABRIC SLEEVE (SLOPE TO SUMP)

10" X 24" CONC. FOOTING W/ 3-#4 CONT.

BUILDING SECT'N @ BASEMENT — C / 14   SC: 1/4"=1'-0"

illustrated. In such cases, the section is cut through a portion of the structure to detail the features of one or more internal spaces and the related construction. These drawings might show cabinetwork, wall wainscots, suspended ceilings, dropped soffits, doors, wall openings, and other interior components. Objects such as cabinetry that are cut through will be seen in a cross-sectional view, as illustrated in Figure 8-9. Sections through interior spaces often resemble a building section in their composition, but are more concerned with the interior aspects of the assembly and don't necessarily show floor thickness and other structural details (Figure 8-10). If objects or assemblies are too small to draw in detail, they are keyed with a symbol on this drawing and enlarged elsewhere, as illustrated in the enlarged corner of the cabinet in Figure 8-11. Interior section drawings are usually drawn at a scale of ⅛" = 1'-0", ¼" = 1'-0", or even ½" = 1'-0" (1:100, 1:50, or 1:20 metric).

Wall Sections

A section that is drawn at a large scale to show the specifics of an interior or exterior building wall is called a wall section (Figure 8-12). The wall section is often keyed to the main building section and permits the designer to enlarge and show more clearly the details for that particular wall, such as the floor and ceiling systems. Again, more than one wall section is often required to delineate the uniqueness of a design or construction assembly. The scale of the drawing depends upon the details to be shown and the paper size. Generally, wall sections are drawn at a scale of ½" = 1'-0" to 1½" = 1'-0" (1:20 to 1:10 metric). It is desirable to draw the wall section in its entirety from the bottom of the wall to the top. However, if the sheet size does not allow this, the section can be cut in one or more areas (where large areas of the wall have the same construction) with break lines to compress the drawing to fit the paper size (Figure 8-13).

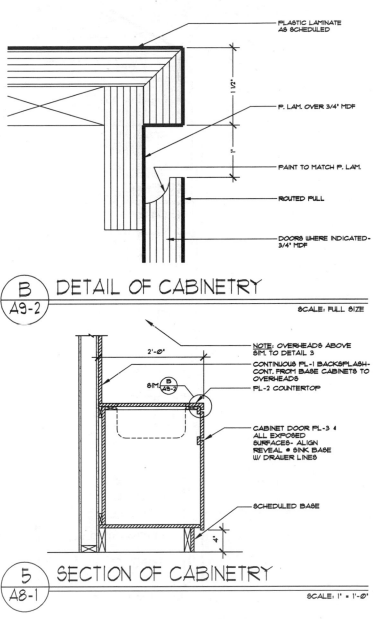

Figure 8-11 A detail of millwork is drawn at a very large scale for clarity and keyed by symbols to the corresponding part of a sectional view of the cabinetry.

Figure 8-12 A wall section is drawn at a larger scale to clearly show the details and materials of the wall assembly.

Figure 8-13 Horizontal break lines are used in this wall section to allow for the drawing to be compressed. This provides for a larger-scale drawing that will fit on the given sheet size.

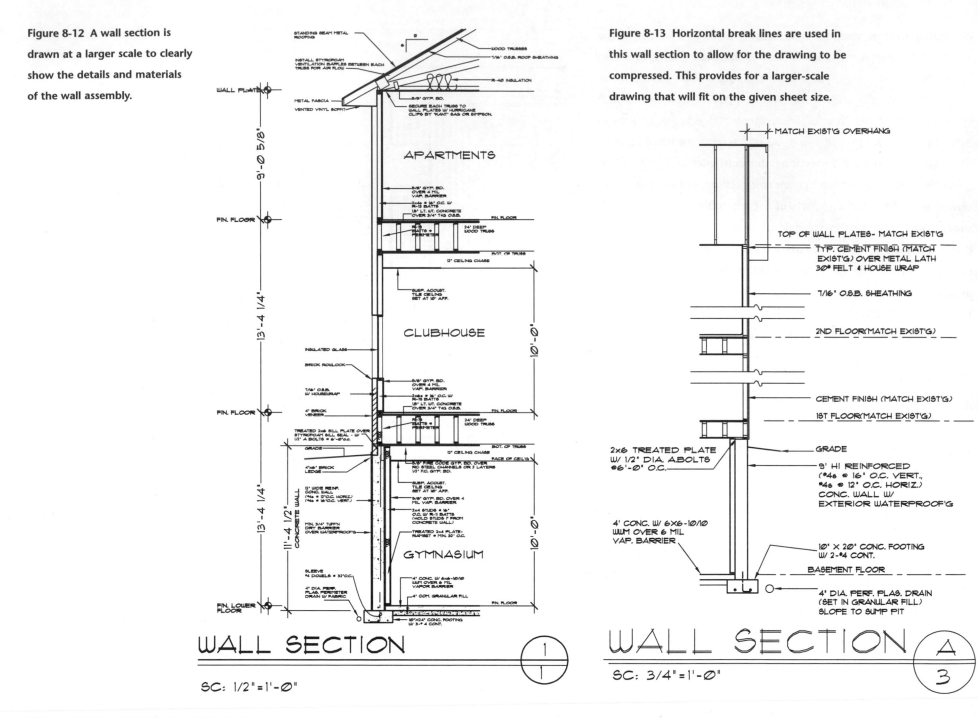

WALL SECTION

SC: 1/2"=1'-0"

WALL SECTION

SC: 3/4"=1'-0"

Detail and Object Sections

Sometimes, a complete building or wall section cannot be drawn large enough to fully explain a portion of the assembly. Or there might be items that are not tied to the building structure in such a way that the wall section needs to be included in the drawing. These might include handrails, as shown in Figure 8-14, or objects such as cabinets and furniture. In such cases, a detailed section or partial section is drawn at a large scale to clearly show the items, as seen in Figure 8-15. The scale of details and partial section drawings is usually a minimum of ½" = 1'-0" (1:20 metric) and can range to a drawing scaled to full size. These detailed sections are cross-referenced to other drawings, indicating where the assembly is located within the whole.

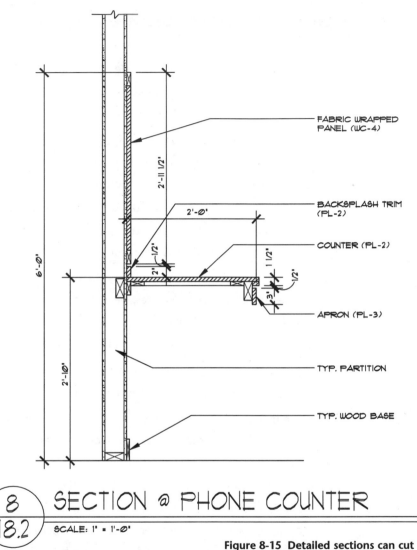

FABRIC WRAPPED PANEL (WC-4)

BACKSPLASH TRIM (PL-2)

COUNTER (PL-2)

APRON (PL-3)

TYP. PARTITION

TYP. WOOD BASE

8 / 18.2 — SECTION @ PHONE COUNTER
SCALE: 1" = 1'-0"

Figure 8-15 Detailed sections can cut through items such as cabinetry and also show the adjacent building structure.

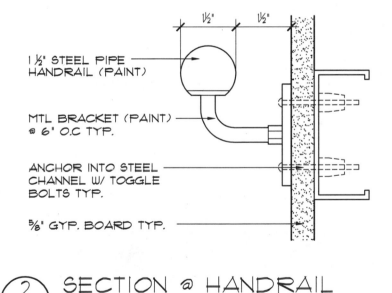

1 ½" STEEL PIPE HANDRAIL (PAINT)

MTL BRACKET (PAINT) @ 6" O.C TYP.

ANCHOR INTO STEEL CHANNEL W/ TOGGLE BOLTS TYP.

⅝" GYP. BOARD TYP.

2 / A4.6 — SECTION @ HANDRAIL
SCALE: N.T.S.

Figure 8-14 A detailed handrail drawn at a large scale for clarity.

Checklist for Section Drawings

General

- Title the drawing and note its scale.

- Key the drawing to other sections, plans, or related drawings.

- Make sure materials rendered in section view are commonly recognized graphic symbols, or place a nearby note or key and legend indicating their meaning.

- Vary the line weights to make the section clearly understandable as to materials shown in section, voids, and objects seen beyond the section cut.

Notations

- Note special materials, features, clearances, alignments, and other important items.

- Call out room/space names or numbers that section refers to.

- Cross-reference the section drawing, carefully checking for accuracy and completeness of information.

- Use manufacturers' templates or CAD images for drawing plumbing fixtures such as water closets and lavatories in the sections where they might show.

- In building and interior sections, draw and note appliances/equipment such as refrigerators, dishwasher, washer/dryer, microwave, trash compactor, etc. If item is not to be supplied by contractor, add note that it is N.I.C. (not in contract).

- Specify or clearly show substitute construction materials.

- Call out (with generic names) wall and cabinet base materials, mirrors, wainscot, moldings, chair rails, and shelves (adjustable or fixed).

- In interior sections, call out generic wall finishes (vinyl, ceramic tile, brick, wood paneling, gypsum board, fabric, etc.), or cross-reference to the finish plans.

Dimensions

- In building and interior sections, add vertical dimensions tying important elements, such as floor levels, together.

- Dimension important items horizontally where they are not shown on referenced plan views.

- Dimension clearances, alignments, and other controlling factors.

- Dimension ceiling heights, soffits, and other headers.

SPECIALTY DRAWINGS AND DETAILS 9

Purpose of Specialty Drawings

There are a number of components, assemblies, and other specialized items in buildings and interiors that do not fall neatly into commonly recognized groupings such as floor plans, elevations, sections, and finish plans. These elements often require a more detailed drawing and even specialized graphic techniques to fully explain them. These pieces of construction and their details often require a series of views that may be done in plan, elevation, section, and even isometric drawings. In most cases, the designer draws the basic sizes, arrangements, materials, and overall details of these components. Then, many elements are redrawn in more detail and submitted back to the designer as "shop drawings" done by one of the subcontractors, such as the cabinetmaker or glazing subcontractor. These shop drawings are highly detailed with expanded views and descriptions of the designer's original design intent and construction drawings. An example is shown in Figure 9-1.

Stairs and Ramps

Stairs, ramps, elevators, and escalators provide access to different floor levels within or on the exterior of a structure. Stairs and ramps are often used in buildings three stories in height and less, whereas elevators and escalators are employed on buildings of four

Figure 9-1 Shop drawings are highly detailed assembly drawings done by a subcontractor. They show a designer's initial design and drawing with expanded views, descriptions, and construction details.

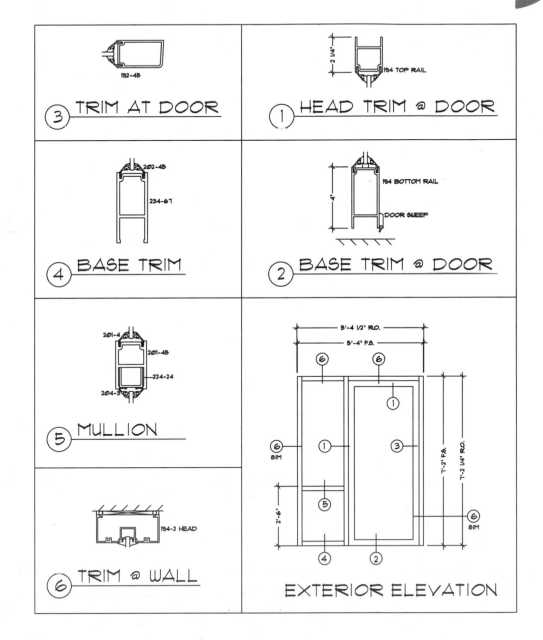

STAIRS

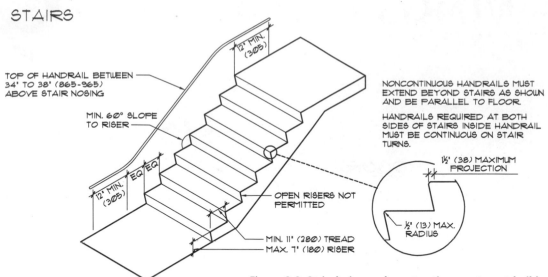

TOP OF HANDRAIL BETWEEN 34' TO 38' (865-965) ABOVE STAIR NOSING

MIN. 60° SLOPE TO RISER

12" MIN. (305)

12" MIN. (305)

EQ EQ

NONCONTINUOUS HANDRAILS MUST EXTEND BEYOND STAIRS AS SHOWN AND BE PARALLEL TO FLOOR.

HANDRAILS REQUIRED AT BOTH SIDES OF STAIRS INSIDE HANDRAIL MUST BE CONTINUOUS ON STAIR TURNS.

1½' (38) MAXIMUM PROJECTION

OPEN RISERS NOT PERMITTED

½' (13) MAX. RADIUS

MIN. 11" (280) TREAD
MAX. 7" (180) RISER

Figure 9-2 Stair design and construction must meet building code and ADA requirements, including rules on configuration, width, risers, treads, landings, and handrails.

RAMPS

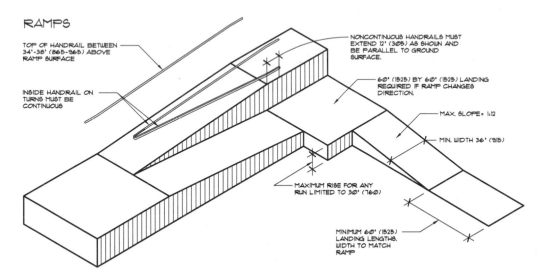

TOP OF HANDRAIL BETWEEN 34'-38' (865-965) ABOVE RAMP SURFACE

INSIDE HANDRAIL ON TURNS MUST BE CONTINUOUS

NONCONTINUOUS HANDRAILS MUST EXTEND 12' (305) AS SHOWN AND BE PARALLEL TO GROUND SURFACE.

60" (1525) BY 60" (1525) LANDING REQUIRED IF RAMP CHANGES DIRECTION.

MAX. SLOPE= 1:12

MIN. WIDTH 36' (915)

MAXIMUM RISE FOR ANY RUN LIMITED TO 30' (760)

MINIMUM 60' (1525) LANDING LENGTHS. WIDTH TO MATCH RAMP

HANDRAILS OMITTED FOR CLARITY, BUT REQUIRED ON BOTH SIDES OF RAMP RUNS WHEN RISE IS OVER 6' (150) OR HORIZONTAL LENGTH IS OVER 72' (1830).

Figure 9-3 Ramps must be constructed in accordance with ADA guidelines and building codes. They provide physically disabled individuals with access to different floors.

floors or more. However, in buildings such as shopping centers, which have high floor-to-floor dimensions and must accommodate a great number of people, escalators are commonly used. The design of stairs should place the least amount of physical strain on the people who use them, while reinforcing the design character of the space and structure of the building. Designs can range from major or monumental stairways to stairways that are strictly for utilitarian purposes.

Stairs are usually constructed from wood, steel, or concrete. Their design and construction must meet a number of building code and Americans with Disabilities Act (ADA) requirements for configuration, width, risers, treads, landings, and handrails (Figure 9-2). In many cases, a stair is augmented by a ramp that provides vertical transit for physically impaired individuals or ease of moving heavy objects (Figure 9-3). Interior design projects might involve the design and construction of a new stair or the remodel of an existing stair. Remodeling is often done to upgrade a stair in an older building to meet the current building codes or ADA requirements.

Stairway Configurations and Terms

Stairs may be designed in a number of configurations to suit the amount of space available, the geometry of the layout, and the vertical/horizontal distance they must traverse. The most common stair configurations are shown in Figure 9-4. Their basic arrangements can be described by the following categories: straight run, right-angle run, reversing run, and some form of circular run. Figure 9-5 illustrates some of the most commonly used stair terms, defined below:

Baluster — the vertical components that hold the handrail. These are spaced to prevent people from falling through. These are governed by building codes and are

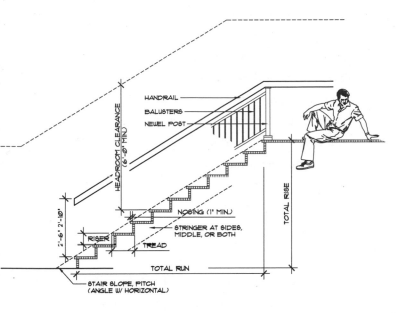

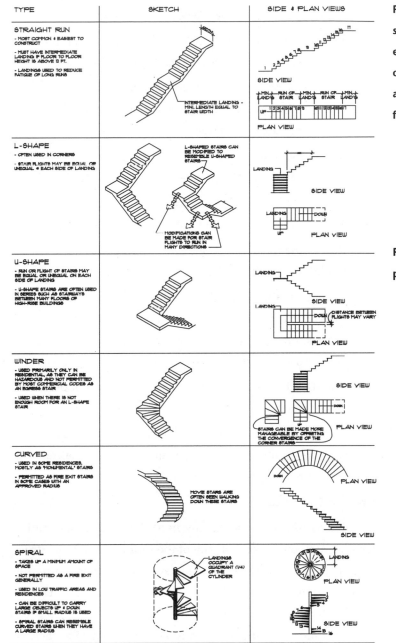

Figure 9-4 Stairs can be constructed in a number of different configurations, depending on the amount of space available and the distance between floors.

Figure 9-5 *(far left)* Typical parts of a stair.

usually a maximum clearance to prevent a 4-inch (101.6 mm) sphere from passing through.

Guardrail — a rail that is used on the landings or floor levels to prevent people from falling between floor levels. It is usually a minimum of 36 inches high in residential and 42 inches high in commercial buildings.

Handrail — a continuous section of railing adjacent to a stair for a person to grasp as an aid when ascending or descending. Building codes closely control whether the railing is on one or both sides of the stair, its height above the floor, and other specifics.

Headroom — the minimum clearance between the edge (or nose) of the tread and any part of an obstruction above.

Landing — the floor or platform at the beginning or end of a stair, or between two or more stair runs.

Newel — the terminating baluster at the bottom or top of a stair, which is usually larger than the other balusters.

Nosing — the part of the tread that overhangs the riser, reducing the problem of a person accidentally kicking the riser as they ascend the stair.

Rise — the total vertical distance that is traveled on a stair. It is the perpendicular measurement between floor levels and the sum of all the riser heights.

Riser — the vertical part of a stair between the treads.

Run — the total horizontal depth of a stair, which is the sum of the treads.

Stringer — the structural support for the stair treads and risers. This is also referred to as a carriage. It might be exposed on a utilitarian stair, or hidden with various finishes on more decorative stairs.

Tread — the horizontal part of a stair that the foot bears down upon.

Winder – the wedge-shaped tread in a turn of the stairway run – found mostly in residential work, because commercial building codes restrict these.

Drafting Standards

The design and drawing details needed to illustrate a stair are dependent upon the complexity of the stair and the basic structural material it is constructed of. Stair systems are made primarily of wood, steel, or concrete. Wood stairs are mostly used in residential construction and are generally the simplest to draw and detail. Stairs are shown on the floor plans and called out as to their basic widths and number of treads and risers. The plan also shows the run and an arrow indicating whether the stairs go up or down from that level. Floor-plan views of stairs often cannot show all the materials and cross-sectional parts of their assemblies. Special stair sections (Figure 9-6) are often drawn to show the construction and finish details. In most cases, the designer does not have to draw every detail of a stairway and its many components. The fabricators of metal, concrete, and some wood stairs often make shop drawings. These detailed drawings are submitted to the designer for review.

Scale of Drawings

The scale of stairway drawings is generally ⅛" = 1'-0" (1:100 metric) or ¼" = 1'-0" (1:50 metric), both in plan and elevation views. The number of treads and risers, as well as their dimensions, are called out here. Generic features such as the handrails and guardrails are also shown in both the plan and elevation views. Generally, handrails seen in elevation views are placed at a uniform height 30–34 inches (762–864 mm) above the stair nosing. In commercial projects with steel or concrete stairs, a large-scale drawing and stair section are required to fully explain these stair details and handrail/guardrail specifics. These are drawn at a scale of at least ½" = 1'-0" (1:20 metric) and cross-referenced to the floor plans.

To determine the number of treads and risers a stair must have, the vertical dimension between floor levels must be known. This vertical dimension is divided by the maximum riser height allowed by the building codes. At this writing, most residential stairs are limited to a maximum riser height of 8 inches (203 mm) and a minimum tread depth of 9¼ inches (235 mm). Commercial codes restrict the maximum height of a riser to 7 inches (178 mm), with

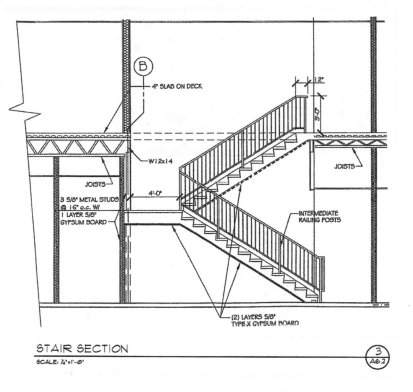

STAIR SECTION
SCALE: ¼"=1'-0"

3
A6.2

Labels in figure: B, 4" SLAB ON DECK, 12", 3'-0", W12x14, JOISTS, JOISTS, 3 5/8" METAL STUDS @ 16" o.c. W/ I LAYER 5/8" GYPSUM BOARD, 4'-0", INTERMEDIATE RAILING POSTS, (2) LAYERS 5/8" TYPE X GYPSUM BOARD

Dimensioning Stairways

Stairways are dimensioned on the floor plans as to their landing sizes, widths, and run of each stair, as seen in Figure 9-7. The total number and dimensions of the risers and runs are also shown on the plan. Vertical heights of the stair rise, handrails, and other particulars are dimensioned on a separate section or elevation drawing that is cross-referenced to the plan view (Figure 9-8).

Designation of Materials

A stair's materials can be indicated in a number of different ways, depending upon how many materials there are and the size and complexity of the construction. Underlying structural materials might be called out with notes or shown in a sectional view. If the structural material is also the finished surface, this should be called out. If a separate finish material covers the stair, this might be called out in the section view, plan view, or on a separate finish plan.

Checklist for Stairways

General

- If a separate enlarged drawing is done for the stairway, key it and cross-reference to the floor plans.

- Show stairs in their entirety where possible, or use break lines where they continue on another floor level.

- Check stair widths, riser heights, tread widths, landing widths, and other particulars against the appropriate building codes and ADA requirements. Verify required dimensions and clearances.

Notations

- Call out direction of travel (up or down) on each section of stairway, and indicate with an arrow.

Figure 9-6 Stair sections are often drawn to detail out the construction and finish components, which are not shown in plan views.

a minimum tread depth of 11 inches (280 mm). In a residential building, the typical vertical dimension might be 9'-10", or 106 inches (2.69 m). The designer divides 106 by 8 to find the minimum number of risers needed, which is 13.2. If only 13 are used, each riser will be slightly over 8 inches, which is not allowed according to the code. Rounding up to 14 will ensure each riser is slightly below the allowed 8 inches.

To find the total number of treads, remember that there is always one tread fewer than number of risers, as the floor levels at each stair end are not counted as treads. In our example, there would be 13 treads at 9 inches (229 mm) each, for a resulting stair run of 13 x 9" = 9 feet, 11 inches (3.02 m).

Figure 9-7 This enlarged plan of a stairway shows the dimensions of the landings, the widths and the run of each stair, risers, treads, and other details.

Figure 9-8 Stair sections show heights of the stair rise, handrails, and other details, cross-referenced to the plan view.

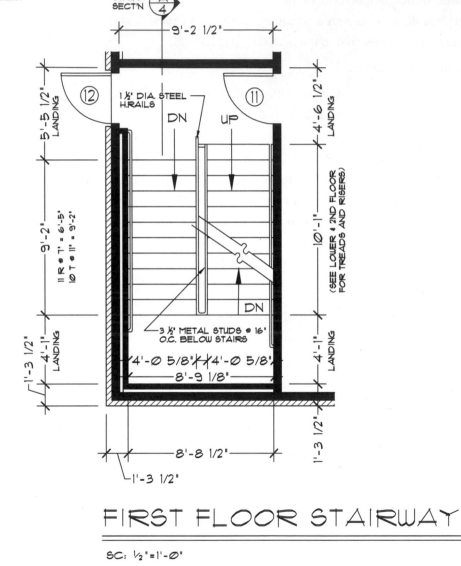

FIRST FLOOR STAIRWAY

SC: 1/2"=1'-0"

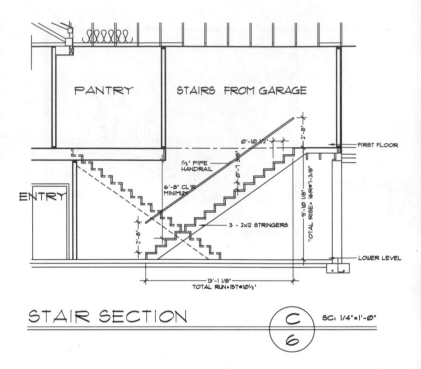

STAIR SECTION C/6   SC: 1/4"=1'-0"

- Note handrails and other trim. Key to where these can be found in more detail.

- Call out materials where stairs are shown in section view, including structural and finish components.

- Cross-reference to any structural plans where they are provided.

Dimensions

- Call out number and widths of treads, as well as number and height of risers.

- Dimension the total run of stairs in both plan and section views.

- Dimension the width of the stairs and any landings.

- Dimension treads, nosings, risers, landings, and handrail locations in sectional views of stairways.

Millwork

Architectural plans are often drawn at a scale too small to show adequate detail for cabinetry and millwork such as moldings, paneling, miscellaneous trim, and casings for doors and windows. These components are drawn and detailed at a large scale and cross-referenced to the basic plans. Millwork and cabinetry, also referred to as architectural woodwork, can include both manufactured stock components and custom woodwork that is assembled on the jobsite (Figure 9-9). Although some designers include cabinetry under the category of millwork, it will be treated here as a separate classification due to the specialized drawings needed to describe it.

Figure 9-9 This large-scale drawing shows the placement of stock-manufactured base cabinets.

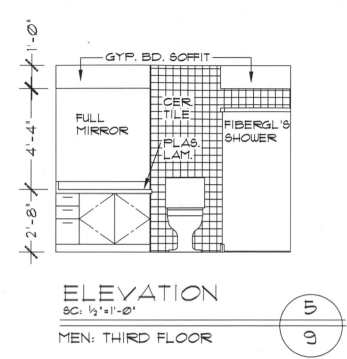

ELEVATION
SC: ½"=1'-0"

MEN: THIRD FLOOR

5
9

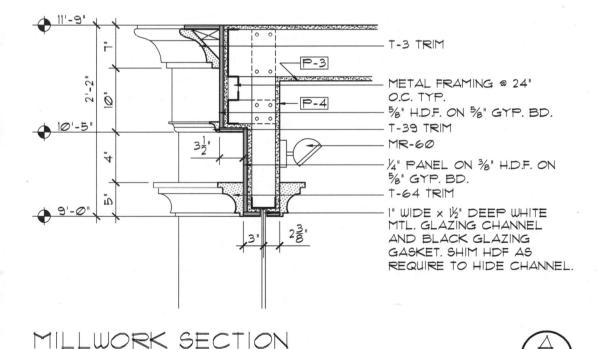

T-3 TRIM

METAL FRAMING @ 24"
O.C. TYP.

⅝" H.D.F. ON ⅝" GYP. BD.

T-39 TRIM

MR-60

¼" PANEL ON ⅜" H.D.F. ON
⅝" GYP. BD.

T-64 TRIM

1" WIDE x ½" DEEP WHITE
MTL. GLAZING CHANNEL
AND BLACK GLAZING
GASKET. SHIM HDF AS
REQUIRE TO HIDE CHANNEL.

Figure 9-10 Molding trim is produced in standard shapes and wood species, as noted in this section detail.

MILLWORK SECTION

SCALE: 3"=1'-0"

A
22

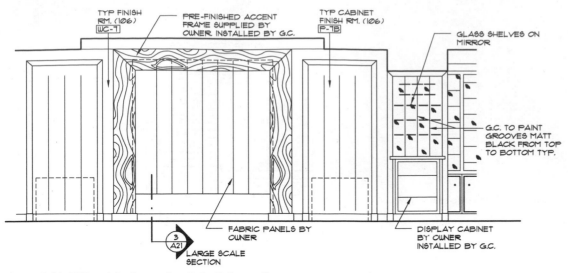

TYP FINISH RM. (106) WC-7

PRE-FINISHED ACCENT FRAME SUPPLIED BY OWNER. INSTALLED BY G.C.

TYP CABINET FINISH RM. (106) P-7B

GLASS SHELVES ON MIRROR

G.C. TO PAINT GROOVES MATT BLACK FROM TOP TO BOTTOM TYP.

FABRIC PANELS BY OWNER

3 A21 LARGE SCALE SECTION

DISPLAY CABINET BY OWNER INSTALLED BY G.C.

Figure 9-11 Millwork is drawn simplistically in small-scale drawings to show overall design, and then referenced to an enlarged scale to show more details.

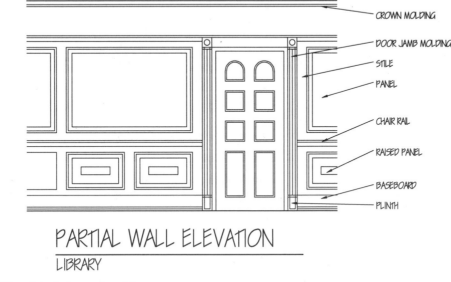

CROWN MOLDING

DOOR JAMB MOLDING

STILE

PANEL

CHAIR RAIL

RAISED PANEL

BASEBOARD

PLINTH

PARTIAL WALL ELEVATION

LIBRARY

Figure 9-12 Millwork includes various trims and panels, as shown in this elevation view.

A variety of styles, sizes, materials, and finishes are used in the construction of millwork. Molding trim is produced in standard shapes and wood species by a manufacturer, or milled and assembled on the jobsite as a custom fit (Figure 9-10). These include wall base, door and window casings, cornices, chair rails, handrails, and a number of other applications.

Scale of Drawings

Millwork elements are drawn simplistically in small-scale drawings, with a reference to a large-scale drawing to show the exact details of the component (Figure 9-11). Particular attention should be paid in drawing details to show both the desired aesthetic results and the methods of construction.

Millwork may include various types of wall paneling such as wood stile and rail paneling, wood flush paneling, and laminate-faced panels with various sorts of trim pieces, as shown in Figure 9-12. Stile and rail paneling is the traditional kind, where separate panels are contained by solid wood or synthetic-material rails, as illustrated in Figure 9-13. Historically, the panels were made from solid wood, but today they are mostly simply covered with a thin layer of wood called a veneer. Wood flush paneling consists of veneers glued to backing panels composed of plywood or particleboard. These panels can be glued end to end, producing a larger smooth surface with a minimum of wood trim at the edges or between panel joints. Laminate faced panels are constructed similar to wood veneer panels and are also installed as a smooth flush system or detailed with trims of wood or plastic laminate.

All of the panel systems are generally drawn in elevation views at ⅛", ¼", or ½" scales, (1: 100, 1: 50, 1:20 metric) depending upon the complexity and size of the assembly.

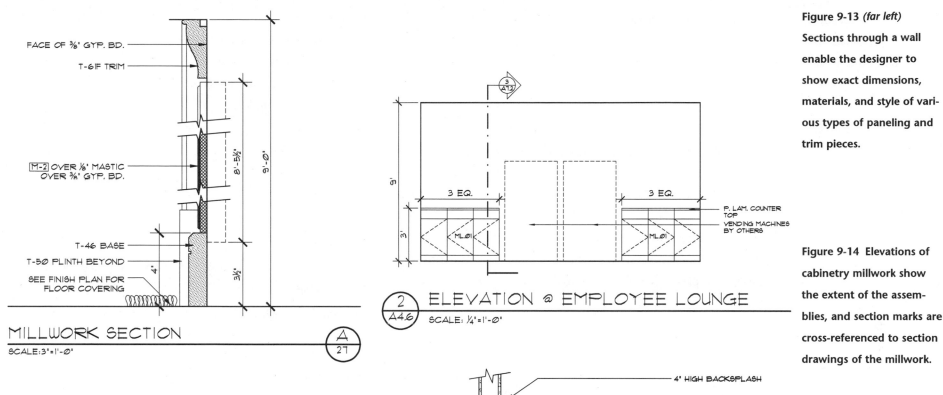

FACE OF ⅜" GYP. BD.

T-61F TRIM

M-2 OVER ⅛" MASTIC OVER ⅜" GYP. BD.

8'-5½"

9'-0"

T-46 BASE

T-50 PLINTH BEYOND

4"

SEE FINISH PLAN FOR FLOOR COVERING

3½"

MILLWORK SECTION
SCALE: 3"=1'-0'

A 27

3 A12

9'

3'

3 EQ.

ML01

3 EQ.

ML01

P. LAM. COUNTER TOP

VENDING MACHINES BY OTHERS

2 ELEVATION @ EMPLOYEE LOUNGE
A4.6   SCALE: ¼"=1'-0'

Figure 9-13 (far left) Sections through a wall enable the designer to show exact dimensions, materials, and style of various types of paneling and trim pieces.

Figure 9-14 Elevations of cabinetry millwork show the extent of the assemblies, and section marks are cross-referenced to section drawings of the millwork.

Figure 9-15 Millwork sections show details such as materials and tolerances needed, as well as panel

Drafting Standards

Millwork is generally drawn in plan view, and if the floor-plan drawing scale is too small to effectively show the components of the millwork, the plan is also keyed to a large-scale plan view. Elevations are also drawn and keyed to the plan view to show the extent of the millwork. In some cases, wood grains may be indicated on the elevation views, as well as panel shapes and joinery. Section marks are then added to the elevations (Figure 9-14) and cross-referenced to details of the panel trims and joints, as illustrated in Figure 9-15. Millwork sections show materials and tolerances needed.

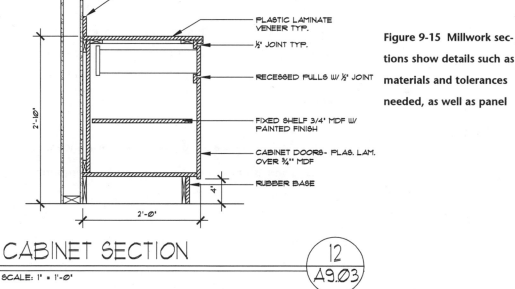

4" HIGH BACKSPLASH

PLASTIC LAMINATE VENEER TYP.

½" JOINT TYP.

RECESSED PULLS W/ ½" JOINT

FIXED SHELF ¾" MDF W/ PAINTED FINISH

CABINET DOORS- PLAS. LAM. OVER ¾" MDF

RUBBER BASE

2'-10"

4"

2'-0"

CABINET SECTION
SCALE: 1" = 1'-0'

12 A9.03

Designation of Materials

Millwork can be drawn at a number of different scales, depending on the size and complexity of the installation. The rendering of materials will depend upon the scale of the drawings and what can be shown without complicating or over-rendering them. Generally, outlines of assemblies are dark, changes in planes are lighter, and any textures that are rendered are done in the lightest line weights. The material features are not necessarily drawn to scale with the rest of the drawing. For example, a tight wood grain is suggested with a few lines, rather than drawn accurately, as attempting to render the material to scale could produce a muddy, unreadable drawing. In most cases, notes are added to describe materials that are too complex or small in scale to draw well.

Dimensioning Millwork

Millwork drawings are dimensioned both horizontally and vertically. Overall dimensions are provided to indicate the limits of the millwork. Then, detailed dimensions are added to fully explain sizes, clearances, and tolerances of the assemblies. In some cases, an enlarged detail or other drawing is needed to fully explain something that is too small to see in the basic drawing. Figures 9-13 and 9-14 illustrate basic dimensioning standards.

Checklist for Millwork

General

- Title the drawings and note the scale below the assembly.
- Use symbols to cross-reference detailed drawings to the floor plans and other drawings.
- Draw the outline (profile) of the objects darker than the textures and minor plane changes.

Notations

- Note materials, clearances, and other items that need to be cross-referenced to these drawings. For example, the cabinet width might be dimensioned, and a note added to verify with floor-plan dimensions.
- Call out related objects that fit within or adjacent to the millwork. These might include doorframes, mirrors, wall bases, hardware, etc.

Dimensions

- Dimension important heights, widths, and limits of the millwork.
- Dimension radii, thickness, and clearances of all millwork assemblies.
- Dimension millwork in relation to built-in features of the building, such as window sizes, door openings, etc.

Cabinetry

Cabinetry includes base and wall cabinets, shelving, desks, planters, mantles, dividers, and many other special items. Cabinetry might be manufactured as a prebuilt unit, partially made at the factory and site-finished, or totally custom-built on site. Manufactured cabinets are made in standard sizes and styles. These are listed in company catalogs (often available on the Internet) so designers and builders can coordinate them into their plans (Figure 9-16). Manufactured cabinetry is available both in stock configurations and finishes, and as semi-custom units with options on door and drawer types, configurations, and other details.

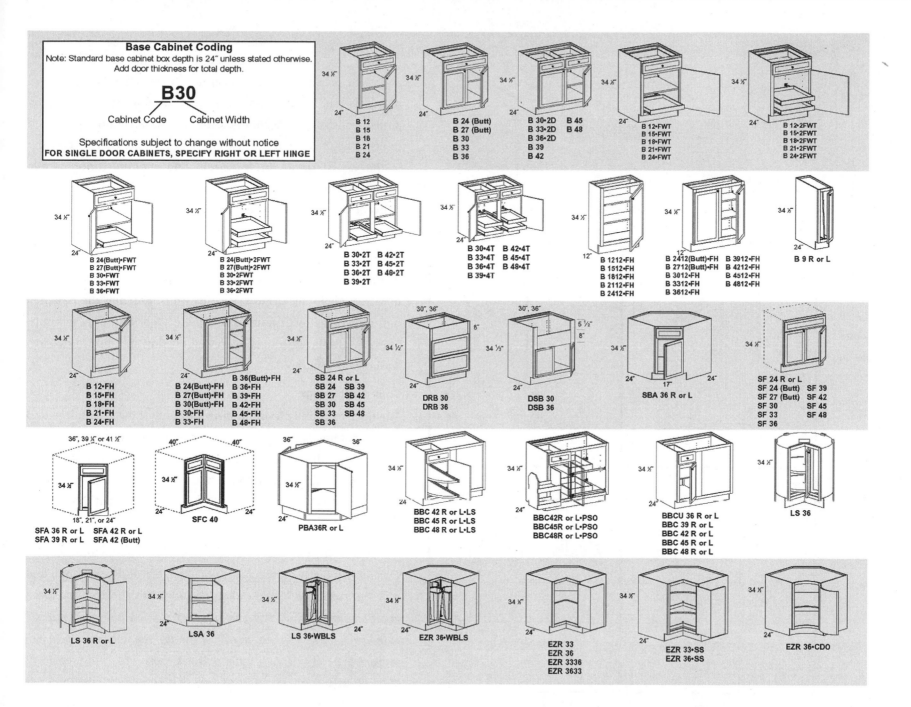

Base Cabinet Coding

Note: Standard base cabinet box depth is 24" unless stated otherwise. Add door thickness for total depth.

B30

Cabinet Code   Cabinet Width

Specifications subject to change without notice

FOR SINGLE DOOR CABINETS, SPECIFY RIGHT OR LEFT HINGE

34 ½" — 24"

B 12
B 15
B 18
B 21
B 24

34 ½" — 24"

B 24 (Butt)
B 27 (Butt)
B 30
B 33
B 36

34 ½" — 24"

B 30•2D   B 45
B 33•2D   B 48
B 36•2D
B 39
B 42

34 ½" — 24"

B 12•FWT
B 15•FWT
B 18•FWT
B 21•FWT
B 24•FWT

34 ½" — 24"

B 12•2FWT
B 15•2FWT
B 18•2FWT
B 21•2FWT
B 24•2FWT

---

34 ½" — 24"

B 24(Butt)•FWT
B 27(Butt)•FWT
B 30•FWT
B 33•FWT
B 36•FWT

34 ½" — 24"

B 24(Butt)•2FWT
B 27(Butt)•2FWT
B 30•2FWT
B 33•2FWT
B 36•2FWT

34 ½" — 24"

B 30•2T   B 42•2T
B 33•2T   B 45•2T
B 36•2T   B 48•2T
B 39•2T

34 ½" — 24"

B 30•4T   B 42•4T
B 33•4T   B 45•4T
B 36•4T   B 48•4T
B 39•4T

34 ½" — 12"

B 1212•FH
B 1512•FH
B 1812•FH
B 2112•FH
B 2412•FH

34 ½" — 12"

B 2412(Butt)•FH   B 3912•FH
B 2712(Butt)•FH   B 4212•FH
B 3012•FH   B 4512•FH
B 3312•FH   B 4812•FH
B 3612•FH

34 ½" — 24"

B 9 R or L

---

34 ½" — 24"

B 12•FH
B 15•FH
B 18•FH
B 21•FH
B 24•FH

34 ½" — 24"

B 24(Butt)•FH   B 36(Butt)•FH
B 27(Butt)•FH   B 36•FH
B 30(Butt)•FH   B 39•FH
B 30•FH   B 42•FH
B 33•FH   B 45•FH
            B 48•FH

34 ½" — 24"

SB 24 R or L
SB 24   SB 39
SB 27   SB 42
SB 30   SB 45
SB 33   SB 48
SB 36

30", 36"
34 ½" — 24" — 8"

DRB 30
DRB 36

30", 36"
34 ½" — 24"
5 ½"
8"

DSB 30
DSB 36

34 ½" — 24" — 17" — 24"

SBA 36 R or L

34 ½" — 24"

SF 24 R or L
SF 24 (Butt)   SF 39
SF 27 (Butt)   SF 42
SF 30   SF 45
SF 33   SF 48
SF 36

36", 39 ½" or 41 ½"
34 ½"
18", 21", or 24"

SFA 36 R or L   SFA 42 R or L
SFA 39 R or L   SFA 42 (Butt)

40" — 40"
34 ½" — 24" — 24"

SFC 40

36" — 36"
34 ½" — 24"

PBA36R or L

34 ½" — 24"

BBC 42 R or L•LS
BBC 45 R or L•LS
BBC 48 R or L•LS

34 ½" — 24"

BBC42R or L•PSO
BBC45R or L•PSO
BBC48R or L•PSO

34 ½" — 24"

BBCU 36 R or L
BBC 39 R or L
BBC 42 R or L
BBC 45 R or L
BBC 48 R or L

34 ½"

LS 36

---

34 ½" — 24"

LS 36 R or L

34 ½" — 24"

LSA 36

34 ½" — 24"

LS 36•WBLS

34 ½" — 24"

EZR 36•WBLS

34 ½" — 24"

EZR 33
EZR 36
EZR 3336
EZR 3633

34 ½" — 24"

EZR 33•SS
EZR 36•SS

34 ½" — 24"

EZR 36•CDO

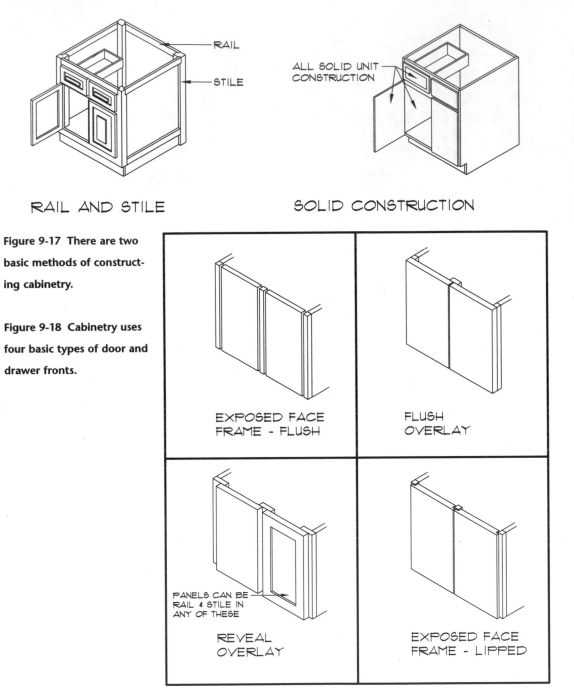

RAIL AND STILE

SOLID CONSTRUCTION

RAIL

STILE

ALL SOLID UNIT CONSTRUCTION

EXPOSED FACE FRAME - FLUSH

FLUSH OVERLAY

PANELS CAN BE RAIL & STILE IN ANY OF THESE

REVEAL OVERLAY

EXPOSED FACE FRAME - LIPPED

Figure 9-17 There are two basic methods of constructing cabinetry.

Figure 9-18 Cabinetry uses four basic types of door and drawer fronts.

Cabinetry can be designed and built in a variety of ways. However, two standard methods of construction are rail and stile and solid construction, as illustrated in Figure 9-17. Cabinetry materials and construction methods are further classified by grades, consisting of Economy, Custom, and Premium, as defined in detail by the Architectural Woodwork Institute (AWI). Economy is the lowest grade in materials and manufacturing, while Premium is the highest and most expensive. The quality and durability of the finishes, joints, fasteners, and hardware also vary greatly according to the grade.

Cabinets are generally manufactured and placed at the jobsite without a countertop. The countertop is then field-fitted to the cabinet and adjoining surfaces, such as walls. Cabinets are designed and constructed with four basic types of door and drawer fronts. These are flush, flush overlay, reveal overlay, and lipped overlay, as shown in Figure 9-18.

Scale of Drawings

The floor-plan and elevation drawings only show the outline and major features of cabinetry. Large-scale drawings are then made showing detailed construction and installation requirements. These are cross-referenced to the basic drawings. Cabinetry that is factory-built is closely referenced to major placement dimensions on the floor plan or elevation.

Drafting Standards

Detailed cabinetry drawings include plan, elevation, sectional, and pictorial views, which are often included with factory-produced components to show proper placement. When a manufacturer's standard cabinetry is placed on the jobsite, the floor plan and elevation generally show the cabinet's positioning dimensions. Alternatively, these might be shown only in one drawing and referenced to the manufacturer's detailed identification units. In some cases, additional drawings might be needed to fully explain other site-built components that interface with the standard cabinetry.

Custom cabinetry and other important woodwork is described in a separate set of drawings specifying basic features and dimensions. Then, an architectural woodworking contractor will take field measurements and produce shop drawings showing every specific detail and condition. These are often drawn at full scale. These drawings are submitted to the designer and contractor to check against the intent of the construction drawings.

Designation of Materials

Cabinetry is drawn in plan view, elevation view, sectional views, and any other details needed to fully describe the units and their particulars. In plan view, the tops of cabinetry are generally shown if they are less than about 4 feet (122 cm) from the finished floor. In small-scale drawings, the materials for the tops of the units are not generally shown, unless the tops are ceramic tile or stone that needs rendering designations.

In elevation views of cabinetry, material designations will depend primarily on the scale of the drawing and how items such as door and drawer designs can be effectively shown, as illustrated in Figure 9-19. Textures and wood grain designations are possible in large-scale drawings, but drawing them can be time-consuming. Most cabinetry elevations are treated simplistically with line varieties and held to a minimum of detailing to designate materials and shapes of doors, drawers, and other decorative items. Notes can be added to call out materials and features that are hard to draw, such as paneled doors and decorative handles.

In sectional views of cabinetry, material designation is done in the manner discussed in Chapter 8. Again, the scale of the drawing will dictate to what extent it is possible to delineate materials.

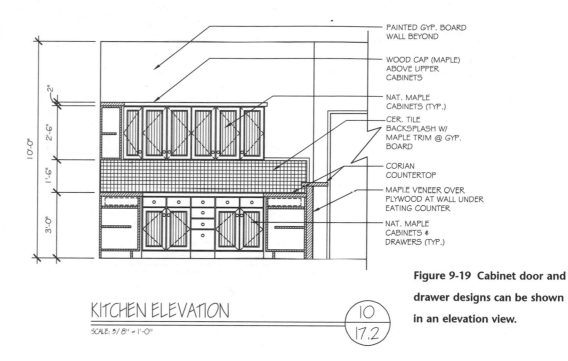

KITCHEN ELEVATION
SCALE: 3/8" = 1'-0"

PAINTED GYP. BOARD WALL BEYOND

WOOD CAP (MAPLE) ABOVE UPPER CABINETS

NAT. MAPLE CABINETS (TYP.)

CER. TILE BACKSPLASH W/ MAPLE TRIM @ GYP. BOARD

CORIAN COUNTERTOP

MAPLE VENEER OVER PLYWOOD AT WALL UNDER EATING COUNTER

NAT. MAPLE CABINETS & DRAWERS (TYP.)

Figure 9-19 Cabinet door and drawer designs can be shown in an elevation view.

Dimensioning Cabinetry

Cabinetry can be dimensioned in a number of different ways. First, if the cabinetry is built in, it is shown on the floor plan. Overall dimensions are given here to match the size of the unit to its location in the building. In turn, symbols or notes might be used to cross-reference this small-scale plan view to a larger and more detailed plan view. Also, an elevation or section symbol is drawn on the floor plan and referenced to a large-scale elevation or section view of each exposed cabinet face. In a large-scale elevation drawing, important vertical heights are dimensioned. Horizontal dimensions might be also added if necessary for clarity. This depends primarily on the standards that are adopted by the firm or individual. Some firms designate the cabinet widths with shorthand for the common manufactured component sizes (Figure 9-20). For example, a 24-inch-wide base cabinet might be desig-

Figure 9-20 Sizes of wall and base cabinets may be designated with the common manufactured component sizes.

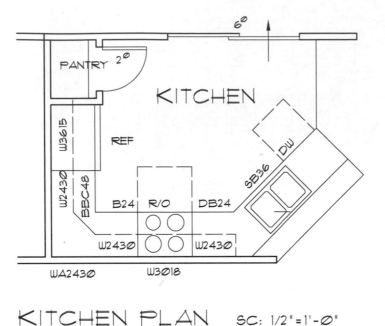

KITCHEN PLAN   SC: 1/2"=1'-Ø"

nated B24, an 18-inch-wide drawer base cabinet would be DB18, and a 24-inch-wide wall cabinet that is 30 inches high would be W2430.

Checklist for Cabinetry

General

- Title the drawings and note their scale.
- Cross-reference the drawings (with correct symbols) to floor plans and other related drawings.
- Adopt commonly accepted designations of materials and their rendering techniques.
- Vary line weights to make the plan, elevation, and section drawings clearly understandable. Draw the outline (profile) of the elevation or plan nice and dark, as it represents the boundaries of the cabinet.

- Show the direction of cabinet door swings (with a dashed line) in elevation views.

Notations

- Use notes to describe special materials, features, clearances, alignments, and other important items.
- In elevation views, call out tops, bases, toe kicks, backsplashes, and other features of the cabinetry.
- Note shelves, brackets, and other items related to the cabinetry.
- Call out generic sizes of manufactured wall and base cabinets.

Dimensions

- Dimension important heights of major items such as base and wall cabinets.
- Dimension toe spaces, height of space between base cabinets and wall cabinets, and other important clearances.
- Dimension miscellaneous items such as grab bars and spacing of shelving.

Fireplaces

Traditionally, fireplaces have been constructed to burn wood as a heat source and for the cooking of meals. Today, we still use fireplaces for some heat, but modern mechanical systems have taken over the need to warm ourselves totally by an open flame. However, many people still like the look and feel of a roaring fire. We now find fireplaces being constructed primarily as a visual element rather than for heating. To this end, the gas fireplace was invented to produce a flame similar to that of wood-burning units, but without the need to collect, burn, and remove ashes of the wood fuel. In fact, there is now more of an emphasis on using gas fireplaces instead of wood-burning units for both convenience and reduction of air pollution.

Wood-burning fireplaces have been constructed for centuries by skilled masons and bricklayers. The proportions and dimensions of such fireplaces and their various parts, such as the flue and openings, are based upon the laws of heat transfer, and on the various building codes. These dimensions and assemblies have developed over the years. Their dimensions are tabulated by various building codes and reference manuals for site-built units and provided by manufacturers for factory-made units (Figure 9-21).

Today, wood-burning fireplaces are of four basic types: those completely constructed on-site; those consisting of a manufactured firebox that is covered with masonry on the jobsite; prebuilt metal units (commonly called zero-clearance models); and freestanding units (Figure 9-22), including both fireplaces and wood-burning stoves. Site-constructed units and some of the heavier types require a structural support or foundation to rest on. Most such foundations are of concrete construction.

Gas fireplaces are manufactured as modular units and are offered with a variety of openings, similar to the wood-burning units. Vented units are sealed from the interior space and have a small round pipe that vents the fumes to the exterior, either vertically or horizontally through an exterior wall. Nonvented models are completely sealed, with no exhausting of fumes.

Scale of Drawings

The floor plans usually show the location of the fireplace, its hearth, and basic dimensions at a scale of ⅛" = 1'-0" (1:100 metric) or ¼"=1'-0" (1:50 metric). These plan views are simplistic, and usually cross-referenced to more detailed drawings done at a larger

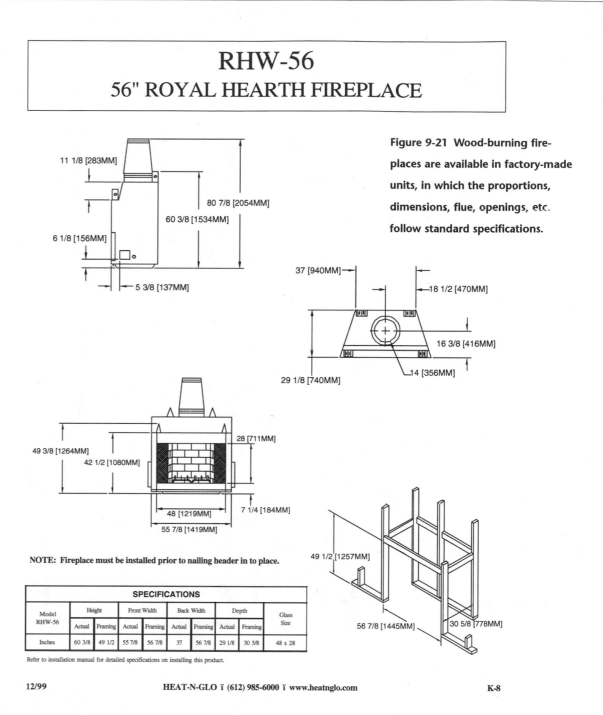

RHW-56
56" ROYAL HEARTH FIREPLACE

Figure 9-21 Wood-burning fireplaces are available in factory-made units, in which the proportions, dimensions, flue, openings, etc. follow standard specifications.

11 1/8 [283MM]
80 7/8 [2054MM]
60 3/8 [1534MM]
6 1/8 [156MM]
5 3/8 [137MM]

37 [940MM]
18 1/2 [470MM]
16 3/8 [416MM]
14 [356MM]
29 1/8 [740MM]

49 3/8 [1264MM]
42 1/2 [1080MM]
28 [711MM]
48 [1219MM]
7 1/4 [184MM]
55 7/8 [1419MM]

49 1/2 [1257MM]
56 7/8 [1445MM]
30 5/8 [778MM]

NOTE: Fireplace must be installed prior to nailing header in to place.

SPECIFICATIONS									
Model RHW-56	Height		Front Width		Back Width		Depth		Glass Size
	Actual	Framing	Actual	Framing	Actual	Framing	Actual	Framing	
Inches	60 3/8	49 1/2	55 7/8	56 7/8	37	56 7/8	29 1/8	30 5/8	48 x 28

Refer to installation manual for detailed specifications on installing this product.

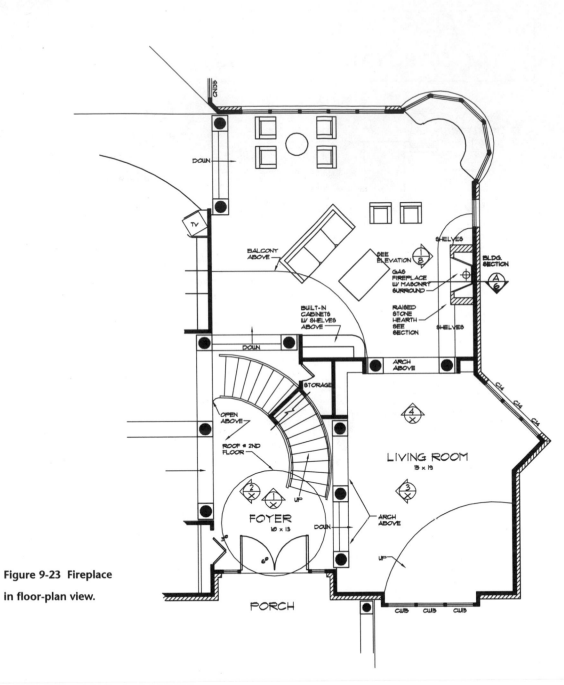

Figure 9-23 Fireplace in floor-plan view.

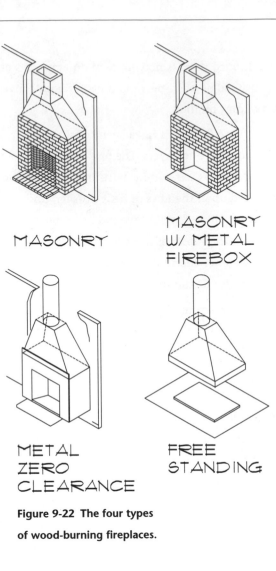

MASONRY

MASONRY W/ METAL FIREBOX

METAL ZERO CLEARANCE

FREE STANDING

Figure 9-22 The four types of wood-burning fireplaces.

scale (Figure 9-23). For example, if the fireplace is a wood-burning masonry unit, large-scale drawings are needed to more fully describe the dimensions and materials of the assembly.

Drafting Standards

The design of a fireplace often requires a series of drawings, including plan views, elevation views, and sections through the firebox. Materials are noted in these drawings, as well as the size of the openings, hearths, chimneys, and other particulars. The plan drawings are referenced to an elevation of the fireplace and further cross-referenced to more detailed large-scale drawings.

For wood-burning, built-in masonry fireplaces, the drawings are placed in the construction set. Many zero-clearance wood-burning units and gas fireplaces are predrawn by the manufacturer and are simply referred to in and included with the designer's drawings. There is no need to redraw all of these details.

Designation of Materials

The materials a fireplace is made of might be shown in a number of different places, as one drawing is generally not enough to accurately describe the unit. The floor plan might show the hearth material and fireplace wall construction, using cross-hatching to represent masonry and firebrick liners. Hearth sizes should be noted for wood-burning units, and further notations added for noncombustible trim work around the fireplace. Building sections and interior elevations would show the design and materials of the front of the fireplace as well as the mantle, as in Figure 9-24.

Dimensioning Fireplaces

The floor plan is dimensioned as to the exact size and location of the exterior surface of the fireplace unit, whether it is of masonry or prefabricated metal. Flues and their vertical chase spaces are dimensioned on floor plans that are above the fireplace, as illustrated in Figure 9-25.

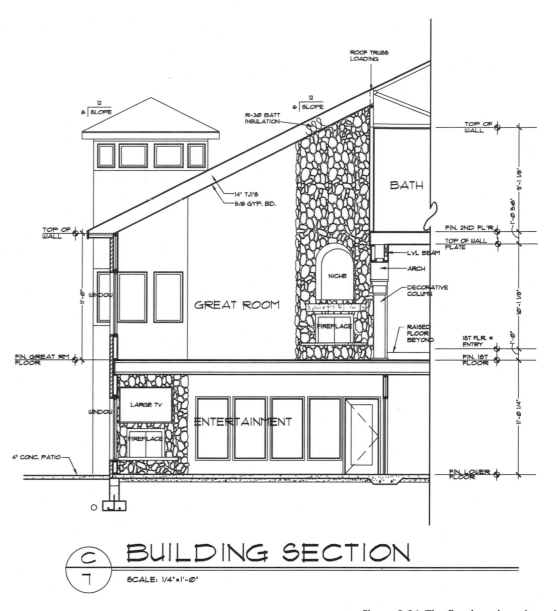

Figure 9-24 The fireplace, hearth, and mantle are shown in the great room as well as in the entertainment area of the basement in this building section.

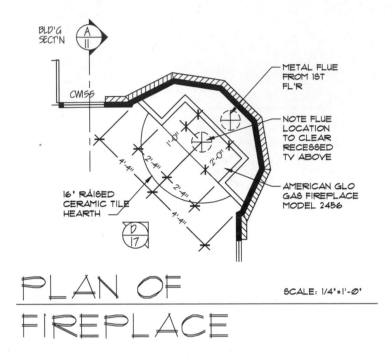

Figure 9-25 Plan view of fireplace showing flues and vertical chases.

BLD'G SECT'N Ⓐ

METAL FLUE FROM 1ST FL'R

CM55

NOTE FLUE LOCATION TO CLEAR RECESSED TV ABOVE

AMERICAN GLO GAS FIREPLACE MODEL 2456

16' RAISED CERAMIC TILE HEARTH

PLAN OF FIREPLACE

SCALE: 1/4"=1'-0"

Checklist for Fireplace Drawings

General

- Draw the firebox to scale in the plan view and cross-reference to other drawings that show more detail.
- Draw or note the flue (if one is required) and its route through the building structure.
- Draw and note the size of the hearth.

Notations

- Call out the basic materials of the fireplace and the hearth. Note if the hearth is raised or flush with the floor.
- Key the plan view with appropriate elevation and section views to fully delineate the fireplace particulars.
- In elevation views, call out the surrounding materials and features adjacent to the basic fireplace. This could include mantles, trim work, cabinetry, and other features.
- Cross-reference to finish plans and other details, as necessary.

Dimensions

- Dimension the firebox opening size, or designate the manufacturer's model number (for premanufactured units), which in turn gives the proper dimensions.
- In elevation views, dimension the size and location of any mantles over the fireplace opening.
- Dimension or call out the size of the hearth.
- Dimension the firebox to any required clearances to wood or other combustible materials.

SCHEDULES 10

Schedules are a convenient way to conserve drawing space and drafting time in construction drawings. They provide detailed information that is keyed to the construction drawings. The schedule is used to clarify sizes, location, finishes, and other information related to the construction of a project. Schedules present a large amount of data in the least amount of space in an organized, easy-to-read tabular fashion, as illustrated in Figure 10-1. Items that appear on interior-design drawings, such as doors, windows, and floor and wall finishes, can be simplistically drawn or represented by generic symbols or keys, such as the graphic indication of ceramic floor tile in Figure 10-2. Such symbols are used to indicate where a particular item or material is to be located and give no specific information about the actual element. The key or symbol is indexed to an entry in the schedule that gives more detailed information on sizes, materials, colors, and other variables. This is a much easier way to convey information than overly complicated drawings or excessive notes.

Interior-design construction drawings commonly include schedules for doors, windows, finishes, kitchen equipment, furniture, millwork, and hardware (Figure 10-3). As most products are available in a variety of different forms and sizes, schedules are used to convey this detailed information. They are keyed to the construction drawings and are located so one can easily relate the information to the drawing. Although the format of schedules varies from office to office, there are some standard practices. Most schedules are presented in tabular form, with rows and columns of data. The method of organization and information shown depends upon the degree of detail desired and the clearest way to show it.

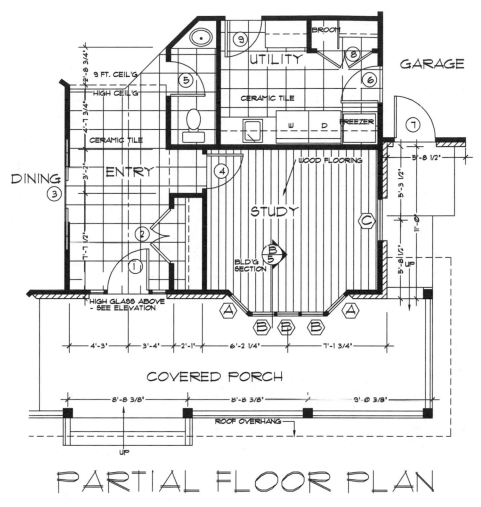

PARTIAL FLOOR PLAN

Figure 10-2 In floor plans, generic symbols can be used to represent items such as doors, windows, and floor or wall finishes.

Figure 10-1 Schedules provide detailed information that is keyed to the construction drawings; they present data concisely in tabular form.

DOOR & WINDOW SCHEDULE

DOOR/WIN NO.	SIZE W & HT	DOOR/WINDOW TYPE	DOOR/WINDOW FINISH	FRAME TYPE	FRAME FINISH	HARDWARE	ELEVATION	RATING	REMARKS
1	6'-0" X 7'-0"	DOOR2	1/4" CLEAR	ALUM	FP	SET#1	B	NONE	USE A SET OF TWO 3'-0" X 7'-0" DOORS W/ TRANSOM ABOVE
2	3'-0" X 7'-0"	DOOR1	P1	HM1	P1	SET#2	G	NONE	
3	3'-0" X 6'-8"	DOOR3	ST	HM2	P1	SET#3	G	NONE	18"x18" TRANSFER AIR GRILL, BREAK ROOM DOOR ONLY
3.9	6'-0" X 6'-8"	DOOR3	ST	HM2	P1	SET#6	F	NONE	USE A SET OF TWO 3'-0" X 6'-8" DOORS
4	3'-0" X 6'-8"	DOOR3	ST	HM2	P1	SET#4	G	NONE	18"x18" TRANSFER AIR GRILL, OFFICE & RESTROOM DOOR ONLY
5	3'-0" X 6'-8"	DOOR3	ST	HM2	P1	SET#3	G	NONE	
6	3'-0" X 4'-8"	DOOR3	ST	HM2	P1	SET#5	H	NONE	
7	6'-4" X 7'-2"	WIN1	1" CLEAR	ALUM	FP	NONE	B	NONE	
8	18'-8" X 7'-2"	WIN1	1" CLEAR	ALUM	FP	NONE	A	NONE	
9	12'-6" X 7'-2"	WIN1	1" CLEAR	ALUM	FP	NONE	E	NONE	
10	9'-5" X 7'-2"	WIN1	1" CLEAR	ALUM	FP	NONE	C	NONE	
11	9'-5" X 9'-0"	WIN1	1" CLEAR	ALUM	FP	NONE	D	NONE	
12	3'-0" X 4'-0"	WIN2	1/4" CLEAR	HM2	P1	NONE	J	NONE	

NOTE: ALL WINDOW DIMENSIONS ARE FROM FRAME TO FRAME

DOOR/WINDOW TYPE

DOOR1 = CURRIES FLUSH GALVANIZED STEEL INSULATED 18 GA. DOOR WITH 12 GA. HINGE & LOCK REINFORCEMENT

DOOR2 = KAWNER 190 COMMERCIAL ALUMINUM DOOR

DOOR3 = SOLID CORE OAK VENNER FLUSH WOOD DOOR

WIN1 = KAWNER 451T TRIFAB ALUMINUM FRAME WITH 1" INSULATED CLEAR GLASS

WIN2 = HOLLOW METAL FRAME WITH 1/4" FIXED GLASS WINDOW

DOOR/WINDOW FINISH

1/4" CLEAR = 1/4" CLEAR TEMPERED GLASS WITH UV BLOCKER

P1 = PAINT ONE COAT PRIMER AND TWO COATS FINISH PAINT SEMI-GLOSS. SHERMAN WILLIAMS, COLOR BY OWNER

ST = ONE COAT STAIN AND TWO COATS OF POLYURETHANE SEMI GLOSS FINISH, COLOR BY OWNER

1" CLEAR = 1" INSULATED CLEAR GLASS WITH UV BLOCKER

N = NONE

FRAME TYPE

HM1 = CURRIES 16GA HOLLOW METAL FRAME GALVANIZED

HM2 = CURRIES 16GA HOLLOW METAL FRAME NON-GALVANIZED

ALUM = KAWNEER TRIFAB 451 FRAME

FRAME FINISH

FP = FACTORY APPLIED FLUROPAN PAINTED FINISH. COLOR SELECTED BY OWNER CUSTOM COLOR, MATCH GLAZED BRICK COLOR

P1 = PAINT ONE COAT PRIMER AND TWO COATS FINISH PAINT SEMI-GLOSS. SHERMAN WILLIAMS, COLOR BY OWNER

N = NONE

HARDWARE

HARDWARE SET#1

2 SETS	PIVOTS	KAWNER TOP/BOTTOM/INTERMEDIATE OFFSET PIVOTS
1 PAIR	FLUSH BOLTS	FB6 X MANUAL
1 EACH	DEADLOCK	MS1850ANSI X THUMBTURN
1 EACH	CLYINER	20-001 X 1 1/8"
2 SETS	PUSH/PULLS	C015 OUTSIDE, CP INSIDE
2 EACH	CLOSER	P4041
2 EACH	DROP PLATE	4040-18PA
2 EACH	B.S. SPACER	4040-61
2 EACH	FLOOR STOP	FB19X
1 EACH	THRESHOLD	171A X 1/2" X 5"
2 EACH	DOOR SWEEPS	315CN
1 SET	WEATHER-STRIP	BY ALUMINUM DOOR SUPPLIER
1 EACH	SIGN	"DOOR MUST REMAINED UNLOCKED DURING NORMAL BUSINESS HOURS"

HARDWARE SET#2

3 EACH	HINGES	TA2314 X 4.5" X 4.5"
1 EACH	ENTRANCE LOCK	D53PD X RHODES
1 EACH	CLOSER	P4041
1 EACH	FLOOR STOPS	FB19X
1 EACH	LATCH GUARD	LP-1
1 EACH	THRESHOLD	2005AV X 1/2" X 5"
1 EACH	DOOR SWEEP	315CN
1 SET	WEATHER-STRIP	330AV

HARDWARE SET#3

3 EACH	HINGES	TA2714 X 4.5" X 4.5"
1 EACH	PRIVACY LATCH	53PD X RHODES
1 EACH	WALL STOPS	60W
3 EACH	SILENCERS	GJ64
1 EACH	SIGN	"RESTROOM"

HARDWARE SET#4

3 EACH	HINGES	TA2714 X 4.5" X 4.5"
1 EACH	STOREROOM LOCK	D40S X RHODES
1 EACH	WALL STOPS	60W
3 EACH	SILENCERS	GJ64

HARDWARE SET#5

3 EACH	HINGES	TA2714 X 4.5" X 4.5"
1 EACH	DRESSING ROOM LOCK	
1 EACH	WALL STOPS	60W
3 EACH	SILENCERS	GJ64

HARDWARE SET#6

3 EACH	HINGES	TA2714 X 4.5" X 4.5"
2 EACH	PULL PLATE	110 X 70B
2 EACH	PUSH PLATE	70C
2 EACH	CLUSTER	4041
2 EACH	KICKPLATES	8" X 2" X L.D.W.
3 EACH	SILENCERS	GJ64

NOTES:
EXIT DOORS SHALL SWING IN THE DIRECTION OF EXIT TRAVEL AND SHALL BE OPERABLE FROM THE INSIDE WITHOUT USE OF ANY SPECIAL KNOWLEDGE OR KEY PER THE UBC.

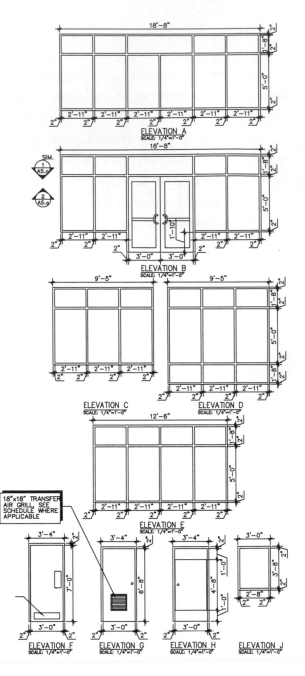

ELEVATION A — SCALE: 1/4"=1'-0"
ELEVATION B — SCALE: 1/4"=1'-0"
ELEVATION C — SCALE: 1/4"=1'-0"
ELEVATION D — SCALE: 1/4"=1'-0"
ELEVATION E — SCALE: 1/4"=1'-0"
ELEVATION F — SCALE: 1/4"=1'-0"
ELEVATION G — SCALE: 1/4"=1'-0"
ELEVATION H — SCALE: 1/4"=1'-0"
ELEVATION J — SCALE: 1/4"=1'-0"

18"x18" TRANSFER AIR GRILL, SEE SCHEDULE WHERE APPLICABLE

ROOM FINISH SCHEDULE

| ROOM | | FLOOR | | WALLS | | | | | | | | WAINSCOT HEIGHT | CEILING | | REMARKS |
| | | | | NORTH | | EAST | | SOUTH | | WEST | | | | | |
NO.	NAME	FIN.	BASE	MTL.	FIN.	MTL.	FIN.	MTL.	FIN.	MTL.	FIN.		MTL./FIN.	HT.	
100	CASHIER	CPT	VCB	GWB	P	GWB	P	GWB	P	GWB	P	–	–	AT/AG	10'–0"	
101	TUX ROOM	CPT	VCB	GWB	P	GWB	P	GWB	P	GWB	P	–	–	AT/AG	10'–0"	
102	DRESSING ROOM	CPT	VCB	GWB	P	GWB	P	GWB	P	GWB	P	–	–	AT/AG	10'–0"	NO CEILING, EXPOSED TO DROP CEILING ABOVE. 8'-0" TALL WALLS
103	BRIDAL ROOM	CPT	VCB	GWB	P	GWB	P	GWB	P	GWB	P	–	–	AT/AG	10'–0"	
104	DRESSING ROOM	CPT	VCB	GWB	P	GWB	P	GWB	P	GWB	P	–	–	AT/AG	10'–0"	NO CEILING, EXPOSED TO DROP CEILING ABOVE. 8'-0" TALL WALLS
105	MECH/ELEC ROOM	VCT	VCB	GWB	P	GWB	P	GWB	P	GWB	P	–	–	GWB/P	12'–0"	
106	WORK ROOM	CONC	VCB	GWB	P	GWB	P	GWB	P	GWB	P	–	–	GWB/P	12'–0"	
107	OFFICE	CPT	VCB	GWB	P	GWB	P	GWB	P	GWB	P	–	–	GWB/P	8'–0"	
108	MECH/ELEC ROOM	VCT	VCB	GWB	P	GWB	P	GWB	P	GWB	P	–	–	GWB/P	12'–0"	
109	BREAK ROOM	VCT	VCB	GWB	P	GWB	P	GWB	P	GWB	P	–	–	GWB/P	8'–0"	
110	UNISEX RESTROOM	VCT	VCB	GWB	P	GWB	P	GWB	P	GWB	P	–	–	GWB/P	8'–0"	
111	DISPLAY ROOM	CPT	VCB	GWB	P	GWB	P	GWB	P	GWB	P	–	–	AT/AG	10'–0"	

Figure 10-3 A room-finish schedule is commonly included in interior construction plans.

FLOOR FINISH

VCT = VINYL COMPOSITION TILE
CPT = CARPET
CONC = CONCRETE

WALL MATERIAL

GWB = 5/8" "X" RATED GYPSUM WALL
        BOARD
N = NONE, EXPOSED TRUSSES

CEILING MATERIAL

GWB = 5/8" "X" RATED GYPSUM WALL
        BOARD
N = NONE, EXPOSED TRUSSES
AT = ARMSTRONG "MINEBOARD CORTEGE"
      2x4 ACOUSTICAL TILE, FISSURED
      PATTERN

BASE TRIM

VCB = VINYL COVE BASE
N = NONE

WALL FINISH

P = PAINT
N = NONE

CEILING FINISH

P = PAINT
N = NONE
AG = CHICAGO METALLIC 200 2x4
      SUSPENDED CEILING GRID WHITE

Schedules should be clear, concise, complete, and easy to read. In order to communicate what is wanted, schedules must be specific and include all of the information needed by the builder to properly furnish the items or complete the construction. The information in the schedule may also be keyed to a specific detail, legend, or written specification for further clarity.

In general, schedules are laid out in a grid format with lines preferably spaced ¼ inch (6.35 mm) apart, but no less than 3/16 inch (4.76 mm), for ease of viewing. Lettering or font sizes should prefer-ably be ⅛ inch (3.17 mm), but no smaller than 3/32 inch (2.4 mm), as sizes less than this can be difficult to read. As many schedules are read during construction in the field, where temporary lighting is dim, information must be clearly readable. The schedule should be organized logically, with titles larger and bolder than the information below them. Heavier borders can also be used to set the schedule apart from other drawings and information on the same sheet, as shown in Figure 10-4.

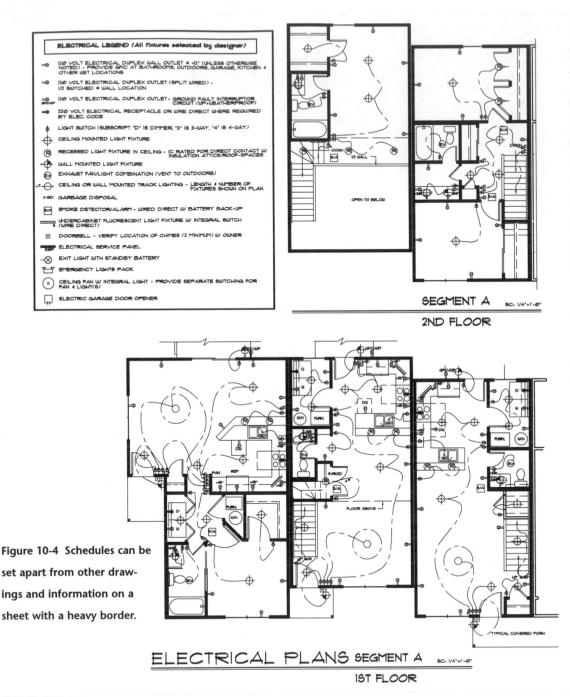

Figure 10-4 Schedules can be set apart from other drawings and information on a sheet with a heavy border.

SEGMENT A SC: 1/4"=1'-0"

2ND FLOOR

ELECTRICAL PLANS SEGMENT A SC: 1/4"=1'-0"

1ST FLOOR

Door Schedules

Door schedules identify each door by a number or other designation that is shown on the floor plan. See Figure 10-5 for an example. Depending on the complexity of a project, door schedules differ in the amount of information required. Door schedules for residential projects usually contain the number of the door, quantity required, size, type of door, material, and remarks (Figure 10-6). More detailed information, such as frame type, hardware, and fire rating, is generally required for large commercial projects (Figure 10-7). Door schedules are generally longer than window schedules, as most projects have many more different types and sizes of doors than windows.

Generally, in more complex projects, the door numbers are the same as the room number into which they open. When more than one door opens into a room, a letter can be added to the number, such as 101 for the first door and 101A for the second, 101B for the third, and so on.

The purpose of a door schedule is to show the type of door being used in a given opening, the type of frame, the size (including width, height and thickness), the material, and any other pertinent details, such as the type of hardware or fire rating, as illustrated in Figure 10-8. Door schedules are generally presented in two parts. The first part is a graphic representation of each type of door that exists in the particular project, as seen in Figure 10-9. The door elevations are typically drawn at a ¼" = 1'-0" (1:50 metric) scale; however, this scale is not a rigid standard. Any special features, such as glazing or wood louvers, should also be drafted, noted, and dimensionally located for clarity. Each door type should be identified with a letter that keys it to the other part of the door schedule.

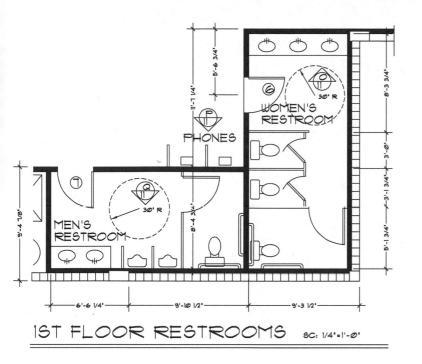

Figure 10-5 Doors in a floor plan are numbered or identified by some other designation, which is referenced to a door schedule that includes more detailed information about each door.

1ST FLOOR RESTROOMS SC: 1/4"=1'-0"

DOOR SCHEDULE

DOOR#	DOOR TYPE	DOOR OPENING			FRAME			HARDWARE
		WIDTH	HEIGHT	THICKN'S	MATERIAL	MATERIAL	FINISH	
①	A	6'-0"	6'-8"	1 3/4"	W'D/GLASS	W'D	SS	LOCKSET/CLOSER
②	A	6'-0"	6'-8"	1 3/4"	W'D/GLASS	W'D	SS	LOCKSET/CLOSER
③	B	3'-0"	6'-8"	1 3/4"	W'D	W'D	SS	LATCHSET
④	B	2'-8"	6'-8"	1 3/4"	W'D	W'D	SS	LATCHSET
⑤	B	2'-6"	6'-8"	1 3/4"	W'D	W'D	SS	PRIVACY LOCK
⑥	B	2'-8"	6'-8"	1 3/4"	WD	WD	SS	LATCHSET
⑦	B	2'-4"	6'-8"	1 3/4"	WD	WD	SS	LATCHSET
⑧	B	2'-6"	6'-8"	1 3/4"	WD	WD	SS	LATCHSET/CLOSER
⑨	B	3'-0"	6'-8"	1 3/4"	WD	WD	SS	LATCHSET/CLOSER
⑩	B	2'-4"	6'-8"	1 3/4"	WD	WD	SS	PRIVACY LOCK
⑪	B	2'-8"	6'-8"	1 3/4"	WD	WD	PT	LOCKSET
⑫	B	2'-4"	6'-8"	1 3/4"	WD	WD	SS	PRIVACY
⑬	C	3'-0"	6'-8"	1 3/4"	MT'L/PT	MT'L	PT	LOCKSET
⑭	C	2'-8"	6'-8"	1 3/4"	MT'L/PT	MT'L	PT	LOCKSET
⑮	D	3'-0"	6'-8"	1 3/4"	MT'L/PT	MT'L	PT	LOCKSET/CLOSER
⑯	D	3'-0"	6'-8"	1 3/4"	MT'L/PT	MT'L	PT	LOCKSET

Figure 10-6 Door schedules, for residential projects, contain information such as the door number, quantity required, size, type, material and remarks.

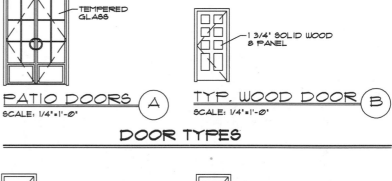

PATIO DOORS Ⓐ
SCALE: 1/4"=1'-0"
— TEMPERED GLASS

TYP. WOOD DOOR Ⓑ
SCALE: 1/4"=1'-0"
— 1 3/4" SOLID WOOD 8 PANEL

DOOR TYPES

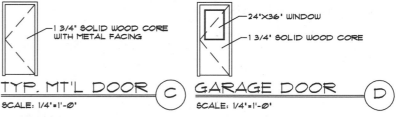

TYP. MT'L DOOR Ⓒ
SCALE: 1/4"=1'-0"
— 1 3/4" SOLID WOOD CORE WITH METAL FACING

GARAGE DOOR Ⓓ
SCALE: 1/4"=1'-0"
— 24"X36" WINDOW
— 1 3/4" SOLID WOOD CORE

GENERAL NOTES:

1. CONTRACTOR TO SUBMIT COMPLETE HARDWARE SHOP DRAWINGS/CUTS AND KEYING SCHEDULE FOR DESIGNERS APPROVAL.

2. SS= STAIN PER DESIGNER'S SAMPLE AND SEAL WITH POLYESTER (TWO COATS MINIMUM)

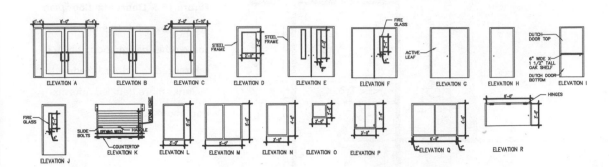

ELEVATION A ELEVATION B ELEVATION C ELEVATION D ELEVATION E ELEVATION F ELEVATION G ELEVATION H ELEVATION I

ELEVATION J ELEVATION K ELEVATION L ELEVATION M ELEVATION N ELEVATION O ELEVATION P ELEVATION Q ELEVATION R

DOOR SCHEDULE

DOOR NO.	SIZE W & HT	DOOR TYPE	DOOR FINISH	FRAME TYPE	FRAME FINISH	HARDWARE	ELEVATION	RATING	REMARKS
1	6'-0" X 7'-0"	DOOR1	ACRO	ALUM	ACRO	SET#1	A	NONE	1'-0" X 7'-0" SIDE LITES EACH SIDE OF DOOR KAWNEER 451T FRAME & 1" INSULATED GLASS
1a	6'-0" X 7'-0"	DOOR1	ACRO	ALUM	ACRO	SET#1.a	A	NONE	1'-0" X 7'-0" SIDE LITE ONE SIDE OF DOOR KAWNEER 451T FRAME & 1" INSULATED GLASS
2	6'-0" X 7'-0"	DOOR1	ACRO	ALUM	ACRO	SET#2	B	NONE	
3	6'-0" X 7'-0"	DOOR1	ACRO	ALUM	ACRO	SET#3	C	NONE	1'-10" X 7'-0" SIDE LITE ONE SIDE OF DOOR KAWNEER 451T FRAME & 1" INSULATED GLASS
4	3'-8" X 7'-0"	DOOR2	P1	HM1	P1	SET#4	D	NONE	
4a	3'-0" X 7'-0"	DOOR2	P1	HM1	P1	SET#4.a	D	NONE	
5	6'-0" X 7'-0"	DOOR3	ST	HM2	P2	SET#5	E	20 MINUTE	HARDWARE MUST MEET 20 MINUTE RATED DOORS
6	6'-0" X 7'-0"	DOOR3	ST	HM2	P2	SET#6	E	20 MINUTE	HARDWARE MUST MEET 20 MINUTE RATED DOORS
7	3'-0" X 7'-0"	DOOR3	ST	HM2	P2	SET#7	H	20 MINUTE	
8	6'-0" X 7'-0"	DOOR3	ST	HM2	P2	SET#8	G	20 MINUTE	
8a	6'-0" X 7'-0"	DOOR3	ST	HM2	P2	SET#8.a	G	20 MINUTE	
9	3'-0" X 7'-0"	DOOR3	ST	HM2	P2	SET#9	H	3/4 HOUR	DOOR FRAME SHALL HAVE MASONRY ANCHORS & 4" TALL HEAD FRAME
9a	3'-0" X 7'-0"	DOOR3	ST	HM2	P2	SET#9	H	3/4 HOUR	DOOR FRAME SHALL HAVE MASONRY ANCHORS & 4" TALL HEAD FRAME
11	3'-0" X 7'-0"	DOOR3	ST	HM2	P2	SET#10	H	NONE	
12	3'-0" X 7'-0"	DOOR3	ST	HM2	P2	SET#10	H	20 MINUTE	HARDWARE MUST MEET 20 MINUTE RATED DOORS
13	3'-0" X 7'-0"	DOOR3	ST	HM2	P2	SET#11	H	NONE	
14	3'-0" X 7'-0"	DOOR3	ST	HM2	P2	SET#11	H	20 MINUTE	HARDWARE MUST MEET 20 MINUTE RATED DOORS
15	3'-0" X 7'-0"	DOOR3	ST	HM2	P2	SET#10	H	NONE	
16	3'-0" X 7'-0"	DOOR3	ST	HM2	P2	SET#11	H	20 MINUTE	HARDWARE MUST MEET 20 MINUTE RATED DOORS
17	3'-0" X 7'-0"	DOOR4	ST	HM2	P2	SET#12	I	20 MINUTE	
18	3'-0" X 7'-0"	DOOR3	ST	HM2	P2	SET#13	H	NONE	
19	3'-0" X 7'-0"	DOOR3	ST	HM2	P2	SET#14	H	NONE	
20	3'-0" X 7'-0"	DOOR3	ST	HM2	P2	SET#13	H	NONE	
21	3'-0" X 7'-0"	DOOR3	ST	HM2	P2	SET#11	J	20 MINUTE	HARDWARE MUST MEET 20 MINUTE RATED DOORS
22	3'-0" X 7'-0"	DOOR3	ST	HM2	P2	SET#11.a	H	20 MINUTE	
23	3'-0" X 7'-0"	DOOR3	ST	HM2	P2	SET#11	H	NONE	
24	3'-0" X 7'-0"	DOOR3	ST	HM2	P2	SET#11	H	NONE	
25	3'-0" X 7'-0"	DOOR3	ST	HM2	P2	SET#15	J	20 MINUTE	
26	3'-0" X 7'-0"	DOOR3	ST	HM2	P2	SET#15	J	20 MINUTE	
27	3'-0" X 7'-0"	DOOR3	ST	HM2	P2	SET#16	J	20 MINUTE	
28	3'-0" X 7'-0"	DOOR3	ST	HM2	P2	SET#17	J	20 MINUTE	
29	3'-0" X 7'-0"	DOOR3	ST	HM2	P2	SET#18	J	20 MINUTE	WINDOW KIT SHALL HAVE ONE WAY MIRRORED GLASS
30	5'-0" X 7'-0"	DOOR3	ST	HM2	P2	SET#17	J	20 MINUTE	
31	3'-0" X 7'-0"	DOOR3	ST	HM2	P2	SET#11	H	NONE	
32	3'-0" X 7'-0"	DOOR3	ST	HM2	P2	SET#11	H	NONE	

CONT'D

1.) ALL LOCKS SHALL OPERATE WITH ONE MASTER KEY & DIFFERENT INDIVIDUAL KEYS. ALL LOCKSET FUNCTIONS TO BE VERIFIED W/ OWNER PRIOR TO ORDERING
2.) HARDWARE FINISH TO BE BRUSHED STAINLESS STEEL

DOOR TYPE

DOOR1 = KAWNEER 350 COMMERCIAL ALUMINUM DOOR
DOOR2 = CURRIES FLUSH STEEL INSULATED 18 GA DOOR WITH 12GA HINGE AND LOCK REINFORCEMENT GALVANIZED.
DOOR3 = SOLID CORE OAK VENEER FLUSH WOOD DOOR
DOOR4 = SOLID CORE OAK VENEER FLUSH WOOD DUTCH DOOR W/ 8" OAK SHELF
DOOR5 = CORNELL IRON WORKS COUNTERTOP ROLL-UP DOOR SURFACE MOUNTED PBI-1F 22GC (COLOR BY OWNER)

FRAME TYPE

HM1 = CURRIES 16GA HOLLOW METAL FRAME GALVANIZED
HM2 = CURRIES 16GA HOLLOW METAL FRAME NON-GALVANIZED
ALUM = KAWNEER TRIFAB 451 FRAME
RAIL = 12GA STEEL GUIDE RAILS BY DOOR SUPPLIER & DRYWALL WRAP JAMBS & HEAD
ALUM2 = ALUM FRAME BY WINDOW SUPPLIER

DOOR FINISH

ACRO = FACTORY APPLIED ACROSLUR SPRAY COLORED FINISH ON DOOR FRAME & CLEAR GLASS. FRAME WILL BE STANDARD COLOR SELECTED BY OWNER
P1 = PAINT ONE COAT PRIMER AND TWO COATS FINISH PAINT. SHERMAN WILLIAMS. COLOR FINISH: SEMI-GLOSS
ST = ONE COAT STAIN AND TWO COATS OF POLYURETHANE SEMI GLOSS FINISH
N = NONE
GC = FACTORY APPLIED SPECTRA SHIELD POWDER COATING COLOR BY OWNER
CLEAR = 1/4" TEMPERED CLEAR GLASS

FRAME FINISH

ACRO = FACTORY APPLIED ACROFLUR SPRAY COLORED FINISH. STANDARD COLOR SELECTED BY OWNER
P1 = PAINT ONE COAT PRIMER AND TWO COATS FINISH PAINT SHERMAN WILLIAMS FINISH: SEMI-GLOSS
P2 = PAINT ONE COAT PRIMER & TWO COATS FINISH PAINT SHERMAN WILLIAMS COLOR: SELECTED BY OWNER FINISH: SEMI-GLOSS
GC = FACTORY APPLIED COATING. COLOR: SELECTED BY OWNER

HARDWARE

HARDWARE SET#1
2 SETS PIVOTS
2 SETS PUSH/PULL SET
1 EACH DEADLOCK
1 EACH CYLINDER
2 EACH CLOSERS
2 EACH DROP PLATES
2 EACH BLADE STOP SPACER
1 EACH FLOOR STOP
1 EACH THRESHOLD
1 SET WEATHERSTRIP

HARDWARE SET#1.a
2 SETS PIVOTS
2 SETS PUSH/PULL SET
1 EACH DEADLOCK
2 EACH CLOSERS
2 EACH DROP PLATES
2 EACH BLADE STOP SPACER
2 EACH WALL STOPS

HARDWARE SET#2
2 SETS PIVOTS
2 SETS PUSH/PULL SET
1 EACH DEADLOCK
1 EACH CYLINDER
1 EACH CLOSER
1 EACH DROP PLATE
1 EACH BLADE STOP SPACER
1 EACH FLOOR STOP
1 EACH THRESHOLD
1 SET WEATHERSTRIP

HARDWARE SET#3
1 SET PIVOTS
1 SET PUSH/PULL SET
1 EACH CYLINDER
1 EACH CLOSER
1 EACH DROP PLATE
1 EACH BLADE STOP SPACER
1 EACH FLOOR STOP
1 EACH THRESHOLD
1 SET WEATHERSTRIP

HARDWARE SET#4
3 EACH HINGES
1 EACH ENTRY LOCK
1 EACH CLOSER
1 EACH LATCH GUARD
1 EACH THRESHOLD
1 SET WEATHERSTRIP

HARDWARE SET#4.a
3 EACH HINGES
1 EACH ENTRY LOCK
1 EACH CLOSER
1 EACH LATCH GUARD
1 EACH THRESHOLD
1 SET WEATHERSTRIP

HARDWARE SET#5
6 EACH HINGES
2 EACH EXIT DEVICE
1 EACH EXIT DEVICE
1 EACH CYLINDER
2 EACH CLOSER
2 EACH KICKPLATES
2 EACH WALL STOPS
2 EACH SILENCERS

HARDWARE SET#6
6 EACH HINGES
2 EACH EXIT DEVICE
1 EACH EXIT DEVICE
1 EACH CYLINDER
2 EACH CLOSERS
2 EACH OVERHEAD HOLDER
2 EACH KICKPLATES
2 EACH SILENCERS

HARDWARE SET#7
6 EACH HINGES
2 EACH EXIT DEVICES
2 EACH CYLINDERS
2 EACH CLOSERS
2 EACH KICKPLATES
1 SET GASKET
2 EACH SILENCERS
1 EACH ELECTROMAG. HOLDBK

HARDWARE SET#8
6 EACH HINGES
1 PAIR FLUSH BOLTS
1 EACH STOREROOM
2 EACH CLOSERS
2 EACH SILENCERS

HARDWARE SET#8.a
6 EACH HINGES
1 EACH STOREROOM LOCK
2 EACH CLOSER
2 EACH KICKPLATE
2 EACH SILENCERS

HARDWARE SET#9
3 EACH HINGES
1 EACH EXIT DEVICES
1 EACH CYLINDER
1 EACH KICKPLATE
1 EACH WALL STOP
1 SET GASKET

HARDWARE SET#10
3 EACH HINGES
1 EACH ENTRY LOCK
1 EACH CLOSER
1 EACH KICKPLATE
3 EACH SILENCERS

HARDWARE SET#11
3 EACH HINGES
1 EACH ENTRY LOCK
1 EACH KICKPLATE
1 EACH WALL STOP
3 EACH SILENCERS

HARDWARE SET#11.a
3 EACH HINGES
1 EACH ENTRY LOCK
1 EACH CLOSER
1 EACH WALL STOP
1 SET GASKET

HARDWARE SET#12
4 EACH HINGES
1 EACH DUTCH DR BOLT
1 EACH CLASSRM LOCK
1 EACH KICKPLATES
3 EACH SILENCERS

HARDWARE SET#13
3 EACH HINGES
1 EACH PRIVACY SET
1 EACH WALL STOP
3 EACH SILENCERS

HARDWARE SET#14
3 EACH HINGES
1 EACH PASSAGE SET
1 EACH WALL STOP
3 EACH SILENCERS

HARDWARE SET#15
3 EACH HINGES
1 EACH ENTRY LOCK
1 EACH CLOSER
1 EACH KICKPLATE
1 EACH WALL STOP
1 SET GASKET

HARDWARE SET#16
3 EACH HINGES
1 EACH PRIVACY SET
1 EACH CLOSER
1 EACH KICKPLATE
1 EACH WALL STOP
1 SET GASKET

HARDWARE SET#17
3 EACH HINGES
1 EACH CLASSROOM LOCK
1 EACH CLOSER
1 EACH WALL STOP
1 SET GASKET

HARDWARE SET#18
3 EACH HINGES
1 EACH CLASSROOM LOCK
1 EACH CLOSER
1 EACH KICKPLATE
1 EACH WALL STOP
1 SET GASKET

HARDWARE SET#19
6 EACH HINGES
1 PAIR FLUSH BOLTS
1 EACH PASSAGE SET
3 EACH SILENCERS

HARDWARE SET#20
ALL HARDWARE BY DOOR MANUFACTURER

HARDWARE SET#21
1 EACH CYLINDER

MANUFACTURERS USED		ACCEPTABLE SUBSTITUTES
HINGE	MCKINNEY	STANLEY, HAGER
LOCKSETS	SCHLAGE	SARGENT
CLOSERS	LCN	SARGENT
STOPS/BOLTS	GLYNN JOHNSON	DCI, ROCKWOOD
KICKPLATES	ROCKWOOD	BURNS
PUSH/PULLS	ROCKWOOD	BURNS
SEALS	PEMKO	NATIONAL GUARD

Figure 10-7 For commercial projects, more detailed information is required, such as specific door types and finishes, frames, and hardware.

DOOR SCHEDULE

DOOR#	DOOR TYPE	DOOR OPENING				FRAME				HARDWARE	HARDWARE GROUP	REMARKS
		WIDTH	HEIGHT	THICKN'S	MATERIAL	HEAD	JAMB	MATERIAL	FINISH			
1	A	6'-0"	9'-0"	1 3/4"	W'D/GLASS	2	2	W'D	SS	LOCKSET/CLOSER	1	
2	A	6'-0"	9'-0"	1 3/4"	W'D/GLASS	2	2	W'D	SS	LOCKSET/CLOSER	1	
3	B	3'-0"	7'-0"	1 3/4"	W'D	1	1	W'D	SS	LATCHSET	2	SOLID CORE/1-HR ASSEMBLY
4	C	6'-0"	7'-0"	1 3/4"	W'D/GL'S/MT'L	2	2	MT'L	PT	CLOSER	3	SOLID CORE WOOD DOOR W/ STAINLESS STEEL FACING
5	D	3'-0"	7'-0"	1 3/4"	W'D/GL'S/MT'L	2	2	MT'L	PT	CLOSER/DB'L ACTION SPRING	3	PAINT 1 (FRAME)
6	B	3'-0"	7'-0"	1 3/4"	W'D	1	1	W'D	SS	CLOSER	4	SOLID CORE/1-HR ASSEMBLY
7	B	3'-0"	7'-0"	1 3/4"	W'D	1	1	W'D	SS	CLOSER	4	SOLID CORE/1-HR ASSEMBLY
8	E	3'-0"	7'-0"	1 3/4"	MT'L/PT	2	2	MT'L	PT	LOCKSET	5	

HARDWARE GROUPS:

1. HIAWATHA SPHERICAL DOOR PULLS - POLISHED STAINLESS STEEL, POLISHED STAINLESS STEEL PUSHPLATE, 4 SCHLAGE HEAVY DUTY DEADBOLT - BRIGHT CHROMIUM PLATED

2. SCHLAGE MEDITERRANEAN ELITE/TREVI LEVER - BRIGHT CHROMIUM PLATED

3. NEWMARK SPRING LOADED/DOUBLE ACTION HINGES

4. HIAWTHA POLISHED STAINLESS STEEL PUSHPLATE AND PULLPLATE WITH DOUBLE ACTION SPRING ON DOOR 5

5. SCHLAGE HEAVY DUTY TULIP KNOB - BRIGHT CHROMIUM PLATED

6. SCHLAGE GRIP HANDLE ENTRANCE LOCK/TREVI PLYMOUTH- BRIGHT CHROMIUM PLATED

GENERAL NOTES:

1. CONTRACTOR TO SUBMIT COMPLETE HARDWARE SHOP DRAWINGS/CUTS AND KEYING SCHEDULE FOR DESIGNERS APPROVAL.

2. SS= STAIN PER DESIGNER'S SAMPLE AND SEAL WITH VARNISH (TWO COATS MINIMUM.)

Figure 10-8 Door schedules are used to give information about the doors being used in a project, such as their type, frame, width, height, thickness, material, and other details such as hardware types and fire rating.

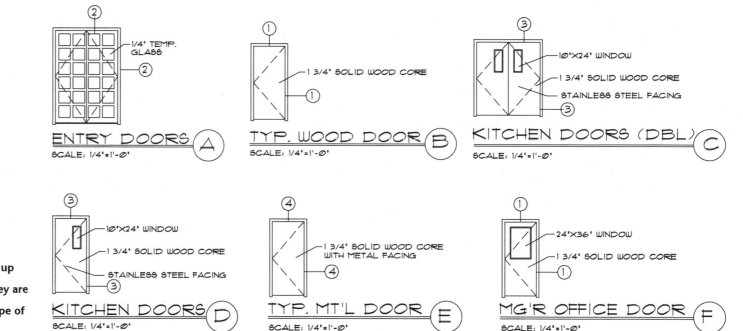

Figure 10-9 Door elevations make up one section of a door schedule; they are graphic representations of each type of door to be used in a project.

DOOR SCHEDULE

IAL	HARDWARE GROUP	REMARKS
W'D	SB-2	SUBMIT SHOP DWGS FOR APPROVAL
W'D	SB-2	
W'D	SB-3	SOLID CORE / 1-HR ASSEMBLY
MT'L	SB-5	MDF CORE W/ MET'L FACING
MT'L	SB-5	MDF CORE W/ MET'L FACING
W'D	SB-3	SOLID CORE / 1-HR ASSEMBLY
W'D	SB-3	SOLID CORE / 1-HR ASSEMBLY
MT'L	SB-5A	

Figure 10-10 The other section of a door schedule is a table listing the bulk of information about the doors used. It includes an area for remarks.

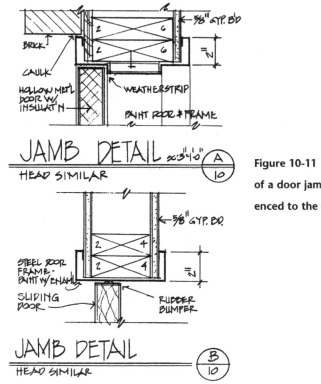

JAMB DETAIL ×:3"=1'0" (A/10)
HEAD SIMILAR

JAMB DETAIL (B/10)
HEAD SIMILAR

Figure 10-11 This enlarged detail of a door jamb is cross-referenced to the door schedule.

The second part of the door schedule is in tabular form and includes the bulk of the information about the given assembly, such as the type of door, material, frame type and material, and the type of hardware. Every schedule should also include an area for remarks for general information not covered in the other columns (Figure 10-10). The door type — solid core flush, sliding, pocket door, etc. — is identified by the letter used in the first section of the door schedule. Door materials might include wood, aluminum, or hollow metal. Frame information might include the head and jamb details of each specific door, if necessary. These details are keyed in the door schedule and are drafted nearby or referenced to another sheet, as illustrated in Figure 10-11. The most common frame materials include wood and aluminum and other metals. The hardware is either called out here or referenced to a more specific hardware group that includes items such as hinges, closers, locksets, and other detailed information. In hand-drafted projects, the door schedule can be easily created by using a spreadsheet or word-processing program. It can then be reproduced on clear plastic film with an adhesive back and adhered to a drawing for blueprinting. It can also be taped on the base sheet and photocopied. In CAD programs, the entire schedule and related drawings can be created simultaneously directly on the sheet.

Checklist for Door Schedules

General

- Start numbering door assignments in a logical sequence on the floor plans. Most systems start with the entry of the building, or work from one side of the plan to the other, trying to place consecutive numbers or symbols where they can easily be followed.

- Title the schedule and cross-reference it to all the plans that it might be used for. Usually only one schedule is included for multiple floors, with a note on each floor plan to see the proper sheet number to find the schedule.
- Make sure lettering, symbols, and line work are clear, concise, and easy to read.

Notations

- Include an abbreviation key near the schedule (or reference to the sheet that explains common abbreviations).
- Cross-reference the schedule to any other drawing that might need clarification.

Dimensions

- Door dimensions can be placed directly on the floor plan in small residential projects.
- Most door sizes and thicknesses are indicated in the door schedule or an elevation view of the door type.

Window Schedules

A window schedule typically includes such information as the window number or identification mark as noted on the floor plan, the quantity required, manufacturer, type, unit size, rough opening, materials, type of glass, and finish (Figure 10-12). A "remarks" column is also useful for special information pertaining to the windows. Window schedules are set up similarly to the door schedule in that they may require two separate parts, depending on the complexity of the project. If there are a wide variety of windows within a project, then elevations and sections may be required to explain how they are to be installed or any special features (Figure 10-13). Interior designers may have to specify exterior windows as

WINDOW SCHEDULE

WINDOW SYMBOL	QUANTITY	MANF. / STYLE	MODEL NO.	UNIT SIZE	ROUGH OPENING	TYPE	FINISH	TYPE OF GLASS	REMARKS
A	7	PELLA / ARCHITECT. SERIES	CM3553	2'-11" x 4'-5"	2'-11 3/4" x 4'-5 3/4"	CLAD CASEMENT	WHITE	5/8" CLEAR TEMPERED	
B	3	PELLA / ARCHITECT. SERIES	CCH35531	5'-10" x 4'-5"	5'-10 3/4" x 4'-5 3/4"	CLAD CASEMENT	WHITE	5/8" CLEAR TEMPERED	3 PAIRS ARCH-TOP WINDOWS
C	5	PELLA / ARCHITECT. SERIES	CCM35536	2'-11" x 4'-5"	2'-11 3/4" x 4'-5 3/4"	CLAD CASEMENT	WHITE	5/8" CLEAR TEMPERED	ARCHED WINDOWS
D	2	PELLA / ARCHITECT. SERIES	CM1711	1'-5" x 5'-11"	1'-5 3/4" x 5'-11 3/4"	CLAD CASEMENT	WHITE	5/8" CLEAR TEMPERED	
E	1	PELLA / ARCHITECT. SERIES	CM3535	2'-11" x 2'-11"	2'-11 3/4" x 2'-11 3/4"	CLAD CASEMENT	WHITE	5/8" CLEAR TEMPERED	

NOTES:
1. CONTRACTOR TO FIELD MEASURE FOR CUSTOM WINDOW SIZES. VERIFY ANY DISCREPANCIES WITH DESIGNER.
2. SUBMIT SHOP DRAWINGS TO DESIGNER FOR APPROVAL BEFORE ORDERING & INSTALLATION.
3. SEE WINDOW TYPES FOR LOCATION OF MULLIONS.

Figure 10-12 Window schedules include information about the windows being used, such as the identification mark, quantity, type, size, rough opening, materials, type of glass, and finish.

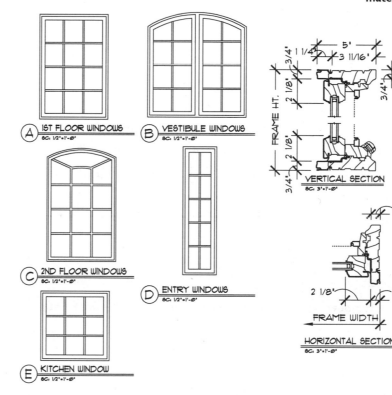

A 1ST FLOOR WINDOWS SC: 1/2"=1'-0"
B VESTIBULE WINDOWS SC: 1/2"=1'-0"
C 2ND FLOOR WINDOWS SC: 1/2"=1'-0"
D ENTRY WINDOWS SC: 1/2"=1'-0"
E KITCHEN WINDOW SC: 1/2"=1'-0"

VERTICAL SECTION SC: 3"=1'-0"
HORIZONTAL SECTION SC: 3"=1'-0"
FRAME HT.
FRAME WIDTH

Figure 10-13 Windows can be further explained with elevations and details showing installation methods or special features.

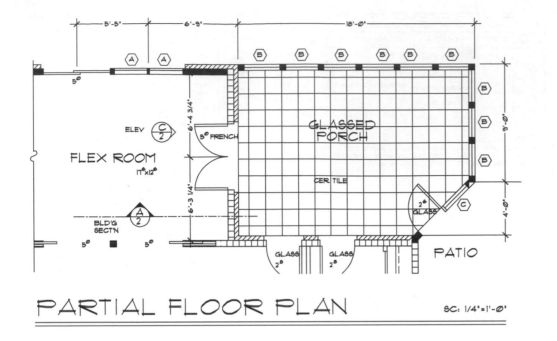

PARTIAL FLOOR PLAN

SC: 1/4"=1'-0"

two or more windows are the same they may share the same number. However, make sure that identical windows have the exact same head, sill, and jamb conditions, because details are referenced from these elevations. The glazing system and glass must also be identical for each window.

Checklist for Window Schedules

General

- Identify the windows with their appropriate symbols in a logical sequence on the floor plans.

- Add a note on the floor plan(s) or sheet index (for a set of drawings) telling where window schedule can be found.

- In elevation views, show the direction operable window units swing.

- Title the schedule and cross-reference it to all the plans that it might be used for. Usually only one schedule is included for multiple floors, with a note on each floor plan to see the proper sheet number to find the schedule.

- Make sure lettering, symbols, and line work are clear, concise, and easy to read.

- Draw window elevations and details where necessary and cross-reference to the window schedule.

Notations

- Include an abbreviation key near the schedule (or reference to the sheet that explains common abbreviations).

- Cross-reference the schedule to any other drawing that might need clarification.

- Note where windows might have special materials, such as tempered glass.

Figure 10-14 Windows are generally noted on a floor plan or elevation with a number or letter inside a polygon-shaped symbol.

well as interior glass windows, or what are commonly referred to as interior glass partitions, depending on the scope of the project, and whether it is a building addition or interior tenant build-out.

Window elevations and sections should be located beside the tabular window schedule so they can refer to one another and be keyed accordingly. Window elevations and sections are typically drawn at a ¼" = 1'-0" scale (1:50 metric); however, ⅛" = 1'-0" (1:100 metric) or ½" = 1'-0" (1:20 metric) may be more appropriate for some projects.

Window types are generally referenced on the floor plan and elevations by means of a polygon-shaped symbol with a number inside it, as illustrated in Figure 10-14. The same symbol and number should also be drafted under the window elevation that is shown. Every window that is different should have a number; if

Finish Schedules

Finish schedules are created to show, in tabular form, the finish materials to be applied to each wall and floor surface of a project. The schedule is generally set up showing each room by name or number along the left side of a sheet. Column heads are then drawn across the top for each wall surface, floor, base, ceiling, and any other special features of a room. A "remarks" column is also a helpful addition for any miscellaneous comments that might be needed to clarify the design intent, as shown in Figure 10-15. Sometimes the walls in a room will have different finishes. For example, three walls may be painted and the fourth wall finished in wood paneling. In order to clarify which wall receives the proper treatment, each wall of each room is noted on the finish schedule. The most common way to record this information is to relate each wall to its orientation: the north, east, south, and west com-

pass directions. In individual rooms or single walls with complex finishes, it may be necessary to supplement the finish schedule with wall elevations for further clarity, as shown in Figure 10-16.

The finish schedule consists of two different parts: the main section, which is in tabular form, and the second section, called the legend or materials key. The first part is used primarily to indicate which floor and wall will receive what type of finish. Therefore, the information provided in the schedule should be generic. Trade or manufacturers' names are indicated in the legend. For example, a P may be used in the schedule to indicate that a particular wall will be finished with paint. The P will then be repeated in the materials key, which will indicate what paint manufacturer will be used as well as what type of paint and what color. If several different types or colors of paint are to be used within the same project, each type and/or color would get a different symbol, such as P-1, P-2, P-3,

ROOM FINISHES SCHEDULE

ROOM NO.	ROOM NAME	FLOOR	BASE	WALLS				CEILING		NOTES
				NORTH	EAST	SOUTH	WEST	HEIGHT	MATERIAL / FINISH	
201	RECEPTION	SEE PLAN	WB-1	WC-1	SEE PLAN	WC-1	WC-1	9'-0"	GYP. BD. / PT-3	SEE DRAWINGS FOR SIGNAGE ON EAST WALL
202	SALES	CPT-1	WB-1	WC-2	WC-2	WC-2	WC-2	9'-0"	GYP. BD. / PT-3	
203	CONFERENCE A	CPT-2	WB-1	WC-2	WC-3	WC-2	WC-3	10'-0"	ACOUSTICAL TILE	PT-3 FOR GYP. BD. CEILING AT BORDERS
204	CONFERENCE B	CPT-2	WB-1	WC-2	WC-4	WC-2	WC-4	10'-0"	ACOUSTICAL TILE	PT-3 FOR GYP. BD. CEILING AT BORDERS
205	KITCHEN	VCT-1	RB-1	PT-1	PT-2	PT-1	PT-1	10'-0"	ACOUSTICAL TILE	
206	CLOSET	VCT-1	RB-1	WC-2	WC-4	WC-2	WC-4	10'-0"	ACOUSTICAL TILE	
207	STORAGE	VCT-1	RB-1	PT-1	PT-1	PT-1	PT-1	10'-0"	ACOUSTICAL TILE	
208	OPEN OFFICE	CPT-3	RB-1	PT-2	PT-2	PT-2	PT-2	10'-0"	ACOUSTICAL TILE	
209	CORRIDOR	CPT-3	RB-1	PT-2	PT-2	PT-2	PT-2	10'-0"	ACOUSTICAL TILE	
210	OFFICE	CPT-1	RB-1	PT-1	PT-1	PT-1	PT-1	9'-0"	ACOUSTICAL TILE	
211	OFFICE	CPT-1	RB-1	PT-1	PT-1	PT-1	PT-1	9'-0"	ACOUSTICAL TILE	
212	WOMENS RESTROOM	CT-1	CT-1	CT-2	CT-2	CT-2	SEE PLAN	9'-0"	GYP. BD. / PT-3	
213	MENS RESTROOM	CT-1	CT-1	CT-2	SEE PLAN	CT-2	CT-2	9'-0"	GYP. BD. / PT-3	

Figure 10-15 Room-finish schedules show the finish materials to be applied to each surface in a room; they should also include a section for notes.

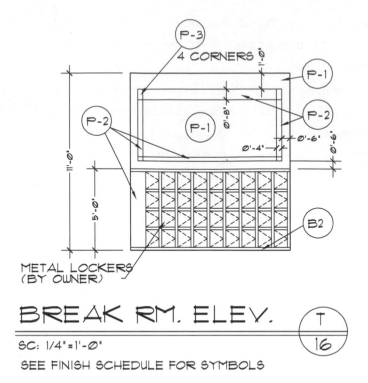

Figure 10-16 An elevation may accompany the finish schedule to show where selected finishes are to be placed.

BREAK RM. ELEV.

T 16

SC: 1/4"=1'-0"

SEE FINISH SCHEDULE FOR SYMBOLS

and so on. This keying system saves a tremendous amount of time and space in preparing the finish schedule. Interior room finish schedules will vary in complexity and presentation, depending upon the amount of information required. For example, in a residential project where all walls of each room will have a common interior finish, the schedule can be rather brief. Commercial projects generally have a much wider range of interior finishes, with wall treatments ranging from simple painted drywall to expensive custom-made paneling. In these situations, the interior room finish schedule must also be coordinated with the floor plan, or drawn as a separate finish plan, as explained in Chapter 11. A variety of symbols are used on the floor plan to identify interior finishes in each room with the interior finish schedule.

Checklist for Finish Schedules

General

- Identify the rooms and finishes and their appropriate symbols in a clear manner in the schedule.

- Title the schedule and cross-reference it to all the plans that it might be used for. Usually only one schedule is included for multiple floors, with a note on each floor plan to see the proper sheet number to find the schedule.

- Make sure lettering, symbols, and line work are clear, concise, and easy to read.

Notations

- Include an abbreviation key near the schedule (or reference to the sheet that explains common abbreviations).

- Cross-reference the schedule to any other drawing that might need clarification.

Dimensions

- Dimensions are generally not needed on a finish schedule, unless a finish has a specific size, such as a 4-inch (101 mm) vinyl base or a 2 feet x 4 feet (60.9 x 122 cm) suspended acoustical tile ceiling.

Other Schedules

A number of other schedules may be used in a set of construction drawings relating to the structure and mechanical, plumbing, and electrical systems. Schedules are also made to delineate the various parties' responsibilities for supplying and installing the materials for a project. For example, a schedule can be used for a custom wall cabinet unit that is supplied by a manufacturer and installed by the general contractor, with custom glass doors furnished and installed by the owner. Examples of other types of schedules and their applications are discussed in the appropriate chapters of this book.

FINISH PLANS 11

There are a variety of ways to communicate what interior finishes are required for a project. Traditionally, a finish schedule is developed in tabular form, listing each room or space and the specific types of finishes that are to be applied to the floors, walls, bases, and ceilings (Figure 11-1). Finish schedules are discussed in more detail in Chapter 10. In residential and small commercial projects where only a single finish is applied on each wall and one or two different floor finishes are used, a finish schedule works fairly well. In some interior projects, however, rooms have more than four walls, and they don't necessarily correspond to the compass directions keyed on the plan as north, south, east, and west. In such cases, it can be difficult to use only a finish schedule to accurately locate the corresponding finishes in the space. A room might also have complex angles and curves that cannot be effectively communicated by means of a finish schedule.

In large or complex interiors, when there is more than one type of finish on each wall, or when there are other complex finish configurations, such as a tile design on a floor, a finish plan is more appropriate. A finish plan, as shown in Figure 11-2, shows the finish material to be applied to wall and floor surfaces graphically, with a corresponding legend (Figure 11-3).

The finish plan codes and graphically indicates where each surface treatment goes. The code is then keyed to a legend and cross-referenced to written specifications, if necessary. The legend specifies the exact material, manufacturer, catalog number, color, fire rating, and any other specific information necessary for a successful application, as illustrated in Figure 11-4. A number or a combination of alphabetical letters and a number generally forms the code. For example, all carpet floor notations could be preceded with a "C" or "FC" for floor covering, and then given numerical designations such as FC-1, FC-2, and so on, as shown in Figure 11-5. The code for a wall treatment may indicate a single wall finish, such as "P" for paint, or a combination of treatments, such as WC-1/WB-2 for wainscot and wall base. Some common abbreviations are shown in Table 11-1. If the wall base finish or the trim is the same through-

ROOM FINISH SCHEDULE

ROOM	FLOOR			BASE			WALLS			CEILING			NOTES
	CARPET	HARDWOOD	CERAMIC TILE	WOOD	VINYL	CERAMIC TILE	WALLPAPER	PAINT	CERAMIC TILE	PTD. GYP. BD.	WOOD	ACOUS. TILE	
FOYER		●		●			●				●		COFFERED CEILING
LIVING ROOM		●		●			●			●			
DINING ROOM		●		●			●			●			
KITCHEN		●				●		●		●			
BREAKFAST NOOK		●				●		●		●			
GREAT ROOM	●			●				●		●			
OFFICE	●			●				●				●	
LAUNDRY/ MUD ROOM		●			●			●		●			
MASTER BEDROOM	●			●			●			●			
MASTER BATH		●				●		●		●			
POWDER ROOM		●					●	●	●	●			CERAMIC TILE WAINSCOT
BEDROOM 1	●			●			●			●			
BEDROOM 2	●			●				●		●			
BATHROOM (2ND FLR)		●				●		●		●			
BONUS ROOM	●			●				●		●			

Figure 11-1 Room-finish schedules are commonly used in interior construction plans.

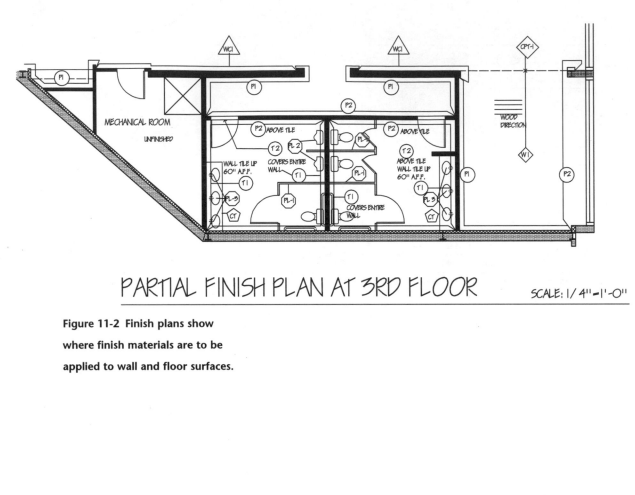

PARTIAL FINISH PLAN AT 3RD FLOOR

SCALE: 1/4"=1'-0"

Figure 11-2 Finish plans show where finish materials are to be applied to wall and floor surfaces.

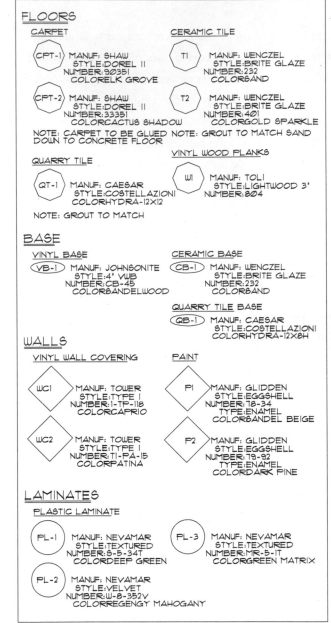

FINISH SCHEDULE

FLOORS

CARPET

CPT-1 MANUF: SHAW
STYLE:DOREL II
NUMBER:90351
COLORELK GROVE

CPT-2 MANUF: SHAW
STYLE:DOREL II
NUMBER:33351
COLORCACTUS SHADOW

NOTE: CARPET TO BE GLUED DOWN TO CONCRETE FLOOR

CERAMIC TILE

T1 MANUF: WENCZEL
STYLE:BRITE GLAZE
NUMBER:232
COLORSAND

T2 MANUF: WENCZEL
STYLE:BRITE GLAZE
NUMBER:401
COLORGOLD SPARKLE

NOTE: GROUT TO MATCH SAND

QUARRY TILE

QT-1 MANUF: CAESAR
STYLE:COSTELLAZIONI
COLORHYDRA-12X12

NOTE: GROUT TO MATCH

VINYL WOOD PLANKS

W1 MANUF: TOLI
STYLE:LIGHTWOOD 3'
NUMBER:804

BASE

VINYL BASE

VB-1 MANUF: JOHNSONITE
STYLE:4' VVB
NUMBER:CB-45
COLORSANDELWOOD

CERAMIC BASE

CB-1 MANUF: WENCZEL
STYLE:BRITE GLAZE
NUMBER:232
COLORSAND

QUARRY TILE BASE

QB-1 MANUF: CAESAR
STYLE:COSTELLAZIONI
COLORHYDRA-12X8H

WALLS

VINYL WALL COVERING

WC1 MANUF: TOWER
STYLE:TYPE I
NUMBER:I-TP-118
COLORCAPRIO

WC2 MANUF: TOWER
STYLE:TYPE I
NUMBER:TI-PA-15
COLORPATINA

PAINT

P1 MANUF: GLIDDEN
STYLE:EGGSHELL
NUMBER:78-34
TYPE:ENAMEL
COLORSANDEL BEIGE

P2 MANUF: GLIDDEN
STYLE:EGGSHELL
NUMBER:79-92
TYPE:ENAMEL
COLORDARK PINE

LAMINATES

PLASTIC LAMINATE

PL-1 MANUF: NEVAMAR
STYLE:TEXTURED
NUMBER:S-5-34T
COLORDEEP GREEN

PL-2 MANUF: NEVAMAR
STYLE:VELVET
NUMBER:W-8-352V
COLORREGENGY MAHOGANY

PL-3 MANUF: NEVAMAR
STYLE:TEXTURED
NUMBER:MR-5-1T
COLORGREEN MATRIX

Figure 11-3 A finish legend that accompanies a finish plan.

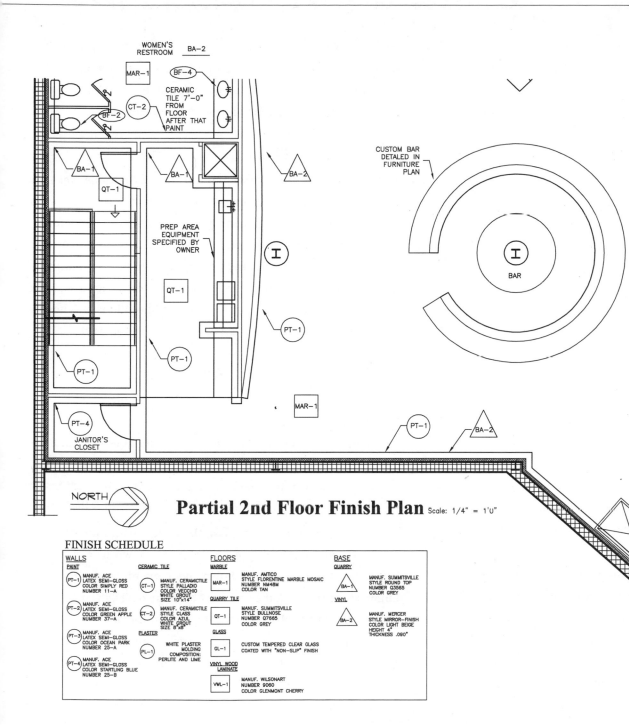

WOMEN'S RESTROOM BA-2

MAR-1   BF-4

CERAMIC TILE 7'-0" FROM FLOOR AFTER THAT PAINT

CT-2   BF-2

BA-1   BA-1   BA-2

QT-1

CUSTOM BAR DETAILED IN FURNITURE PLAN

PREP AREA EQUIPMENT SPECIFIED BY OWNER

QT-1

BAR

PT-1

PT-1

PT-1

MAR-1

PT-4

JANITOR'S CLOSET

PT-1   BA-2

NORTH

Partial 2nd Floor Finish Plan Scale: 1/4" = 1'0"

FINISH SCHEDULE

WALLS

PAINT

(PT-1) MANUF. ACE LATEX SEMI-GLOSS COLOR SIMPLY RED NUMBER 11-A

(PT-2) MANUF. ACE LATEX SEMI-GLOSS COLOR GREEN APPLE NUMBER 37-A

(PT-3) MANUF. ACE LATEX SEMI-GLOSS COLOR OCEAN PARK NUMBER 25-A

(PT-4) MANUF. ACE LATEX SEMI-GLOSS COLOR STARTLING BLUE NUMBER 25-B

CERAMIC TILE

(CT-1) MANUF. CERAMICTILE STYLE PALLADIO COLOR VECCHIO WHITE GROUT SIZE 10"x14"

(CT-2) MANUF. CERAMICTILE STYLE CLASS COLOR AZUL WHITE GROUT SIZE 6"x6"

PLASTER

(PL-1) WHITE PLASTER MOLDING COMPOSITION: PERLITE AND LIME

FLOORS

MARBLE

[MAR-1] MANUF. AMTICO STYLE FLORENTINE MARBLE MOSAIC NUMBER NM48M COLOR TAN

QUARRY TILE

[QT-1] MANUF. SUMMITSVILLE STYLE BULLNOSE NUMBER Q7665 COLOR GREY

GLASS

[GL-1] CUSTOM TEMPERED CLEAR GLASS COATED WITH "NON-SLIP" FINISH

VINYL WOOD LAMINATE

[VWL-1] MANUF. WILSONART NUMBER 9060 COLOR GLENMONT CHERRY

BASE

QUARRY

(BA-1) MANUF. SUMMITSVILLE STYLE ROUND TOP NUMBER Q3565 COLOR GREY

VINYL

(BA-2) MANUF. MERCER STYLE MIRROR-FINISH COLOR LIGHT BEIGE HEIGHT 4" THICKNESS .090"

Figure 11-4 The symbols on the finish plan are keyed to a legend that specifies the materials, manufacturer, catalog number, color, fire rating, and any other information necessary for successful installation.

FLOOR COVERING SCHEDULE

FLOOR COVERING

FC-1	CARPET MANF: WINFIELD STYLE: CIRCUS COLOR: GREEN APPLE WIDTH: 12'-0'	
FC-2	RESILIENT FLOORING MANF: JOHNSTON STYLE: METRO (VINYL) COLOR: ELECTRIC BLUE SIZE: 12' x 12' TILES	*BASE: 2 1/2' VINYL COVE BASE - JOHNSTON/ OCEAN #621
FC-3	MARBLE MANF: IGRL STYLE: REGENCY COLOR: ROYAL CREAM SIZE: 18' x 18' x 3/8'	* GROUT: GRISSOM/ BEIGE #422-1
FC-4	CERAMIC TILE MANF: FLORIDIAN TILE STYLE: SEABREEZE COLOR: TANGERINE SIZE: 12' x 12' x 3/8'	* GROUT: GRISSOM/ BEIGE #422-1

FLOOR COVERING NOTES

1. GROUT TO BE SUPPLIED & INSTALLED BY G.C. TILES TO BE INSTALLED WITH CONSISTENT GROUT WIDTH THROUGHOUT - APPROX. 1/16' GROUT JOINT WIDTH.

2. CERAMIC TILE TO BE SUPPLIED BY OWNER, INSTALLED BY G.C. TILES TO BE INSTALLED WITH CONSISTENT GROUT WIDTH THROUGHOUT - APPROX. 1/4' GROUT JOINT WIDTH.

Figure 11-5 An example of a floor-covering schedule for a commercial project.

PAINT SCHEDULE

SUPPLIED AND APPLIED BY THE GENERAL CONTRACTOR, UNLESS NOTED OTHERWISE.
NOTES:

1. PAINT MANUFACTURER IS SPECIFIED AS GLIDDEN PAINTS. SUBSTITUTIONS ALLOWED ARE BENJAMIN MOORE AND SHERWIN-WILLIAMS.

2. PREFERRED METHOD OF PAINT APPLICATION IS BY SPRAY APPLICATION.

P-1	GLIDDEN 1067 - SEMI-GLOSS LATEX - LT. BEIGE
P-2	GLIDDEN 1064 - FLAT FINISH LATEX - IVORY
P-3	GLIDDEN 2364 - SEMI-GLOSS LATEX - LT. PINK
P-4	GLIDDEN 1254 - SEMI-GLOSS FINISH LATEX - MEDIUM PINK

PAINT NOTES

1. CONTRACTOR TO REVIEW DETAIL SHEETS, FINISH PLANS, AND ELEVATIONS FOR PAINTED SURFACES.

2. ALL FACTORY WHITE SPEAKER PLATES TO BE SPRAY PAINTED TO MATCH ADJACENT SURFACES.

3. ALL WOOD SURFACES ARE TO BE PRIMED WITH OIL-BASED PRIMER AND FINISHED W/OIL-BASE SEMI-GLOSS PAINT.

4. ALL METAL SURFACES TO BE PAINTED SHALL FIRST BE PRIMED WITH METAL PRIMER AND FINISHED WITH SEMI-GLOSS OIL-BASED PAINT.

5. FINISH COATS MUST NOT SHOW BRUSH MARKS, IF THIS METHOD IS USED VS. SPRAYING OF ANY MISCELLANEOUS ITEM.

Figure 11-6 A detailed paint schedule is helpful in commercial projects where several walls and details are to be painted.

out the project, a general note will be sufficient. Also, if the majority of the walls are finished the same, this could be indicated in a general note and only the exceptions graphically drawn on the plan or in an accompanying schedule (Figure 11-6).

Scale of Finish Plans

Finish plans are drawn at as small a scale as possible, yet large enough to accurately convey information critical for placing finishes. The finishes are drawn in plan view simplistically, preventing clutter for ease of recognition. As there is often not a lot of detailed information that needs to be drawn in the floor-plan view, a scale of ⅛" =1'-0" (1:100 metric) is generally used. However, if sufficient detail is needed to clarify exact configurations or details of the pieces, a scale of ¼" = 1'-0" (1:50 metric) can be used.

Drafting Standards for Finish Plans

The advantage of the dedicated finish plan is that more detailed information can be given to the workers on locations of specific finish treatments. A finish plan helps eliminate questions and mistakes that might arise if a finish schedule alone were used. However, remember that items such as installation instructions are not included on the finish plan, but in the written specifications.

When drawing the finish plan, the designer uses lines to show the extent and location of each finish, as shown in Figure 11-7. When the finish lines are drawn, door openings are generally ignored to ensure that the surfaces above the doors, in corners, and between doors are also covered. Finishes on the doors and frames are either specified in a note or referred to on the door schedule; they are not generally a part of the finish plan. However, some designers prefer to list their colors here on this sheet to coordinate with other finish and color selections. Floor finishes and wall finishes can generally be indicated on one drawing. However, if complex floor patterns are designed, a separate large-scale floor-finish drawing may be needed for clarity, as illustrated in Figure 11-8.

Designation of Materials in Finish Plans

If the plan or detail of a particular area is drawn at a scale of ½" = 1'-0" (1:20 metric), material sizes might be shown in the plan view. However, the plans are generally too small to accurately represent the size of most materials. For example, 4 x 4 in. (101.6 mm) is too small to draw at the ⅛" (1:100 metric) or ¼" (1:50 metric) scales. Likewise, the attempt at drawing wood grain in floors or even the widths and lengths of random floor planks is not necessary in these small-scale drawings. The most critical item to include in such cases is the start and stop of the flooring, and the direction of the pattern if it has one. In many CAD programs, the software for rendering finish materials is available, but the readability of the drawing should take precedence over drawing them to scale. A different scale can be selected and assigned to the patterns for ease of visibility. As mentioned before, this can be done on a large blow-up drawing of the finish material, cross-referenced to the main plan. See Figure 11-9 for a detail of a tile floor pattern.

Sometimes a texture, color, fabric, or other feature cannot be accurately specified in the finish schedule. In such instances, a swatch of material or paint color chip is often attached to the drawing or put in the specification booklet. Or a material can be scanned and placed digitally in the schedule, as illustrated in Figure 11-10.

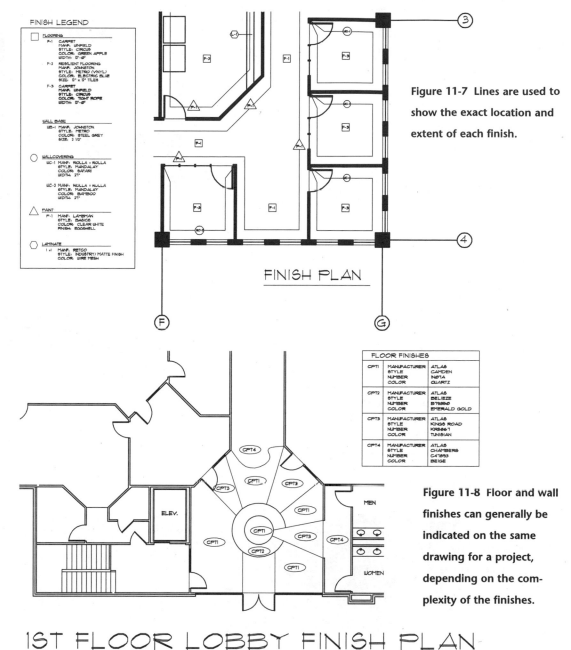

Figure 11-7 Lines are used to show the exact location and extent of each finish.

FINISH PLAN

Figure 11-8 Floor and wall finishes can generally be indicated on the same drawing for a project, depending on the complexity of the finishes.

1ST FLOOR LOBBY FINISH PLAN

SC: 1/8" = 1'-0"

Figure 11-9 Enlarged detail of a custom tile floor pattern.

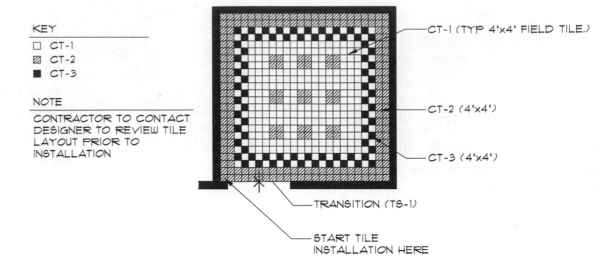

KEY

☐ CT-1
▨ CT-2
■ CT-3

NOTE

CONTRACTOR TO CONTACT DESIGNER TO REVIEW TILE LAYOUT PRIOR TO INSTALLATION

CT-1 (TYP 4'x4' FIELD TILE.)

CT-2 (4'x4')

CT-3 (4'x4')

TRANSITION (TS-1)

START TILE INSTALLATION HERE

Figure 11-10 A specification using an actual material swatch.

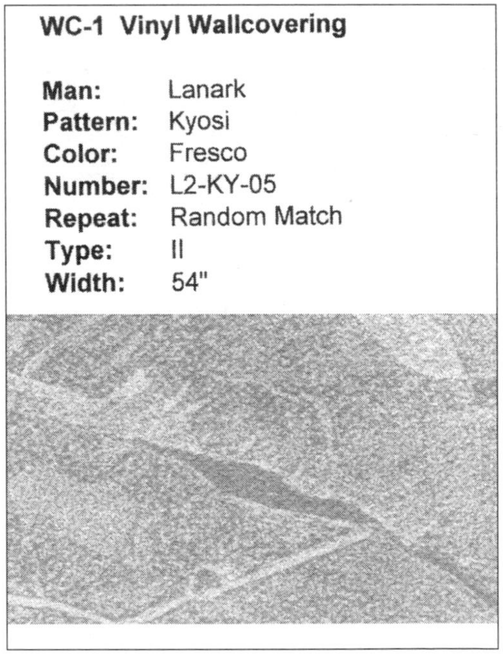

12 / A5.2   CERAMIC TILE FLOOR PATTERN

SC: 1/4"=1'-∅"

WC-1 Vinyl Wallcovering

Man:	Lanark
Pattern:	Kyosi
Color:	Fresco
Number:	L2-KY-05
Repeat:	Random Match
Type:	II
Width:	54"

Dimensioning Finish Plans

Generally, there is not a lot of dimensioning on the finish plan. As long as the plan is drawn to scale and the dimensions of the spaces and structure are indicated on the floor plan(s), the finishes can be estimated from these or other drawings. However, in some cases, dimensions are needed to describe limits of finishes or start and stop points occuring in areas that are not easily referenced in the plan view. Alignment and direction of patterns might need to be dimensioned directly on the plan, as illustrated in Figure 11-11. In these instances, references should be given that are easily obtainable in the field. Dimensions should be referenced from the face of a wall, column, or imaginary centerline of a room.

Checklist for Finish Plans

General

- Title the drawing, note its scale, and identify north (or reference direction).

- Title the accompanying finish schedule and key it to the plan.

- Place finish schedule on the same sheet as the finish plan (if possible) or on a sheet immediately preceding or following the plan.

- Clean up the plan (or in CAD, turn off superfluous information) so the walls, spaces, and key codes are clear, dark, and very legible.

- Number or name all applicable rooms/spaces where necessary.

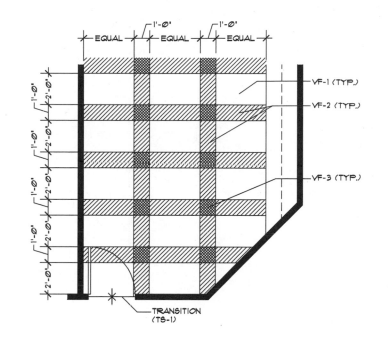

Figure 11-11 A detail for a custom floor pattern with dimensions.

Table 11-1 Common Abbreviations for Interior Finishes

FLOORS
_____

FC - FLOORCOVERING
C - CARPET
CPT - CARPET
CT - CERAMIC TILE
VCT - VINYL COMPOSITION TILE
W - WOOD
VWP - VINYL WOOD PLANKS
SV - SHEET VINYL
ST - STONE

BASES
_____

VB - VINYL BASE
RB - RUBBER BASE
CB - CERAMIC BASE
QB - QUARRY TILE BASE
WB - WOOD BASE
STB - STONE BASE

WALLS
_____

WT - WALL TREATMENT
WC - WALLCOVERING
P or PT - PAINT
VWC - VINYL WALL COVERING
CT - CERAMIC TILE

LAMINATES (OR COUNTERTOPS)
_____

PL - PLASTIC LAMINATE
SS - SOLID SURFACE

PLUMBING
_____

PF - PLUMBING FIXTURES

Notations

- Cross-reference the plan (and schedule if applicable) to other drawings that might contain information critical to the finish plan.

- Note special features, clearances, alignments, and other important items.

- Cross-reference the finish plan and finish schedule, carefully checking for accuracy and completeness of information.

- Add notes on issues for the installer to be alert to when placing the finishes.

- Show or call out directions of linear patterns, such as strip wood flooring.

- If the designer is to approve a trial layout (such as floor or wall tile) in the field, add a note to this effect.

Dimensions

- Dimension clearances, alignments, and other controlling factors.

- Call out for the installer or contractor to verify existing dimensions of the space/structure with those shown on the finish, and verify these with the designer before installation.

FURNITURE INSTALLATION PLANS 12

The selection of furniture is an integral phase in the design of interior spaces, as it affects human functions and desires. Spaces can also be personalized by furniture, which reflects individual preferences, activities, and needs. This chapter will discuss furniture in both residential and commercial buildings. In commercial spaces, furniture generally reflects the concept, theme, or image an establishment wants to convey to the public or their clients. The selection of furniture in residential spaces often reflects the personal tastes and lifestyles of the individuals who occupy them.

Furniture is often included in what interior designers call the furniture, furnishings, and equipment (FF&E) package. (This terminology is found in many documents available through professional design societies, such as ASID, IIDA, and AIA.) Furniture provides for users' daily needs and completes the humanization of the environment. Furniture is often planned for early in an interior-design project. It may even be a design generator. For example, space can be organized around the placement of furniture to define traffic patterns or provide conversation areas.

Most interior projects involve the reuse of some existing furniture. Depending on the budget for the project and the condition of the existing furniture, such pieces might be reused in their original condition or refurbished for coordination with the designer's new concepts.

The design of interior environments with furniture often begins during the programming and space planning. These intial steps define the furniture needs in terms of type, size, and quantity. It then continues throughout the project, with the exact placement

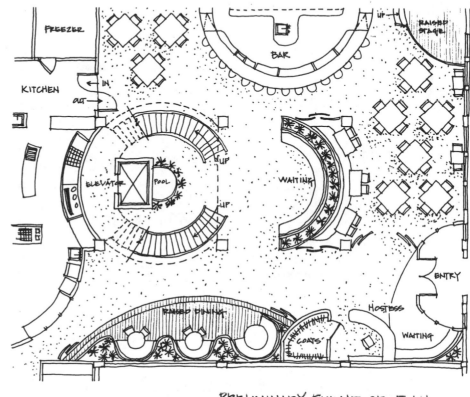

PRELIMINARY FURNITURE PLAN

and selection of individual characteristics often occurring after the initial programming and planning.

For specifying, ordering, and placing furniture, several steps are needed. The first step is to ascertain the client's activities in a space and what furniture is needed to perform these. During this phase, the furniture selection is often generic, which means the exact furniture pieces are not selected. For example, a conference table

Figure 12-1 A preliminary furniture plan for a proposed restaurant.

161

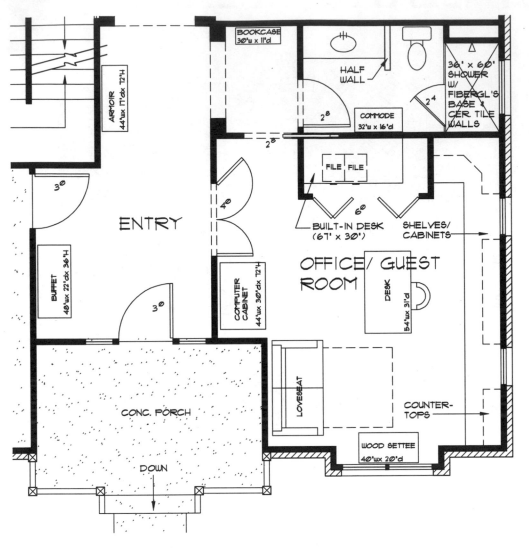

Figure 12-2 In small projects, furniture selections can be noted directly on the plan view.

might be specified as requiring seating for eight people. At this time, the designer might not even determine whether the table will be round, rectangular, or oval. However, this selection of form will occur soon, as it could have a major impact on the space planning by affecting clearances around the table for seating and circulation. The next step is the creation of a preliminary furniture plan to determine furniture number, groups, and orientation to support user activities, as illustrated in Figure 12-1. Next, a scaled furniture plan is drawn using the actual dimensions of the furniture pieces and an accompanying schedule is made. The next process is the creation of what is referred to as a job or control book or catalog, listing the specifications of each piece of furniture involved in the project. These are cross-referenced to the written specifications as to the standards to be met in the performance of the work, for the materials and the installation. The written specifications have the same contractual weight as the construction drawings and are part of the contract documents.

The exact placement of furniture is important in interior-design projects. In many projects, a separate drawing is created to show the final placement and orientation of the selected furniture. This is the furniture plan, or what is commonly called the furniture installation plan. It may include new, existing, and future pieces of furniture and related items. The selected pieces of furniture might be keyed directly to the plan view, as illustrated in Figure 12-2. However, most furniture plans in commercial projects include an accompanying key or schedule that is referenced to the plan view (Figure 12-3). Code numbers identify each piece of furniture. Information on pricing and ordering, as well as the final placement of the furniture, will generally be included in the job or control book.

FURNITURE SCHEDULE (PARTIAL EXAMPLE)

MARK	QUANTITY	MANUFACTURER	DESCRIPTION	FABRIC/ FINISH	REMARKS	MARK	QUANTITY	MANUFACTURER	DESCRIPTION	FABRIC/ FINISH	REMARKS
C-1	90	MIKE INDUSTRIES, INC.	20-485 NELSON CHAIR 20W, 22D, 35H	SEAT: NUANCE, LIZ JORDON-HILL, MAHOGANY FRAME: POLISHED CHROME	CLASS A FLAME SPREAD FABRIC	T-3	11	FALCON PRODUCTS	CUSTOM WOOD TABLE TOP 30"X36"	SOLID OAK TOPS W/ NATURAL MAPLE STAIN	FIELD FINISH TO MATCH DESIGNER'S EXAMPLE
C-2	30	MIKE INDUSTRIES, INC.	35-670 SONAR BARSTOOL 19W, 19D, 45H - 30"SH	SEAT: 2057-701 TALISMAN DESIGNTEX FRAME: NATURAL MAPLE CAPS: BRUSHED CROME	CLASS A FLAME SPREAD FABRIC	T-4	6	FALCON PRODUCTS	CUSTOM WOOD TABLE TOP 36" DIA. ROUND	SOLID OAK TOPS W/ NATURAL MAPLE STAIN	TOP WITH STAINLESS STL INSET STRIP - SEE DETAIL, SHT 22
T-1	16	FALCON PRODUCTS	CUSTOM WOOD TABLE TOP 48" DIA. ROUND	SOLID OAK TOPS W/ NATURAL MAPLE STAIN	BASE TB BRUSHED CHROME - SEE LISTING UNDER TB	T-5	5	FALCON PRODUCTS	CUSTOM WOOD TABLE TOP 42" DIA. ROUND	SOLID OAK TOPS W/ NATURAL MAPLE STAIN	FIELD FINISH TO MATCH DESIGNER'S EXAMPLE
T-2	12	FALCON PRODUCTS	CUSTOM WOOD TABLE TOP 42"X42"	SOLID OAK TOPS W/ NATURAL MAPLE STAIN		T-6	7	BROWN JORDON	2901-4800 DINING TABLE 42" DIA. ROUND	FRAME: POLISHED STAINLESS STEEL W/ VENEERED TOP	

Figure 12-3 A furniture plan shows the placement of each piece of furniture. It is referenced by a symbol to an accompanying furniture schedule that details the specifications of the component.

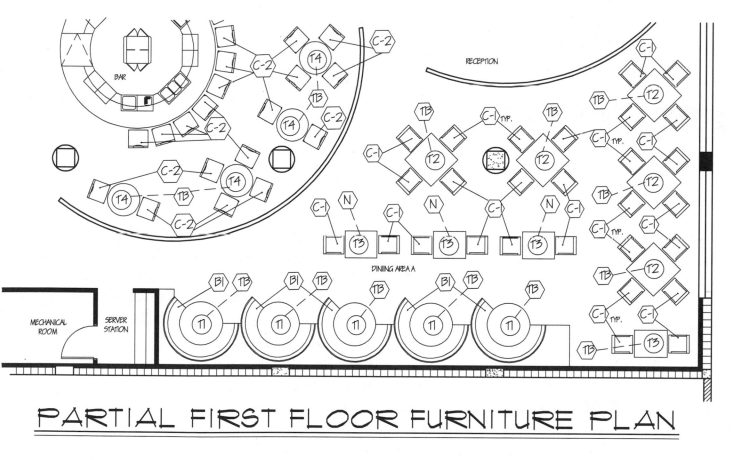

PARTIAL FIRST FLOOR FURNITURE PLAN

PROJECT:	JOHNSON & KLINKER, INC.
ITEM #:	T11
QUANTITY:	4
MANF:	VECTA
MODEL:	GINKGO BILOBA - 606902
DESCRIPTION:	ROUND CONFERENCE TABLE WITH WOOD VENEER TOP AND ALUMINUM TUBE BASE
	W: 48" DIA.
	H: 29"
FINISH:	NATURAL CHERRY
LOCATION:	CONFERENCE ROOM 2004
ILLUSTRATION:	

DATE: _____   **REVISION**: _____

The schedule, which is located adjacent to the furniture plan, may simply be in the form of a legend indicating codes and the generic types of furniture they refer to, such as C for chair or TA for table, and not specific product information. The codes must then be explained in more detail in the job or control book, as seen in the example in Figure 12-4. In the job or control book, trade names, product numbers, color names, and other specific details are given. A photograph or line drawing may be included as well as an actual piece of the finish or upholstery fabric. Figure 12-5 shows a page from a job book in which a chair is specified for a project.

For a more complex project, the code may consist of a combination of letters and numbers, such as C014/409, where C stands for chair, 014 stands for the 14th type of chair, and 409 after the slash refers to the room number where the chair is to be located. These codes must be explained in the control book and specifications.

On large office-building projects with open-plan workstations, each workstation and panel cluster may be coded as a unit and keyed to the "systems" furniture division of the furnishings specifications. That is, instead of identifying each piece of furniture and component on the plan, each workstation may be designated by a code. The code may be a simple designator, such as S1 or S5, meaning merely systems furniture group one or five. Codes may also be more complex and have designators that relate to the size and/or job function of the workstation, such as A being the largest, for executives; B for middle management; C for secretaries, and so on. These may be further broken down as A1, A2, etc., depending on the number of different configurations and/or components. Other prefixes, such as WS for open-plan workstations or PO for private offices, may also be added to the code for clarity as to the specific type of workspace and location. Thus, a code such as POA1 or WSC3 may appear on the plan and in the schedule (see Figure 12-6).

Furniture plans are also used to itemize the furnishings for pricing and ordering as well as to show the installers the exact location and orientation of each piece during move-in. The furniture plan is sometimes aligned with the electrical and power/communication plans, because the exact location of many of these outlets is directly related to the location and orientation of the furniture. See Figure 12-7 for an example of a combined power/communication and furniture plan.

Scale of Furniture Installation Plans

Furniture installation plans are drawn at as small a scale as possible to reduce the amount of space they take up on the sheet. The furniture drawn in plan view may be simplistic in form to prevent clutter. For example, a chair could be drawn as a rectangle, with no back or arms depicted. However, most designers prefer to portray the furniture shape in more detail. Today, this is particularly easy as many manufacturers supply furniture templates that can be directly transferred into the designer's CAD program. As there is often not a lot of detailed information that needs to be drawn in the floor-plan view, a scale of ⅛" = 1'-0" (1:100 metric) is generally used. However, if more detail is needed to clarify the exact configurations or elements of pieces, a scale of ¼" = 1'-0" (1:50 metric) or larger can be used.

Drafting Standards for Furniture Installation Plans

Furniture can be identified on plans using numerical codes, graphic depictions of the object, or a combination of these, depending on the complexity and size of the project. Most design firms prefer a simple

PROJECT:	JOHNSON & KLINKER, INC.
ITEM #:	C3
QUANTITY:	16
MANF:	KNOLL
MODEL:	BULLDOG MANAGEMENT (7A1-1-B5G-H-K722/2)
DESCRIPTION:	MEDIUM BACK UPHOLSTERED CONFERENCE CHAIR WITH ARMS

W: 25 ½"
D: 21 ¼"
SEAT H: 16" – 21"
ARM H: 23 ¾" – 28 ¾"
OVERALL H: 30" - 39"

FINISH:	DARK GREY
UPHOLSTERY:	KNOLL TEXTILES/ CHOPSTICKS/ JADE
LOCATION:	CONFERENCE ROOM 2004

ILLUSTRATION:

DATE: REVISION:

Figure 12-5 The job book often includes a piece of the fabric and a drawing of the item, such as this chair, Item # C3.

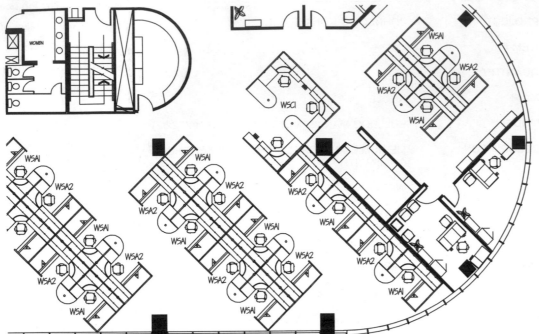

Figure 12-6 In this furniture plan, workstations are coded WSA1, WSC1, etc. — then specified in detail in the job book or schedule.

drawing convention that labels furniture based on their generic category. For example, a chair is designated C-1, C-2, C-3, etc. Sofas are called S-1, S-2, S-3, and tables are T-1, T-2, and T-3. An identifying symbol is drawn around the designation on the floor plan to isolate the key clearly from other information on the drawing (Figure 12-8). In some cases, symbols can be used to identify generic groups of furniture. For example, hexagons might be used for chairs, rectangles for desks, and circles for tables. In all of these methods, it is imperative that the coded information be clear, concise, and legible.

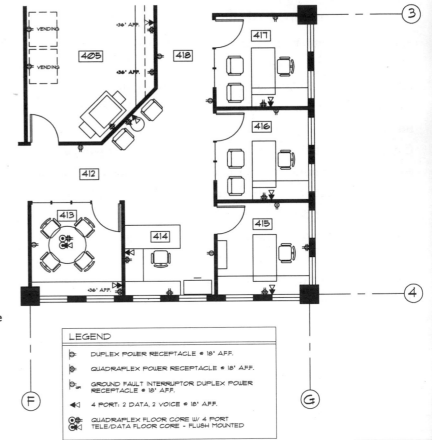

LEGEND

⊖ DUPLEX POWER RECEPTACLE @ 18" A.F.F.

⊜ QUADRAPLEX POWER RECEPTACLE @ 18" A.F.F.

⊖ GROUND FAULT INTERRUPTOR DUPLEX POWER RECEPTACLE @ 18" A.F.F.

◄ 4 PORT: 2 DATA, 2 VOICE @ 18" A.F.F.

⊕ QUADRAPLEX FLOOR CORE W/ 4 PORT TELE/DATA FLOOR CORE - FLUSH MOUNTED

Figure 12-7 This plan combines the power/communication and furniture plans in order to accurately locate electrical devices in relation to furniture and other cabinetry.

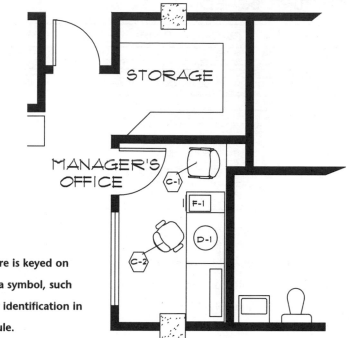

Figure 12-8 Furniture is keyed on the floor plan with a symbol, such as this hexagon, for identification in the furniture schedule.

Another method of coding furniture on an installation plan is to use the coding system on specifications or accompanying schedule for easy cross-referencing. This convention assigns a reference number to each item. For example, all tables are indexed as belonging to the 15,000 series. Specific tables could then be itemized as 15100, 15200, and so forth, as illustrated in Figure 12-9. The first two digits reference all tables to the specifications and the last four digits can be used to identify and describe the specific table.

A variety of information can be included in the schedule accompanying a furniture installation plan. Figure 12-10 shows the basic information to be included in the furniture schedule. Design firms may augment this basic information as necessary for the scope, size, and complexity of the project. Firms vary as to

Figure 12-9 In this example, the furniture is coded with a series of numbers. The chairs are all in the 16000 series. Their specific characteristics are reflected in the numbers following the 16 in each code.

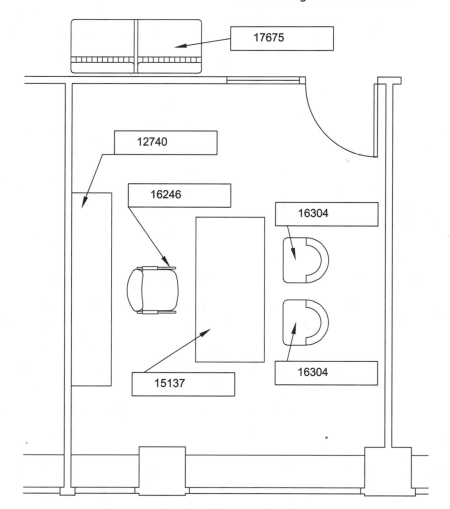

FURNITURE SCHEDULE

Figure 12-10 The furniture schedule lists the specifics represented by the symbol in the floor plan. Other columns might be added for the quantity, size, manufacturer, fabric/finish, room location, and other information needed to order and install the furniture.

KEY	QUANTITY	ITEM	MFG'R / CATALOG NO.	FABRIC / FINISH	REMARKS
C1	12	CHAIR	BROWN JORDAN± 4320-2001	WALL-PRIDE, INC. KL 1267 KALEIDOSCOPE WIDTH:54'± NO REPEAT	FINISH: NATURAL± CLASS A FLAME SPREAD
B1	7	BOOTH	SHELBY WILLIAMS 81-564 LOUNGE SETTEE-CUSTOM SIZE PER PLANS	A. BACK: WAVERLY FABRICS 6071, WIDTH 54' B. SEAT: MAHARAM FABRICS 4538 WOOL "28 FOREST± WIDTH 54' REPEAT Ø.	FLAME PROOF PER CHICAGO BUILDING CODE
T1	4	TABLE	ICF: CARIBE TABLE± L1 MARI	A. BASE: POLISHED BRASS (SMOOTH SURFACE "458) B. TOP: PLASTIC LAMINATE FORMICA NATURAL ALMONDD361. ONE INCH BRASS BAND INSET INTO TOP PERIMETER 2' FROM TABLE EDGE	36 INCHES SQUARE, WITH DROP LEAVES TO 54 INCHES
S1	5	SOFA	KRIES, INC / SHOWPLACE SERIES 9507	BODY: SCHUMACHER AMETHYST PALLADIO TEXTURE, WIDTH 54', REPEAT Ø PILLOWS: MADDEN DESIGNS, JADE SERIES A713	YARDAGE: 17 YARDS FLAMEPROOF PER CHICAGO BUILDING CODE

whether the "quantity" column is to be included in this schedule. Some firms prefer to leave the exact count of the pieces up to the furniture representative supplying the items, whereas other firms want to make sure of the exact count before the final order is placed. In such cases, the furniture items can be cross-checked between the purchase orders and the location on the floor plan.

Dimensioning Furniture Installation Plans

Generally, there is not a lot of dimensioning placed on the furniture installation plan. As long as the plan is drawn to scale and the exact sizes are known, the pieces should fit into their assigned spaces and arrangements. However, in some cases, such as with systems furniture, critical clearances and alignment with other items might need to be dimensioned directly on the plan. In these instances, references should be given that are easily obtainable in

the field. For example, a dimension might be from the face of a wall, column, or imaginary centerline of a room, as illustrated in Figure 12-11.

Designation of Materials

If the furniture installation plan is drawn at a scale of ½" = 1'-0" (1:20 metric), material designations might be included on the piece shown in the plan view. However, this designation of materials is often reserved for presentation drawings rather than included in the construction drawings. Designers must use their discretion or the office standard when deciding whether to include material designations. In many CAD libraries, the software for rendering the material is available, but retaining the scale of the drawing and the clear placement of the furniture should take precedence over making the drawing a visual delight.

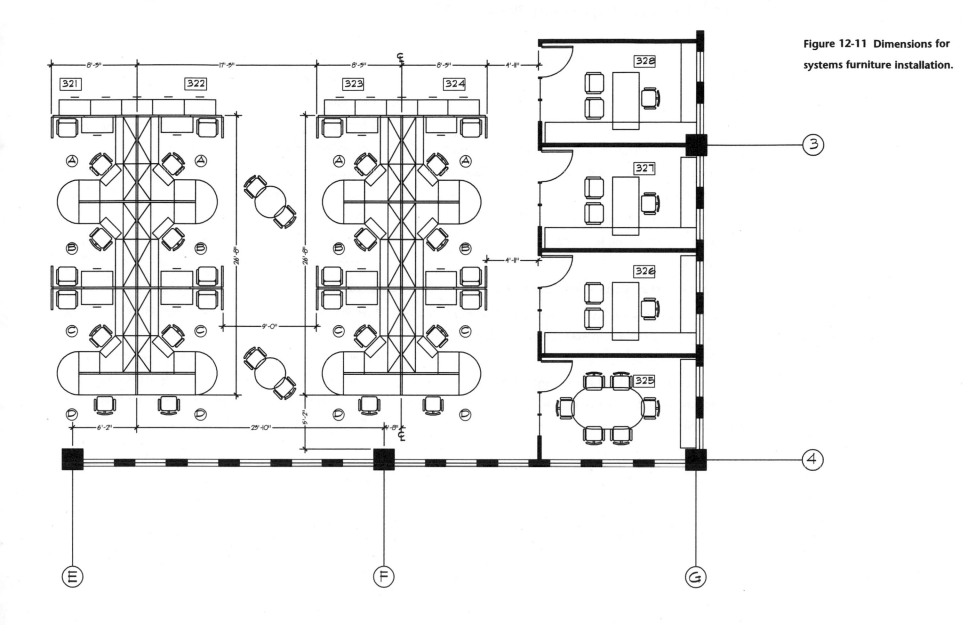

Figure 12-11 Dimensions for systems furniture installation.

Checklist for Furniture Installation Plans

General

- Title the drawing, note its scale, and identify north (or reference direction).

- Title the accompanying furniture schedule and key it to the plan.

- Place the furniture schedule on the same sheet as the furniture plan (preferred) or on a sheet immediately preceding or following the plan.

- Clean up the plan (or in CAD, turn off superfluous information) so the furniture and key codes are clear, dark, and legible.

- Number or name all applicable rooms/spaces.

- Dot in wheelchair access circles and other special furniture items to show compliance with ADA standards (where applicable).

- Carefully check placement of furniture against the electrical and lighting plans for coordination with electrical and luminaire devices.

Notations

- Cross-reference the plan (and schedule if applicable) to other drawings that might contain information critical to the furniture installation plan.

- Note special features, clearances, alignments, and other important items.

- Cross-reference the furniture installation plan and schedule, carefully checking for accuracy and completeness of information.

- Add notes about issues the installer should be alert to when placing the furniture.

Dimensions

- Dimension clearances, alignments, and other controlling factors.

- Call out for installer or contractor to verify existing dimensions of the space/structure against those shown on the installation plan, and to verify these with the designer before furniture installation.

FURNISHINGS AND EQUIPMENT PLANS 13

Interior spaces are composed of more than just floors, walls, ceilings, and furniture. Other elements are often needed to enrich and support a space to make it more "completed" and habitable. Furniture, furnishings, and equipment comprise what is commonly referred to as the FF&E program. Furniture was discussed in Chapter 12. The last two areas of the FF&E program, furnishings and equipment, are discussed in this chapter. Furnishings and equipment are an integral part of the interior environment and generally selected by the interior designer. They are not items that are just "thrown together" and placed in the interiors. Sometimes interior designers, when referring to furnishings and some specialized equipment, such as for retail spaces, use the term *fixtures.*

Furnishings are those items that add the finishing touch to spaces. Furnishings can be utilitarian or decorative, and serve to enhance the architectural features of the space as well as meet user needs and aspirations. The selection and display of furnishings can impart a person's individual character to a space. Generally, furnishings can include accessories, artwork, plants, graphics, and special freestanding or constructed items, as illustrated in Figure 13-1. Accessories could include baskets, figurines, collections, clocks, pottery, or many other items. Accessories might provide a sense of uniqueness or freshness, or be in a serious vein. The selection and display of furnishings follows the principles of design, with attention to their suitability for the total environment.

Most people like to surround themselves with objects that have special meaning. Items such as personal collections or cherished

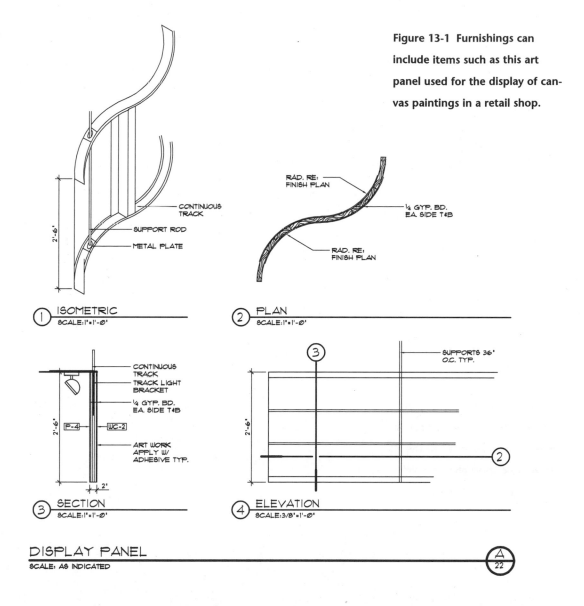

Figure 13-1 Furnishings can include items such as this art panel used for the display of canvas paintings in a retail shop.

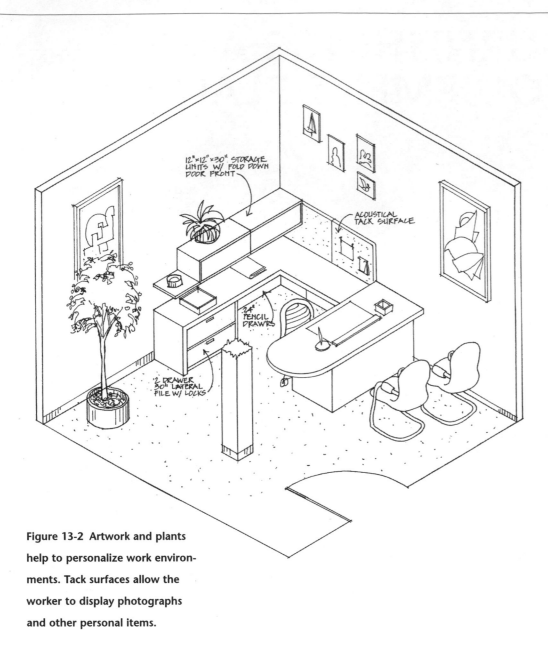

12"x12"x30" STORAGE UNITS W/ FOLD DOWN DOOR FRONT

ACOUSTICAL TACK SURFACE

24" PENCIL DRAWER

2 DRAWER 30" LATERAL FILE W/ LOCKS

Figure 13-2 Artwork and plants help to personalize work environments. Tack surfaces allow the worker to display photographs and other personal items.

photographs elicit fond memories and create the sense of continuity in our lives. Placing these items can be difficult for the interior designer, as their intrinsic aesthetic qualities may not be as strong as the personal connection the client feels for them. However, it is best to coordinate these items and their placement with the client, rather than have the client misplace them later.

Nonresidential or commercial furnishings might be keyed to a theme, for example, a Mexican or seaside motif in a restaurant. In work environments, people like to surround themselves with personal items, just as they do in their residences. This often gives them a feeling of territoriality and supports them emotionally. Office workers often use elements such as pictures and other personal mementos to personalize their work environment, as illustrated in Figure 13-2. It is generally perceived that these items can add to the worker's feelings of self-worth and perhaps even increase productivity. The interior designer should strive to coordinate the whole environment while providing for the significant humanization of spaces by the people who will occupy them as part of their daily routine. In some situations, special display equipment must be designed to show accessories, whether they belong to an individual or are being presented for sale (Figure 13-3).

Equipment consists primarily of those specialized items that are necessary for occupants to carry out their activities. For example, equipment might include tools used in commercial kitchens, or teller equipment needed in banking facilities. Equipment is not generally recognized as a part of the building systems, furniture, or furnishings. However, in some cases, equipment might be physically attached to the building, as with retail display equipment or specialized chairs and other equipment in dental treatment rooms, as shown in Figure 13-4.

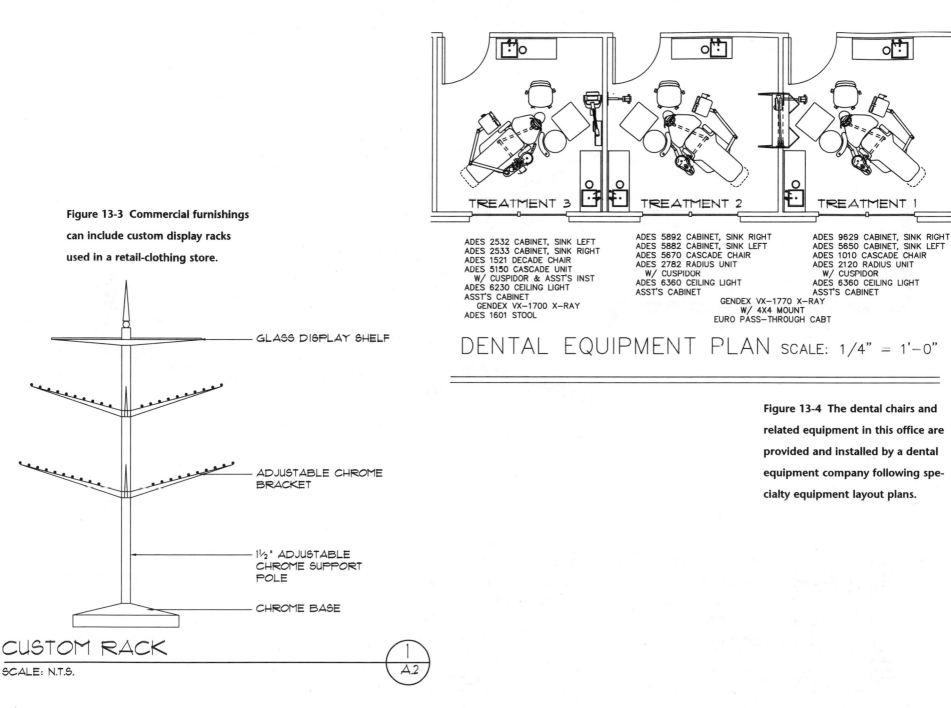

Figure 13-3 Commercial furnishings can include custom display racks used in a retail-clothing store.

GLASS DISPLAY SHELF

ADJUSTABLE CHROME BRACKET

1½" ADJUSTABLE CHROME SUPPORT POLE

CHROME BASE

CUSTOM RACK

SCALE: N.T.S.

1
A.2

TREATMENT 3   TREATMENT 2   TREATMENT 1

ADES 2532 CABINET, SINK LEFT
ADES 2533 CABINET, SINK RIGHT
ADES 1521 DECADE CHAIR
ADES 5150 CASCADE UNIT
  W/ CUSPIDOR & ASST'S INST
ADES 6230 CEILING LIGHT
ASST'S CABINET
  GENDEX VX-1700 X-RAY
ADES 1601 STOOL

ADES 5892 CABINET, SINK RIGHT
ADES 5882 CABINET, SINK LEFT
ADES 5670 CASCADE CHAIR
ADES 2782 RADIUS UNIT
  W/ CUSPIDOR
ADES 6360 CEILING LIGHT
ASST'S CABINET

ADES 9629 CABINET, SINK RIGHT
ADES 5650 CABINET, SINK LEFT
ADES 1010 CASCADE CHAIR
ADES 2120 RADIUS UNIT
  W/ CUSPIDOR
ADES 6360 CEILING LIGHT
ASST'S CABINET

GENDEX VX-1770 X-RAY
W/ 4X4 MOUNT
EURO PASS-THROUGH CABT

DENTAL EQUIPMENT PLAN SCALE: 1/4" = 1'-0"

Figure 13-4 The dental chairs and related equipment in this office are provided and installed by a dental equipment company following specialty equipment layout plans.

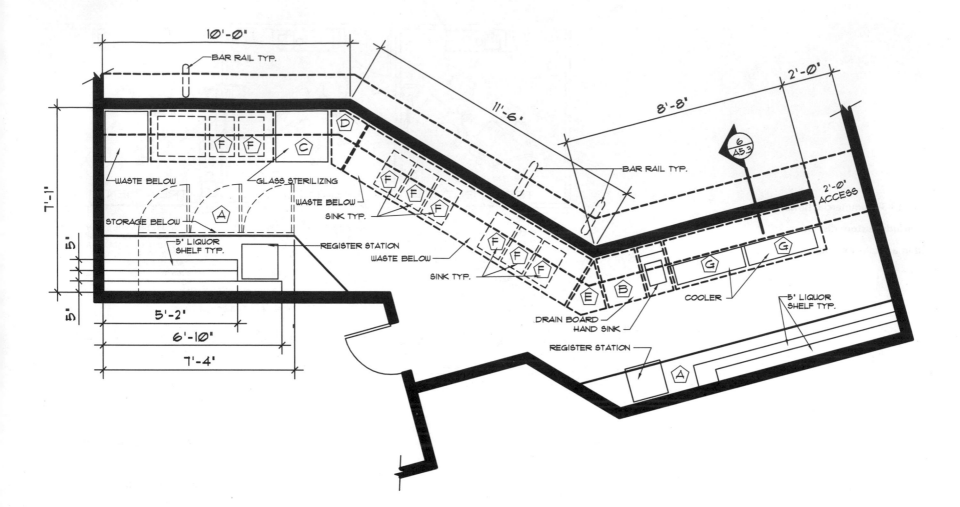

KEY	QUANTITY	DESCRIPTION	DIMENSIONS	COMMENTS
A	2	36' UNDER BAR #CJ5150	36"Hx23½'D	SELF CONT. / S.S. DOORS
B	1	DRAIN BOARD # CJ1500	30"Hx24'Dx18W	30"Hx24'Dx18W
C	1	GLASS STERILIZER #CJ0804	30"Hx24'Dx24W	S.S. FRONT
D	1	CUSTOM CORNER	V.I.F.	S.S. TOP / CUSTOM
E	1	CUSTOM CORNER	V.I.F.	S.S. TOP / CUSTOM
F	8	SINK	30"Hx24'Dx16W	S.S.
G	2	COOLER	33"Hx24'Dx72W	S.S. FRONT

Figure 13-5 A commercial kitchen supplier provides the equipment, specification schedule, and installation plans for this small bar area.

Equipment information, guidelines, and location of electrical and plumbing interfaces are often supplied by the manufacturer or supplier and coordinated by the interior designer. He or she works with the manufacturer, installer, and user when selecting this equipment. In residential work, equipment might include appliances, security systems, or built-in ironing boards. Office equipment in the nonresidential area might include computers, printers, copiers, and other work-related devices. In some situations, consultants such as commercial kitchen specialists might do the actual equipment installation plan if it is complex, as in the bar plan in Figure 13-5. In many cases, the manufacturers supply their equipment templates and detailed information on CD files, or make them available on the Internet. They can often be downloaded directly into the designer's CAD drawings.

Scale of Drawings

The placing of furnishings in small commercial or residential projects might not need any drawings. The interior designer might locate many of the furnishings after the spaces are almost complete, either alone or with the owner. When drawings are needed for specifying and locating furnishings, a variety of scales can be used, depending on the complexity of the project. In some cases, partial sections of the floor plan or interior elevations might be drawn at a large scale, such as ½" = 1'-0" (1:20 metric) to convey the information for locating items.

Equipment is often best located with the help of drawings, as much of it is related to the electrical, communication, and other architectural features of the building. Most of these drawings are in a plan view and drawn at a scale of ⅛" = 1'-0" (1:100 metric) or ¼" = 1'-0" (1:50 metric). However, if more detail is needed to clarify exact configurations or elements of equipment, a larger scale such as ½" = 1'-0" (1:20 metric) can be used, as shown in Figure 13-6.

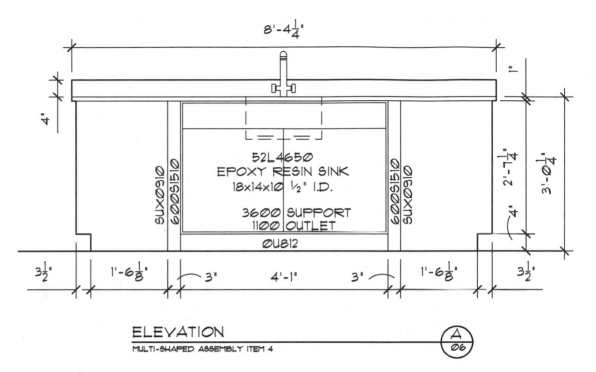

ELEVATION
MULTI-SHAPED ASSEMBLY ITEM 4

Figure 13-6 Some equipment drawings, such as this scientific workstation elevation, are drawn at a large scale to detail out the components of the assembly.

Drafting Standards

Many of the furnishings for interior spaces are small in scale. The drawing of these items is often simplified in plan or elevation view, as their exact appearance is often too complicated to represent in a small-scale drawing. In such cases, the basic outline shape and important surface qualities might only be shown. Some items may be left undrawn, and will have to be physically located in the space by the interior designer in conjunction with the client. However, it is best to portray in at least a general way, to provide drawings that can be the governing principle for the price and location of the installation. This can prevent confusion and relocation costs at a later date if the items are difficult to move.

Figure 13-7 A plan view is needed to indicate the equipment and remodeling work needed in this small commercial kitchen.

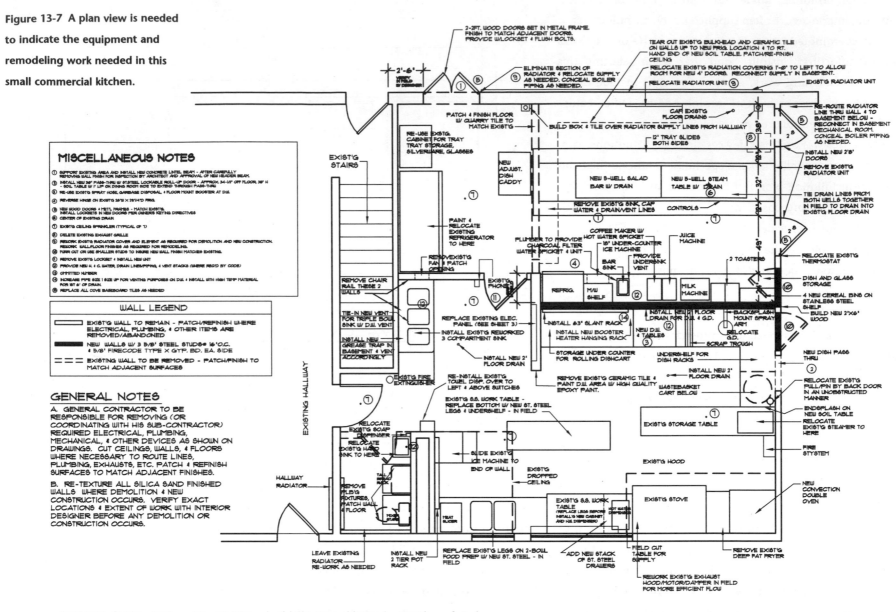

FIRST FLOOR KITCHEN PLAN

SC: 1/2"=1'-0"

T-3 TRIM

METAL FRAMING @ 24"
O.C. TYP.

⅝" H.D.F. ON ⅝" GYP. BD.

T-38 TRIM

MR-60

¼" PANEL ON ⅝" H.D.F. ON
⅝" GYP. BD.

T-64 TRIM

1" WIDE x 1½" DEEP WHITE
MTL. GLAZING CHANNEL
AND BLACK GLAZING
GASKET. SHIM HDF AS
REQUIRE TO HIDE CHANNEL.

A/22

FIXTURE / RESPONSIBILITY SCHEDULE

		QUANTITY	FURNISHED			INSTALLED			REMARKS
			OWNER	GENERAL CONTRACTOR	FIXTURE CONTRACTOR	OWNER	GENERAL CONTRACTOR	FIXTURE CONTRACTOR	
	MISCELLANEOUS CONT								
MS-1	SECURITY KEY PAD		●				●		
MS-2	FIRE EXTINGUISHER			●			●		
MS-3	HAT RACKS		●			●			
	HARDWARE								
R-1	2'x48' U-RAIL				●		●		
R-2	5'x48' U-RAIL				●		●		LINGERIE FIXTURES
R-3	8'x36' U-RAIL				●		●		LINGERIE WALL
R-4	12'x42' U-RAIL				●		●		
R-5	14'x36' U-RAIL SHELF				●		●		
R-6	U-RAIL BRACKET				●		●		FOR SHELF @ HANDBAG DEPT.
R-7	3' FACEOUT				●		●		
R-8	3' SLIP OVER FACEOUT				●		●		
R-9	6' SLIP OVER FACEOUT				●		●		
R-10	14' FACEOUT				●		●		
F-1	14' SLIP OVER FACEOUT				●		●		
B-1	BOW RAIL				●		●		
H-1	SINGLE HAT FACEOUT				●		●		

Figure 13-8 Schedules can help coordinate the work of equipment suppliers and installers.

Equipment plans should be drawn accurately, with the size and configuration of the items shown in a scaled plan or elevation view, as illustrated in Figure 13-7. Drawings can be produced in CAD using templates provided by the manufacturers or in a software library in the designer's office. The drawings should be produced in sufficient detail to accurately portray the item, with a key to cross-reference it to a nearby legend that gives more specific information. Some equipment legends not only show specific items, but also list whose responsibility it is to furnish or install them, as shown in Figure 13-8.

Designation of Materials

As mentioned earlier, many materials cannot be accurately drawn in a small-scale plan or elevation view. However, some materials can be delineated or described in drawings if they are not overly complicated, as seen in the three-way mirror design in Figure 13-9. Designers should use their discretion as to how much detail is really needed to convey the material qualities in an architectural drawing. Most of the material information that cannot be drawn clearly is placed in the accompanying schedule or cross-referenced to the specifications — which are often located elsewhere in the

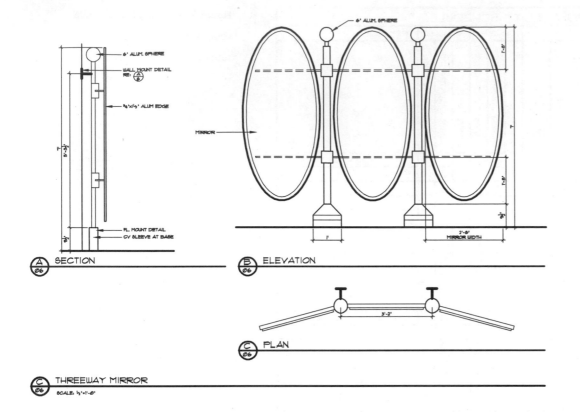

Labels on the drawing (as visible):
6" ALUM. SPHERE
WALL MOUNT DETAIL RE: (A)
3/4"x1 1/2" ALUM EDGE
MIRROR
FL. MOUNT DETAIL
CV SLEEVE AT BASE
6" ALUM. SPHERE

SECTION (A/06)
ELEVATION (B/06)
PLAN (C/06)

2'-8" MIRROR WIDTH
3'-2"

THREEWAY MIRROR (C/06)
SCALE: 1/2"=1'-0"

Figure 13-9 These drawings show the dimensions of a three-way mirror, as well as its location in relation to the floor and adjacent wall.

drawings or in a separate booklet. In some cases, photographs or scanned images of the items can be placed on the drawing sheets, both in two- and three-dimensional work.

Dimensioning of Furnishings and Equipment Plans

Furnishing installation plans, equipment plans, and other drawings are dimensioned as needed. Generally, the most important dimensions are those used to accurately locate the items in relation to physical objects such as walls, ceilings, and columns. Heights above finish floor, in elevation views, and location from fixed architectural elements in plan view, are often referenced, as seen in the example in Figure 13-10.

Checklist for Furnishings and Equipment Plans

General

- Title the drawing, note its scale, and identify north (or reference direction).

- Title the accompanying furnishings or equipment schedule and key it to the plan.

- Place the furnishings and equipment schedule on the same sheet as the furnishings or equipment plan (preferred) or on a sheet immediately preceding or following the plan.

- Clean up the plan (or in CAD, turn off superfluous information) so the furnishings or equipment key codes are clear, dark, and very legible.

- Number or name all applicable rooms/spaces.

- Dot in wheelchair access circles and other special items to show compliance with ADA standards (where applicable).

Notations

- Note special features, clearances, alignments, and other important items.

- Cross-reference the plan (and schedule if applicable) to other drawings that might contain information critical to the furnishings or equipment installation plan.

- Cross-reference the furnishings and equipment plans and related schedules, carefully checking for accuracy and completeness of information.

- Add notes on issues the installer should be alert to when placing the furnishings or equipment.

- Add notes to refer to other consultant drawings that might have input on the furnishings or equipment plans.

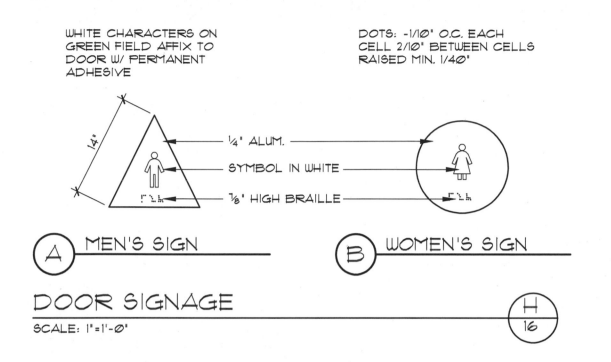

WHITE CHARACTERS ON
GREEN FIELD AFFIX TO
DOOR W/ PERMANENT
ADHESIVE

DOTS: -1/10" O.C. EACH
CELL 2/10" BETWEEN CELLS
RAISED MIN. 1/40"

14"

¼" ALUM.

SYMBOL IN WHITE

⅞" HIGH BRAILLE

A MEN'S SIGN

B WOMEN'S SIGN

DOOR SIGNAGE

SCALE: 1"=1'-0"

H
16

Figure 13-10 A combination of notes and drawings is used to present the specifics of the door signage in this dressing area.

- Call for the submission of shop drawings where applicable, either on these sheets or cross-referenced to the general specifications.

Dimensions

- Dimension clearances, alignments, and other controlling factors. Refer to manufacturers', suppliers', or installers' dimensional standards.

- Call out for installer or contractor to verify existing dimensions of the space/structure against those shown on the installation plan, and verify these with the designer before installation of any items or equipment.

REFLECTED CEILING AND ELECTRICAL PLANS 14

Electrical systems in a building include lighting, electrical outlets, telephone lines, and other communication systems such as computer networks. A designer's objective is to communicate the nature and locations of these systems in a clear, uncluttered manner. Several approaches are commonly used to do this. The particular method and type of drawing selected will depend on the size and complexity of the project and the office drafting standards. This chapter will discuss electrical system drawings in both residential and commercial projects, both small and large in scale.

The interior designer is responsible for developing the lighting design and for documenting it in a reflected ceiling plan. The reflected ceiling plan is included with the overall architectural drawings and shows the construction of the ceiling, the location of all the lighting, and the location of sprinklers, smoke detectors, and any other objects in or on the ceiling, such as the mechanical (HVAC) air diffusers and grilles. In residential projects and some small commercial projects, the switching and electrical outlets may also be indicated, as illustrated in Figure 14-1.

In larger projects, primarily in commercial work, after the interior designer develops the reflected ceiling plan, an electrical engineering consultant is contacted to prepare a separate plan, called the lighting plan, that includes switching and circuitry. A separate electrical plan, which is sometimes referred to as the power and signal plan, specifies the exact type of circuiting, wire sizes, and other aspects of the systems needed for lighting, convenient outlets, and other fixed equipment. All three plan types are shown in Figure

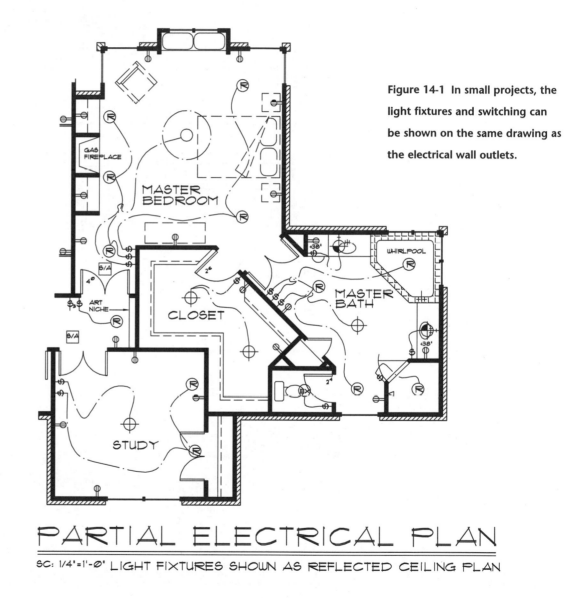

Figure 14-1 In small projects, the light fixtures and switching can be shown on the same drawing as the electrical wall outlets.

PARTIAL ELECTRICAL PLAN
SC: 1/4'=1'-0' LIGHT FIXTURES SHOWN AS REFLECTED CEILING PLAN

Figure 14-2 In large commercial projects, electrical drawings often include a reflected ceiling plan that shows elements on the ceiling, a lighting plan for fixtures and switching, and a power plan for electrical supply devices

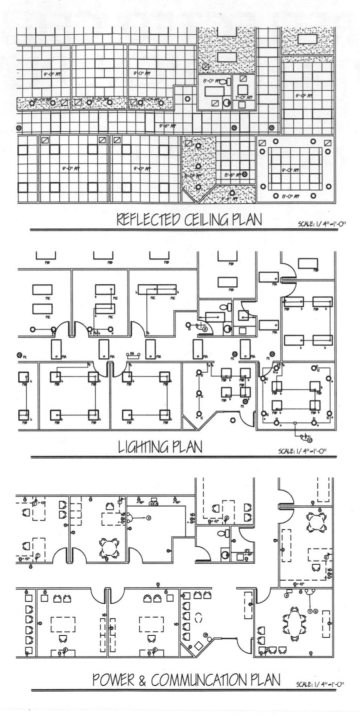

REFLECTED CEILING PLAN SCALE: 1/4"=1'-0"

LIGHTING PLAN SCALE: 1/4"=1'-0"

POWER & COMMUNICATION PLAN SCALE: 1/4"=1'-0"

14-2. As the electrical requirements vary a great deal from project to project, a careful analysis of equipment needs will help to determine what type(s) of drawings will be necessary.

Note that the lighting plan and the reflected ceiling plan appear similar, but differ in some important ways. The reflected ceiling plan is often drawn first by the interior designer, showing the various ceiling materials and other particulars. The light fixture types and locations are planned on this drawing to coordinate with other items such as mechanical ceiling diffusers, dropped soffits, a suspended ceiling, sprinklers, and other items, as illustrated in Figure 14-3. Since the lighting fixtures, referred to as luminaires, are shown on the reflected ceiling plan in a schematic form, a legend is used to cross-reference this drawing to the lighting plan for the exact specifications of the luminaires' wattages, sizes, wall switches, and the various circuits and wiring for these fixtures, as shown in Figure 14-4.

Reflected Ceiling Plans

The lighting of interiors is important to our activities and our perception of the world. By creatively controlling natural and artificial light, the interior designer can create striking designs while providing for the visual needs of the user. Lighting design is a combination of art and applied science. It guides our vision, and can affect our attitudes and behavior. The designer can also ensure the conservation of energy by employing efficient luminaires. The switching of lighting controls and systematic maintenance programs can also affect energy conservation.

The type of lighting system the interior designer selects determines the amount of detail the construction drawings need. Lighting systems can refer to the individual types of luminaires or

Figure 14-4 A lighting plan indicates the luminaires' wattage and sizes and the location of wall switches and circuits.

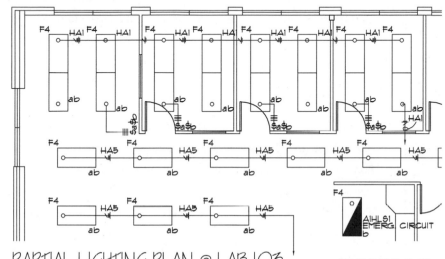

PARTIAL LIGHTING PLAN @ LAB 103

SCALE: 1/4" = 1'-0"

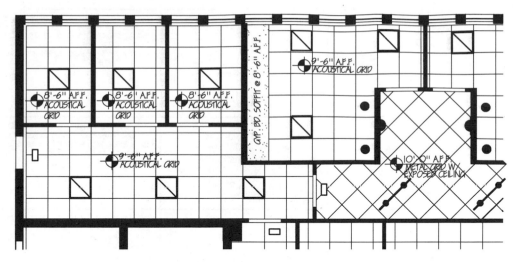

PARTIAL REFLECTED CEILING PLAN

LIGHT FIXTURE LEGEND

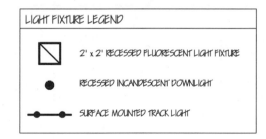

2' x 2' RECESSED FLUORESCENT LIGHT FIXTURE

RECESSED INCANDESCENT DOWNLIGHT

SURFACE MOUNTED TRACK LIGHT

Figure 14-3 This reflected ceiling plan shows light fixture locations in reference to other items. Details about lamps, housing trim, and switching for the fixtures are provided separately in a legend or in written specifications.

SYMBOLS LEGEND

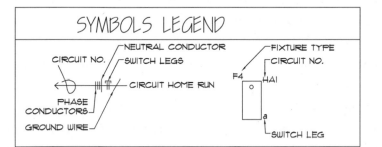

LIGHT FIXTURE SCHEDULE

TYPE	DESCRIPTION	VOLTAGE	LAMPS	MOUNT'G	LENS	MANUFACTURER
F4	2'x4' TROFFER, BAKED WHITE ENAMEL, RETURN AIR SLOTS	277	(4) 32W F32T8 3500K	RECESSED CEILING	PATTERN #12, 0.125 NOMINAL PRISMATIC (ACRYLIC)	HE WILLIAMS

TYPE	LIGHT DISTRIBUTION	CHARACTERISTICS
DIRECT-WIDE BEAM		90-100% OF LIGHT OUTPUT IS DIRECTED DOWN. WIDE BEAM DIRECT LIGHTING CAN BE USED FOR EMPHASIS AND HIGHLIGHTING.
DIRECT-NARROW BEAM		90-100% OF LIGHT OUTPUT IS DIRECTED DOWN. NARROW BEAM DIRECT LIGHTING CAN BE USED FOR EMPHASIS AND HIGHLIGHTING.
INDIRECT		90-100% OF LIGHT OUTPUT IS DIRECTED UP TOWARD THE CEILING. CAN CREATE A FEELING OF HEIGHT AND PREVENT DARK CEILINGS.
DIRECT / INDIRECT		EQUAL AMOUNT OF LIGHT DIRECTED DOWN AS WELL AS UP WITH LITTLE PROVIDED TO THE SIDES. DIRECT GLARE IS REDUCED.
DIFFUSE		LIGHT OUTPUT IS DIRECTED IN ALL DIRECTIONS. DIRECT GLARE CAN BE PREVENTED BY DIFFUSE ENCLOSURES.
SEMI-DIRECT		10-40% OF LIGHT OUTPUT IS DIRECTED UPWARD, WHILE 60-90% OF LIGHT IS DIRECTED DOWN. SHADOWS ARE NOT AS HARSH.
SEMI-INDIRECT		60-90% OF LIGHT IS DIRECTED UPWARD. SOME LIGHT IS DIRECTED DOWN, WHICH SOFTENS HARSH SHADOWS.

to the total installation. They are described as direct, indirect, direct-indirect, diffuse, semi-direct and semi-indirect, as illustrated in Figure 14-5.

The reflected ceiling plan shows the ceiling in plan view and anything that is attached to it, such as light fixtures, sprinkler heads, visible HVAC devices, and soffits. Material indications and any change in ceiling height are also shown. It is referred to as a reflected ceiling plan because it is the view that one would see if looking down at a mirrored floor, reflecting what is on the ceiling. Note, however, that the ceiling plan is not a mirrored or reversed image of the floor plan. This "reflected" view is in the same orientation as the floor plan and objects on it. It is drawn as if the ceiling were a clear glass sheet and one were looking downward through this at the floor plan. If the floor plan is oriented with north toward the top of the sheet, then the reflected ceiling plan should also be oriented with north toward the top of the sheet, as shown in Figure 14-6. This provides consistency in the construction documents.

The reflected ceiling plan is particularly useful for coordinating all ceiling-mounted building systems and checking on the ceiling appearance and finished ceiling heights above the finish floor. Before the design of the lighting system begins, the clearance above the finished ceiling must be verified by reviewing the architectural building sections and mechanical drawings. For recessed lighting systems, there must be enough space above the ceiling to install the fixtures. Most recessed fluorescent troffers used in commercial projects are only 4–10 inches (101–254 mm) in depth and are usually not a problem. However, recessed downlights can be as deep as 16 inches (406 mm), which may cause problems with other above-ceiling construction such as HVAC ductwork, electrical conduit, or plumbing pipes. See Figure 14-7 for some typical sizes of various recessed luminaires.

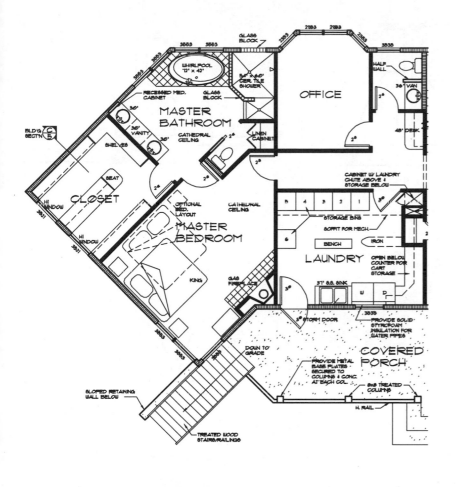

PARTIAL 1ST FLOOR PLAN

SC: 1/4"=1'-0"

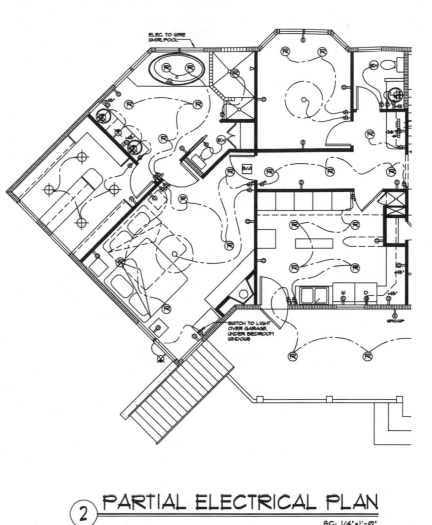

PARTIAL ELECTRICAL PLAN

SC: 1/4"=1'-0"

Figure 14-6 The reflected ceiling plan is oriented in the same direction as the floor plan.

Figure 14-5 *(opposite page)* This chart illustrates luminaire beam spread patterns and the percentage of light directed upward or downward.

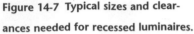

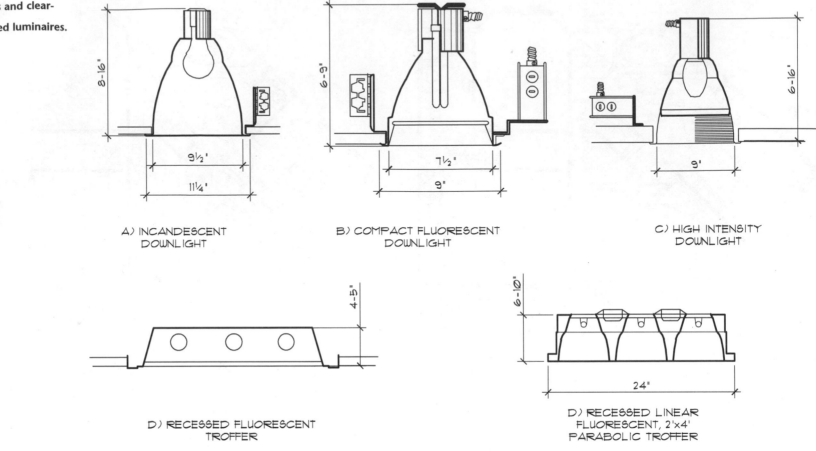

A) INCANDESCENT
DOWNLIGHT

8-16"
9½'
11¼'

B) COMPACT FLUORESCENT
DOWNLIGHT

6-9"
7½"
9"

C) HIGH INTENSITY
DOWNLIGHT

6-16'
9'

D) RECESSED FLUORESCENT
TROFFER

4-5"

D) RECESSED LINEAR
FLUORESCENT, 2'x4'
PARABOLIC TROFFER

6-10"
24"

Scale of Reflected Ceiling Plans

Reflected ceiling plans should be drawn at the same scale as the floor plans. Depending on the complexity of the project and ceiling treatment, the most common scale for residential and small commercial projects is ¼" = 1'-0" (1:50 metric) and ⅛" = 1'-0" (1:100 metric) for large commercial projects. The scale the ceiling plan is drawn at should be noted and placed directly below the drawing, either adjacent to or directly below the title. If an enlarged detail is needed to explain a feature in the ceiling, it is keyed with a note or symbol to a separate, larger-scale drawing (Figure 14-8).

The luminaires should be drawn as simple rectangles, squares, or circles that depict the actual fixture as closely as possible (Figure 14-9). Simplistic forms prevent clutter in the view for ease of recognition. In most cases, the lighting fixture is drawn to the scale of the actual fixtures. However, in some cases such as miniature spotlights, the size may have to be exaggerated, as the properly scaled unit would be too small to show up on the plan.

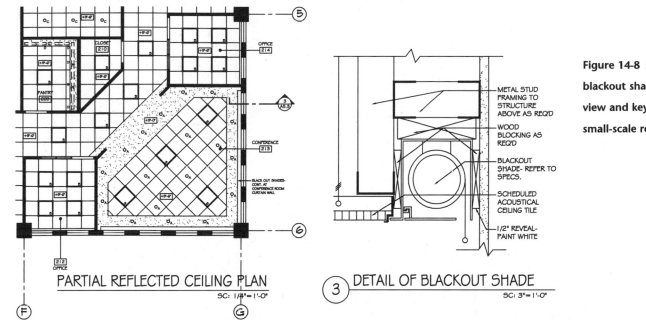

METAL STUD
FRAMING TO
STRUCTURE
ABOVE AS REQ'D

WOOD
BLOCKING AS
REQ'D

BLACKOUT
SHADE- REFER TO
SPECS.

SCHEDULED
ACOUSTICAL
CEILING TILE

1/2" REVEAL-
PAINT WHITE

Figure 14-8 An enlarged detail of a blackout shade is drawn in section view and keyed to its location in the small-scale reflected ceiling plan.

PARTIAL REFLECTED CEILING PLAN
SC: 1/4"= 1'-0"

③ DETAIL OF BLACKOUT SHADE
SC: 3"= 1'-0"

Figure 14-9 Simple symbols are used to denote the various types of light fixtures and ceiling treatments.

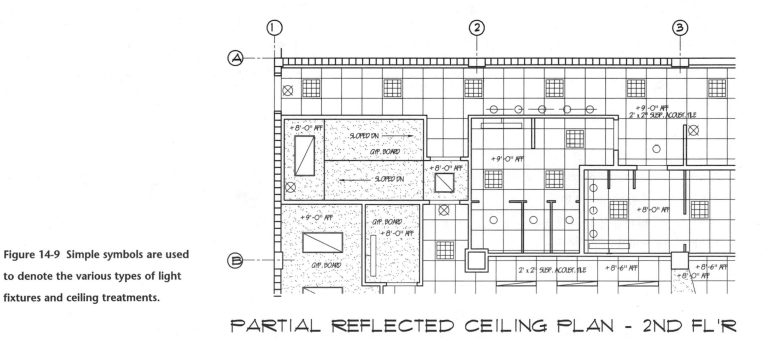

PARTIAL REFLECTED CEILING PLAN - 2ND FL'R

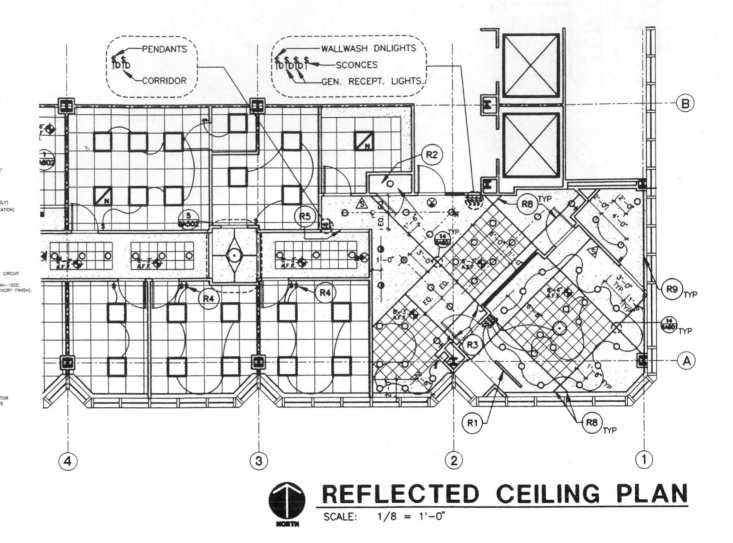

SYMBOL LEGEND

REFLECTED CEILING PLAN

SCALE: 1/8 = 1'-0"

Figure 14-10 Lighting fixtures are represented with symbols in the reflected ceiling plan and keyed to a legend showing specifications.

Drafting Standards for the Reflected Ceiling Plan

A reflected ceiling plan must clearly show all walls, partitions, and soffits that intersect with the ceiling. It should also specify changes in ceiling elevations and materials, such as lights, sprinklers, smoke detectors, and HVAC diffusers that attach to or penetrate the ceiling. In drafting reflected ceiling plans, the designer should reproduce the floor plan walls and openings such as doors and windows, but without showing items such as built-in cabinetry, plumbing fixtures, etc.

The lighting fixtures and other electrical features shown on the reflected ceiling plan are given symbols that are keyed to a legend (Figure 14-10). It is advisable to draw in all the electrical symbols on the plan before it is dimensioned or notes are added. If not, a symbol may fall on top of a dimension, thus requiring the dimension to be moved. Locate the light fixtures in the ceiling plan in accordance with the lighting design concept. Common types of light fixtures on the lighting plan include surface-mounted, recessed, pendant, and track-mounted. See Figure 14-11 for a list of standard lighting and electrical symbols.

On commercial projects where there is a suspended ceiling, the reflected ceiling plans would show any partitions that extend through the ceiling plane as well. The ceiling grid lines (called "T" bars) should also be shown (Figure 14-12). Other information included in the reflected ceiling plan are the ceiling materials, ceiling heights, ceiling slopes, changes in ceiling heights, locations of all lighting fixtures (including exit and emergency lights), air diffusers and vents, access panels, speakers, sprinkler heads (if used), and other items that touch or are part of the ceiling plane.

Next, the interior designer should determine how the lights in the space are to be switched. For residential or small commercial

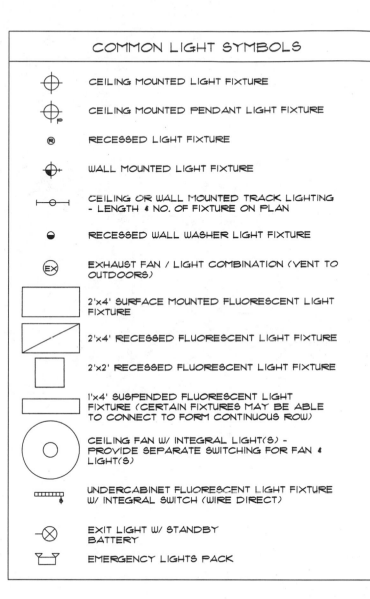

Figure 14-11 Standard lighting and electrical symbols.

COMMON LIGHT SYMBOLS

CEILING MOUNTED LIGHT FIXTURE

CEILING MOUNTED PENDANT LIGHT FIXTURE

RECESSED LIGHT FIXTURE

WALL MOUNTED LIGHT FIXTURE

CEILING OR WALL MOUNTED TRACK LIGHTING - LENGTH & NO. OF FIXTURE ON PLAN

RECESSED WALL WASHER LIGHT FIXTURE

EXHAUST FAN / LIGHT COMBINATION (VENT TO OUTDOORS)

2'x4' SURFACE MOUNTED FLUORESCENT LIGHT FIXTURE

2'x4' RECESSED FLUORESCENT LIGHT FIXTURE

2'x2' RECESSED FLUORESCENT LIGHT FIXTURE

1'x4' SUSPENDED FLUORESCENT LIGHT FIXTURE (CERTAIN FIXTURES MAY BE ABLE TO CONNECT TO FORM CONTINUOUS ROW)

CEILING FAN W/ INTEGRAL LIGHT(S) - PROVIDE SEPARATE SWITCHING FOR FAN & LIGHT(S)

UNDERCABINET FLUORESCENT LIGHT FIXTURE W/ INTEGRAL SWITCH (WIRE DIRECT)

EXIT LIGHT W/ STANDBY BATTERY

EMERGENCY LIGHTS PACK

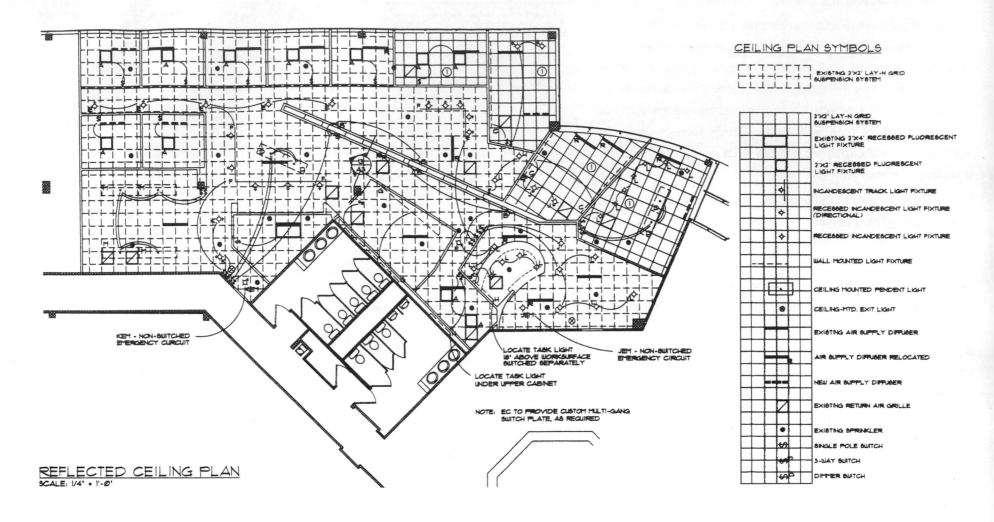

CEILING PLAN SYMBOLS

⊏⊐⊏⊐⊏⊐	EXISTING 2'X2' LAY-IN GRID SUSPENSION SYSTEM
	2'X2' LAY-IN GRID SUSPENSION SYSTEM
▭	EXISTING 2'X4' RECESSED FLUORESCENT LIGHT FIXTURE
◻	2'X2' RECESSED FLUORESCENT LIGHT FIXTURE
⟶	INCANDESCENT TRACK LIGHT FIXTURE
◇	RECESSED INCANDESCENT LIGHT FIXTURE (DIRECTIONAL)
◇	RECESSED INCANDESCENT LIGHT FIXTURE
	WALL MOUNTED LIGHT FIXTURE
▭	CEILING MOUNTED PENDENT LIGHT
⊗	CEILING-MTD. EXIT LIGHT
	EXISTING AIR SUPPLY DIFFUSER
▮	AIR SUPPLY DIFFUSER RELOCATED
▬	NEW AIR SUPPLY DIFFUSER
◻	EXISTING RETURN AIR GRILLE
●	EXISTING SPRINKLER
S	SINGLE POLE SWITCH
S³	3-WAY SWITCH
S⁰	DIMMER SWITCH

KEM - NON-SWITCHED EMERGENCY CIRCUIT

JEM - NON-SWITCHED EMERGENCY CIRCUIT

LOCATE TASK LIGHT 18' ABOVE WORKSURFACE SWITCHED SEPARATELY

LOCATE TASK LIGHT UNDER UPPER CABINET

NOTE: EC TO PROVIDE CUSTOM MULTI-GANG SWITCH PLATE, AS REQUIRED

REFLECTED CEILING PLAN
SCALE: 1/4" = 1'-0"

Figure 14-12 The ceiling grid, as well as lights and other items located within it, are shown to scale.

projects, the switching can either be shown on the reflected ceiling plan or on the electrical lighting plan. The switching design should be based on how much individual control is needed and the function of the lighting. Energy conservation needs and maximum circuit loads within the circuits will also determine the number and location of the switches. Generally, switches are located near the door or opening leading into the space. Large spaces that have more than one entry may require multiple switching locations.

After locating the switches, determine which luminaires they should control and delineate this on the plan. This can be done in two ways, depending on the size and complexity of the lighting plan.

The first method is to draw a line from the wall switch to the fixtures it controls. This connecting line should be dashed and curved to distinguish it from other objects and items on the drawing. Curved lines are preferred, as straight lines may get mixed up with wall lines or other items that are drawn in the plan. The connecting curved line should touch the outlet or fixture symbol, as illustrated in Figure 14-13. The symbol for switches can be a simple S. If a particular lighting fixture is switched from two locations, the symbols will be S_3 to indicate that three items (two switches and one lighting fixture) are connected electrically. Common switch symbols are shown in Figure 14-14.

The second method of showing light-fixture switching is to assign a number or letter to the switch and to place this same number in or near the light fixture shown in the ceiling plan (Figure 14-15). This method is used primarily in commercial spaces, where there might be a lot of multiple switching and other items placed on the ceiling plan, so that the use of lines (the first method) could complicate the drawing.

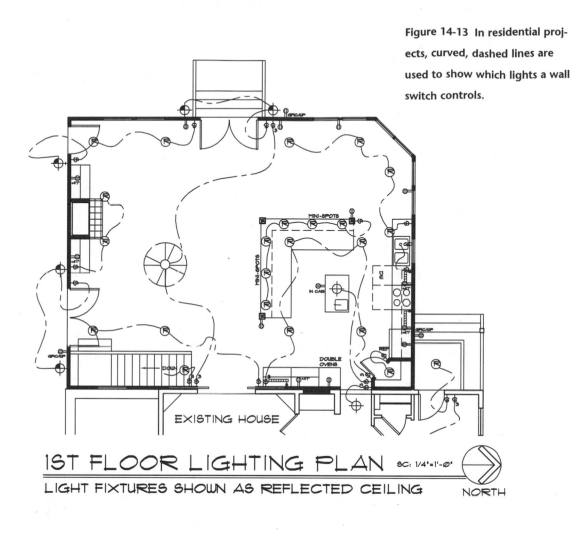

Figure 14-13 In residential projects, curved, dashed lines are used to show which lights a wall switch controls.

1ST FLOOR LIGHTING PLAN SC: 1/4"=1'-0"
LIGHT FIXTURES SHOWN AS REFLECTED CEILING
NORTH

After the interior designer lays out the lighting and switching, the drawing is given to an electrical engineer, who indicates the exact circuitry, wire sizes, and other specifications required for the electrical system. In residential spaces, the drawing might be given directly to the electrical contractor, as the circuitry and requirements here are not as complex as those in commercial work.

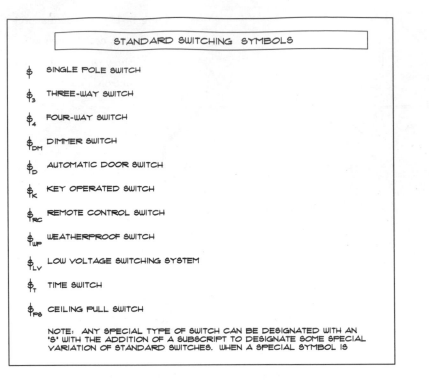

STANDARD SWITCHING SYMBOLS

S SINGLE POLE SWITCH

S_3 THREE-WAY SWITCH

S_4 FOUR-WAY SWITCH

S_{DM} DIMMER SWITCH

S_D AUTOMATIC DOOR SWITCH

S_K KEY OPERATED SWITCH

S_{RC} REMOTE CONTROL SWITCH

S_{WP} WEATHERPROOF SWITCH

S_{LV} LOW VOLTAGE SWITCHING SYSTEM

S_T TIME SWITCH

S_{PS} CEILING PULL SWITCH

NOTE: ANY SPECIAL TYPE OF SWITCH CAN BE DESIGNATED WITH AN
'S' WITH THE ADDITION OF A SUBSCRIPT TO DESIGNATE SOME SPECIAL
VARIATION OF STANDARD SWITCHES. WHEN A SPECIAL SYMBOL IS

**Figure 14-14 Common switch
symbols for light controls.**

Figure 14-15 Another method of denoting light-switch controls in large commercial projects is by the use of subscript letters that match the light fixture to the proper wall switch.

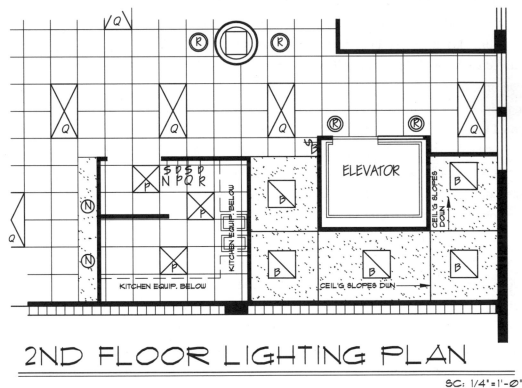

2ND FLOOR LIGHTING PLAN

SC: 1/4"=1'-0"

Designation of Materials

When preparing the reflected ceiling plan, the designer must call out types and locations of specific ceiling materials. This can be done by placing notes on the plan, or symbols that are referenced to a ceiling material legend. The two most common ceiling systems used are gypsum board ceilings that are attached to the structure above, and suspended acoustical ceilings. Other ceiling finishes might include wood facing, linear metal, or even exposed wood joists and beams (Figure 14-16).

Dimensioning Reflected Ceiling Plans

As the reflected ceiling plans are generally drawn to a scale that matches the floor plans, there is no need for a lot of dimensioning on the plan, unless ceiling breaks or changes of materials occur where they are not obviously located at a door, wall, or column location. As long as the reflected ceiling plan is drawn to scale, the dimensions of the spaces and structure can be reserved for the floor plan. However, in some cases, the sizes of the units and the fixture locations do need to be dimensioned. This is particularly true for large expanses of gypsum board ceiling, where the scale cannot be as easily determined as in a gridded suspended ceiling assembly (where, for example, one can count units to locate the light fixture).

When dimensioning the reflected ceiling plan, either "finish" dimensions or "framing" dimensions can be used, but the choice must be noted on the plans. Elements such as recessed light troffers can be precisely located in the finished space. If a downlight in a gypsum wallboard ceiling is to be used, it generally is dimensioned to its center point so the electrical contractor knows where to install

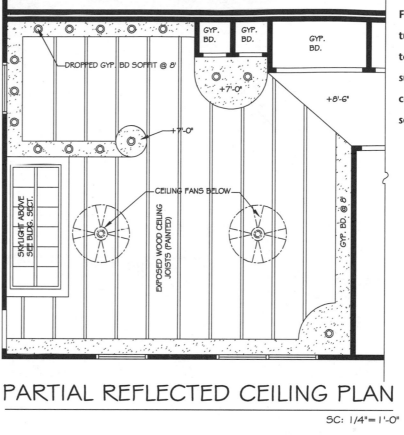

PARTIAL REFLECTED CEILING PLAN

SC: 1/4"= 1'-0"

Figure 14-16 A variety of textures and notes can be used to designate ceiling types, such as this exposed wood ceiling with gypsum board soffits.

it. Alignment and direction of patterns might need to be dimensioned directly on the plan. In these instances, references should be given that are easily obtainable in the field. Dimensions should be referenced from the face of a wall, column, or imaginary centerline of a room, as illustrated in Figure 14-17.

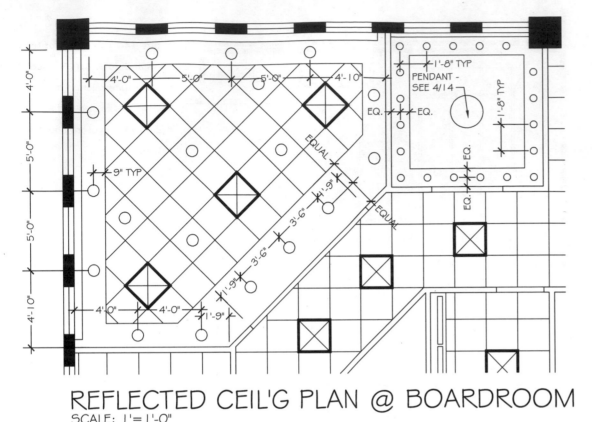

REFLECTED CEIL'G PLAN @ BOARDROOM
SCALE: 1"=1'-0"

Figure 14-17 The recessed down lights in this reflected ceiling plan are dimensioned in relation to each other and various wall elements and soffits.

Checklist for Reflected Ceiling Plans

General

- Title the drawing, note its scale, and identify north (or reference direction).

- If needed, develop a ceiling type material schedule and key it to the plan.

- Develop a lighting symbol legend and locate it on the same sheet as the first reflected ceiling plan (if more than one is required), or on a nearby sheet.

- Clean up the plan (or in CAD, turn off superfluous information) so the walls, spaces, and key codes are clear, dark, and very legible. Don't show items unless they are on the ceiling plane or intersecting it.

- Draw in major soffits or openings above and call them out in a note, including attic access panels.

- Pouche walls, if applicable.

- Decide on the switching patterns of the light fixtures (if the interior designer has this responsibility) and show by the curved-line method or use of numbers/letters.

- Cross-reference the reflected ceiling plan to other drawings (if applicable), carefully checking for accuracy and completeness of information.

Notations

- Note where the ceiling level changes or slopes if this has a direct effect on the light fixtures and their installation.

- Note special features, clearances, finished ceiling heights above finish floors, alignments, and other important items.

- Cross-reference the plan with symbols and reference to the lighting schedule, details, and other drawings as needed.

Dimensions

- Dimension the locations of light fixtures and changes in ceiling types that are not readily apparent. Locate to such items as columns or existing walls.

- Dimension clearances, alignments, and other controlling factors.

- Dimension lighting coves and other structural lighting, or create large-scale drawings of these and cross-reference.

Electrical Plans

Electrical plans can include electrical outlets, telephones, communication devices, and other items requiring electrical power. In small projects, these items can be shown together with the lighting. An example of this type of drawing is illustrated in Figure 14-18. On large commercial projects, the electrical plan, often referred to as a power or power/communication plan, shows the outlets and related electrical devices separately (Figure 14-19). In most cases, the plumbing fixtures and items such as cabinetry and other built-in items are shown in order to more closely coordinate the location of electrical power devices. In some instances, such as in open-office situations, designers also prefer to show the furniture, as many times it relates directly to the electrical outlet locations (Figure 14-20). The interior designer prepares the power plan and then forwards it to the electrical engineer to detail the circuitry, wire sizes, panel boxes, and other electrical specifications. On small residential plans, the drawing is given directly to the electrical contractor to install the work according to accepted practices.

The telephone and other communication systems are also generally shown on the electrical plan. Locations of telephones, public address systems, computer terminals, intercommunication devices, and security systems are the responsibility of the interior designer in consultation with specialists. The designer draws a power/communications plan that schematically shows where power is needed for special equipment. Symbols for electrical devices are generally keyed to a legend that is on the same sheet as the plan. The electrical engineer or other system specialists do most of the detailed specifications for these devices.

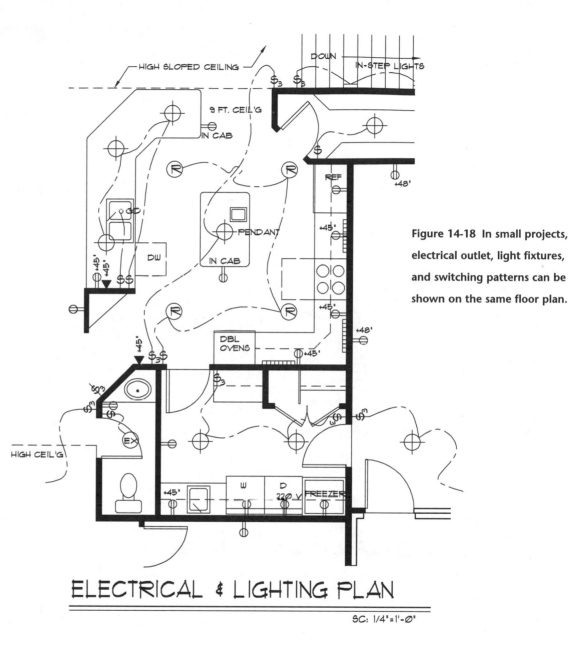

Figure 14-18 In small projects, electrical outlet, light fixtures, and switching patterns can be shown on the same floor plan.

ELECTRICAL & LIGHTING PLAN

SC: 1/4"=1'-Ø'

Figure 14-19 In large commercial projects, a separate electrical/power plan with a legend specifies outlets and circuitry. Many architectural features and other systems are left out so that the electrical plan can be easily read.

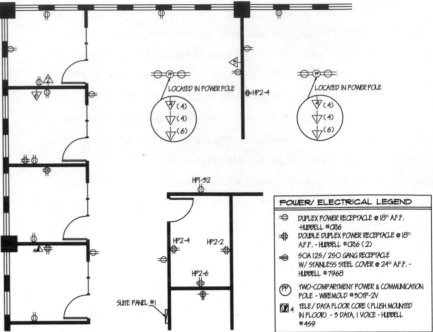

PARTIAL POWER/ ELECTRICAL PLAN
SCALE: 1/4"=1'-0"

POWER/ ELECTRICAL LEGEND

⊖	DUPLEX POWER RECEPTACLE @ 18" A.F.F. -HUBBELL #CR16
⊕	DOUBLE DUPLEX POWER RECEPTACLE @ 18" A.F.F. - HUBBELL #CR16 (2)
⊜	50A 125/250 GANG RECEPTACLE W/ STAINLESS STEEL COVER @ 24" A.F.F. - HUBBELL #7968
(PP)	TWO-COMPARTMENT POWER & COMMUNICATION POLE - WIREMOLD #30TP-2V
▼₄	TELE/ DATA FLOOR CORE (FLUSH MOUNTED IN FLOOR) - 3 DATA, 1 VOICE - HUBBELL #459

Figure 14-20 A power plan often includes telephone and other communication devices.

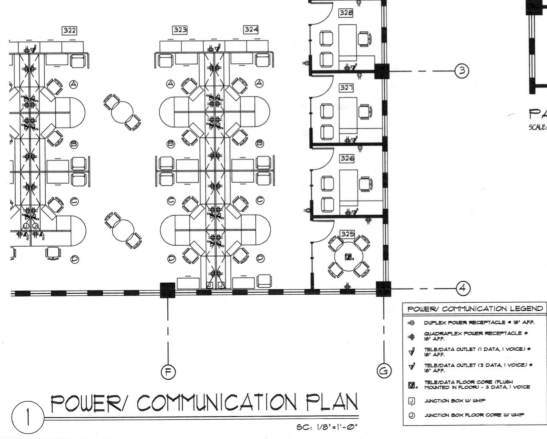

POWER/ COMMUNICATION PLAN
SC: 1/8"=1'-0"

POWER/ COMMUNICATION LEGEND

⊖	DUPLEX POWER RECEPTACLE @ 18" A.F.F.
⊕	QUADRAPLEX POWER RECEPTACLE @ 18" A.F.F.
▽	TELE/DATA OUTLET (1 DATA, 1 VOICE) @ 18" A.F.F.
▼	TELE/DATA OUTLET (3 DATA, 1 VOICE) @ 18" A.F.F.
▼₄	TELE/DATA FLOOR CORE (FLUSH MOUNTED IN FLOOR) - 3 DATA, 1 VOICE
⊡	JUNCTION BOX W/ WHIP
⊙	JUNCTION BOX FLOOR CORE W/ WHIP

Scale of Electrical Plans

Electrical plans in commercial spaces are generally drawn at the same scale as the floor plans. The most common scale for commercial projects is ⅛" = 1'-0" (1:100 metric). However, in complex installations, the scale might be increased to ¼" = 1'-0" (1:50 metric). The scale the plan is drawn at should be noted and placed either adjacent to or directly below the title.

Drafting Standards for Electrical Plans

Electrical plans must show all interior and exterior walls, stairs, and large devices, such as furnaces, water heaters, etc., that require power. Built-in fixtures and cabinetry, such as in bathrooms and kitchens, should also be drawn to better locate the electrical outlets and other devices. The walls should be drawn with lighter line weights so they do not dominate the drawing. Locate the convenience outlets on the walls where they are to be mounted, and call out the dimension above the finished floor (A.F.F.). Remember to note any special requirements such as weatherproof (WP), split-wired, or special-purpose connections. Common electrical symbols are shown in Figure 14-21.

Designation of Materials

Electrical plans are primarily diagrammatic. Although they are drawn to a scale that matches the floor plans, the electrical devices are often too small to portray in the drawing at their exact scale. They are drawn as an oversize symbol to be easily recognized. To keep the drawing simple, materials such as finish flooring and other items are not delineated.

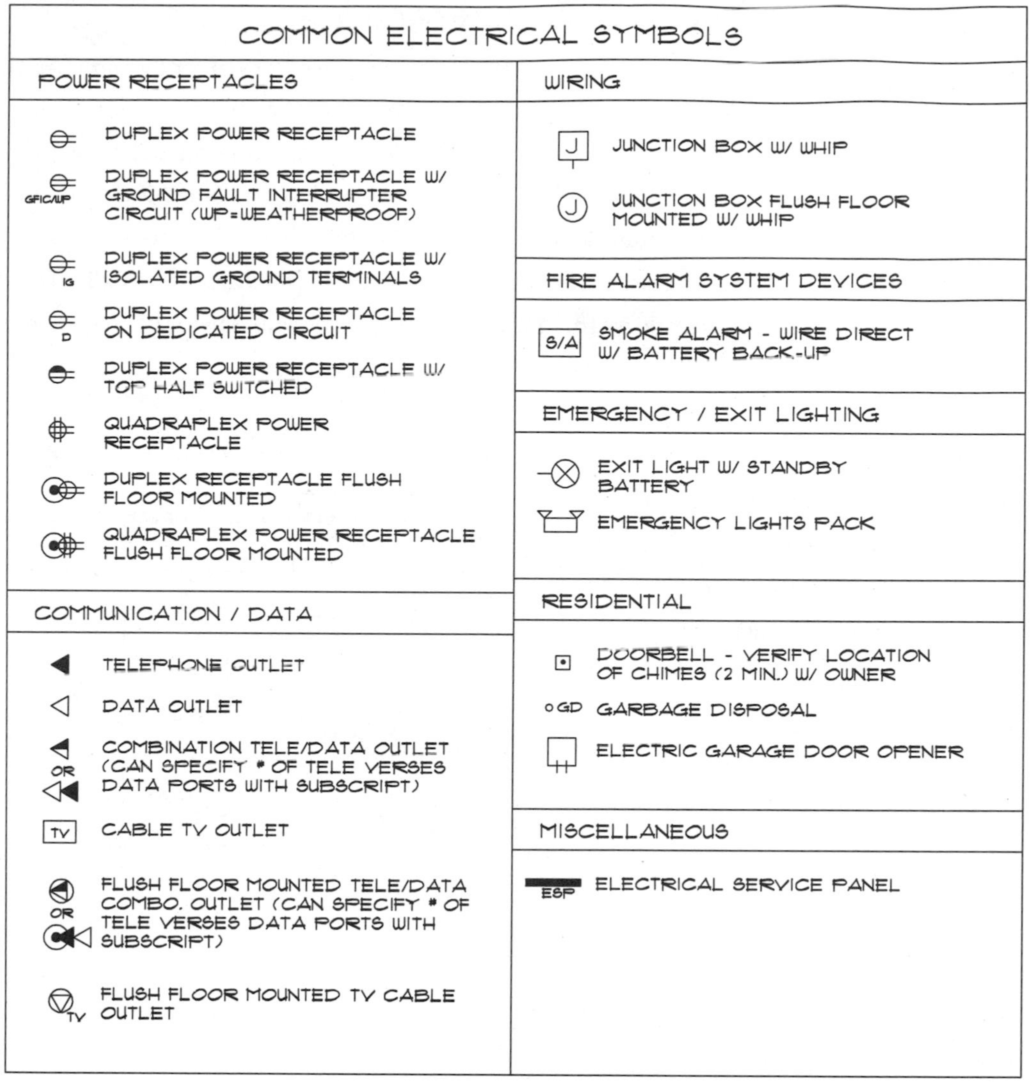

Figure 14-21 Common electrical symbols.

Dimensioning Electrical Plans

Electrical plans are drawn to a scale that generally matches the floor plans. There is no need for a lot of dimensioning on the electrical plan, as items can be located to scale on the floor plans. However, in some cases, electrical outlets and other devices do need to be dimensioned to accurately place them where they can be easily accessed when the building is occupied (Figure 14-22). This is particularly true for large expanses of wall where the scale cannot be accurately determined by scaling the drawing. In such instances, references should be given that are easily obtainable in the field, dimensioning from the face of a wall, column, or imaginary centerline of a room. If a horizontal dimension is not given for a wall outlet, the electrician will place it as close as possible to the designer's plan. The electrician might choose to attach the outlet to a wall stud rather than locating it between two studs if the designer has not dimensioned a specific location.

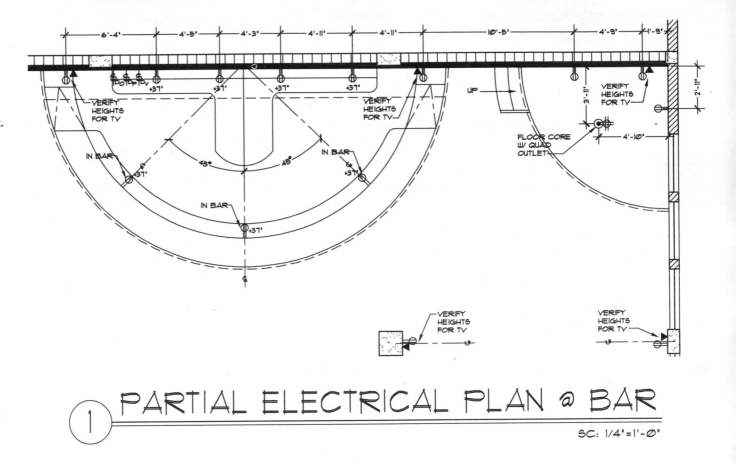

Figure 14-22 Although most electrical outlets do not need to be exactly located, there are some exceptions, such as in this bar area, where outlets must coordinate with equipment.

PARTIAL ELECTRICAL PLAN @ BAR

SC: 1/4"=1'-0"

Checklist for Electrical Plans

General

- Title the drawing, note its scale, and identify north (or reference direction).

- Title the accompanying electrical schedule and key it to the plan.

- Add notes to clarify any abbreviations that are not commonly recognized.

- Clean up the plan (or in CAD, turn off superfluous information) so the walls, spaces, and key electrical codes are clear, dark, and very legible.

- Cross-reference the electrical plan to other drawings and schedules, carefully checking for accuracy and completeness of information.

Notations

- Note special situations, such as devices supplied by owner or others.

- Note special features, clearances, outlet locations above finish floors, cabinetry, and other items.

- Note alignments and other important items that affect the electrical plan.

Dimensions

- Dimension location of outlets and changes in floor or wall types that affect the outlet installation.

- Dimension outlets to walls, wall corners or intersections, and other items such as columns.

- Dimension the appropriate outlets to the proper distance above the finished floor (A.F.F.).

- Dimension clearances, alignments, and other controlling factors.

MECHANICAL AND PLUMBING PLANS 15

The mechanical systems of a building are commonly referred to collectively as the HVAC (heating, ventilating, and air-conditioning) system. The HVAC system ensures that the occupants of a building are provided with a comfortable environment. The system does more than provide heating for winter and cooling for summer. It brings in fresh air, circulates it through the interiors, and exhausts stale air and odors. It can also treat air to control humidity, dust, pollen, and other undesirable conditions.

The plumbing system in a building serves a number of different functions, such as delivering water to people and machines through pressurization (water supply), and ejecting water to be removed through gravity (drainage). Plumbing serves three basic needs: it provides water for human consumption, sanitary drainage of wastes, and mechanical systems. Water might be used for equipment or serve an automated sprinkler system, as discussed later in this chapter under plumbing plans. Some commercial buildings might also have a storm drainage system that rids the roof or other areas of rainfall or flooding. Such systems are separate from the sanitary sewage piping and collect into a storm sewer or are routed to a curbside drainage. A building might also have a waterfall feature, fountain, pond, or other decorative element that has a specialized, recirculating water system.

Mechanical and plumbing drawings involve a lot of communication, coordination, and teamwork among the various design professionals and the contractors. The professional offices that produce the HVAC and plumbing drawings must be aware of one

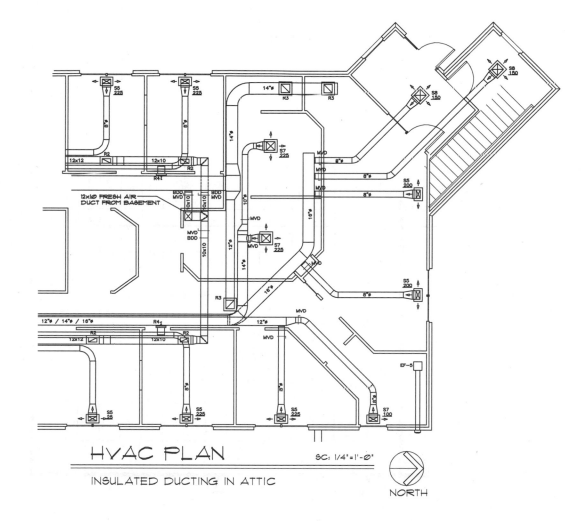

Figure 15-1 Heating, ventilating, and air-conditioning ductwork and related ceiling grilles are designed and drawn over the floor plan.

201

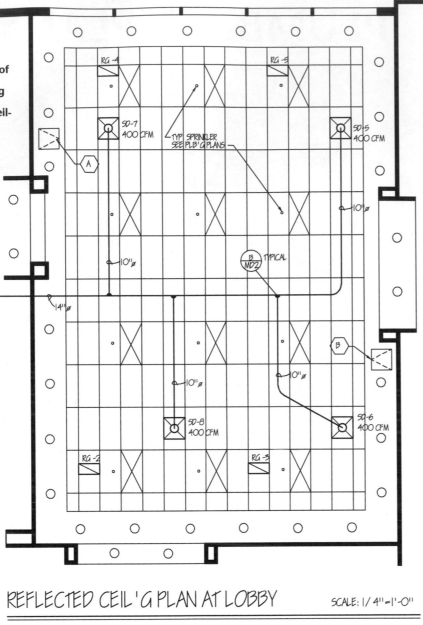

Figure 15-2 This ceiling plan shows the location of HVAC ducting and ceiling registers in relation to ceiling light fixtures and dropped soffits.

REFLECTED CEIL 'G PLAN AT LOBBY   SCALE: 1/4"=1'-0"

another's responsibilities to avoid conflicts, such as the location of a light fixture and air diffuser in the same position. At the same time, both of these types of drawings are schematic in nature, allowing the contractor some latitude in the placement of the parts during field installations. Great care and forethought should go into the drawings, but existing conditions and the many variables present during the construction process may cause small deviations in the placement and installation of these systems.

Mechanical (HVAC) Plans

Engineers, architects, and mechanical contractors are the primary designers of HVAC plans (Figure 15-1). However, interior designers are often called on to coordinate the way the HVAC is installed and to monitor how it will affect the interiors of a building. A designer needs to be able to interpret the basic HVAC plans (particularly the reflected ceiling plan) for coordination of light fixtures, registers, grilles, thermostats, and other items that interface with the system (Figure 15-2). For example, an air diffuser in a wood-paneled ceiling needs to be carefully dimensioned to fall in the center of a panel, rather than at a joint or other haphazard position. The interior designer should understand the basic layout of the HVAC system and take care that furniture, furnishings, and miscellaneous equipment does not obstruct the operation of the system.

HVAC systems utilize a number of different mediums to regulate the environment in a building. The two most common are air and liquid. These carry energy produced by electricity, oil, or renewable sources such as solar and wind power. Liquid systems primarily use water as a transport medium; however, other fluids, such as refrigerants and oils, are also used. In the water system, a boiler is used to create steam. The steam is circulated through piping to radiators placed in the building spaces, creating a heating mode. In the cooling mode, water is chilled at the central plant and circulated to individual radiator units that cool the surrounding air and absorb heat, which is piped back to the central plant. In the air system, heated or cooled air is transported to the interior spaces with supply and return ducts. In residential projects, these ducts are generally run below floor joists, above the ceiling, or even in an attic space. In commercial work, the ducting is run in the space between a suspended ceiling and the structure above, such as the next floor, as shown in Figure 15-3. When this space is also used as a return air space or plenum, building codes limit the use of combustible and other hazardous materials in the plenum. In other cases, raised floor systems can be placed above the structural floor, and ducting runs in this accessible system. In both residential and commercial work, ducting is also sometimes run in wall cavities, although the space is generally limiting in large systems due to the larger sizes of ductwork required for moving large amounts of air.

Access is needed to HVAC components such as fire dampers, valves, and adjustable dampers. In suspended acoustical ceilings, a tile or two can be removed to gain access to the necessary parts. In gypsum board ceilings, special access doors are installed in strategically located areas. The interior designer should be able to read the plans and take note where these items might cause physical or aesthetic conflicts with the ceiling design.

The HVAC system also includes various controls such as thermostats and other monitoring equipment. The position of the thermostats is generally specified by the mechanical engineer. They are placed away from heat sources such as fireplaces, exterior walls, large expanses of exterior glass, and other features that may hinder their operation. Generally, they are located on the walls, and must be coordinated with other interior finishes and equipment

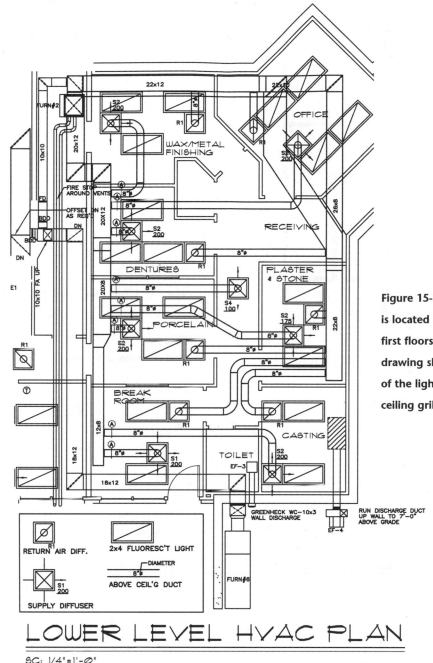

Figure 15-3 The HVAC ductwork is located between the lower and first floors of this dental lab. The drawing shows the coordination of the light fixtures and the HVAC ceiling grilles.

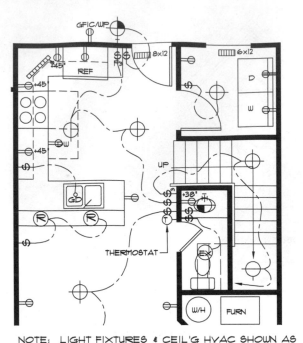

NOTE: LIGHT FIXTURES & CEIL'G HVAC SHOWN AS REFLECTED CEIL'G PLAN

ELECTRICAL PLAN

Figure 15-4 The thermostat for the first floor of this apartment is located on an inside wall, next to the light switches.

Figure 15-5 Furnaces and ducting are drawn at a large scale in this sectional view of the attic for a small commercial building.

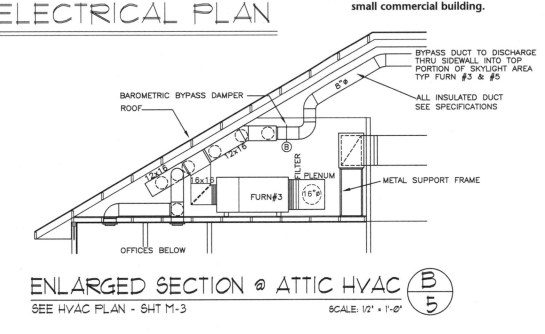

ENLARGED SECTION @ ATTIC HVAC B/5

SEE HVAC PLAN - SHT M-3   SCALE: 1/2' = 1'-0'

such as wall switches, wall sconces, etc., as illustrated in Figure 15-4. In large projects, there may be several thermostats to control heating and cooling in multiple zones of a building.

Scale of HVAC Plans

HVAC plans are generally drawn at the same scale as the floor plans. The most common scale is $\frac{1}{4}$" = 1'-0" (1:50 metric) for residential and small commercial projects and $\frac{1}{8}$" = 1'-0" (1:100 metric) for large commercial ones. The scale the HVAC plan is drawn at should be noted either adjacent to or directly below the drawing title. Other detailed and related equipment drawings might be enlarged with their respective scales shown on the drawing and referenced to the HVAC plan (Figure 15-5).

Drafting Standards for HVAC Plans

As HVAC systems carry water, air, electrical currents, or a combination of these, detailed drawings are made to show the layout of each system and its operation. The drawings for HVAC air supply equipment reflect the ductwork system and sizes needed to deliver and return the proper amount of air to each space, as shown in Figure 15-6. HVAC systems that carry water use drawings to indicate boiler equipment, piping sizes, and layouts.

In all of these systems, the equipment, piping, ducts, and other features are shown in a plan view. These floor plans should not be cluttered with notes, dimensions, room names, and other notations that might make the HVAC part of the plan difficult to read. Wall lines are often drawn lighter and thinner than the HVAC system lines in order to make the system particulars stand out clearly. In some instances, the ductwork might even be shaded for easier identification. The HVAC plans are schematic, using symbols to denote the various parts such as furnaces, ducts, control devices, and piping. Although professional firms might vary in the symbols they

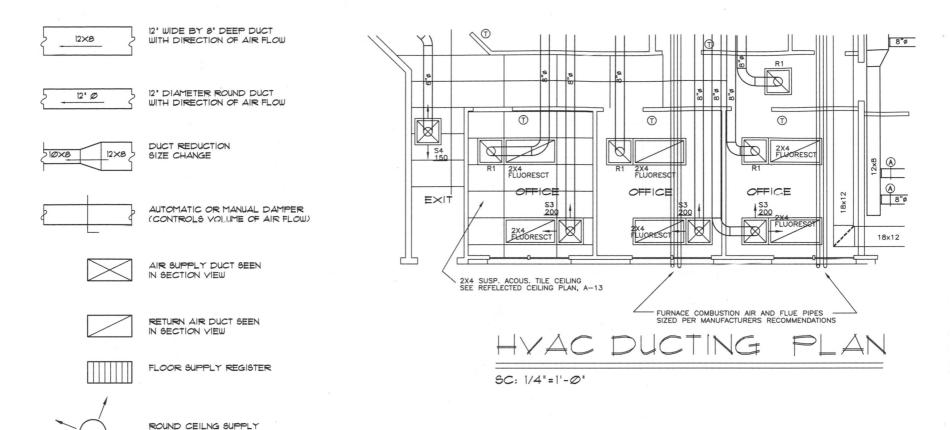

HEATING AND AIR CONDITIONING SYMBOLS

Symbol legend (left column):

- 12×8 — 12' WIDE BY 8' DEEP DUCT WITH DIRECTION OF AIR FLOW
- 12' Ø — 12' DIAMETER ROUND DUCT WITH DIRECTION OF AIR FLOW
- 10×8 / 12×8 — DUCT REDUCTION SIZE CHANGE
- AUTOMATIC OR MANUAL DAMPER (CONTROLS VOLUME OF AIR FLOW)
- AIR SUPPLY DUCT SEEN IN SECTION VIEW
- RETURN AIR DUCT SEEN IN SECTION VIEW
- FLOOR SUPPLY REGISTER
- ROUND CEILNG SUPPLY DIFFUSER OUTLET — ARROWS INDICATE DIRECTION OF AIR FLOW
- RECTANGULAR CEILNG SUPPLY DIFFUSER OUTLET
- LINEAR AIR DIFFUSER
- THERMOSTAT

HVAC DUCTING PLAN

SC: 1/4"=1'-0"

Labels within the plan: 2X4 SUSP. ACOUS. TILE CEILING SEE REFELECTED CEILING PLAN, A–13; FURNACE COMBUSTION AIR AND FLUE PIPES SIZED PER MANUFACTURERS RECOMMENDATIONS; EXIT; OFFICE; 2X4 FLUORESCT; R1; S4 150; S3 200; 12×8; 18x12; 8"ø

use, some are fairly standard, as seen in Figure 15-7. The symbols are cross-referenced to a schedule that fully describes the piece of equipment or assembly. In some cases, a single line is used to represent the ductwork or piping (Figure 15-8). A note is then added next to the run indicating the size of the duct or pipe. In ducting, the first number generally refers to the width and the second number to the height of the assembly. In air systems, arrows are used to indicate the direction of flow through the ducting and at the diffusers. Isometric drawings are also used to explain HVAC assemblies or particulars of the system, as illustrated in Figure 15-9. These are prepared by the mechanical engineer to more clearly show the components of system.

Figure 15-6 This reflected ceiling plan shows the HVAC duct sizes and location of the supply and return registers where they penetrate the ceiling.

Figure 15-7 *(left)* HVAC drawings employ basic symbols to illustrate components.

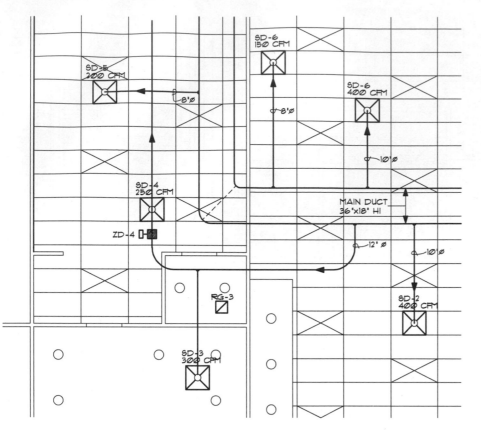

PARTIAL HVAC DUCTING

In the ductwork diagram:

- SD-5 200 CFM
- SD-6 150 CFM
- SD-6 400 CFM
- 8'ø
- 8'ø
- 10'ø
- SD-4 250 CFM
- ZD-4
- MAIN DUCT 36"x18" HI
- RG-3
- 12"ø
- 10'ø
- SD-2 400 CFM
- SD-3 300 CFM

Figure 15-8 In this office building, the above-ceiling ductwork that radiates from a central main supply is shown as a single line, with size noted next to each duct.

Figure 15-9 An isometric is an effective way to illustrate certain equipment and ducting in the HVAC system, as seen in this furnace room.

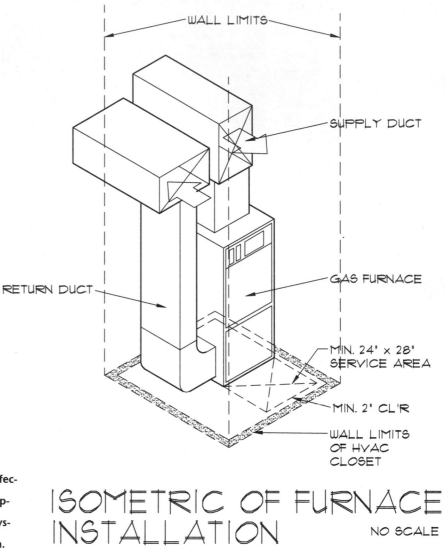

ISOMETRIC OF FURNACE INSTALLATION
NO SCALE

- WALL LIMITS
- SUPPLY DUCT
- RETURN DUCT
- GAS FURNACE
- MIN. 24" x 28" SERVICE AREA
- MIN. 2' CL'R
- WALL LIMITS OF HVAC CLOSET

Designation of HVAC Materials

HVAC materials are generally not indicated on the plan drawings. They are primarily indicated by a note or in the specifications. The notes might specify a duct as 1-inch (25 mm) fiberboard or 20-gauge sheet metal. In a water system, copper piping or other materials might be called out in notes as to their diameter and grade of copper. Elbows, tees, and other connector assemblies are drawn simplistically as they are commonly shown in HVAC standards.

Checklist for HVAC Plans

General

- Title the drawing, note its scale, and reference it to north or another plan locator.

- Completely fill out the symbol legend for a clear understanding by the reader.

- Cross-reference equipment on the plans to schedules or specifications.

- Show thermostat locations. Check these locations against the floor plans for coordination with electrical receptacles, counters, cabinets, and other built-ins.

- Show the exterior location for air-conditioning equipment, such as compressors and coils.

- Call out access panels and controls as required by the equipment and building codes.

- Cross-reference the drawing with the reflected ceiling plan and other drawings for coordination and to avoid conflicts in installation of lights, etc.

Notations

- Call out exhaust vents (bathroom and kitchen equipment) to the exterior or note if they are recirculating.

- Call out domestic dryer vents to the exterior.

- Note furnaces and boilers, and cross-reference to specifications.

- Note proper clearances and access to equipment for adjustments, repair, etc.

- Note fresh-air intakes where applicable.

- Note piping sizes, whether they are supply or return, and the type of fluid they carry (chilled water, hot water, etc.).

- Note (and coordinate with mechanical engineer) whether air diffusers are to be a particular color or painted to match adjacent surfaces.

Dimensions

- Dimension the sizes of ducts by calling them out on the plan by width and height or diameter. With water systems, call out the pipe sizes and transitions.

- Call out the sizes of grilles and diffusers.

Plumbing Plans

Plumbing plans are prepared to show how pressurized fresh water and gravity-drained wastes are routed through the building. These plans are coordinated with the other structural and architectural plans to ensure proper location, operation, and protection of the plumbing systems. Plumbing drawings are often done in plan view (Figure 15-10) and elevation views, and sometimes an isometric drawing is provided. A number of plumbing materials are used in both residential and commercial projects, such as cast iron, copper, steel, and plastic pipe. Although the materials might vary, the drawing techniques and symbols used are primarily the same in all systems.

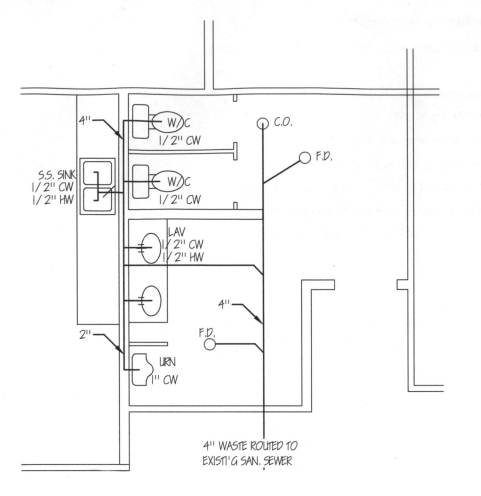

PLUMBING PLAN @ MEN'S RM 302

SCALE: 1/4"=1'-0"

Figure 15-10 The sanitary sewer system in this small apartment is drawn as heavy lines over the base floor plan, with sizes noted. Domestic waterline sizes are also specified.

The fire-protection system, which is considered separate from the plumbing, is usually a sprinkler system utilizing its own separate water system. This system is fed from dedicated water mains that in turn connect through piping to the individual sprinkler heads. In the case of a fire, heat sensor devices activate these heads to open and allow the directionally controlled flow of water to the fire's source. In most buildings, these sprinkler heads are visible, and they can be located on ceilings and walls, depending on the amount of coverage needed. However, recessed sprinkler heads that have a smooth cover flush with the ceiling are available at a higher cost. The cover is dropped away when the head activates and lowers below the ceiling to spray the water.

Although interior designers do not design these sprinkler systems, it is important to recognize the location of the heads in a drawing and coordinate them with other ceiling-mounted items. For example, the designer should consider how the individual heads will fit with the design scheme of the reflected ceiling plan, as well as check for interference with light fixtures, ceiling treatments, and other features.

Scale of Plumbing Drawings

A variety of scales may be used to draw plumbing systems, depending whether the drawings are depicted in plan views, isometrics, or enlarged details. The most common scale is ¼" = 1'-0" (1:50 metric) for residential and small commercial projects and ⅛" = 1'-0" (1:100 metric) for large commercial ones. Floor plans serve as the base drawing and are turned into plumbing plans by the addition of piping, controls, and other devices. Domestic water lines and sanitary sewer lines are drawn as an overlay on the floor plans. It can be difficult to show a lot of piping details and other components that are close together in a space, such as a boiler room and other heavy water-usage equipment. In these instances, a portion of this area is drawn at a larger scale and referenced to the plans (Figure 15-11). As most plumbing plans show only the horizontal positions of pipes and fixtures, a schematic is drawn to show the vertical elements of the system. This is often done with an isometric and is generally not drawn to scale to conserve space on the drawings, as illustrated in Figure 15-12.

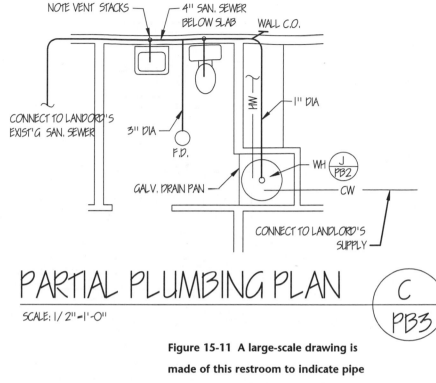

PARTIAL PLUMBING PLAN

SCALE: 1/2"=1'-0"

(C)
PB3

Figure 15-11 A large-scale drawing is made of this restroom to indicate pipe sizes and related information that could not be shown on a small-scale floor plan.

Figure 15-12 An isometric drawing is often made to show the complete layout and piping sizes of the sanitary sewer system in a building.

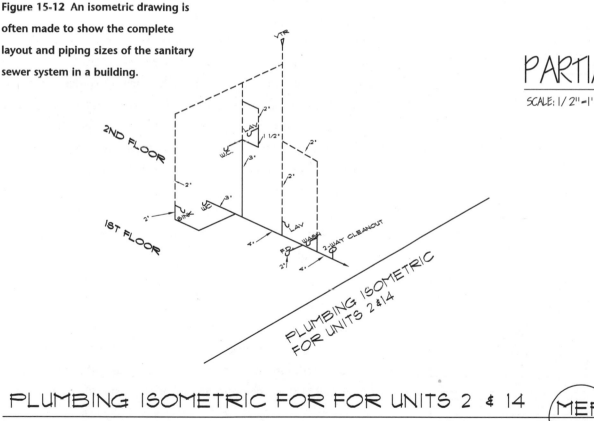

PLUMBING ISOMETRIC FOR FOR UNITS 2 & 14

(MEP
12)

Figure 15-13 Standard plumbing symbols used in construction drawings.

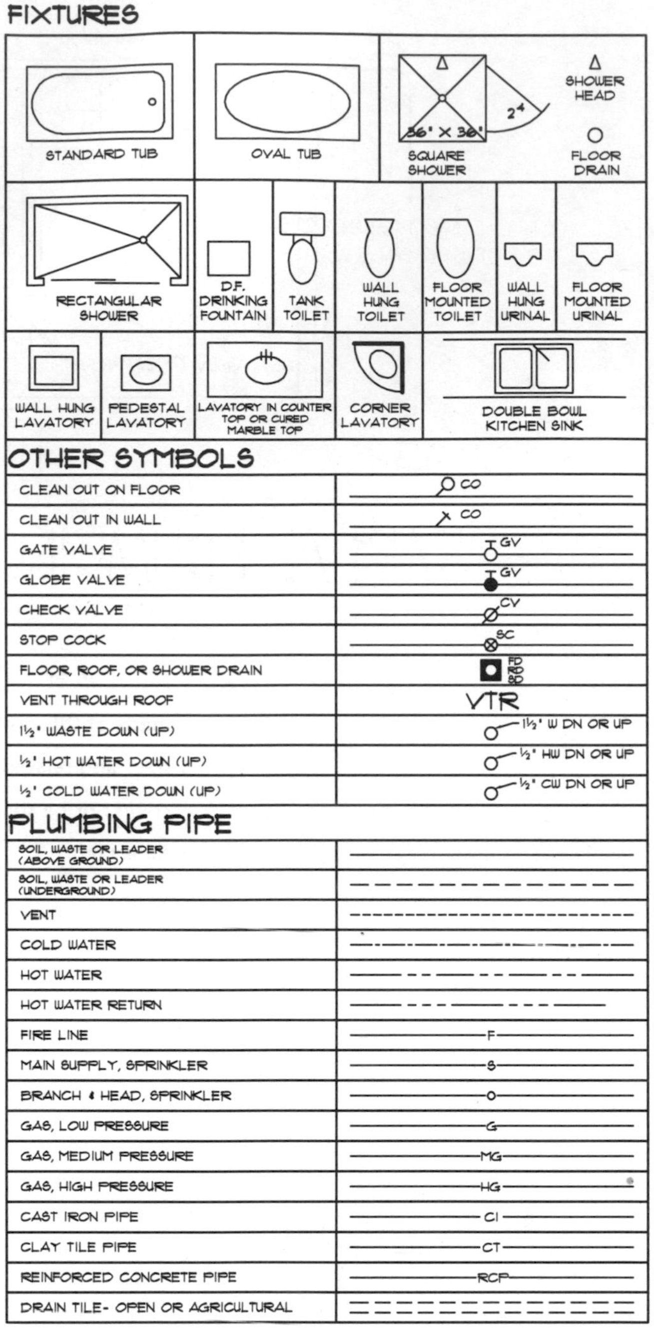

FIXTURES

STANDARD TUB	OVAL TUB	SQUARE SHOWER 36" X 36"	SHOWER HEAD / FLOOR DRAIN
RECTANGULAR SHOWER	D.F. DRINKING FOUNTAIN / TANK TOILET	WALL HUNG TOILET / FLOOR MOUNTED TOILET	WALL HUNG URINAL / FLOOR MOUNTED URINAL
WALL HUNG LAVATORY / PEDESTAL LAVATORY	LAVATORY IN COUNTER TOP OR CURED MARBLE TOP	CORNER LAVATORY	DOUBLE BOWL KITCHEN SINK

OTHER SYMBOLS

CLEAN OUT ON FLOOR	CO
CLEAN OUT IN WALL	CO
GATE VALVE	GV
GLOBE VALVE	GV
CHECK VALVE	CV
STOP COCK	SC
FLOOR, ROOF, OR SHOWER DRAIN	FD RD SD
VENT THROUGH ROOF	VTR
1½" WASTE DOWN (UP)	1½" W DN OR UP
½" HOT WATER DOWN (UP)	½" HW DN OR UP
½" COLD WATER DOWN (UP)	½" CW DN OR UP

PLUMBING PIPE

SOIL, WASTE OR LEADER (ABOVE GROUND)	————————
SOIL, WASTE OR LEADER (UNDERGROUND)	– – – – – –
VENT	- - - - - - - -
COLD WATER	—·—·—·—
HOT WATER	— — — — —
HOT WATER RETURN	— – – — – –
FIRE LINE	——F——
MAIN SUPPLY, SPRINKLER	——S——
BRANCH & HEAD, SPRINKLER	——O——
GAS, LOW PRESSURE	——G——
GAS, MEDIUM PRESSURE	——MG——
GAS, HIGH PRESSURE	——HG——
CAST IRON PIPE	——CI——
CLAY TILE PIPE	——CT——
REINFORCED CONCRETE PIPE	——RCP——
DRAIN TILE- OPEN OR AGRICULTURAL	===========

Drafting Standards for Plumbing Drawings

In small projects, domestic water supply and sanitary sewer systems are drawn on the same plan, as they are not often overly complicated. Solid, dashed, and other line types are developed to distinguish between the systems. In the sewage system, the waste line is shown as well as the various required vent lines as dictated by the building codes.

Lines are drawn to depict the various sizes of piping in vertical risers and vents as well as the horizontal runs. However, a plumbing system consists of more than runs of piping. Pipe elbows, fittings, valves, traps, faucets, and numerous other items are sized to work with the piping system and must be accurately called out. In addition to adding notes to the drawings, standard symbols have been developed and are placed on the sheet to coincide with the proper item, as shown in Figure 15-13. A legend is included to accurately identify the type of pipe, and other specific elements that must be connected. A schedule or legend is also developed to indicate a fixture's type, manufacturer, size, color, and other special features — such as a lavatory and faucet set, as illustrated in Figure 15-14. Special plumbing systems such as the automatic fire-extinguishing system are generally drawn by a fire-protection engineer and coordinated into the designer or architect's drawings.

Designation of Materials for Plumbing Plans

Plumbing materials are basically shown in a simplistic manner. Double lines are primarily used to indicate sizes of air ducting, and water-piping systems are indicated mostly with single lines. The actual material might be called out in the plan, although it is usually found in the accompanying schedule or specifications.

Dimensioning Plumbing Plans

Plumbing plans are basically diagrammatic. Although they are scaled to the floor plans, exact dimensions are generally not noted, except in special cases. For example, the scale of the floor plan and building section will indicate fairly accurately the length of piping, but an exact measurement can only be made in the field during installation. For this reason, a note is added to most plans stating, "Piping shown is diagrammatic and must be accurately measured in the field." Many designers, architects, and engineers dimension the centerlines of important elements such as sinks, water closets, lavatories, and drains. But in small residential projects, it is often left up to the builder or plumber to determine their exact placement.

Checklist for Plumbing Plans

General

- Title the drawing, note its scale, and indicate north (or reference direction). Cross-reference this drawing to related drawings.

- Title any accompanying schedules and key them to the plan.

- Place schedules on the same sheet as the plumbing plan (preferred) or on a sheet immediately preceding or following the plan.

- Clean up the plan (or in CAD, turn off superfluous information) so the plumbing information and key codes are clear, dark, and very legible.

- Clearly show the directional run of each pipe and draw its line weight and style to match that shown in the accompanying legend.

- Indicate special features such as valves, faucets, sinks, etc. with a standard symbol on the plan. Cross-reference to the specifications or a legend that details information such as manufacturer and model.

PLUMBING FIXTURES

PF-1	TOILET PARTITIONS GENERAL PARTITIONS SERIES 30 STAINLESS STEEL	PF-4	URINAL ELGER 164-2457 256 BONE
PF-2	URINAL SCREENS GENERAL PARTITIONS SERIES 30 STAINLESS STEEL	PF-5	BOWL UNIT DUPONT CORIAN 387-2 BONE WHITE
PF-3	WATER CLOSET ELGER 111-8675 256 BONE	PF-6	GRAB BARS GENERAL PARTITIONS FF STAINLESS STEEL

Figure 15-14 An example of a plumbing legend that accompanies a plumbing plan drawing.

- Include an abbreviations legend on this sheet or cross-reference to the title sheet (where all the abbreviations are listed).

Notations

- Note the minimum fall required for the gravity sanitary sewer (often ¼" per foot of horizontal run).

- Call out pipe sizes on the plan and their use (hot water, cold water, sanitary sewer, vents, etc.).

- Label the plumbing fixtures and cross-reference to a schedule or the specifications.

- Call out special devices such as vents through the roof (VTR), floor drains, clean-outs, and hose bibs where applicable.

- Note where existing and new plumbing lines are to be extended, removed, or connected.

Dimensions

- Dimension to centerlines of sink, lavatories, drains, faucets, supply lines, and other items where required.

- Dimension maximum runs, lengths, and sanitary sewer line fall.

REPRODUCTION METHODS AND COMPUTERS 16

Once the construction drawings are complete, the designer must decide how to distribute them to the various parties involved in a project. This might be done by making multiple copies through a reproduction process or by sending them electronically through a computer system, such as the Internet.

Along with reproduction processes, the use of computers in design schools and professional offices will be addressed in this chapter. The focus will be on CAD, which is an acronym for computer-aided design or computer-aided drafting. Design involves creating, sketching, drawing, and rendering two-dimensional and three-dimensional spaces and objects. Traditionally, drawings were all done by hand, but now we see the computer taking over many of the repetitive and labor-intensive parts of the process. But even more exciting is that designers can use CAD to do much of their exploration, creation, and presentation. Most designers now see CAD as a tool, similar to the pencil or pen, but much more powerful and dynamic.

This chapter will not attempt to describe the most popular model of computer and its peripherals (hardware) and programs (software), as there is a large variety on the market today, and the technology changes rapidly. Also, preferences for particular software programs differ widely among professional firms, depending on their needs. The reader is encouraged to research the many computers and programs that are available to find those suited to their specific needs.

Figure 16-1 A xerographic machine performs a number of operations for copying drawings and other materials, such as multiple copies, different sizes of paper, reduction, enlargement, and collating.

Reproduction of Drawings

Multiple copies are often made of drawings and used for presentations and as check prints for construction drawings. Copies are also used for competitive bidding and generally distributed to parties such as owners, contractors, subcontractors, and material suppliers during the construction of the project.

Blueprints

For over a hundred years, the prime method of copying drawings was the blueprint process. Originally, the photographic copy process produced a blue background (the white space on the original) with lettering and lines converted to white. From this process, the name *blueprint* was derived, and can still be heard today when dealing with copies of original drawings. However, the historic method of white print on blue ink is no longer used.

Whiteprint Reproduction

After the blueprint process came the development of the whiteprint, produced through a diazo process. For a whiteprint, the original copy, which must be on translucent vellum or plastic film, is fed through a machine and the image is transferred to a piece of yellow diazo paper. The machine uses ultraviolet light that is directed through the original, bleaching out the diazo dye, except where the pencil or pen lines are. The sheet is then fed through a developer system that fixes the lines permanently in blue, black, or brown — depending on the type of diazo paper used. The blue-line prints are still generally referred to as "blueprints." As with the historic blueprint process, most offices and print shops are phasing out this method of copying in favor of advanced technology.

Electrostatic Reproduction

Today, the xerographic process is the preferred method of making reproductions of drawings. It is fast, very accurate in reproduction quality, and becoming more economical each year. This system produces multiple copies in black lines on white paper (Figure 16-1). Variations can include colored lines on a variety of colored papers or on bond, vellum, plastic, and other surfaces. These copiers can handle a number of paper sizes, multiple copies, collating, and even reducing and enlarging images. One advantage of these machines is that the original does not have to be made on translucent vellum or plastic film, as with the whiteprint process.

Facsimile Copies

A facsimile machine (fax) can be used to copy and transmit drawings over a telephone line to a receiver that reproduces the original drawing (Figure 16-2). The process is fairly fast and convenient, but in most cases, the size is limited to the size of the original that can be placed in the machine. Also, most fax copies on the receiving end do not match the exact size and visual quality of the original. However, the speed of the process makes it a handy tool in the design office.

Digital Printers, Plotters, and Copiers

Although the diazo process is being phased out, it is still an economic method of reproduction and used by some firms for making "blueprint" copies from transparent originals. However, this process is fairly labor-intensive. For example, to reproduce 40 sets of 80 original drawings, an operator must feed each of the 80 originals through the machine one at a time and wait for the 40 copies of each sheet. With the advent of large-format plotters and plain-paper copiers (Figure 16-3), multiple copies can be made that are less labor-intensive. As the costs of using xerographic copiers comes down, the diazo process will fall into history, as did the blueprint process.

Today, high-speed digital printers are making copying even more economical and improving the quality of the images. Even the photographic process used in the photocopier machines is being replaced with digital and laser technology. Digital technology and Internet usage has also reduced the time required to deliver the designer's originals to the printing company for reproductions, and then to get the originals back again. Now CAD plans can be electronically transferred in a print-ready format to a remote print station or separate print company, while the original file is retained in the design office.

When printing out a drawing from a CAD file, the designer has several basic ways to create the image. The most basic is the use of a small-scale ink-jet plotter that can do multiple copies at 8½ x 11 inch (216 x 279 mm) formats, either in black-and-white or color. Fairly economical machines can also increase these sizes up to 11 x 17 inch (279 x 432 mm) formats (Figure 16–4). For large-scale drawings, the large-scale plotter can reproduce the large sheet sizes commonly used in architectural and engineering offices. This plotter can also print in black-and-white or color (Figure 16–5). However, large-scale machines are generally slower and more costly than the small ink-jet units. Also, rather than making multiple copies on one of these devices, a print is made on a vellum sheet and then physically sent to a print company for the making of multiple copies. Now we are seeing more plot files e-mailed, rather than hand-carried, to the printer.

Figure 16-2 A facsimile machine can be used to copy and transmit drawings over a telephone line.

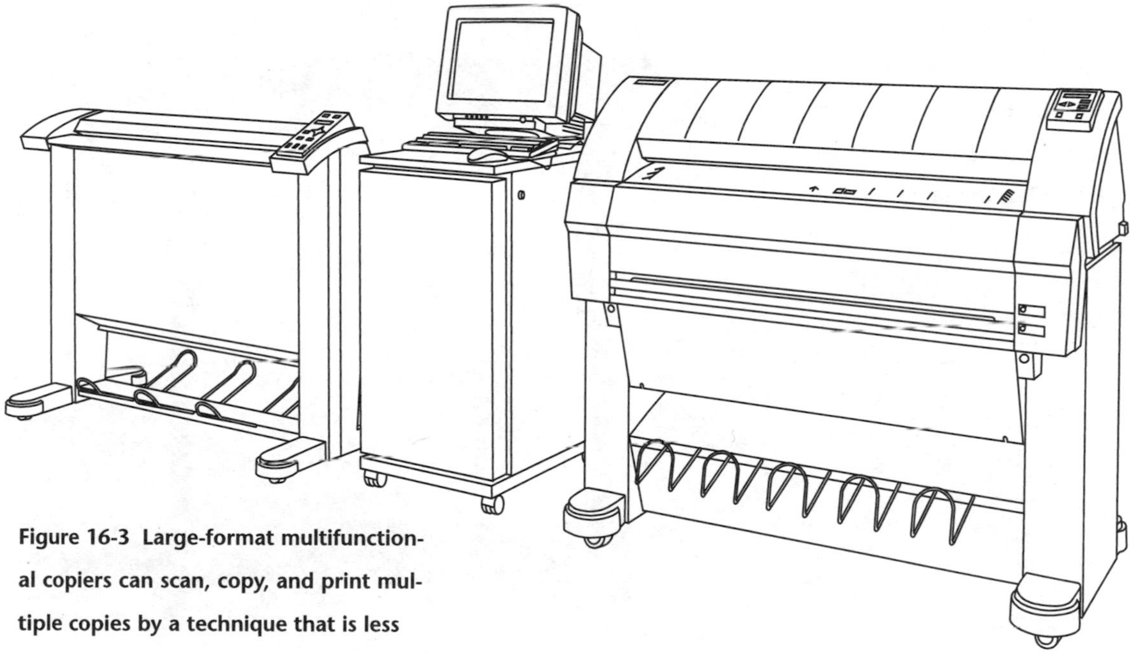

Figure 16-3 Large-format multifunctional copiers can scan, copy, and print multiple copies by a technique that is less labor-intensive than the diazo process.

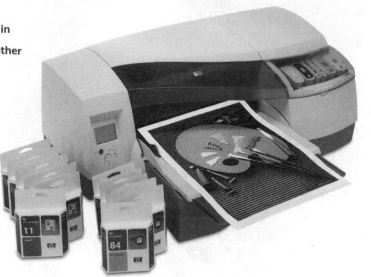

Figure 16-4 Small-scale ink-jet printers can do multiple copies in formats up to 11 x 17 inches, either in black-and-white or color.

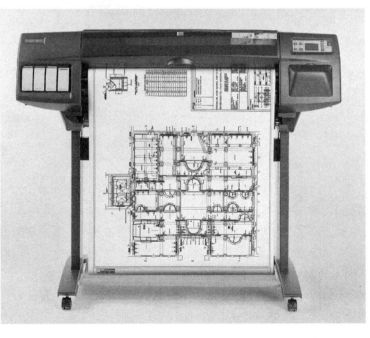

Figure 16-5 For large-format printing, this Hewlett Packard DesignJet plotter can produce D-size black-and-white or color plots in less than four minutes.

The other method of printing small drawings is by laser printer, which can accommodate the same sizes as the ink-jet system. Generally, laser printers can create more precise images and are often faster than the ink-jet printers.

Using Computers for Design, Communication, and Drafting

The use of computers has exploded in both design schools and the professional office. Computers are fast and very accurate, which has increased their use for complicated procedures. Hardware and software were originally used primarily for data processing and mathematical calculations. The next step was the use of the computer for drafting and producing construction drawings, and only occasionally for design process drawing. Today, with ever-evolving software and the reduction in size and cost of computers, many designers and students use computer-aided design (CAD) systems throughout the design process. The computer is used to create preliminary designs, photorealistic renderings, and construction drawins. Besides CAD, a wide variety of programs are available for estimating, tracking time on projects, word-processing, creating data spreadsheets, exchanging e-mail, and many other uses. Some of the programs are effective for increasing productivity, whereas others — such as games and other accessories — offer a refreshing break from our everyday work schedule.

Many designers still find it quicker to create a rough drawing by hand than with a CAD system. They prefer to use CAD for more complex drawings, particularly ones that involve repetitive operations or similar shapes. CAD can also be more effective and faster than manual drafting for making changes to drawings. Editing functions allow the designer to change only part of the file or drawing, or enlarge/reduce something very quickly. In addition to its use for repetitive tasks and other time-saving needs, the computer is also very effective as a design and presentation tool for creating and drawing three-dimensional objects and spaces. Larger memories and processor speeds have enabled designers to create very realistic and accurate images, which can also be explored in movement or in what is termed *virtual reality*. For example, buildings and their interiors can be created on screen in real-time three-dimensional space, allowing the observer to "walk" through them. Some programs are interactive, allowing the transformation of objects and spaces in accordance with the viewer's directives.

CAD programs allow the designer to assign lines and objects their own unique layer. Each layer can then be assigned its own individual line weight, or thickness. Line weights in the computer are referred to as pen weights. In this layering system, line work can be easily controlled. The designer can "turn off" layers that are not needed in a particular drawing. These types of programs allow base drawings to serve as "reference" drawings for all others to build off. For example, in AutoCAD® programs, the floor plan can serve as the base drawing for the electrical plan and the furniture-installation plan. When a change is made to the floor plan, it will automatically update the configuration in the electrical and furniture-installation plans, by using the x-referencing command.

CAD drawings and programs also allow a designer to share files with others, such as clients, vendors, colleagues, and consultants. These files can be stored on disks and given to other parties for viewing, printing, and even modifying. Today, however, we see more of this sharing done electronically, by e-mail, or through file-transfer protocol (FTP).

CAD programs are becoming increasingly interconnected, so that one can change a three-dimensional drawing and automatically cause a related change in the two-dimensional drawing stored in the program. This dynamic linking can also produce automatic changes in the 3-D drawing as the designer changes the 2-D drawing.

Although we speak of the interconnectivity of programs, today's computer hardware is also becoming more "unconnected," or wireless. Until recently, the networking of computers and other devices has been accomplished primarily through the use of cables, wiring, and optical lines. Now more and more devices are being "unplugged" by the use of wireless technology — using transmitting and receiving technology to connect multiple devices. We will soon be less hindered by the hardwiring of our individual components, with the freedom to use a basic server that can wirelessly present through a portable video screen or input to a laptop — unfettered with wiring connections. However, security is a concern with these new wireless connections, as direct-wired networks are more secure. New programs are being developed to overcome these obstacles.

Again, it is not the intent of this chapter to present or review all the hundreds of software and hardware selections available today. New developments in computers and programs are made every six months or less, complicating the timing of writing on items that may have changed drastically since the date of this writing. In some cases, new software is introduced and other software is discontinued. The computer will no doubt continue to improve our work habits and needs, affecting how we design and communicate to others. But behind these wonderful machines is still the need for input and direction from a human designer.

Appendix A MasterFormat™ Level Two Numbers and Titles

Introductory Information

00001	Project Title Page
00005	Certifications Page
00007	Seals Page
00010	Table of Contents
00015	List of Drawings
00020	List of Schedules

Bidding Requirements

00100	Bid Solicitation
00200	Instructions to Bidders
00300	Information Available to Bidders
00400	Bid Forms and Supplements
00490	Bidding Addenda

Contracting Requirements

00500	Agreement
00600	Bonds and Certificates
00700	General Conditions
00800	Supplementary Conditions
00900	Addenda and Modifications

Facilities and Spaces

Facilities and Spaces

Systems and Assemblies

Systems and Assemblies

Construction Products and Activities

Division 1	***General Requirements***
01100	Summary
01200	Price and Payment Procedures
01300	Administrative Requirements
01400	Quality Requirements
01500	Temporary Facilities and Controls
01600	Product Requirements
01700	Execution Requirements
01800	Facility Operation
01900	Facility Decommissioning
Division 2	***Site Construction***
02050	Basic Site Materials and Methods
02100	Site Remediation
02200	Site Preparation
02300	Earthwork
02400	Tunneling, Boring, and Jacking
02450	Foundation and Load-Bearing Elements
02500	Utility Services
02600	Drainage and Containment
02700	Bases, Ballasts, Pavements, and Appurtenances

02800	Site Improvements and Amenities		05700	Ornamental Metal
02900	Planting		05800	Expansion Control
02950	Site Restoration and Rehabilitation		05900	Metal Restoration and Cleaning

Division 3	**Concrete**		**Division 6**	**Wood and Plastics**
03050	Basic Concrete Materials and Methods		06050	Basic Wood and Plastic Materials and Methods
03100	Concrete Forms and Accessories		06100	Rough Carpentry
03200	Concrete Reinforcement		06200	Finish Carpentry
03300	Cast-In-Place Concrete		06400	Architectural Woodwork
03400	Precast Concrete		06500	Structural Plastics
03500	Cementitious Decks and Underlayment		06600	Plastic Fabrications
03600	Grouts		06900	Wood and Plastic Restoration and Cleaning
03700	Mass Concrete			
03900	Concrete Restoration and Cleaning		**Division 7**	**Thermal and Moisture Protection**
			07050	Basic Thermal and Moisture Protection Materials and Methods
Division 4	**Masonry**			
04050	Basic Masonry Materials and Methods		07100	Dampproofing and Waterproofing
04200	Masonry Units		07200	Thermal Protection
04400	Stone		07300	Shingles, Roof Tiles, and Roof Coverings
04500	Refractories		07400	Roofing and Siding Panels
04600	Corrosion-Resistant Masonry		07500	Membrane Roofing
04700	Simulated Masonry		07600	Flashing and Sheet Metal
04800	Masonry Assemblies		07700	Roof Specialties and Accessories
04900	Masonry Restoration and Cleaning		07800	Fire and Smoke Protection
			07900	Joint Sealers
Division 5	**Metals**			
05050	Basic Metal Materials and Methods		**Division 8**	**Doors and Windows**
05100	Structural Metal Framing		08050	Basic Door and Window Materials and Methods
05200	Metal Joists		08100	Metal Doors and Frames
05300	Metal Deck		08200	Wood and Plastic Doors
05400	Cold-Formed Metal Framing		08300	Specialty Doors
05500	Metal Fabrications		08400	Entrances and Storefronts
05600	Hydraulic Fabrications		08500	Windows
05650	Railroad Track and Accessories		08600	Skylights

08700	Hardware		10550	Postal Specialties
08800	Glazing		10600	Partitions
08900	Glazed Curtain Wall		10670	Storage Shelving
			10700	Exterior Protection
Division 9	**Finishes**		10750	Telephone Specialties
09050	Basic Finish Materials and Methods		10800	Toilet, Bath, and Laundry Accessories
09100	Metal Support Assemblies		10880	Scales
09200	Plaster and Gypsum Board		10900	Wardrobe and Closet Specialties
09300	Tile			
09400	Terrazzoo		**Division 11**	**Equipment**
09500	Ceilings		11010	Maintenance Equipment
09600	Flooring		11020	Security and Vault Equipment
09700	Wall Finishes		11030	Teller and Service Equipment
09800	Acoustical Treatment		11040	Ecclesiastical Equipment
09900	Paints and Coatings		11050	Library Equipment
			11060	Theater and Stage Equipment
Division 10	**Specialties**		11070	Instrumental Equipment
10100	Visual Display Boards		11080	Registration Equipment
10150	Compartments and Cubicles		11090	Checkroom Equipment
10200	Louvers and Vents		11100	Mercantile Equipment
10240	Grilles and Screens		11110	Commercial Laundry and Dry Cleaning Equipment
10250	Service Walls		11120	Vending Equipment
10260	Wall and Corner Guards		11130	Audio-Visual Equipment
10270	Access Flooring		11140	Vehicle Service Equipment
10290	Pest Control		11150	Parking Control Equipment
10300	Fireplaces and Stoves		11160	Loading Dock Equipment
10340	Manufactured Exterior Specialties		11170	Solid Waste Handling Equipment
10350	Flagpoles		11190	Detention Equipment
10400	Identification Devices		11200	Water Supply and Treatment Equipment
10450	Pedestrian Control Devices		11280	Hydraulic Gates and Valves
10500	Lockers		11300	Fluid Waste Treatment and Disposal Equipment
10520	Fire Protection Specialties		11400	Food Service Equipment
10530	Protective Covers		11450	Residential Equipment

11460	Unit Kitchens
11470	Darkroom Equipment
11480	Athletic, Recreational, and Therapeutic Equipment
11500	Industrial and Process Equipment
11600	Laboratory Equipment
11650	Planetarium Equipment
11660	Observatory Equipment
11680	Office Equipment
11700	Medical Equipment
11780	Mortuary Equipment
11850	Navigation Equipment
11870	Agricultural Equipment
11900	Exhibit Equipment

Division 12   *Furnishings*

12050	Fabrics
12100	Art
12300	Manufactured Casework
12400	Furnishings and Accessories
12500	Furniture
12600	Multiple Seating
12700	Systems Furniture
12800	Interior Plants and Planters
12900	Furnishings Restoration and Repair

Division 13   *Special Construction*

13010	Air-Supported Structures
13020	Building Modules
13030	Special Purpose Rooms
13080	Sound, Vibration, and Seismic Control
13090	Radiation Protection
13100	Lighting Protection
13110	Cathodic Protection

13120	Pre-Engineered Sptructures
13150	Swimming Pools
13160	Aquariums
13165	Aquatic Park Facilities
13170	Tubs and Pools
13175	Ice Rinks
13185	Kennels and Animal Shelters
13190	Site-Constructed Incinerators
13200	Storage Tanks
13220	Filter Underdrains and Media
13230	Digester Covers and Appurtenances
13240	Oxygenation Systems
13260	Sludge Conditioning Systems
13280	Hazardous Material Remediation
13400	Measurement and Control Instrumentation
13500	Recording Instrumentation
13550	Transportation Control Instrumentation
13600	Solar and Wind Energy Equipment
13700	Security Access and Surveillance
13800	Building Automation and Control
13850	Detection and Alarm
13900	Fire Suppression

Division 14   *Conveying Systems*

14100	Dumbwaiters
14200	Elevators
14300	Escalators and Moving Walks
14400	Lifts
14500	Material Handling
14600	Hoists and Cranes
14700	Turntables
14800	Scaffolding
14900	Transportation

Division 15   **Mechanical**

15050   Basic Mechanical Materials and Methods

15100   Building Services Piping

15200   Process Piping

15300   Fire Protection Piping

15400   Plumbing Fixtures and Equipment

15500   Heat-Generation Equipment

15600   Refrigeration Equipment

15700   Heating, Ventilating, and Air Conditioning Equipment

15800   Air Distribution

15900   HVAC Instrumentation and Controls

15950   Testing, Adjusting, and Balancing

Division 16   **Electrical**

16050   Basic Electrical Materials and Methods

16100   Wiring Methods

16200   Electrical Power

16300   Transmission and Distribution

16400   Low-Voltage Distribution

16500   Lighting

16700   Communications

16800   Sound and Video

Appendix B
Section Format Outline

PART 1 GENERAL

SUMMARY

Section Includes

Products Supplied But Not Installed
  Under This Section

Products Installed But Not Supplied
  Under This Section

Related Sections

Allowances

Unit Prices

Measurement Procedures

Payment Procedures

Alternates

REFERENCES

DEFINITIONS

SYSTEM DESCRIPTION

Design Requirements,
  Performance Requirements

SUBMITTALS

Product Data

Shop Drawings

Samples

Quality Assurance/Control Submittals
  Design Data, Test Reports,
  Certificates,

Manufacturers' Instructions,
  Manufacturers' Field Reports,
  Qualification Statements

Closeout Submittals

QUALITY ASSURANCE

Qualifications

Regulatory Requirements

Certifications

Field Samples

Mock-ups

Pre-installation Meetings

DELIVERY, STORAGE, AND HANDLING

Packing, Shipping, Handling, And Unloading

Acceptance at Site

Storage and Protection

Waste Management and Disposal

PROJECT/SITE* CONDITIONS

Project/Site* Environmental
  Requirements

Existing Conditions

SEQUENCING

SCHEDULING

WARRANTY

Special Warranty

SYSTEM STARTUP

OWNER'S INSTRUCTIONS

COMMISSIONING

MAINTENANCE

Extra Materials

Maintenance Service

PART 2 PRODUCTS

MANUFACTURERS

EXISTING PRODUCTS

MATERIALS

MANUFACTURED UNITS

EQUIPMENT

COMPONENTS

ACCESSORIES

MIXES

FABRICATION

Shop Assembly

Fabrication Tolerances

FINISHES

Shop Priming, Shop Finishing

SOURCE QUALITY CONTROL

Tests, Inspection

Verification of Performance

PART 3 EXECUTION

INSTALLERS

EXAMINATION

Site Verification of Conditions

PREPARATION

Protection

Surface Preparation

ERECTION

INSTALLATION

APPLICATION

CONSTRUCTION

Special Techniques

Interface with Other Work

Sequences of Operation

Site Tolerances

REPAIR/RESTORATION

RE-INSTALLATION

FIELD QUALITY CONTROL

Site Tests, Inspection

Manufacturers' Field Services

ADJUSTING

CLEANING

DEMONSTRATION

PROTECTION

SCHEDULES

*Project Conditions is the preferred term in the U.S.,
Site Conditions is the preferred term in Canada

Appendix C
Sample ADA Guidelines

The Americans with Disabilities Act (ADA) was enacted into law in 1990 to establish Accessibility Guidelines for commercial and public facilities. These guidelines are set forth in civil rights legislation and outline many specifics that must be addressed in new and remodeled buildings. The drawings that follow illustrate some common areas within these facilities that are outlined in the ADA Guidelines. More specific information and drawings of the ADA may be found on the United States Government website.

STAIR HANDRAILS

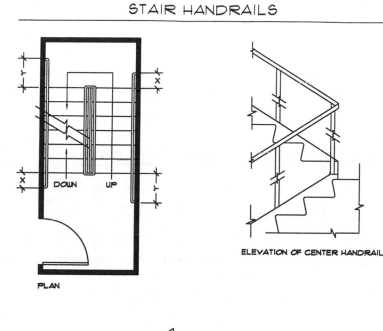

PLAN

ELEVATION OF CENTER HANDRAIL

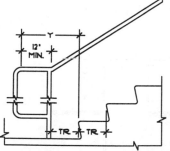

EXTENSION AT BOTTOM OF RUN

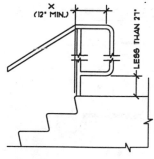

EXTENSION AT TOP OF RUN

NOTE:
X IS THE 12" MIN. HANDRAIL EXTENSION REQUIRED AT EACH TOP RISER
Y IS THE MIN. HANDRAIL EXTENSION OF 12" + THE DEPTH OF ONE TREAD (TR) THAT IS REQUIRED AT EACH BOTTOM RISER

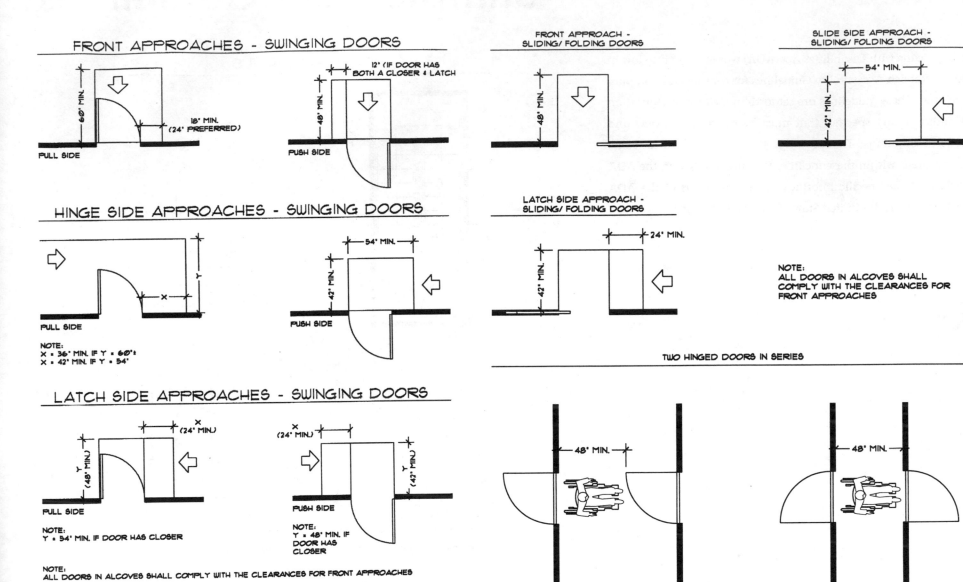

FRONT APPROACHES - SWINGING DOORS

60" MIN.

18" MIN.
(24" PREFERRED)

PULL SIDE

12" (IF DOOR HAS
BOTH A CLOSER & LATCH)

48" MIN.

PUSH SIDE

HINGE SIDE APPROACHES - SWINGING DOORS

PULL SIDE

Y

X

NOTE:
X = 36" MIN. IF Y = 60"
X = 42" MIN. IF Y = 54"

54" MIN.

42" MIN.

PUSH SIDE

LATCH SIDE APPROACHES - SWINGING DOORS

X
(24" MIN.)

Y
(48" MIN.)

PULL SIDE

NOTE:
Y = 54" MIN. IF DOOR HAS CLOSER

X
(24" MIN.)

Y
(42" MIN.)

PUSH SIDE

NOTE:
Y = 48" MIN. IF
DOOR HAS
CLOSER

NOTE:
ALL DOORS IN ALCOVES SHALL COMPLY WITH THE CLEARANCES FOR FRONT APPROACHES

FRONT APPROACH -
SLIDING/ FOLDING DOORS

48" MIN.

LATCH SIDE APPROACH -
SLIDING/ FOLDING DOORS

24" MIN.

42" MIN.

SLIDE SIDE APPROACH -
SLIDING/ FOLDING DOORS

54" MIN.

42" MIN.

NOTE:
ALL DOORS IN ALCOVES SHALL
COMPLY WITH THE CLEARANCES FOR
FRONT APPROACHES

TWO HINGED DOORS IN SERIES

48" MIN.

48" MIN.

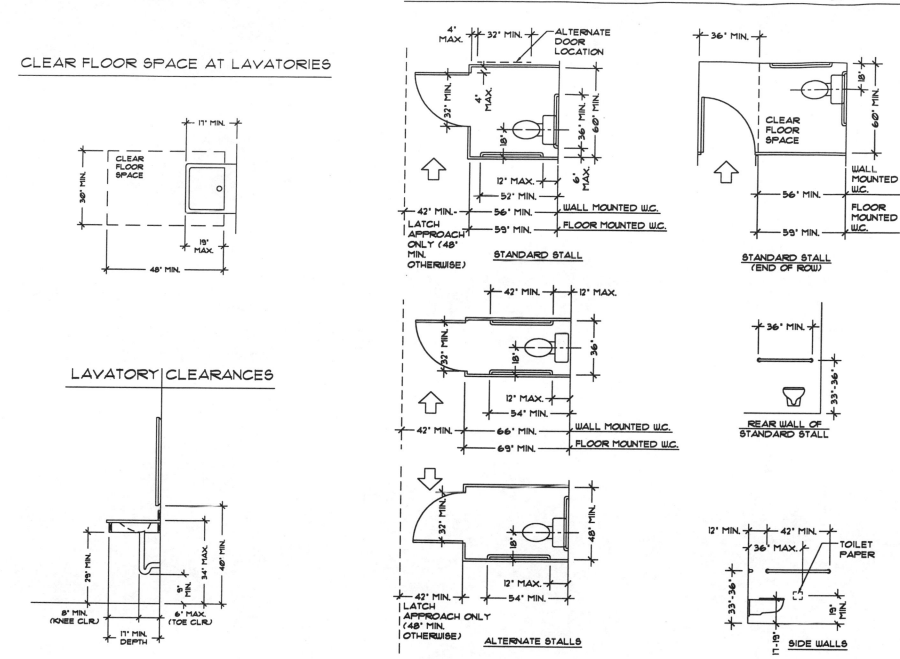

CLEAR FLOOR SPACE AT LAVATORIES

17" MIN.

CLEAR FLOOR SPACE

30" MIN.

19" MAX.

48" MIN.

LAVATORY CLEARANCES

29" MIN.

34" MAX.

40" MIN.

8" MIN. (KNEE CLR.)

6" MAX. (TOE CLR.)

17" MIN. DEPTH

4" MAX.

32" MIN.

ALTERNATE DOOR LOCATION

32" MIN.

4" MAX.

18"

36" MIN.

60" MIN.

12" MAX.

52" MIN.

42" MIN. LATCH APPROACH ONLY (48" MIN. OTHERWISE)

56" MIN. — WALL MOUNTED W.C.

59" MIN. — FLOOR MOUNTED W.C.

6" MAX.

STANDARD STALL

36" MIN.

18"

CLEAR FLOOR SPACE

60" MIN.

56" MIN.

59" MIN.

WALL MOUNTED W.C.

FLOOR MOUNTED W.C.

STANDARD STALL (END OF ROW)

42" MIN.

12" MAX.

32" MIN.

18"

36"

12" MAX.

54" MIN.

42" MIN.

66" MIN. — WALL MOUNTED W.C.

69" MIN. — FLOOR MOUNTED W.C.

36" MIN.

33"-36"

REAR WALL OF STANDARD STALL

32" MIN.

18"

48" MIN.

42" MIN. LATCH APPROACH ONLY (48" MIN. OTHERWISE)

12" MAX.

54" MIN.

ALTERNATE STALLS

12" MIN.

42" MIN.

36" MAX.

TOILET PAPER

33"-36"

17"-19"

19" MIN.

SIDE WALLS

AB	Anchor Bolt	CIR	Circle	DIM	Dimension	FFE	Finished Floor Elevation
AC	Acoustical	CJ	Control Joint	DIN. RM.	Dining Room	FHS	Fire Hose Station
A/C	Air Conditioning	CK	Check	DISP	Garbage Disposal	FIN	Finish
ACT	Acoustical Tile	CLG	Ceiling	DN	Down	FIX. GL	Fixed Glass
ADJ	Adjacent/Adjustable	CLK	Caulk	DP	Dam proof	FLR	Floor
AFF	Above Finished Floor	CLOS	Closet	DR	Door	FLUR	Fluorescent
AL	Aluminum	CLR	Clear	DTL	Detail	FND	Foundation
ASPH	Asphalt	CLS	Close or Closure	DW	Dishwasher	FOC	Face of Concrete
AUTO	Automatic	CM	Centimeter	DWG	Drawing	FOM	Face of Masonry
BR or BDRM	Bedroom	CMU	Concrete Masonry Unit	DWR	Drawer	FOS	Face of Studs
BD	Board	CNTR	Counter	E	East	FTG	Footing
BEL	Below	C.O.	Cleanout	EA	Each	FURR	Furred/Furring
BET	Between	COL	Column	EF	Each Face	GA	Gauge
BIT	Bituminous	CONC	Concrete	EL	Elevation	GB	Grab Bar
BLK	Block	CONST	Construction	ELEC	Electrical	GC	General Contractor
BLDG	Building	CONT	Continuous	EWC	Electric Water Cooler	GFI	Ground Fault Interrupter
BLKG	Blocking	CONTR	Contractor	ELEV	Elevator	GFIC	Ground Fault Interrupter
BM	Beam	CPT	Carpet	EMERG	Emergency		Circuit
BOT	Bottom	CS	Counter Sink	ENCL	Enclose/Enclosure	GI	Galvanized Iron
BRG	Bearing	CSMT	Casement	EQ	Equal	GLS	Glass
BRZ	Bronze	CT	Ceramic Tile	EQP	Equipment	GYP	Gypsum
BRK	Brick	CTR	Center	ESC	Escalator	GYP BD	Gypsum Board
BSMT	Basement	D	Drain	EX	Existing	HB	Hose Bib
BVL	Bevel	DBL	Double	EXH	Exhaust	HBD	Hardboard
CAB	Cabinet	DEM	Demolish	EXT	Exterior	HC	Hollow Core
CEM	Cement	DH	Double Hung	FD	Floor Drain	HDR	Header
CER	Ceramic	DIA	Diameter	FFCE	Finish Face	HDW	Hardware
CI	Cast Iron	DIAG	Diagonal	FF	Finish Floor	HM	Hollow Metal

HOR	Horizontal	MULL	Mullion	REQD	Required	SYS	System
HT	Height	N	North	RET	Return	T	Tread
HT'G	Heating	NO or #	Number	REV	Revise/Revision	TEL	Telephone
HVAC	Heating, Ventilating,	NIC	Not in Contract	RFG	Roofing	TEMP	Tempered
	Air Conditioning	NOM	Nominal	RFL	Reflected	T&G	Tongue and Groove
HWD	Hardwood	NTS	Not to Scale	RH	Right Hand	THK	Thick(ness)
ID	Inside Diameter	OC	On Center	RL	Rail	THR	Threshold
INCL	Include	OD	Outside Diameter	RM	Room	THRU	Through
INSUL	Insulate (ion)	OH	Overhead	RO	Rough Opening	TRTMT	Treatment
INT	Interior	OPG	Opening	MIN	Minimum	TV	Television
JST	Joist	OPH	Opposite Hand	MIR	Mirror	TYP	Typical
JT	Joint	OPP	Opposite	MISC	Miscellaneous	UNF	Unfinished
KIT	Kitchen	PAR	Parallel	MLD	Molding	UTIL	Utility
KO	Knockout	PED	Pedestrian	SC	Solid Core	V	Volts
LADR	Ladder	PERI	Perimeter	SCH	Schedule	VAT	Vinyl Asbestos Tile
LAM	Laminate	PFB	Prefabricate	SCN	Screen	VERT	Vertical
LAUND	Laundry	PKT	Pocket	SEC	Section	VTR	Vent Thru Roof
LAV	Lavatory	PL	Plate	SERV	Service	VTW	Vent Thru Wall
LBL	Label	PLAS	Plastic	S4S	Surfaced Four Sides	VNR	Veneer
LH	Left Hand	PLAST	Plaster	SHR	Shower	ROW	Right of Way
LIV. RM	Living Room	PNL	Panel	SHT	Sheet	RR	Restroom
LOC	Locate/Location	PNT	Paint	SIM	Similar	RWD	Redwood
M	Meter	PT	Point	SL	Slide (ing)	S	South
MAS	Masonry	PTN	Partition	SOFT	Soffit	WWF	Welded Wire Fabric
MAX	Maximum	PVC	Polyvinyl Chloride	SPEC	Specification	W/	With
MECH	Mechanical	PWD	Plywood	SPK	Speaker	W	West
MED	Medium	QT	Quarry Tile	SQ	Square	WC	Water Closet
METL	Metal	R	Riser	S&R	Shelf and Rod	WD	Wood
MFR	Manufacturer	RA	Return Air	SS	Service Sink	W/D	Washer/Dryer
MILWK	Millwork	RAD	Radius	STD	Standard	WG	Wire Glass
FPL	Fireplace	RAG	Return Air Grille	STL	Steel	WH	Water Heater
FR	Frame	RAFT	Rafter	STR	Structure(al)	WH	Wall Hung
MM	Millimeter	REF	Reference	SUSP	Suspended	WM	Wire Mesh
MOD	Modular	REFR	Refrigerator	SYM	Symmetrical	WSCT	Wainscot
MTL	Material	REM	Remove	SYN	Synthetic		

Glossary

Acoustical tile — Fiberboard, fiberglass, or similar material used to absorb sound rather than reflect it. Often used as a ceiling material.

Air exchanger — An HVAC unit designed to exhaust stale air and draw in fresh air. In cold climates, the units often capture latent heat in the air and redirect it to the heating system.

Acrylic paint — A water-based paint made with synthetic resins.

Ampere — The unit used to measure the rate of flow of electrical current.

Alcove — Recessed niche or space connected to the side of a larger space or room.

Alloy — A substance produced by the combination of two or more metals, or a nonmetal fused with a metal.

Ampere — The unit used to measure the rate of flow of electrical current.

Alcove — Recessed niche or space connected to the side of a larger space or room.

Anchor bolt — A threaded rod cast or shot into concrete (or masonry) and used for anchoring — e.g., securing a sill plate to the foundation.

Anodize — Use an electrolytic process and a combination of chemicals to place a protective oxide film on metal.

Architect — A professional who designs and draws up instruments such as construction drawings for buildings and other structures in the built environment.

Areaway — An open area below grade that allows light and ventilation toward a basement door or window.

Ashlar — Stone that is cut in rectangular shapes and fitted together.

Ash pit — A recessed pit below a fireplace hearth that is used to collect ashes.

Atrium — An open space or court within a building.

Awning — A covering made of canvas, metal, or another material. The term is also used to describe a window that is hinged at the top and swings outward.

Attic — A space between the ceiling and roof of a building.

Baffle — A device used to block the flow of sound, light, or wind.

Baluster — A row of posts that supports a rail, such as a handrail used on a stairway.

Banister — Another term for a handrail.

Baseboard — A finish and protective board (or other material) covering where a wall and floor meet.

Basement — Lowest story of a building, generally entirely or partially below ground.

Base plate — A steel plate used at the bottom of a column to spread vertical loads out and anchor the column to the floor.

Batt — A blanket of insulating material (such as fiberglass) manufactured in specific widths to be installed between framing members.

Batten — Narrow strip of material (usually wood) that conceals the spacing between larger boards — such as in board and batten siding.

Batter — A wall that slopes away from perpendicular and is seen mostly in concrete or masonry construction.

Bay window — A window element projecting from a building, which generally has three sides.

Beam — A horizontal structural member that supports loads.

Beam ceiling — A ceiling treatment that exposes ceiling beams to view.

Bearing wall — A wall that supports vertical loads.

Bib — A faucet with threads for the attachment of a water hose. Also called a hose bib.

Blocking — Wood framing pieces used to reinforce, secure, or provide backing for other members or materials.

Board and batten — Siding technique using narrow strips of wood (battens) placed in a pattern over wooden siding. The original intent of the battens was to hide the cracks between the vertical boards.

Bookmatch — A wood veneer pattern produced by alternating sheets (flitches) similar to the leaves of a book.

Brick veneer — A facing of brick installed in front of a frame, concrete, or concrete block wall.

BTU — An abbreviation for "British Thermal Unit," which is the standard measurement for heat loss and gain.

Building inspector — An official whose job is to inspect remodeling or new building construction for safety and compliance with the various building codes.

Built-up beam — A roofing type composed of several smaller beams, all secured together.

Built-up roof — Roofing type composed of layers of felt and asphalt, commonly top-coated with gravel.

C.O.M. — Customer's own material. The customer purchases upholstery from another party rather than the furniture manufacturer.

CAD — Computer-aided design

CADD — Computer-aided design and drafting. However, this term is not used as much as the former designation.

Cant strip — A triangular strip of material used to support or eliminate sharp turns in roofing materials or flashings.

Cantilever — A projected structure that is supported only at one end.

Carriage — The supporting linear frame that holds the treads and risers in a stair.

Casement — A window that is hinged on the vertical side.

Casing — The frame around a window or door.

Caulking — A waterproof material used to seal small spaces between adjoining surfaces.

Cavity wall — A hollow wall made up by two layers of masonry walls constructed a few inches apart.

Cement — An adhesive masonry material.

Circuit breaker — A device that opens or closes an electrical circuit. It opens (breaks) a circuit automatically if an unusually high level of current passes through it.

Chamfer — Easing or angling of the edge of two adjoining planes, often at a 45-degree angle.

Channel — A standardized structural steel shape, which resembles a U.

Chase — A space within a building for routing pipes, ducts, wiring, or other utilities.

Checking — Cracks or splits in a board caused by drying or seasonal changes.

Chimney — A flue used to exhaust gases and smoke from a building. See also Flue.

Chord — The bottom, top, or diagonal member of a truss.

Cinder block — A concrete masonry unit made of cinders and cement.

Cleanout — Removable cover or insert in a sewer waste line for cleaning or inspection of the line.

Clerestory — High windows placed in an interior or exterior wall, used mostly for admitting light to a space.

Collar beam — A horizontal member used to connect opposing rafters in roof framing.

Column — A perpendicular load-carrying member.

Concrete — A mixture of cement, gravel, sand, and water that hardens to a strong solid state.

Concrete block — A precast hollow or solid masonry unit of concrete. See also Cinder block.

Concrete masonry unit (CMU) — A concrete block made of hardened concrete, with or without hollow core cells.

Conduit — An outer channel (primarily of metal) used to contain electrical wiring for protection and safety.

Control joint — A groove troweled or cut in concrete slabs that permits the regulation of cracks.

Corbel — The projecting of masonry construction by placing courses cantilevered beyond the lower ones.

Cornerbead — A metal molding used in plaster or drywall construction to protect and finish corners.

Cornice — The projecting element of a roof or wall.

Course — A continuous row of masonry laid with the same uniform height.

Court — A partial or full open space within a building.

Cripple — A vertical structural member in a door or window that is less than full-height.

Curtain wall — The exterior portion of a building that does not support loads.

Damper — The adjustable plate in a chimney or air duct that regulates the draft or air flow.

Duct — A rectangular- or circular-shaped material (metal, fiberboard, etc.) that is used to transfer air from one space to another.

Diffuser — A device that scatters (diffuses) air, light, or sound into a space.

Dormer — A housing projecting from a sloping roof that accommodates a window.

Double-hung — A window that has bottom and top sashes, either of which can be slid up and down.

Drip — A groove or projecting edge incorporated below a surface to carry water or cause it to drip away from a vertical surface below.

Dimension line — A line that shows the distance (in measured increments) between two points. It consists of a line and arrowheads, dots, or slash marks to mark the exact point of reference.

Drywall — Construction using premade gypsum board panels (versus lath and plaster, which is a wet system).

Eave — The section of a roof that projects over a wall below.

Edge band — Thin veneer of material (such as wood) applied to the edge of a panel, such as plywood.

Efflorescence — Powdery deposit on the surface face of masonry. It is a result of water leaching to the surface and transporting chemical salts from within the structure.

EIFS — Exterior insulation and finish system. Coating system of reinforced stucco applied to the surface of an insulated plastic foam board.

Elevation — A drawing of the front, side, or rear of an object.

Escutcheon — A cover plate on door hardware; or cover for the gap around piping where it enters a surface.

Fascia — A vertical band (wood or other material) secured to the cornice or roof overhang.

Fenestration — The placement of windows on a wall surface.

Finished lumber — Wood that has been dressed (milled or sanded) to be used for constructing cabinetwork and other building trim.

Firebrick — A brick that is hard and withstands great heat. It is used to line fireplaces, furnaces, etc.

Fire door — A door that resists fire and prevents it from spreading between spaces. Fire doors are rated as 20-minute, one-hour, two-hour, etc.

Fire resistant — Capable of slowing the spread of or providing a barrier to fire.

Firestopping — Fire-resistant material installed to close the opening through or around the edge of a floor, to prevent the spread of fire between levels.

Firewall — A wall assembly that prevents fire from spreading between adjacent spaces. Firewalls are rated as one-hour, two-hour, three-hour, and four-hour.

Fixed window — A sealed, nonopening window or glass section.

Fixture — An item of plumbing or electric equipment. The term is also used to denote other specialty items such as medical, laboratory, and display elements (as used in retailing and commercial facilities).

Flagstone — A flat stone used for flooring, steps, walls, and walks.

Flange — The horizontal top and bottom sections of a steel beam.

Flashing — The sheet metalwork used to make a construction assembly weathertight.

Flitch beam — A structural beam utilizing a steel plate sandwiched and bolted between two wood members.

Float — To use a trowel (or tool called a float) to spread cement, stucco, plaster, gypsum joint compound, or other workable materials.

Floor joist — A horizontal structural member that supports and distributes floor loads.

Floor plan — A view from above in a building where an imaginary horizontal cut has been made about four feet above the floor plane.

Flue — A vertical shaft that exhausts smoke from a wood or gas fireplace; also, the piping used to exhaust gases from water heaters and furnaces.

Flush — Aligned, level, or even.

Footing — An enlarged base that supports a wall, pier, or column and distributes the weights of a structure onto the ground.

Framing — The wood or steel construction of a building's framework.

French door — Pair of glazed doors hinged at the door frame jambs, and swinging to meet in the center of the opening.

Frieze — A decorative board of cornice trim fastened to a structure.

Frost line — The depth at which frost penetrates the ground during the winter season.

Furred — Lined with a separate surface material, as on a wall, ceiling, or other assembly.

Furring — Narrow strips of wood or metal secured to a wall or ceiling for the purpose of providing a new ground (surface) to attach other finish materials.

Galvanized — Treated with zinc and lead to prevent rusting.

Gauge — Measure designating the diameter of a wire or thickness of a sheet of material, such as metal.

GFIC — Ground fault interrupter circuit. An electrical device in a circuit that quickly disconnects when current is leaked to the ground — often used in moist spaces.

Glass block — Masonry unit made of glass, with a hollow center.

Glazing — Installing glass in windows or doors.

Glue-laminated beams — Structural beams composed of layers of wood glued together under pressure. Abbreviated as glulam.

Grain — Direction of longitudinal axes of wood grain fibers found in wood members.

Grout — A pastelike mixture of cement, sand, and water used for laying and filing joints in masonry construction.

Gusset plate — A metal plate used to connect various portions (chords) of a truss.

Gypsum — Material made of hydrated sulfate of calcium, used to make sheets of wallboard.

Hardboard — A sheet material made by compressing and gluing fine fibers of wood.

Head — The top of a door or window.

Hearth — Noncombustible horizontal surface immediately outside of a fireplace opening.

Heartwood — Center region of cells in a tree trunk.

Heat pump — Mechanical unit that can heat or cool buildings using refrigeration cycles of air or liquid mediums.

Hollow-core door — Door made with face veneers separated by an inner core of gridded spacers, with solid material around the four edges.

Hose bib — An exterior mounted water faucet. It is frost-proofed in cold climates.

Insulation — Various materials used primarily for the reduction of heat gain or loss through floors, walls, and ceilings of buildings.

Jalousie — Horizontal windows composed of a number of long, hinged glass panels that are operated in unison.

Jamb — The vertical side of a door or window.

Joist — Structural members of wood, steel, or concrete used to support floors, ceilings, and roofs.

Kiln-dried — Refers primarily to lumber that has been dried in a kiln to reduce its moisture content.

Knee brace — Short diagonal brace joining a beam and column.

Lag screw — Large structural wood screw turned with a wrench. Has hexagonal or square head.

Landing — Platform at the beginning or end of a stair, or between runs.

Lath — A base material (often metal) that serves as a base for plaster or stucco.

Lattice — Open framework of wood or other material arranged in a grid-like pattern.

Lavatory — A washbasin in a bathroom. The term sink is often reserved for kitchens, laundry rooms and other spaces.

Lintel — The horizontal structural member that spans openings and supports loads from above, such as at a doorway or above a window.

Live Load — The nonstatic weights of people, snow, furniture, and equipment on a floor, roof, or structural member.

Lockset — Hardware assembly for a door, which includes a deadbolt and latch.

Louver — An assembly used to admit or exhaust air, such as a gable vent or other device.

LVL — Laminated veneer lumber. Thin wood veneers glued together to make a larger structural member.

Mantel — Decorative trim piece or member around a fireplace opening.

Masonry — Materials of brick, stone, concrete block, and burned clay (such as ceramic tile).

Masonry veneer — A layer of masonry units such as brick, stone, or tile facing a frame or masonry wall.

MDF — Medium-density fiberboard.

Metal lath — Expanded metal mesh used as base for applying stucco or plaster.

Millwork — Wood building products used for finish work, such as cabinetry, moldings, and other trim.

Moisture barrier — Sheathing made of various materials that retards transfer of water vapor through walls, floors, and ceilings in buildings.

Mullion — Vertical divider placed between doors or windows.

Muntin — Thin divider trim that separates panes of glass in a window assembly.

Newel — Post that serves as termination for guardrails and handrails.

Nonbearing wall — Wall that has no load-bearing capacity to support other elements other than its own weight.

Nominal — Refers to common size terminology for standard items, rather than their actual size, such as a 2x4 stud, which is actually 1.5 inches by 3.5 inches.

Nosing — Portion of the stair tread that projects beyond the riser below. Also used to describe projection of front edge of a countertop.

Ogee — S-shaped curve mostly found in trim and roof gutters.

Oriented strand board (OSB) — Construction panel composed of adhesives and shreds /flakes of wood fiber oriented in specific directions.

Parapet — The portion of a building's exterior wall that extends above the roofline.

Pier — A concrete or masonry footing used to support a load from above, such as a column.

Pilaster — Vertical columnlike element in a wall that provides support or stiffening.

Pitch — The incline of a roof or other plane expressed as a ratio of the span to the height.

Plaster — Cementitious material made of portland cement or gypsum. Applied in paste form to a substrate of lath or masonry, and hardens to a finishable surface.

Plate — A horizontal bottom or top member in wall framing.

Plenum — Space used primarily for HVAC ducting. Usually found between ceiling of a space and floor above, or an elevated area constructed for HVAC purposes.

Plumb — Vertical.

Rafter — Structural member that supports the roof assembly and its finished roofing material.

Raze — Demolish existing construction.

Reinforced concrete — Concrete that has steel reinforcing added to increase its ability to handle various loading forces.

Register — Grille installed at the termination of a mechanical duct for supplying, returning, or exhausting air flow, usually in a directional manner.

Riser — The vertical part of a stair step.

Rough opening — The initial framing size of an opening used to accept a door, widow, or other assembly.

Rowlock — In masonry construction, a brick laid on its long edge, with the end exposed in the wall face.

Run — The horizontal distance of a stair.

R-value — Numerical measurement of a material's resistance to the flow of heat.

Sash — The frame that holds window glass in place.

Scribe — The process of fitting materials such as woodwork or counter backsplashes to irregular faces of a wall or floor surface.

Sealer — Coating that closes the porous surface of a material such as concrete.

Shim — Tapered piece of wood or other material used between two parts for filing voids and to aid in leveling.

Sill — The lowest part or bottom of a window or door. Also can refer to rough wood member that rests on a foundation wall.

Soffit — The horizontal exposed part of a building overhang, such as a roof or balcony.

Soldier — In masonry, a brick (or other masonry unit) laid on its end, with the narrow face to the outside or finished wall face.

Specifications — Written documents that accompany drawings and contain specific information that cannot be conveyed by the drawings alone. They address the materials and the workmanship needed to construct various parts of a building.

Spline — Thin material inserted in grooves cut in two joining pieces of material. Used to hold or align the mating materials.

Split jamb — Preassembled door frame that is made in two halves, installed and locked from opposite sides of an opening.

Sprinkler head — A wall or ceiling device that sprays water in a predetermined coverage pattern, primarily for extinguishing fire.

Stile — The vertical piece in a door panel.

Stringer — The sloped member of a stairway that supports the treads and risers.

Strip flooring — Finished wood flooring manufactured in narrow widths of tongue-and-groove boards.

Stucco — Mixture of portland cement base and sand, which is applied to the exterior of a building. A similar coat applied to the interior of a building is called plaster.

Stud — Vertical wood or steel framing member that is primarily used to build walls.

Sub floor — The under floor sheathing that provides the proper surface for the finished flooring.

Tempered glass — Heat-treated glass that resists breakage.

Terrazzo — Durable flooring made of small stone or other materials embedded in a strong cement-bonding agent and ground smooth.

Thermostat — Electrical or mechanical device that controls the HVAC system by maintaining a preset temperature or providing an override setting.

Threshold — Strip of material used under doors to cover the joint between the finished floor and sill.

Thru — Architectural slang and abbreviation for the word through.

Timber — Wood that is larger in cross-section than 4 x 6 in. (102 x 152 mm).

Top plate — The horizontal framing member on top of a stud wall.

Transom — Small window located directly above a door.

Tread — The horizontal plane of a stairway that one steps on.

Truss — A structural assembly of wood or steel used to span great distances with the minimum amount of material.

Type X gypsum board — A specialized type of gypsum board used for greater fire resistance.

Vapor barrier — Material, generally a sheeting, that prevents water vapor migration into unwanted areas of a building.

Varnish — A tough transparent coating made of a combination of resinous substances with alcohol or oil. Applied with a brush or sprayer.

Veneer — Thin sheets of wood or other material used in surface applications to other materials.

Vent — The vertical pipe in a plumbing system that exhausts sewer gas and provides pressure equalization.

Vestibule — The entry or open area dedicated to the entrance of a building.

Waferboard — Sheathing material or panel made by pressing and gluing flat flakes of wood.

Wainscot — Lower section of a wall finish, usually a different material than the upper section.

Water closet — Common name for a toilet that contains a bowl of water.

Water resistant gypsum board — Panel of gypsum board that is manufactured to resist dampness. Often used in bathrooms as a subsurface for ceramic tile.

Weep hole — A small aperture in masonry construction that allows the drainage of water to the exterior of the building.

Weld — To fuse together two pieces of metal using intense heat from an electrode or rod.

Welded-wire fabric (WWF) wires — A grid for concrete slab reinforcing, made of various diameters and strengths welded together.

Winder — The triangular tread found on a stairway.

Wood molding — Wood assemblies curved or angled in various convex or concave shapes used for trim.

Wrought iron — Soft, malleable iron that can be forged into different shapes.

Dyed yarn — Yarn that is colorized before knitting or weaving into a fabric.

Zero-clearance fireplace — A metal prefabricated fireplace designed to be placed directly against wood framing, without causing combustion of the wood.

Index